The Westward Crossings

THE
Westward
Crossings

Balboa

Mackenzie

Lewis and Clark

JEANNETTE MIRSKY

ALFRED A. KNOPF, New York 1946.

This is a Borzoi Book, published by Alfred A. Knopf, Inc.

Copyright 1946 by Jeannette Mirsky

Published simultaneously in Canada by The Ryerson Press.

FIRST EDITION

This book is inscribed to my husband

EDWARD B. GINSBURG

whose many-sided encouragement,
whose unending patience and stout belief
created an atmosphere that nourished
and sustained my effort.

> *Here I have but gathered a nosegay of strange floures, and have put nothing of mine unto it, but the thred to binde them.*
>
> MONTAIGNE, Of Phisiognomy

Acknowledgments

THIS BOOK, based on research, was written far from any sizable library. That obstacle would have been insuperable except for the understanding help of librarians. On short hurried trips to New York I surveyed as well as I could the vast mass of material pertinent to my subject, and because I was so fortunate as to enlist the bibliographical knowledge and ready co-operation of Sylvestre Vigilante, head of the American History Reading Room of the New York Public Library, these forays were rewarding. My good luck held after I had decided what books I should study intensively: Isaac Copeland of the Presbyterian College Library at Clinton, South Carolina, was miraculously able to borrow them for me from the Library of Congress and other large libraries.

Two eminent historical scholars helped solve certain problems: John Bartlet Brebner in stimulating and illuminating conversations, Lesley Byrd Simpson in correspondence. Their generous suggestions were of the greatest assistance. To Professor Brebner I owe the title of the last section, *Commerce for the Nation,* and with it the proper emphasis and direction.

I wish to thank Harcourt, Brace and Co., Inc. for permission to quote from Vernon Louis Parrington's *Main Currents in American Thought,* and the American Philosophical Society and Dodd, Mead & Company for permission to quote from the *Original Journals of the Lewis and Clark Expedition,* edited by Reuben Gold Thwaites.

Specific references were contributed by my nephew Ralph Colp, Jr., to the enrichment of the book, which was carried from manuscript to typescript and through revisions by the patience and skill of Pauline Q. Garber.

My first version was read by Dorothy Teall, whose suggestions helped immeasurably in fashioning the final form.

To all these friends my warmest thanks.

J. M.

Laurens, S. C.

Contents

Illustrations and Maps

Foreword

This book is part of the story of North America from its earliest settlement to the emergence of the United States into continental power. Its framework is the transcontinental explorations of Balboa, Mackenzie, and Lewis and Clark. The impelling motives, the social terms in which they were expressed, and the rewards harvested by each of these three expeditions, which all together stretched over three centuries, have historical continuity; there is illumination even in their contrasts.

The story of Vasco Núñez de Balboa, the first European to cross the continent from the Atlantic to the Pacific, introduces a number of extraordinary figures: Peter Martyr, Cortés, Las Casas. A united Spain was sending great numbers of her sons who knew how to conquer or die to the New World Columbus had found. This was the moment of the first European settlements on the American mainland, brave, pathetic colonies that lived for gold and pearls and died for want of bread. Balboa's achievement and his senseless death throw the two extremes of sixteenth-century Spain into sharp relief: colonial Spain, young and inchoate, yet aware of the ideals befitting a virile and Christian nation, and fanatic, feudal, Catholic Spain.

Alexander Mackenzie, the next explorer to accomplish the avowed purpose of reaching the Pacific, was one of a long line of French, American, and British fur traders whose far-flung ventures were business trips—fantastic business trips that delineated much of northern North America, yet whose success was measured not in added knowledge but in increased profits. Mackenzie's enterprise secured the vastness and resources of western Canada for Great Britain just when she had, by her conservatism, lost thirteen of her colonies.

The Lewis and Clark expedition was a conscious historical gesture with social implications. Part of Jefferson's western

[xiii

dream, it was boldly directed toward the future. By it the continent was explored not only for the immediate rewards of gold or furs but also as a dwelling-house for a growing nation. The expedition opened up the valley of the Missouri, more than half a million square miles in the heart of North America; it secured a foothold on the Pacific Coast, which was already being pre-empted by the European powers, Spain, Great Britain, and Russia; it reflected at once Jefferson's urgent concern for our participation in the enriching global flow of commerce and his vision that demanded room for the growing States he had helped create, for the people who were pouring across the Appalachians into the valley of the Mississippi.

Considering North America as a whole gives unity to elements that are commonly separated into preludes to Latin American history, or Canadian history, or the history of the United States. For a long time North America was almost as empty as it is vast, but nevertheless it was responsive to varied impacts from Europe —from the Spanish, the French, the Dutch, the English, the Russians.

No, Balboa, Mackenzie, and Lewis and Clark are not three stories, they are three episodes in one story—the penetration and exploration of the continent. These episodes are tied together by a solid line of continuous development; an identical pressure of hopes and needs was felt by all, a single idea renewed itself throughout their explorations. Before North America became the end of many long trails it was a mighty obstacle interposing itself between Europe and the East she desired; before North America became a home for many nations, it was a treasure house to be looted—for these men and for many others.

For us here in the United States it would be well if we learned to think of Spanish America as one of our own antecedents. A full century before Englishmen established Jamestown and the Pilgrims landed, Spaniards had their settlement of Santa María de la Antigua del Darién. If we acknowledge England as our mother, we should remember that we were sired by Spain. If, for most of us, our history starts with the passionate, awkward, heart-stirring act of British colonists' proclaiming their political coming of age, it should be understood that that act did not make them Americans; they had to be Americans before they could declare themselves for freedom.

The ennobling idea of freedom—the right to life, liberty, and the pursuit of happiness—was, like so much else, brought to North America from many parts of Europe; here it was but adapted to our demands, our dreams. The cry that was raised in Spain, back in the sixteenth century, against Negro slavery and Indian exploitation in the Americas lies on the same watershed as our own struggles for freedom. Hope is universal and thought is international. Through devious channels the naked savage whose cause Las Casas espoused evolved into the natural man of Rousseau, and the violated rights of the savage were indicated in the political philosophy of the rights of man.

From each of the three ventures recounted here there shines the bold, radiant quality of youth that marks Spain, Great Britain, and the United States as each successively pushed across North America toward the constantly expanding frontier of freedom. Balboa to the south, Mackenzie to the north, Lewis and Clark in the middle—each expedition blazed a trail, made a westward crossing. . . .

PART I
Gold for the Crown

(*Balboa*)

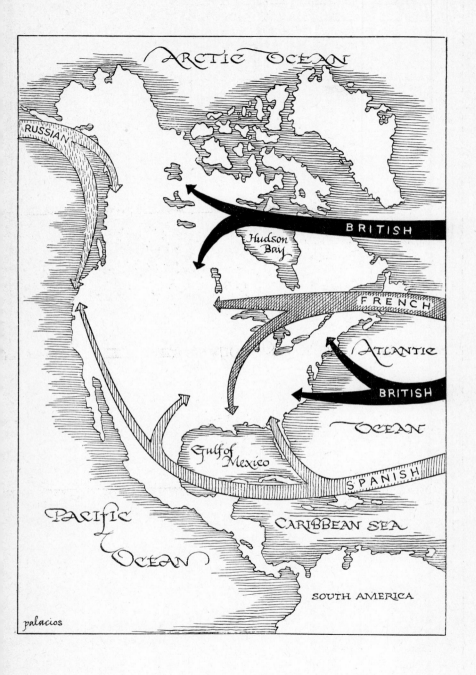

ARCTIC OCEAN

RUSSIAN

BRITISH

Hudson Bay

FRENCH

ATLANTIC

BRITISH

OCEAN

Gulf of Mexico

SPANISH

PACIFIC

OCEAN

CARIBBEAN SEA

SOUTH AMERICA

palacios

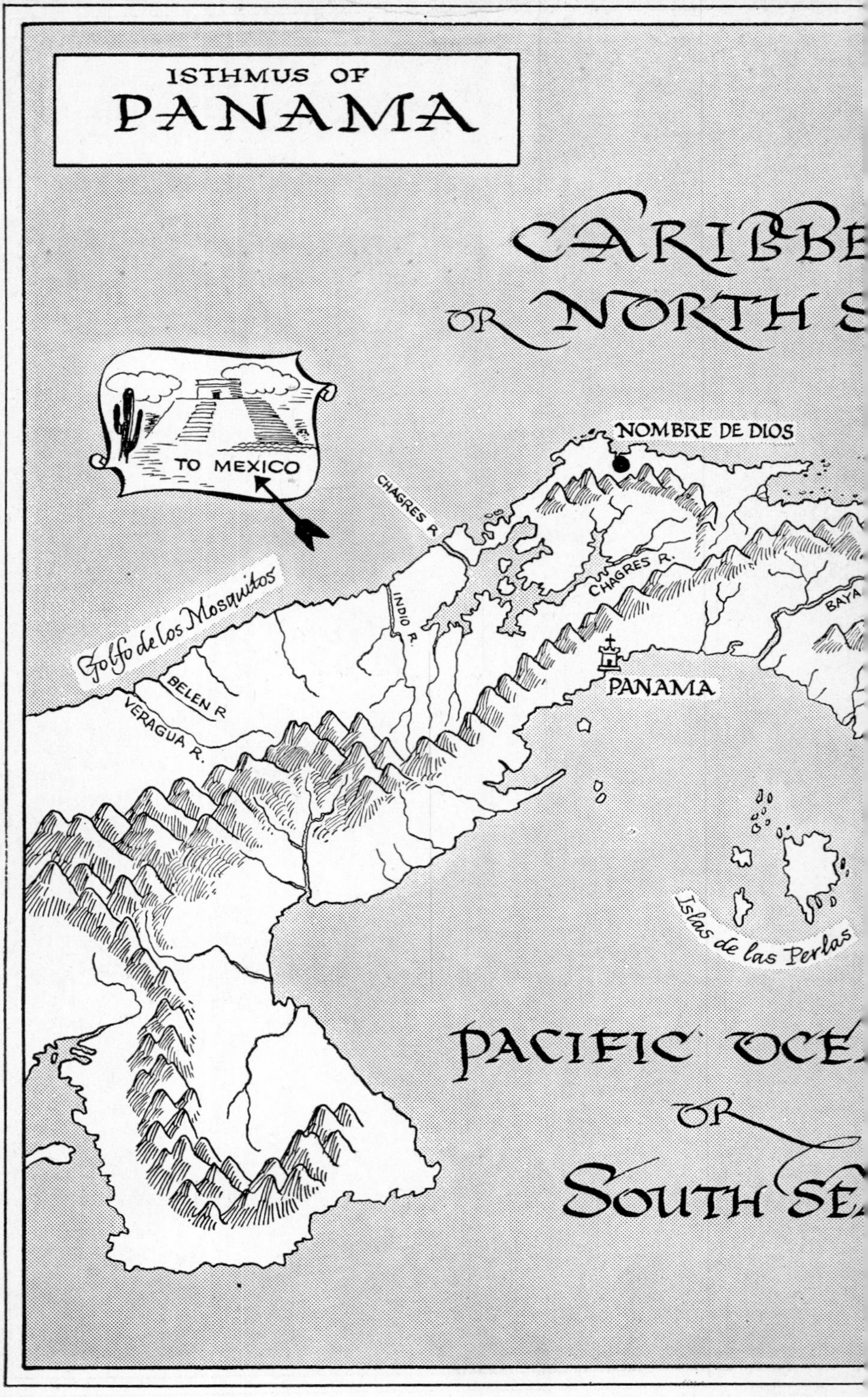

ISTHMUS OF
PANAMA

CARIBBE
OR NORTH S

TO MEXICO

NOMBRE DE DIOS

CHAGRES R.

CHAGRES R.

Golfo de los Mosquitos

INDIO R.

BELEN R.

VERAGUA R.

BAYA

PANAMA

Islas de las Perlas

PACIFIC OCE

OR

SOUTH SE

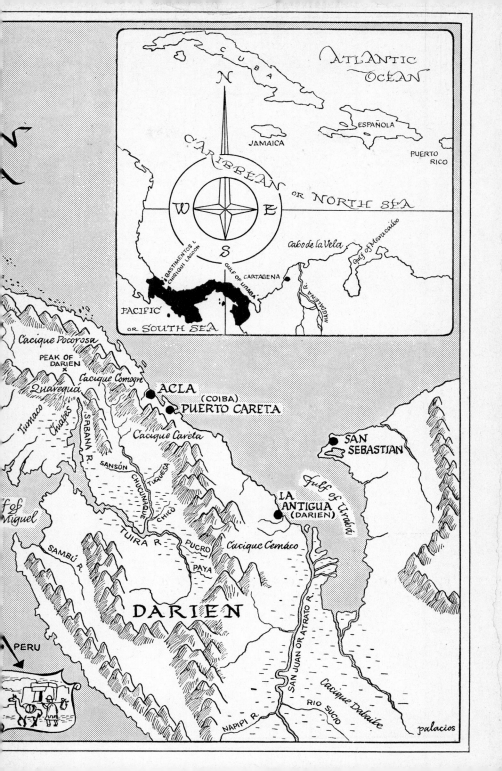

Peter Martyr

To be a great letter writer it is necessary to write constantly, indefatigably, with ever-recurring zest; it is almost necessary to live to a good old age.

LYTTON STRACHEY

THE year was 1487, and the fifteenth century was dispiritedly coming to an end. The Church, cynical, corrupt, and mercenary, watched its frontiers contract before Islam; it was equally indifferent to the subsidence of faith within its European stronghold. For many people their inner despair translated the end of the century to mean the end of the world, while intellectuals by-passed the present and dwelt happily on the undying grandeur of Greece and Rome. Christopher Columbus, the Genoese, the great mariner and greater mystic, was proclaiming that the world of the Mediterranean must yield before the new and vaster world of the Atlantic. Unknown, unnamed, still dreamed of, was the Pacific Ocean.

Peter Martyr was not one of those filled with the sense of impending doom, nor was he content to walk forever along the ilex-bordered paths of antiquity; he was neither mariner nor mystic. He was a scholar informed, inquisitive, ardent, restless, devout. He knew that by the marriage of Ferdinand and Isabella, Spain was a united country and was blessed with peace within her Christian boundaries, in marvelous and striking contrast to his own Italy; he heard how powerful, wilful feudal lords were being transformed there into obedient courtiers vying for royal favor; he listened to endless stories of the fight against the Moors that was presently to draw to a successful close. To Spain would Peter Martyr go.

The news that Peter Martyr had decided to accompany Iñigo López de Mendoza, Count of Tendilla, the Spanish ambassador to Pope Innocent VIII, on his return to the court of their Catholic Majesties was completely incomprehensible to his many friends. How can you leave Rome? they urged. How can

3

you leave the Academy, where eloquence and wit are daily fare, where enthusiastic and learned scholars devote themselves to recovering from oblivion the glorious literature of Greece and Rome? His intimate friends—Pomponius Laetus, Theodore of Pavia, Peter Marsus, and Cardinal Ascanio Sforza—entreated and reproached him. Isn't Rome the center of the world? Isn't Rome the glittering goddess who draws to herself all men of talent, of ambition? How can you leave?

Peter Martyr might have replied: "I am thirty. From Arona, near Lago Maggiore, I went to Milan; from there I came here to Rome. Among you, my friends, I am a pygmy among giants, whereas in Spain men of learning are few, and therefore the need and opportunities for their talents is greater. To you Rome is the world; but I am eager to go to its western edge and feel the wind that sweeps in from the unknown. Rather than bewail, you should envy me my going." He must have sensed the great drama he was going to see, the role he was going to play.

Peter Martyr lived until 1526, long enough for him to know that the first adventures he had recorded had revealed themselves to be not isolated and exotic material for his letters, but the decisive beginning of something new, continuous, and vast. Before he died it was clear that the course of empire lay westward, that its proper prelude was western exploration. The original discovery by Columbus had earned for him, by the terms of his contract, an immense but vague viceroyalty with a handsome share of the profits; his honors and emoluments amounted, in prospect, to a prodigious monopoly. No other could sail to the New World without the Admiral's personal license. But the forces arrayed against the carrying out of such a contract were too strong and too many. His disastrous experiences on Hispaniola embittered many against him, and his repeated failures to find the cities of the East made the rest impatient. Great numbers of Spanish adventurers had been left without occupation or income by the final triumph over the Moors; for them Ferdinand and Isabella had no further use at home. Their Catholic Majesties, now that they had conquered all of Spain, were ready to start on their great domestic program of welding it into the first strong national monarchy of Europe. The needs of the crown itself, already reaching out toward European hegemony, also worked against Columbus's interests. Too much was at stake, the prom-

ises were too rich for the crown to forgo complete control over
exploration and colonization. Properly, these were imperial
enterprises. The Genoese had opened a dam that released a flood
of energy, which cried to be curbed and was soon to be strictly
channeled.

Rare, in that human flood and its human controls, were spirits
balanced between personal motives and political sagacity. One
such was Balboa, the redhead, who ran his short impetuous course
more than a century before the Pilgrims came to Plymouth. Peter
Martyr spread news of the luminous young man in those letters
of his that record the Spanish overseas venture. Balboa was a
discoverer not greatly inferior to Columbus in spirit and mind;
he was markedly superior to the stubborn and mystical Admiral
in human relationships. There is a fascinating mixture of elements in the Balboa story: the impetuous and the accidental, the
adventurous, the shrewd, and the inevitable; there is the touch
of genius and the imprint of inspiration. All this Peter Martyr's
sharp mind discerned, though he never saw Balboa and learned
of him at second hand.

The first serious colonization of the American mainland is
identified with the brief, brilliant, hardy career of Balboa: here
was the seed of the Spanish expansion that was to cover so much
of what is now the United States, an expansion that enriched the
New World with food plants, horses, cattle, peaceable and gracious and civilized ways of life, all carefully implanted by the
mother country. The small, secure foothold established by Balboa on the Isthmus that connects North and South America was
a funnel through which Spanish energy and empire poured out
north and south. His successors profited by his spirit and courage, though none but Cortés had quite his quality of greatness.

When, ten years after Columbus's first great discovery, the
Admiral set out on his fourth and final voyage, the man who had
found a world knew that his contract had been broken and
would soon be shattered. Already other expeditions had been
licensed without his knowledge, let alone consent; one of these
had brought home from the Pearl Coast of Venezuela the first
rich haul from the Americas. Thus Columbus's last venture was
a fevered search for the gold that might restore his fortunes and
reputation; but even more, it was a search for a strait that would
vindicate his theories and lead easily to the Orient. Traces of gold

he found, but nowhere was there a break in the coastline that would let his ships through. The discovery of the only strait between the two oceans was left for Magellan—the difficult waterway near the southern tip of the hemisphere. Not the Strait of Magellan but the overland route across the Isthmus of Panama gave the Spaniards domination of mainland America. This route was Balboa's gift.

Peter Martyr, a Lombard by birth, Roman by culture, became the matchless source of contemporary reportage of Spain's enterprise in America. Attached to the court of Spain as tutor to the young nobles, or handling a delicate mission for their Catholic Majesties in Egypt, he dashed off accounts of his experiences and impressions at white heat to his friends in Rome; the letter-writing habit was firmly fastened on him by the time he became Bishop of Jamaica (an office that gave him a substantial income without requiring him to leave Spain) and a member of the Council of the Indies, the bureaucratic fountainhead of colonial administration, which was seated in the Iberian peninsula. Peter Martyr is revealed in his letters not only as a scholar and a critic, but as a man who had learned how to deal wisely and to practical effect with men and affairs. His curious mind was alive both to the details and to the widest implications of the discoveries in the New World. Each caravel that arrived gave him material for his letters; he questioned the captains, the pilots, the cosmographers; he entertained Columbus, Cabot, and Cortés; he listened to the sailors and soldiers; he knew what ships were licensed and how they were financed and equipped; he watched as the fabulous cargoes passed through the Casa de Contratación, Spain's colonial board of trade.

The full impact of the wonderful and terrible flowering of the Spanish genius is felt in his letters—the start of a new age, the discovery of a New World, the beginning of what is still, for Americans north and south, the greatest story of our civilization.

Balboa

Balboa has attempted and accomplished a deed so great that not only has he been pardoned for his treasonable conduct, but distinguished by honorable titles. Partly by force, partly by conciliation and by pacifying the native Kings with our presents, he scaled the mountains and saluted the ocean. Marvelous things are written. . . . And so farewell.

PETER MARTYR
23 July 1514. Valladolid.

VASCO NÚÑEZ DE BALBOA was the most famous stowaway ever to come to the New World. His luck in Santo Domingo had run true to local form: he had acquired nothing there but debts. It was in the hope of escaping them that in 1509 he stowed away on a vessel that was to sail westward. He could hardly have chosen more injudiciously than to hide himself in a large cask on a ship owned and commanded by the lawyer Martín Fernández de Enciso. Enciso had amassed a small fortune—did not all lawyers amass fortunes in Spain, where litigation was as costly as it was common?—and this fortune he was gambling for rich returns by conveying provisions to a party that had already gone out under command of Alonso de Ojeda. All of Enciso's funds were tied up in a ship and brigantine that carried one hundred and fifty soldiers; a dozen horses and swine, both male and female, for propagating the species; fifty cannon; a good supply of lances, shields, swords, and other fighting material; flour, cheeses, biscuit, wine, and other provisions. Ojeda, before setting sail, had acknowledged Enciso's contribution by naming him *alcalde mayor* or chief judge of the settlement that he intended to found.

Enciso was consumed with his own importance. It is never wise to cross a lawyer, certainly not a quick-witted, word-twisting, puffed-up lawyer like Enciso, who was alert to protect his investment and his status. No one needed to tell Enciso why

7

Vasco Núñez had stolen on board his ship; the very fact that he had done so was proof that he was a blackguard, riffraff, scum. Vasco Núñez had debts. He was guilty of poverty, and this, to Enciso, was an unforgivable vice. Both as lawyer and as man of property Enciso thought highly of the law that forbade debtors to leave Hispaniola without having paid off their creditors. As administrative head of a prospective settlement he feared and detested people who took laws lightly. Many debtors had sought to join his party; only this stowaway had managed to elude the vigilant authorities and board the ship. Enciso assessed Balboa's shrewdness, and he did not like it. He was to prove a persistent and powerful enemy to Balboa; he was to oppose him in the first significant mainland settlement of Santa María de la Antigua del Darién, and he was to work and whisper against him at the court of Spain. But for good or evil their destinies were joined in the great adventure on Tierra Firme, as the mainland was then called.

Enciso questioned the stowaway closely, but Balboa was reluctant to supply him with more than a few meager facts.

As if to give diginity to his sorry position, the young man boasted that he came from the illustrious lineage of the Balboas. He had been born in 1475, in the town of Jérez de los Caballeros in the province of Badajoz, and had served as page to Don Pedro Puertocarrero, lord of Moguer. A master of the sword, he had brought nothing aboard with him but his sword and his dog Leoncico.

As the questioning proceeded, a story gradually took shape.

Balboa had sailed from Spain in 1500 with Don Rodrigo de Bastidas, a wealthy notary, who put his savings into two caravels that set out to trade for pearls along the coast where Columbus had learned these jewels were to be had. Balboa had seen the license issued to Bastidas by their Catholic Majesties; it authorized him to secure gold, silver, copper, lead, tin, quicksilver, and any other metals; pearls, jewels, and precious stones; slaves, Negroes and mixed breeds; monsters, serpents, fish, and birds; spices and drugs, and every other kind of whatsoever name or quality or value it might be. Bastidas had secured for his venture the services of the able chart-maker and pilot, Juan de la Cosa, who had sailed with Columbus on his second voyage and who had then just returned from piloting the first successful fortune hunter to the Pearl Coast.

Bastidas's crossing had been easy. The caravels went even farther than Cabo de la Vela, the point in what is now western Venezuela at which Cosa had turned back for Spain on his previous pearling voyage. Leisurely and without untoward incident they had cruised along the coast, trading as they went. For a needle, a bell, a fragment of mirror, the Indians gladly gave as much in gold or pearls as was asked of them. At first the Indians had spurned the needles because, wearing no clothes, they were puzzled as to their use. But when the shrewd Spaniards showed them that needles were useful for extracting thorns from the flesh and for cleaning the teeth, they set a high value on them. Soon Bastidas's caravels were loaded with pearls as other ships were loaded with straw—pearls as big as almonds, resembling oriental pearls, but not so valuable because they were badly pierced.

Enciso's greed and hopes glowed on his face. The sailors exchanged smiles.

Well beyond Cabo de la Vela the mouth of a great river had been found. Bastidas called it the Magdalena. Still farther west they found a fine harbor, which they named Cartagena. They sailed on till suddenly the shoreline bent southward, and they believed that they were about to discover the strait that would provide the much-desired short cut to the Orient. But soon they observed that the waters on which they were sailing had a sweet, fresh taste, and they named them Golfo Dulce. Subsequently the gulf was renamed Urabá. It marked the western end of the lands that Ferdinand had assigned to Ojeda, Enciso's superior.

Bastidas did not stop at the Gulf of Urabá. Continuing along the coast, he found Indians who wore only cunningly wrought necklaces and nose plugs. Then disaster struck. Without warning, without having run on a reef or dragged over shoals, the ships began to leak in every part. The bottoms had been pierced through and through in many places by the worm known as broma, a scourge never encountered before. Pumping and bailing, day and night, Bastidas and his men set an eastward course and ran for home.

And what happened to those fair ships carrying pearls and gold that had been so easily gathered?

At an islet not far short of Hispaniola they stopped to make repairs as best they could before attempting an Atlantic crossing. But the infested ships hung together only long enough to reach Hispaniola. They were some distance from the town of Santo Domingo, and the whole party, lacking provisions, was too large to live off the land while making their way to it. Bastidas prudently divided his men into three groups, each carrying not only part of the precious cargo but also trade goods to be bartered for food with the Indians along the way. Each detachment in turn, as it arrived at Santo Domingo, was arrested and thrown into prison. Don Francisco de Bobadilla, the governor who the year before had sent Columbus home in chains, accused Bastidas of having conducted an illicit trade with the natives. In vain Bastidas protested that he had traded only for food or guides, he had not sought nor taken any gold; after a year in prison he was finally dispatched to Spain to stand trial.

The rest of the story, Balboa said, was known to all. But Enciso and his men called for his version of it. Not many venturers had such luck as Bastidas, and happy endings bear repetition.

Bastidas started homeward in June 1502, on the return voyage of the fleet of thirty ships that had brought out Don Nicolás de Ovando as the new governor of Hispaniola. Accused as he was, Bastidas was assigned to the meanest of the vessels. His persecutor Bobadilla, the retiring governor, embarked with his retinue, a large number of Indian captives, including a famous chieftain, and a fortune in gold worth two hundred thousand *castellanos* and the largest nugget ever found in the West Indies, of the fabulous weight of thirty-six hundred *pesos*. Before they weighed anchor, Columbus, on his last voyage, sent word advising Ovando to have the sailing delayed in view of the many signs announcing a severe hurricane. But the fleet spread its canvas to the wind. The very next day the full fury of the storm broke over it. Twenty ships went down with all hands and the gold they carried. A few vessels crept back to Santo Domingo before falling apart; only one reached Spain, and that the one bearing Bastidas and his treasure. Bobadilla and his party, the Indian chieftain and his fellow captives, five hundred altogether, perished. In Spain Bastidas was tried and acquitted; the huge sums he had to spend in clearing himself of Bobadilla's charges were raised by the sale of his pearls and gold, which also discharged the expenses of his expedition and the crown's share and still left him a substantial fortune.

Enciso gazed at the tall, well-built fellow with the open, pleasant face who had already seen the coast for which they were bound. Balboa's calm and self-assurance disturbed him. How could a stowaway, a man loaded with debts, be so much at ease with decent people? Was it possible that Balboa expected his creditors to hold Enciso liable for what he owed them? Enciso was worried. Perhaps he had best maroon Balboa and be free of future trouble. But it had already become plain that the soldiers and sailors were no less conscious than Enciso of Balboa's distinction. Enciso knew that his men would never let him strand Balboa on some distant shore. So Balboa became one of the expedition. To the men the young man with nothing but his sword and his dog had an intrinsic worth, a magic almost, for a venture into what to them was the completely unknown.

Balboa's assurance was related to nothing outside himself, but sprang from the deep well of his own wild strength and terrific energy. There was neither vulgarity nor pettiness in him; he was forged of the true steel of the adventurer, and it was the qualities and achievements of men of his caliber that gave substance and flavor to the very name of conquistador. In such men the yeast of restlessness ferments from early years; they seek out danger; they must have fame, glory, laurels; they are prepared for any sacrifice, any privation. In some things they are simple, in others cunning. They are reckless both in the means they use and of danger itself. They possess a formidable persistence. They combine a consuming desire to have their ears filled with shouts of adulation, their heads wreathed in glory, with an unflinching heroism in the face of disaster and death; and only death can check natures of such impetus. These men absorb early the hard but essential lesson of self-control, the art of keeping their own counsel before judges and even among friends.

Balboa, in telling Enciso and the others the story of Rodrigo de Bastidas, had withheld three things. With Bastidas he had learned when to fight the Indians and when to conciliate them; where, along the Gulf of Urabá, there was an Indian village surrounded by gardens; and where the Indians were who did not use poison on their arrows. Each of these bits of knowledge was an invaluable key to success in such an enterprise. He knew the time would come to utilize these scraps of information. And at that time and in the telling lay the moment and chance for which he had unconsciously been preparing.

2.

I have opened the gates and others enter at their pleasure and follow in my tracks.
COLUMBUS

[You are] loosing the barriers of the Ocean Sea which had been closed with such strong chains.
(The words Columbus heard in a trance on his fourth voyage.)

Others besides Bastidas had taken part in the initial exploration and exploitation of the Pearl Coast. He had been preceded by Alonso de Ojeda, who commanded four ships outfitted by wealthy Seville merchants because he had no funds of his own. Juan de la Cosa, to whom the tracks of the ocean were as well known as the rooms of his own house, was Ojeda's pilot, Amerigo Vespucci his cartographer. Ojeda acquired nothing but rich adventures and the friendship and esteem of Cosa, which he had won by his courage and high spirit. There had also been the quiet, modest, businesslike voyage of Peralonso Niño, a pilot who had twice sailed with Columbus; his pearling expedition netted the richest returns obtained from the New World up to that time. Then Vicente Yáñez Pinzón, one of the three brothers who had helped Columbus on his great enterprise of discovery, after an amazing voyage brought his two battered ships home to Palos with a cargo of brazilwood, valued for dye, to pay off his irate and threatening creditors. Pinzón's greatest accomplishment, the discovery of Brazil and the mouth of the Amazon, netted him nothing. Within the three years before 1500 these men, poaching on the lands that by lawful contract belonged to Columbus—poaching with the full knowledge, consent, and assistance of Fonseca, to whom, as head of the Indies enterprise, Columbus had sent his reports and charts—had extended knowledge of the mainland from the Isthmus of Panama three thousand miles along the coast of South America.

The report brought back by Columbus of his fourth and final

voyage was even more tempting. He had discovered gold. Sailing
along the Isthmus of Panama, where the trees crowded to the
water's edge and rose in mountains to touch the clouds, he had
hoped and tried to find a strait that would lead him through to
the Indian Ocean. The Admiral did not find the strait; but along
that coast, which was called Veragua, the men and women were
bedecked with necklaces and breastplates wrought of pure polished gold. His disappointment as a discoverer and his unshak-
able belief that he was close to the Indies led him to identify
Veragua as the site of Solomon's mines. He assumed that he had
reached the mines of Ophir, whose gold was lavished inside and
outside the fabulous temple built by the wisest of kings. With
that to sustain him, Columbus came home, stricken, to die.
Shrewd and greedy, Ferdinand of Spain wanted to be as rich as
Solomon—his wisdom he did not covet—and the death of Columbus made his plans more practicable. With the adamant Admiral
he could not abrogate the contract he and his late queen had
signed, but with the heirs he would be able to settle that obnoxious clause which gave them, free of taxes, a tenth of all precious
metal and gems, pearls, spices and all other valuables produced
by mining or obtained by barter. With Columbus dead and the
regency of Spain safely in his own hands, Ferdinand planned to
get the gold of Veragua.

Hungry people have hallucinations, and Europe at that time
was hungry for gold and silver. The gold myth that from the
days of Marco Polo had troubled the daydreams of Europe
assumed the size and shape and glitter that surrounded Solomon
as he received the Queen of Sheba in his golden temple. Ferdinand needed gold to finance his vast enterprises, and that meant
having more than any other king in Europe. Like everyone else,
he knew that Columbus had found a new continent, a New
World; and as he was the regent of Castile, the heir of Isabella,
it belonged to him, not to Spain—to the crown, not to the nation.
The treasures of the New World would be his. Dominated by
cupidity, versed in cunning, Ferdinand sought among the young
adventurers for men who would do his bidding on his terms. His
agent, who fully understood and shared his motives and methods,
was Juan Rodríguez de Fonseca, Bishop of Burgos.

Fonseca is the type of officeholder met with in all countries at
all times. Ambitious, wary, and selfish, Fonseca possessed the

unshaken confidence of his masters; energetic and with a real capacity for business, he organized and equipped the great fleet for Columbus's second voyage—was it he who suggested using the monies appropriated from the Jews exiled from Spain the previous year to help finance this venture?—and in time became head of the predominant Council of the Indies; overbearing, prejudiced, unscrupulous, and petty, he held power for thirty years and enjoyed the unique distinction of having opposed Columbus, Balboa, and Cortés. A second-rate nature, he did not plot against them when, as yet, they had only visions and hopes; but he could not tolerate them in the greatness of their accomplished achievements and schemed to reduce them to his level. He mocked at the prophetic intimations that haunted Columbus, and he feared the qualities that drove Balboa to find the Pacific, Cortés to conquer Mexico.

Fonseca found the very men to serve Ferdinand. There was little to choose between the merits and qualities of Alonso de Ojeda and of Diego de Nicuesa, and so the wily king did not make a choice, but, dividing the command between them, granted to each patents and dignities that cost him nothing and promised rich returns. There was very little to choose between Ojeda and Nicuesa. Both were small-statured, but of prodigious courage; with only slight variations in the trimming, they were cut from the same cloth. They came from good families and had served in the households of great noblemen; they were superb horsemen, accomplished courtiers, and skilful with weapons and words. Nicuesa had served as carver to the king's uncle, was famous as a lute player, and had made a fortune in Hispaniola. Ojeda could not carve or play the lute, and possessed nothing but debts, but he had faithful friends and powerful connections. He was cousin to one of the first Inquisitors General of Spain and an intimate friend of Fonseca, who had already demonstrated his warm regard by privately showing him Columbus's chart of the Pearl Coast. Cosa had been Ojeda's pilot on his first voyage; now he showed affection and high regard for him by placing his earnings at Ojeda's disposal and also by advancing his cause with Fonseca.

In 1509 King Ferdinand issued licenses to both Nicuesa and Ojeda. Their districts met at a boundary line running through the Gulf of Urabá. Nicuesa was to have the lands westward from that line along the coast of the Isthmus of Panama, while Ojeda's territory extended in the other direction as far as Cabo de la Vela. Both were to use the island of Jamaica as their base of supplies from which to renew their provisions. Their licenses gave them a ten years' right to all profits from gold. In return each was to erect two fortresses within his district and to pay a royalty to the crown of one tenth the first year, one ninth the second year, one eighth the third year, one seventh the fourth, and one fifth for each of the remaining years. They were allowed to recruit additional men from Hispaniola.

The two arrived at Santo Domingo at the same time. Nicuesa, with his own fortune to spend, had a fleet of four vessels and two brigantines well stocked with arms and supplies to do honor to his position as governor of the golden mines of Veragua. Ojeda, using only the modest savings of Cosa, who served as his captain general, had only one ship and two brigantines, with equipment for a much smaller force than Nicuesa's.

Ojeda was mortified when he compared the two fleets anchored in the harbor. There must be someone in Hispaniola whom the bait of imposing titles and still more imposing riches would win over as an additional backer. Ojeda met the lawyer Enciso. Here was his man: Enciso had a modest fortune, he was a little bored with his dull routine, he was eager for the immense returns that Ojeda said an investment would bring. As Enciso's restless, speculative nature responded, Ojeda added the irresistible item that, as lawyer and investor, he would be *alcalde mayor* in the government to be set up on Tierra Firme. The bargain was properly and legally signed by both parties. Ojeda's pride had been restored, for now everyone knew that his ships and men and supplies would be augmented; his fleet almost matched that of his rival Nicuesa.

With a near equilibrium established, Santo Domingo was too small for such rivals. Large and operatic gestures were made on both sides. Which should control Jamaica? In whose province was Darién (the Indian name for Veragua)? The confused maps and charts might be taken to substantiate both men's claims. The quick tongue of Ojeda mentioned a duel as the only way to settle the problem of Darién. The quicker wits of Nicuesa added a substantial side-bet as a prize for the winner. This, and the discreet urging of his friend Cosa, checked the impecunious Ojeda;

the duel and the wager were shelved. A compromise was agreed upon: the boundary between their districts should be the Darién River. The contention over Jamaica was taken out of their hands by Columbus's son and heir. Don Diego Colón, irritated at the manner in which both these men had been given rights over an island that was his by inheritance, sent Juan de Esquivel as his lieutenant to colonize Jamaica. Ojeda did not learn of this until he was on the point of sailing, and his last words before leaving were a threat to cut off Esquivel's head if he so much as landed on Jamaica. This he swore, and no one present doubted that the hot-tempered, intrepid little swordsman would do just as he said.

Ojeda was the first to sail. Early in November, 1509, his two ships and two brigantines, carrying three hundred men and twelve mares, left Santo Domingo. Enciso was to follow as soon as he was ready. With Ojeda went Francisco Pizarro, the future conqueror of Peru. Hernán Cortés, who was to topple the Aztec empire, was also to sail with him, but a knee badly wrenched in escaping from an irate husband detained him ashore. Balboa, who wanted to go too, was prevented by his debts.

Nicuesa had hoped to be the first to leave, but he was delayed from day to day. First he was so deluged by volunteers eager to make their fortune in the golden province of Veragua that he had to find another ship to accommodate them. Then he was delayed by the shrewd manipulations of Don Diego Colón, who sought by involving him in endless litigation to prevent his going. Thick and vexatious and insistent, the legal gnats pestered him until his funds and his patience were both exhausted. Nicuesa's eager heart despaired. Then something like a miracle happened. A notary public who was distressed at the threatened ruin of such a charming courtier and alarmed that the whole brave expedition might founder shamefully in a court of law supplied the needed sum himself. Seven hundred men and six horses sailed with Nicuesa. He arranged to have a thousand big, beautiful sides of bacon, from five hundred of his own pigs, and other additional supplies sent out to him later on.

Ojeda had a ten-day head start. The rivals raced toward Darién, disaster, death.

3.

The natives poisoned their arrows with the juice
of a death-dealing herb.

PETER MARTYR

Juan de la Cosa set the course of Ojeda's expedition almost due south from Santo Domingo. As pilot for Bastidas, he had traced the coast that stretched from Cabo de la Vela to Cartagena, the harbor set midway along the coast of Ojeda's grant. Under Cosa's expert direction the boats sailed sweetly and truly for their goal.

Again and again Ojeda told of his voyage ten years before to the Gulf of Paria (now the Gulf of Venezuela), when he had sought for pearls. The memory of that trip was vivid. He described the spacious, tranquil landlocked gulf into which his ships had probed and along whose shore was a marvelous village: twenty large bell-shaped houses lifted themselves above the shallow water on piles sunk deep into the bottom of the gulf. Each house had its drawbridge for safety and many canoes for transportation, and because it had reminded him of Venice and its gondolas he called it Venezuela, Little Venice. Still within the gulf he had reached a village called Maracaibo by the natives. There, he remembered, the Spaniards were treated like gods. There for nine blessed days the Indians had feasted and worshipped them and danced for them; the women were very fair, and their men did not have even a word for jealousy. And Ojeda remembered with delight that there the loveliest of them all, his Isabel, had joined him. To Ojeda it had been an earthly paradise and its people of the golden age: the land belonged to everyone just as the sun and water do, and they knew no difference between *mine* and *thine*, that source of all evils. Little was required to satisfy them, for there was always more than enough land for all. Neither ditches nor hedges nor walls enclosed their domains; they lived in gardens open to all, without laws, without judges. But what good was the fertility of their land and of what use were the gentle, sociable qualities of the natives, if they did not possess the gold or precious stones the Spaniards sought? And torn between his need of gold and his capacity for love, Ojeda had sailed away to search for gold and sigh for that lost land where life had been lovely as a dream.

Ojeda questioned Cosa about the province of which he was governor, the land to which they were sailing, the land Cosa had visited with Bastidas.

The natives, Cosa told him, despite their nakedness were ferocious and were armed with poisoned arrows and lances whose sharp points had been hardened in fire. Of Carib stock, they were cannibals. These monsters hunted for humans as other hunters chase wild beasts. They captured children, whom they castrated like chickens being fattened for the table, and, when the captives were grown and had become fat, ate them. Older victims the cannibals killed and cut into pieces for food; they also ate the intestines and extremities, which they salted like hams. With the exception of lions, tigers, and crocodiles, the animals were not dangerous. In many places bats as large as pigeons flew about and, as soon as twilight had fallen, bit men cruelly. There were certain trees that bore sweet-tasting fruit, but eating it was unwise, for it produced worms; and still more noxious was the shade of these trees, for whoever slept beneath their branches awoke with a swollen head and a temporary blindness. And now Cosa warned Ojeda:

"It is not the animals or bats or trees that are to be feared and guarded against; it is the people, odious and unyielding. They have huge swords fashioned out of palm wood that cut as do the finest Toledo blades. Yet the weapon most to be feared is their arrows. Respect their arrows! Be brave, but do not be foolhardy in reckoning with their slender reedy arrows, for the tips dipped in a sly poison are deadly."

Cosa wanted to avoid Cartagena. His sagacity and experience argued that it was better to shun that harbor, proceeding directly to the Gulf of Urabá, where poisoned arrows were not used. Prudence ruled him, for he had much at stake—his savings, his position as captain general, his very life. He urged Ojeda not to land at Cartagena. But Ojeda's pride translated his warning into a challenge, and he refused to allow that naked infidels could bar him from any place in the New World. They landed.

Like Cassandra, Cosa, gifted to foresee his brutal, bloody death and with the courage to walk steadily through the door that led to doom, accompanied Ojeda's large landing party. The Indians

had had experience with white men and were not to be conciliated with kindly gestures. Loudly they blew upon their conch
shells. For the last time Cosa urged discretion. Ojeda was deaf
to all but his need to fight. The Spaniards charged and in a brief
skirmish killed some Indians, took a few prisoners, and routed the
rest. To Ojeda the encounter was as it should be, and he yielded
to the joy of battle. He followed the fleeing enemy inland. Again
Cosa cautioned against reckless action, and again, when his counsels failed, followed his commander faithfully and valiantly.
Miles inside the thick forest, the landing party reached an Indian
village. Another determined fight, and the village fell into their
hands with seventy captives. A second time Ojeda pursued
fleeing warriors deeper into the forest and at twilight reached
another village, whence the inhabitants had fled. This silent,
deserted village satisfied Ojeda that at last he had accomplished
his end: he had cowed and terrified the Indians. The Spaniards
scattered and ran eagerly into the houses, looking for gold and
loot. Suddenly, with a yell of triumph and fury, the Indians fell
upon the dispersed Spaniards, surrounding small groups, fighting
with envenomed strength, with poisoned arrows. And thus,
hemmed in by maddened natives and with a strange and hostile
forest between him and the sea he knew so well, the great Juan
de la Cosa died. And with him was lost to Ojeda the knowledge
of where in that region arrows were not dipped in poison.

Only two Spaniards escaped alive: Ojeda, who had fought
with all the mastery, endurance, nerve, and luck for which he
was known, and a soldier who had stood beside Cosa and had
been charged by him to dash for safety and tell Ojeda of his
doom.

The men who had remained on board waited for their leaders
to return. Days passed while they watched, but no one stepped
out of the darkness of the great forest. Only a sound, not human,
not Spanish, came through the trees—the distant sound of shouts,
of drums, of long-blown conch shells. The Spaniards could not
stay idle, waiting, and they sailed on along the shore, calling with
their trumpets, signaling with their guns, looking . . . looking.
At last they sighted Ojeda, a small figure, weak from hunger and
cold and fatigue, crushed by his loss.

At this terrible moment ships were sighted. It was Nicuesa's
fleet, fresh from Santo Domingo, untouched by any accidents.

Here was an occasion for Spanish chivalry. In Hispaniola the two leaders had been rivals and had quarreled. But both were Spaniards and aristocrats. Gently and generously Nicuesa placed his large force at Ojeda's disposal. Their first task, it was evident to both, was to avenge Cosa's death. This was the tonic Ojeda needed. His strength and spirits returned and, accompanied by Nicuesa, he led a party of four hundred back into the forest. It was night when they reached the fatal village. The unsuspecting Indians were asleep. Revenge was quick and complete. The village was burned and all its inhabitants save six young children killed. The shame of Cosa's death had been wiped out; his body, bristling with arrows, swollen and black with poison, was found lashed to a tree. Death itself now wore a terrifying new appearance.

The Spaniards returned to their ships. The two leaders, sworn to friendship, parted. Nicuesa headed toward Veragua.

Ojeda called his first settlement San Sebastián. That saint, who had died of arrow wounds, was invoked to give heavenly protection against poisoned arrows. The spot chosen was the eastern extremity of the Gulf of Urabá, whither Ojeda had sailed, belatedly heeding the advice of the slain Cosa, for Cosa had known, as Balboa did, where along that coast there were no poisoned arrows. San Sebastián was still within the danger zone. Ojeda and his men worked hard to build a fort and a stockade to protect themselves. Soon they realized that they were ringed in by hostile Indians; it was only within the stockade that the men were safe from the sudden strike of poisoned arrows. Now they trembled when they heard the jaguars; they trembled when they stumbled on large snakes; they trembled when they saw alligators, evil and powerful, sunning themselves; and most of all they trembled when the Indians fought them along the trail. After a short time the panic-stricken men would not leave the settlement, and hunger and disease struck down both the wounded and the well. Daily men died, and each day brought new despairs.

The next stage in the settlement's disintegration came when the disillusioned, fearful men turned on Ojeda. Their supplies were exhausted, and though they were famished, they dared not venture out in search of food. They spent their strength in accusing Ojeda of having lied to them. Where were the additional supplies that had been promised them? Where was Enciso? They did not believe Ojeda when he told them that Enciso was due with a shipload of food, that he himself was astonished at the delay.

Just then, as though sent from heaven, a ship was sighted, though not Enciso's. It was captained by Bernardino de Calavera, a desperado who with sixty other ruffians had seized a ship loaded with bread and meat and come out in it for gold. The good supplies they brought made them and their unsavory proposition acceptable. But the food was only a temporary palliative that eased the men's hunger. More days passed, days that stretched out, one after another, in unhurried succession, days that were endless to the starving men, waiting and watching for Enciso's boat loaded with bread and cheese, bacon and wine. Soon the newcomers, too, hungered; and as the men chewed on roots and herbs, some conspired to steal a boat while yet they had the strength to act and sail away from their misery. Hearing these mutinous murmurings, Ojeda knew that he must work quickly if he was to save his command: he would return to Hispaniola and there beg Don Diego Colón for aid for his struggling colony.

Ojeda called the men together; of the three hundred who had started, only sixty were left. He looked at them, so starved, so thin, that death had only to take off the skin—the skeleton was ready. He urged them not to abandon the village they had built. It was a foothold that in time would give them control over the whole region. Narrow and dangerous it might be, but it was the first step toward gold and riches. He himself would go with Calavera and his desperadoes to Santo Domingo to learn why Enciso was delayed. Either he would return within fifty days with help and food, or they could abandon San Sebastián and sail for Hispaniola. He spoke with energy and assurance and renewed his men's hope and trust in him. He appointed Pizarro his lieutenant, and the men pledged themselves to stay at San Sebastián for fifty days pending his return. The agreement was written down and notarized, according to Spanish custom.

Ojeda, at the mercy of Calavera and his cutthroat crew, sailed to seek help. He never returned to San Sebastián, that pin-point of authority set in the luxuriant wilderness over which he had been duly appointed governor. His return to Hispaniola, an incredible odyssey, was a relentless succession of hardships.

Blown by a storm to Cuba, the party spent thirty terrible days crossing a vast, bottomless salt marsh, knee-deep, waist-deep, neck-deep in slime, crazy with thirst; their bread and cheese rotted, and they had but a few raw potatoes to gnaw on; they pulled themselves onto mangrove roots and slept a while before pushing on; rivers and inlets had to be crosed, and those who could not swim were drowned; a path had to be hacked through a wall of vines and creepers. Half of the seventy men died. Half lived through that nightmare and stumbled into the village of some peaceful Indians. There they got food and rest and sent out a canoe to Jamaica to beg for help. Esquivel, the governor of Jamaica, immediately sent a caravel for them; and though he remembered that Ojeda had once threatened his life he gallantly welcomed him and tended and housed him. From there Ojeda returned to Santo Domingo, where he learned that Enciso had been gone a long while, carrying men and ample supplies as he had promised, and that as yet nothing had been heard from him. Ojeda, fearful lest some misfortune prevent Enciso's reaching San Sebastián, tried to get other aid for the colony. But no longer could he dazzle backers and attract recruits.

Some accounts say that Ojeda, broken in spirit and in health, died a pauper. Others say that he took the vow of poverty and died in the odor of sanctity, in the habit of Saint Francis.

Pizarro and the men with him waited fifty days, as they had pledged themselves to do. No help came. They wanted to abandon San Sebastián and sail away in their two brigantines, but that raised a new problem. They were too many for those two small ships, and it was impossible to choose who should sail and live and who should be left behind to die. The solution they arrived at was very simple, impartial, direct: they would stay where they were while death picked the winners. They did not have to wait too long. Getting the boats loaded was easy. Four horses that were still alive and had been used to terrify the Indians were killed and salted for food; they had very little else to take. Six months after they had landed there with Ojeda, they sailed away from San Sebastián.

Their number was further reduced when one of the brigantines sank with all hands in a bad storm. The surviving brigantine, carrying thirty-five men and commanded by Pizarro, sailed along the coast toward Cartagena. There they met Enciso's ship and brigantine, which, too late, were bringing relief to San Sebastián.

The condition of the colonists and the story Pizarro told made Enciso tremble for his investment and position. These men must be mutineers, malefactors seeking to escape. Impossible that these few specters eating salted horse meat were all who still lived! Enciso refused to believe them. His worst suspicions were aroused when they offered all their gold, of which they had plenty, to be allowed to continue to Hispaniola. Only when Pizarro showed his authorization signed by Ojeda would Enciso believe him; but, deaf to all their entreaties, he invoked his authority as Ojeda's *alcalde mayor* and forced them to return with him to San Sebastián. Together they reached that ill-fated spot.

It was now Enciso's turn to experience the misfortune and danger and uncertainty of this hostile New World. The twelve horses and swine, the fifty cannons and good supply of lances, shields, swords, and other fighting equipment, all that he had bought with his savings, everything he relied on for existence— all, in a few moments, was gone. For as they were about to enter the port the ship struck a sandy reef and was engulfed by the waves; the animals were drowned; the weapons sank; and the men, peeling off their clothes so as to swim, reached the shore almost naked. They managed to save twelve barrels of flour, a few cheeses, and a small amount of biscuit. Stripped of everything but life itself, Enciso reached the shore with thoughts of other things than gold.

Not a dwelling was left. San Sebastián, its thirty houses, its fortress and stockade, was ashes and charred logs; the Indians had set fire to the abandoned settlement. For a few days the Spaniards lived off the meat of some wild swine, small herds of which were found in the near-by swamps, cabbage palms, and green wild plums; then Enciso had to face the task of feeding his hundred and eighty-five men. He was as aggressive with the sword as he had been with the law, and at the head of a hundred men, he started out to forage. This first sortie showed them what they could expect. The party was waylaid by a few Indians who, with lightning speed, shot their load of arrows and disappeared before they could be killed. Picking up their wounded, the Spaniards turned and ran. Again they were encircled by the same swift, silent Indians, struck by the same deadly poisoned arrows. How could they escape now that their ship had sunk? Enciso could not cope with the nameless terror that walked among them. He might, with a few chosen friends, seize the brigantine and steal away; but the desperate vigilance of the men prevented such action. Must they rot there, dying off one by one, until the small brigantines could carry away the pitiful survivors?

This was the moment and this the setting in which Vasco Núñez revealed himself. He held the solution to their plight.

4.

Behold them! alive and safe on the land they had
desired with their whole hearts.

PETER MARTYR

"I remember that in past years, coming along this coast with Rodrigo de Bastidas to discover"—Balboa addressed himself to Pizarro and the others who had not heard his story on Enciso's boat—"I remember that we entered this gulf and disembarked on the western shore, where we found a town seated amid abundant fertile fields, and inhabited by people who did not put the herb on their arrows." *Herb* meant poison. His words filled them with hope as a fine wind fills flabby sails and gives a boat sudden power and direction. Arrows without poison! With hope came courage, strength flowed back into their arms, and dreams and plans found room within their hearts; gratitude to God who showed them His favor flooded their spirits, and questions came pouring from their mouths. Arrows without poison?

Vasco Núñez told them that the Gulf of Urabá was wide and deep, and lands strangely different from one another were washed by its waters. He reminded them that they had seen how poor and unprofitable were the regions where the Indians ate men. In contrast the villages on the other side of the Gulf were rich. The Indians had well-tilled fields, cotton cloth, and gold, finely and cunningly wrought. The particular village that ought to be conquered rested on the bank of a river that flowed into the Gulf: the town, the river, and that whole region were called Darién by the natives. They were brave people, but they did not use poisoned arrows. The men listened to him and knew he spoke the truth. They knew how the children of Israel had felt when the Red Sea parted and let them pass toward the Promised Land.

Enciso appointed Balboa guide, and the strongest and most courageous men were chosen to go with him. In the two brigantines they crossed the gulf and arrived at the river and thus at the village. Everything was as Balboa had described it. Cémaco, chief of the Dariéns, saw these strange, large ships with sails carrying armed men and prepared to defend his capital. He ordered the women and children to leave the town and hide in the forest, and while his medicine men invoked the supernatural, Cémaco with five hundred of his warriors waited on a hill to destroy the bearded white intruders.

In orthodox Spanish fashion, Enciso, kneeling with his men, prayed for victory and vowed to give gold and silver and jewels to adorn the statue of the Virgin in Seville—a statue most honored there and known as Santa María de la Antigua—and to name for her the town they would build and the church they would erect. Then, to overcome any fear of poisoned arrows that might still remain in them, all bound themselves by a vow not to retreat. Thus Enciso, the lawyer, having contracted with Heaven and his men, was ready for battle. Two things gave the Spaniards great courage: their empty bellies and the knowledge that their steel swords and lead bullets must triumph over wooden swords and lances, even when the latter, hurled from throwing sticks, had great impact at a distance.

The Indians fought fiercely and well. They fought until the bodies of their dead told them with solemn finality that wooden swords were powerless against the invader's shields, that naked bodies could be cut in two by his steel weapons; they fought until the invader threw lightning and thunder among them with deadly effect while not a single Spaniard was killed. The battle was soon over. Cémaco and his men ran for the forest, where their women and children were hiding. The Spaniards, with Enciso at their head, marched into the village.

Balboa had told them the truth, for on entering the village they found plenty of food, coverlets woven of cotton, utensils of wood and earthenware. Best of all, they found gold. Marvelously worked bracelets, coronets, anklets, and plates as fine as the finest objects Mexico was to yield were collected and heaped up; the shining pile was reflected in their eyes as an incredible token of the treasure they had come so far, had suffered so much, to find. Joy and greed filled their hearts. They were giddy at their sudden deliverance. They stilled their hunger with fruits, vegetables, and cassava and corn bread. Here were houses, ready built for their shelter; here would be their new town; and this town would forever bear the sweet, proud name of Santa María de la Antigua del Darién.

At last a bridgehead in the New World had been secured.

Morning came and the Spaniards reconnoitered this country of theirs. Set back from the gulf, a little way up the Darién River, the town was accessible only to very small boats and native canoes. River, town, and gardens filled the deep valley. Beyond were swamps and then a great forest filled with valuable woods—mahogany, ebony, satinwood, and rosewood, the Bombax or silk cotton, brazilwood. The river itself differed from the rivers they knew in Spain; it was more like a perpetual spring freshet, irresponsible, capricious, carrying to the sea the vegetative vigor of the forests that crowded to the top of the mountain range.

The rich gardens promised food for the morrow. In the gardens were roots that the natives called potatoes. To the men they looked like Milanese turnips or huge mushrooms except that their skins were rougher and earth-colored, their insides quite white. Raw, they tasted a little sweeter than green chestnuts; but when cooked, either roasted or boiled, they were equal to any delicacy. The Spaniards also found a kind of millet that reminded them of that which grew plentifully among the Andalusians: the length of a palm and the thickness of the upper part of a man's arm, it was studded with grains of the form and size of peas. While still growing, they noticed, its grains were white; ripened, they became black, but when ground made a flour whiter than snow. This kind of grain the natives called *maiz*. And so Europe first saw corn, the great staple of the New World. And again they marveled at the bread the natives ate, made from cassava. The root itself, from which the flour came, had a juice of deadly poison. But when that poison had been carefully washed away, the root gave a food both appetizing and wholesome. To the Spaniards, the greatest delicacy was a fruit having the form and color of a pine-nut, the firmness of a melon, and a skin of scales.

It did not grow upon a tree like an orange or plum, but was rather like an artichoke or an acanthus. Tasting the pineapple, they vowed that no other fruit excelled its flavor.

The Spaniards settled down, and soon the natives came, eager to give gold, which the white men craved, for the articles of value to themselves that they had abandoned—their cotton coverlets, their utensils of wood and clay. Law and order inexorably came to Darién: on pain of death Enciso forbade all private trading with the natives for gold. This was consonant with the royal order under which, as head of the government, he operated, but it struck an ominous chord among these individualistic, adventurous men who had endured so much for just such an opportunity. Had his enemies planned his downfall they could not have wrought it more directly and easily than he himself did. Every man was against him, for he stood squarely between each man and his self-interest. Law and order come slowly to the frontier—but this Enciso could not, would not understand. He was too pleased with what had happened: Ojeda was gone, and he was in control; his investment had been sunk, but here he had enough treasure to repay him many times. Greedily he clung to the authority that had been given him, indifferent to the needs and wishes and hopes of the people he ruled.

The aggressive, inflated lawyer did not even notice the dissatisfaction. The men did nothing cruel or violent; rather, with exquisite mockery they turned on him with his own techniques: politely they asked—knowing that he had come ashore as naked as any of them—to see the contract from Ojeda under which he held power. They then turned on him, called him a miser, accused him of being a tyrant who had assumed illegal control. The break had been made, and Enciso was never again to exert authority in Darién.

Had Balboa, aiming at leadership, mobilized and directed the discontent that ousted Enciso? Some believed it. But for such ambitions patience and guile are needed; had Balboa possessed these two qualities, they would have saved him from the trap that was to cost him his life. Cortés had these weapons in his personal armory, and with them he outmaneuvered and conquered his most puissant Spanish enemies and Mexico. It seems rather that the men, having turned against Enciso, looked for a capable, sympathetic directing hand. Had not Balboa saved them from San Sebastián and sent them forward to Darién? And Balboa could have little love for Enciso, who had threatened to maroon the stowaway. So the men reasoned, and turned to Balboa. Surely he would know how to deal with the lawyer. Vasco Núñez did not question Enciso's authority. He admitted it, but reminded him that his position derived from Ojeda, not from the King, and that the Gulf of Urabá was the boundary between Ojeda's province and that accorded Nicuesa. Darién lay within Nicuesa's territory, where Enciso had no status. If Enciso would be *alcalde mayor*, let him return to San Sebastián, which lay within Ojeda's district; but if he wanted to stay here at Darién, then before God and his Catholic Majesty, Enciso was no *alcalde mayor*, there was no government, and all were equal. This clinching argument coincided with the wishes of the men, and Enciso was deprived of his position. Thenceforth he was to be the embittered, venomous, tireless enemy of Vasco Núñez, who had displaced him.

Tradition had provided an implement that these men now used. In Castile and Aragon, local assemblies, self-respecting and self-reliant, were a valuable appendix to the royal power; traditional municipal liberties were recognized by Ferdinand and Isabella, who encouraged the initiative and creative vigor these bodies fostered. Thus anarchy did not succeed Enciso's removal from office. Instead, the men met in orderly meeting and, according to familiar procedures, elected their officers by popular vote. Here, in the first European colony planted firmly in the New World, the first town meeting was held, by Spaniards functioning under Spanish custom. By this action the officials of Darién took their power directly from the King, the source of power. Their government, of necessity, was temporary: should Nicuesa appear, they must yield to him; or should Don Diego Colón exercise his viceregal will from Hispaniola, they must recognize his jurisdiction; or should the King appoint a new head, they must bow to his pleasure.

The men elected two alcaldes, Balboa and Martín de Zamudio; and, with authority thus divided, factions arose. The more lethargic favored waiting for Nicuesa; some adhered to Zamudio, and others followed Balboa; and everywhere, fomenting dissension, creating distrust, was Enciso. Affairs were in a state of flux, and the contending factions had not yet completely re-

vealed their composition or strength when suddenly the thunder
of distant cannons was heard. Answering this civilized sound
with their own cannon, the colonists saw two ships coming from
the direction of San Sebastián. In a short time the ships were
anchored near Darién, and Rodrigo de Colmenares came ashore.

Colmenares, Nicuesa's lieutenant, who was bringing out to his
governor men and ammunition and food—including Nicuesa's
own thousand sides of big, beautiful bacon—had coasted the
length of Ojeda's province, and when at San Sebastián he saw
charred remains, he feared lest the whole party had perished.
The silence everywhere amazed him. Hoping to locate and
attract any survivors, he had signaled with his guns, and here in
Darién he found them, a mere one hundred and eighty out of
the hundreds who had started. Their story moved him to pity,
and he gave them liberally of the provisions he carried. His generosity and his tactful reference to the position accorded him by
Nicuesa won him authority over the settlement. It was decided,
after a little discussion, to send two representatives from the
town with Colmenares to find Nicuesa and invite the rightful
governor to Darién. As soon as this had been arranged, Colmenares sailed. The sight of Ojeda's men, the terrible sufferings
they described, spurred him to seek his commander speedily.
Colmenares dreaded to imagine what calamity might have befallen his friend, the charming and distinguished Diego de
Nicuesa.

Only a man gifted with an evil imagination could have antici-
pated the frightfulness of Nicuesa's fate.

5.

*Nicuesa was the most wretched of men, reduced
to a skeleton, covered with rags.*
                                        PETER MARTYR

Ojeda had used his head start to court catastrophe at Cartagena;
then it was Nicuesa's turn to outrival him even in disaster. His
fine fleet of ships carrying seven hundred and eighty-five volunteers headed for the coast of Veragua, where before them only
Columbus had sailed. If it was poisoned arrows that defeated
Ojeda, Nicuesa's first misfortunes were due to mediocre sea-

manship in waters that had almost broken the stout heart of the
great Admiral of the Ocean Sea.

To get his bearings, Nicuesa sailed for the Gulf of Urabá and
thence toward his destination, the Veragua River. He cruised
along a coast where only a narrow plain cut between a sullen sea
and an unfriendly jungle that covered high rugged country.
Here the trade winds blew, here the rain fell furiously, monot-
onously. Long sand beaches separated by rocky bluffs offered
no shelter, and even a landing in small boats called for skill and
caution. This region was to destroy Nicuesa's proud fleet. A
storm changed this dangerous coast into a hostile one. And in
the face of a threatening tempest, Nicuesa turned from the land
where there was no safety and, as night approached and hid the
peril of reefs and shoals, he put farther out to sea. Between the
storm and the darkness his ships lost each other. When morning
came Nicuesa was alone.

Where were the other ships? And should he go eastward or
westward to find the Veragua River? Coming in to land, he
decided that the Veragua lay to the west. Soon he came to the
mouth of a river that seemed large enough for his vessel to
enter. He did not know that in this region, where the earth is
saturated from the constant beating of moisture-laden trade
winds on the high mountains, any rain floods the little streams
that masquerade as rivers until they have dumped their extra
load into the sea, when, as suddenly, they resume their original
size. Hardly had his boat crossed the bar when the waters sub-
sided and his boat grounded. Caught between the pounding
waves and the receding water, the ship keeled over, her seams
opened. It was no longer a question of saving the ship; Nicuesa
and his men had to save their lives. Struggling to the river bank,
they stood and watched their ship, their food, their arms, their
clothes, everything, destroyed or carried away.

Of Nicuesa's once fine fleet, nothing was left him but the
dinghy; a pathetic procession, his crew still traveled westward
along that terrible coast. Days stretched into weeks. Death
claimed a few, and they seemed the more fortunate; for each
day and night brought new miseries as hunger and despair
enveloped them.

And then one day, in that remote and lonely ocean, a sail was
seen. The ship came straight for an island on which the survivors

had been stranded when their dinghy had disappeared. Aboard the ship were four sailors who had vanished with the dinghy. Their story was simply told. They had become convinced that Nicuesa was marching in the wrong direction, that the Veragua River lay east, not west, of where they had lost their boat. They did not say that because it was impossible to convince Nicuesa of his mistake they had taken the only other course and, marooning their comrades on a little island so they could be sure of finding them again, had retraced their steps and continued to the east until they had found the rest of the expedition. When the sailors on the brigantine saw the emaciated, translucent bodies of those who were still alive on that island, they felt they had assisted not at a rescue, but at a resurrection. This terrible experience, the fruit of his own stubborn persistence in going in the wrong direction, had done something to Diego de Nicuesa. In Spain, he had been talented and distinguished; in Hispaniola, he had been charming and successful; here, on the shore of the New World, he saw his proud undertaking reduced to nothing, his golden ambitions frustrated; he had tasted wormwood and gall; he had lived with death. Someone, not something, was responsible for all this; for his own sanity he had to find a scapegoat, someone on whom to pour his bitter anger, his unbearable fear. From then on his swift tragedy was of his own making.

Nicuesa accused his pilot of being a traitor, and would have had him beheaded had not the men begged for his life. Grudgingly at last he yielded to them. But his vindictiveness had to be satisfied: the culprit was put in chains, awaiting the first ship that would take him back to Spain to stand trial for high treason. Now the only thing Nicuesa knew was to sail eastward. His men were without food, and whenever they landed to secure provisions warlike Indians drove them off, for the Spaniards were so weakened by hunger that they could not fight. And so, worn and starving and despairing, they reached a lovely harbor, surrounded by tended gardens.

"Here," said Nicuesa, "let us stop *en el nombre de Dios!*"

Taking his words as a happy omen, the men started to build a small fort for protection and hopefully called it Nombre de Dios. But building this fort took the last strength of many men, and still Nicuesa drove them to complete the work. To those who protested that they were too ill to work, he sternly, in-

humanly answered: "Begone to the dying place!" Of the seven
hundred and eighty-five men who had crowded his boats when
he left Hispaniola, only sixty were alive.

This was the half-crazed Nicuesa that his good and loyal
friend Colmenares finally found. Warmly Colmenares embraced
his friend, cheered him with the news of the successful settlement in Darién, dazzled him with its stores of gold; he had food
brought ashore for a banquet. Nicuesa once again was gay and
dashing, and at the feast he recalled his skill and former office
as carver and carved a fowl in midair with undiminished adroit-
ness. But his greed was as inflexible as his authority.

Drunk with his sudden change of fortune, his appetite satisfied
for the first time in many months, Nicuesa talked airily of his
intentions: he would immediately confiscate all the gold that
had been collected. He amplified this statement when later he
spoke to the two representatives who had accompanied Colmenares from Darién: as governor he would not only force all
to give up what they possessed, but he would punish them for
having trespassed on his monopoly. These ideas and his arrogance
dismayed the two men; their fears were thoroughly aroused
when that night they found his pilot, still a prisoner, who urged
them to be warned by his story and his chains. Nothing more
was needed to convince the two men from Darién, and they
resolved that never would Nicuesa inflict his kind of gratitude,
his greed, his will, on the struggling but promising settlement
of Darién.

Taking their leave with courtly bows and hints of preparing
a welcome, the two men hastened back to warn their fellow
colonists of Diego de Nicuesa, Governor of Veragua. To the
men of Darién they gave their report, exaggerated perhaps, but
with enough solid truth to dispel any doubts that might have
persisted in the governor's favor. "What folly is it in you," their
argument ran, "being your own masters and in such free condition to send for a tyrant to rule over you?"

Nicuesa's reception was brief and bitter. As his boats approached the mouth of the Darién River he beheld the colonists
drawn up along the beach. They were not there to do him honor,
as he fatuously imagined, but to back up the loud voice of the
town crier who called on Nicuesa not to land but to return
immediately to Nombre de Dios. Vainly Nicuesa pleaded and

promised any concession if only he might be allowed to land. And then Balboa, who with Zamudio stood at the head of the men, bade the notary read the paper that he had witnessed: in the sight of God and the King the officers of the town, followed by all of the people, had taken a solemn oath not to receive Nicuesa as their ruler; any of his men who chose to stay at Darién were permitted to do so, and any men who preferred to follow Nicuesa were to be allowed to depart with him. Seventeen men, out of loyalty or fear or sympathy, departed with Nicuesa. The most telling evidence of Nicuesa's impossible behavior is that his friend Colmenares chose to stay in Darién.

In an evil hour Nicuesa sailed, and somewhere and somehow he and his men found death.

Alonso de Ojeda and Diego de Nicuesa, those two appointed leaders who represented to their contemporaries all "the human graces and perfection to be found in Castile," had, with an unerring flair for doing the wrong thing, wasted twenty thousand pesos and over a thousand human lives. The contrast between them and Balboa is striking. Balboa took the scant remnants of men and material of these two impressive undertakings, established them in a colony, subdued or conciliated many native tribes, and led one hundred and ninety of his men far from his base, across the cordillera to the Pacific Ocean. The great secret of Balboa's success, and it was to be true of Cortés's also, was his instinctive generosity with his men. Each received his portion of the spoils, and all were satisfied. Ojeda and Nicuesa were of the generation that, in Spain, witnessed the shift from a feudal society to a strong centralized national monarchy; to the feudal concept of the noble class they had added a new idea of authority vested in the sovereign. Neither Ojeda nor Nicuesa knew generosity. That those who faced hunger and disease and death should expect their share of the spoils of the New World was in the sweet smell of America, and it was wafted far out to sea for the commonest sailor to breathe in. And their right to share in the opportunity was the reason, unvoiced but apperceived, why the Darién settlers refused Nicuesa permission to land.

Nicuesa's expulsion did not resolve the difficulties besetting Darién. Factions still divided the settlers, and food was still a problem. Balboa, Zamudio, and Enciso were contending for power. Each had his following, and until the political question should be resolved, the simple matter of food slid into the background. Enciso had few adherents. His brief period of authority had been resented by the original settlers; his imperious manner reminded many of the newcomers of Nicuesa. Zamudio had a certain number of friends, active, vociferous, united, determined; but it was Balboa who had the largest following. The men did not forget that it was he who had saved them from the poisoned arrows of San Sebastián, while his open, engaging nature, his thoughtfulness, his confidence emanating from his own inner assurance, marked him as a leader whose nature held his cachet of authority. Balboa first showed his potentialities by the manner in which he disposed of his two rivals.

With Zamudio's support, proceedings were started against Enciso. He was accused of having used his appointment from Ojeda to usurp power in a region outside the latter's jurisdiction. Enciso defended himself adroitly at his trial. But the facts were plain, and his manner had so prejudiced all against him that he was found guilty; his property was confiscated, and he, the former chief judge, was thrown into jail. Enciso's friends pleaded for him, and Balboa was faced with a delicate decision: If, as they requested, he freed Enciso and sent him back to stand trial in Spain, he would be decently rid of a rival, but he would have sent a powerful, persuasive enemy back to the court, where he could do plenty of harm. If—and here Balboa tried a subtle expedient—if Zamudio accompanied Enciso as a representative of the town, he would be an antidote to Enciso's poison, and at one stroke Balboa would have rid himself of both rivals. Balboa presented this program to the town council, but kept his reasons to himself.

The King must be informed of all that had occurred; that was essential. Some assistance must be found, too, until the colony could feed itself. The council acted on Balboa's suggestions to these effects, and a boat was immediately made ready to sail to Hispaniola, where the viceroy, Don Diego Colón, was to be petitioned for provisions and additional volunteers. This task was assigned to Juan de Valdivia, a man who had been as greatly respected in Hispaniola as he was in Darién. Valdivia was entrusted by Balboa with a large sum of gold to be presented to the influential royal treasurer at Hispaniola; this was an additional precaution taken by Balboa to obtain favorable reception both there and at the court in Spain. At Hispaniola, Zamudio and Enciso were to take passage on a boat returning to Spain. Zamudio was urged to impress upon the King the great riches to be found in Darién, and carried with him some choice native pieces in evidence.

As the boat sailed away from Darién at the beginning of April 1511, Balboa stood on the shore, the undisputed leader of the colony. He knew that wealth and fame and deeds of grandeur were now possible; he was gambling on time, on realizing these dreams before the intrigues of the court could crystalize and a successor to Ojeda and Nicuesa appear bearing the King's authority. He was realist enough to know that Ferdinand of Spain would not allow him any credit against the future, but would insist on a *fait accompli* before giving him personal recognition. All his energies and everything he had learned were directed toward such an accomplishment. The region abounded in clues. He would follow each in turn until somewhere he would discover mines that would dim the ancient glory of Ophir. He would find gold, and he would care for his men: those were his main concerns.

The first clue pointed to the neighboring region of Coiba, whose chief, Careta, was reputed very wealthy. Balboa sent out a small reconnoitering party under Pizarro, but they had gone only a few miles when they were ambushed by a large force of Indians led by the vengeful and watchful Cémaco. After a short, fierce fight both groups withdrew, the Indians leaving many dead and wounded, the Spaniards leaving one man too wounded to return to Darién. When Pizarro, himself wounded, reported this encounter to Balboa, the latter listened to him in amazement and anger and ordered him to return and bring in his wounded comrade. This small but significant incident boosted the morale of the men; they knew they had a leader whose first thought was for their safety.

The men had further proof of Balboa's preoccupation with their welfare when he sent Colmenares to Nombre de Dios to bring to Darién those of Nicuesa's party who remained there. On their return voyage the brigantines, coasting close to the shore, sighted two men who, though they looked as naked and painted as any Indian, hailed them in Spanish. Nicuesa's men recognized these two as comrades who more than a year before had fled rather than submit to an unjust punishment. And then the two men told how they had found refuge with local Indians and had been well received by Careta, the chieftain; all this time they had lived in his town. They confirmed his reputation for great wealth and added that he also possessed great stores of provisions. Without a thought of gratitude toward Careta, they planned how best they might betray him. One returned with Colmenares to Darién to act as a guide, while the other remained with the Indians, alerted for treachery.

When the brigantines reached Darién, and Balboa learned about Careta from the guide, he knew at once that this was the announcement, the summons of good fortune, for which he had been waiting. Losing no time, he selected one hundred and thirty of his strongest men and with the guide proceeded the hundred miles overland to Puerto Careta; he also sent the ships so that he could use them to transport the gold and food he expected to acquire.

With the resident Spaniard acting as interpreter, Careta, surrounded by two thousand warriors, welcomed the Spaniards to his village and offered them food and drink. Balboa asked him for provisions, and the chief graciously answered that he had to refuse only because he had been so busy waging war that he had none to spare. Balboa had to try another method. The Spanish interpreter secretly reassured him that Careta had lied and that the best way to get the food would be to surprise the village at night. Dissembling to keep relations cordial and gracious, Balboa said farewell and left. When darkness concealed their movements, the Spaniards returned, and before the sleeping natives knew what had happened, Balboa had captured Careta, his family, and many others. The spies showed Balboa where the provisions were hidden; captives and food were quickly loaded onto the brigantines, and Balboa returned to Darién.

After the first shock and bitter humiliation, Careta decided that it would be better to have Balboa and his powerful men as friends than spend his strength and the lives of his people in fighting them. And so when the brigantines arrived at Darién, Careta spoke to Balboa in gentle reproach and offered his people's friendship: "Set me and my family and my people free and we will remain your friends. We will cultivate your fields and supply you with provisions. We will reveal to you the riches of the land. Do you doubt my faith? Here is my daughter. Take her for your wife and be assured of the fidelity of her family and her people!"

Balboa was wise enough to understand that a friend and ally would be no mean spoil of victory. For three days Careta, no longer his captive, but now his father-in-law, remained as Balboa's guest. His wondering eyes saw horses for the first time, saw them put through their paces and watched them bridled and saddled; guns were shot off in his honor and for his edification; he examined and marveled at the spaciousness and seaworthiness of the tiny brigantines, and he was delighted by a concert performed for his pleasure. Before he left, Balboa gave his word that he would join in fighting Careta's Indian foes; and then, loaded with presents, his daughter safely installed by the side of his great new ally, Careta returned to his country.

Of Careta's daughter little is known. That she, like her father, was dazzled by the power and strangeness of the white men and their way of life must be assumed. It is known that Balboa accorded her a status congruent with her father's importance, that she was devoted and loyal to Balboa, and that he respected the wise advice she gave him. She remained with him to the very end, and it is as she emerges then for a brief moment that the affection that bound them together is glimpsed, her faithfulness to him that inadvertently was to lead to his death.

As he had promised, Balboa soon returned to Puerto Careta and from there invaded the territory of Careta's enemy, Ponca. News of the alliance between Careta and the white men had been brought to Ponca, and when he saw Careta's allies approach his villages, he fled to the mountains with his people, leaving gardens and houses unprotected. The Spaniards took what food they found, obtained a few pounds of wrought gold pieces, and then, burning the villages, returned triumphantly to Puerto Careta. Here Balboa's delighted father-in-law entertained him and suggested that he make an alliance with his powerful friend, the chief Comogre, who ruled the country to the west and commanded three thousand fighting men.

Comogre's scouts told him that the Spaniards were coming toward his country, and he was advised by a relative of Careta's who lived with him to make friends with this strong new chief of Darién. So Comogre, surrounded by his seven sons, each by a different wife, all handsome and all naked, received the Spaniards as his guests. He conducted them to his great palace, where rooms and attendants and food awaited them. Solid and impressive, the palace was one hundred and fifty paces in length by eighty in width and was set off from the village by an encircling stone wall. Great beams supported an intricately carved ceiling, and the floors were smooth and polished. Commodious storerooms were full of the provisions of the country —maize, cassava bread, meats, dried fruits—and huge earthenware containers, some holding a fermented liquor elaborately prepared from manioc, some a fermented maize drink, and still others a palm wine. But it was not the spirituous liquors nor the food bins nor the spacious living apartments that commanded the amazed awe of the Spaniards; it was the sight they saw when they entered the sacred inner apartment of the chief. Here were bodies, reduced to skin and bone by a careful drying process over a slow fire, preserved with great care; in cotton robes, they hung suspended from the ceiling according to the rank they had occupied in life. Golden masks richly decorated with pearls and precious stones covered their faces. The ancestors of Comogre guarded with their presence the life and strength of their tribe.

The eldest of the seven sons of Comogre was a young man of extraordinary intelligence. Perceiving that the Spaniards were, as Peter Martyr said, "a wandering kind of men living only by shifts and spoils," he did not want them to find any pretext for burning and looting, as they had done to Ponca's villages. He therefore presented four thousand ounces of wrought gold and seventy slaves captured in war to Vasco Núñez and Colmenares, the two leaders. Immediately the Spaniards brought out their scales and smelting instruments and started weighing out the gold to set aside the royal fifth and divide the rest according to agreement. Several disputes arose as they weighed and counted and apportioned; and the eldest son of Comogre, the wise youth who was present, scornfully struck the scales with his fist, scattering the gold in all directions, and then spoke to the thunderstruck Spaniards:

"What thing then is this, Christians? If your thirst of gold is such that in order to satisfy it you disturb peaceable people, if

you exile yourselves from your country in search of gold, I will
show you a country where it abounds and where you can satisfy
the thirst that torments you. You destroy the artistic beauty of
these necklaces, melting them into ingots. We place no more
value on rough gold than on a piece of clay before it has been
transformed into a vase that pleases our taste or serves our
need."

Then he pointed to the mountain range and said,

"Once on the other side of these mountains, you will gaze on
another sea, which has never been sailed by your little boats.
The people there go naked as we do, but like you they use both
sails and oars. On the other side of the mountains, all the streams
are very rich in gold. More than all other, the King Tubanamá
will oppose your advance; his is the richest kingdom of all;
Tubanamá has his kitchen utensils and other common articles
made of gold, for gold has no more value among them than iron
among you."

The Spaniards thought he must be jesting; they did not dare
believe him. He paused a moment, thinking how he might convince them. Then he said:

"Listen to me, Christians. We people who go naked are not tormented by covetousness, but we are ambitious and we fight one
another for power, each seeking to conquer his neighbor. This,
therefore, is the source of frequent wars and of all our misfortunes. Just as you see prisoners of war among us, so likewise
have our enemies captured some of our people. Many prisoners
as well as freemen are here who have traversed that country and
know these facts. Nevertheless, to convince you of the truth
of my information and allay your suspicions, I will myself go
as your guide. You may bind me, you may hang me to the first
tree, if you find I have not told you the exact truth.
"Summon, therefore, a thousand soldiers well armed for fighting, so that by their help and assisted by the warriors of my
father, Comogre, we may shatter the power of our enemies. In
this way you shall obtain the gold you want, and our reward for
guiding and helping you will be our deliverance from hostile

attacks, from the fear under which our ancestors lived and which destroys our enjoyment of peace."

The words rang with authority and truth, and the love of gain and the hope of gold fairly made the Spaniards' mouths water.

Only the most precious gift in Balboa's possession could repay his debt to Comogre and his people: he would make them Christians. For the wise youth, the eldest son, he personally chose the name of Carlos, in honor of the son of their Queen, Mad Juana, who was soon to rule Spain.

The door to everything Vasco Núñez de Balboa had planned and hoped for—gold, fame, the longed-for South Sea—this door, opened by Carlos, dazzled him. And thus Europeans first heard of the fabulous lands whose gold and silver were to flow back to Spain and thence over the old continent, nourishing the new commerce, financing the new enterprises that from many countries were to spread over the face of the world.

6.

A certain Vasco Núñez, who, in the opinion of most people was a man of action rather than judgment.

PETER MARTYR

Nothing was heard in Darién but talk of the treasure that, since the day God created the earth, had been awaiting the Spaniards by the shore of the southern sea.

Soon after Balboa had returned from Puerto Careta, the envoy Valdivia returned from Hispaniola. Six months had passed, six eventful months. Valdivia brought with him as much food as could be loaded onto his small boat, but best of all he brought Don Diego's appointment of Vasco Núñez as governor and captain general of Darién. Valdivia told Balboa how the wanton loss of men by Ojeda and Nicuesa had angered and saddened Don Diego, and how both he and the royal treasurer had written urging the King to secure Balboa in authority as the one man capable of maintaining the colony of Darién. Don Diego had also informed the King that he was sending provisions to the

colonists and would continue to supply them regularly. Just
as Don Diego had tried to prevent Nicuesa and Ojeda from
sailing to their provinces on Tierra Firme, which he claimed was
under his jurisdiction, so now he sought to reaffirm his viceregal status by assisting Balboa. Ferdinand, acting on the reports
from Hispaniola, was later to approve Don Diego's appointment
of Balboa as temporary governor, but Valdivia did not know this
when he returned to Darién.

The provisions were soon consumed, and again the men were
back on limited rations. Peter Martyr might write glowingly of
the admirable fecundity of Urabá, where everything sowed or
planted grew marvelously well; he might compose panegyrics
in praise of cabbages, beets, lettuces, salads, and other garden
stuffs that ripened in ten days. But this amazing rate of growth
and fertility were offset by the sudden, devastating fury of the
elements, hurricanes and cloudbursts that in a few hours ruined
the colonists' labors and hungry hopes. The crops were washed
out and the gardens smothered under debris carried down from
the surrounding hills. Before he could seek treasure, Balboa had
to solve the immediate problem of providing food. He decided
to implore Don Diego a second time for prompt assistance. Also
he was eager to announce to his superiors the wonderful, joyful
news told him by Don Carlos, the eldest son of Comogre. Ad-
dressing letters to Don Diego and the King, he explained in
detail everything he had done and everything he had been told,
and he begged for a thousand soldiers, armed and supplied, to
follow him across the mountains separating the two seas.

Again Valdivia was entrusted with the commission. In addition to the letters, he was charged to deliver two thousand four
hundred ounces of gold, the King's fifth, to the royal treasurer;
and again Balboa propitiated the latter with some choice bits
for his own pocket. Many colonists took this opportunity to
send their shares of gold back to their families or creditors in
Spain. In January 1512 the little caravel with Valdivia and
seventeen men, freighted with desperate needs and astounding
news and gold given by the Indians or stolen from them, put
out for Hispaniola. It never reached port, but sank with its gold
and carried down with it its hopes; its crew had a strange and
terrible fate.

(When the little vessel sailed from Darién it passed out of the story of Balboa; the subsequent adventures of its crew are a proper prologue to the story of Cortés. Here is the frail link that connects those two great conquistadors, an incident worth recalling. Seven years later—in 1519—when Cortés was ready to start his march into Mexico, he shrewdly guessed from certain clues that there might be some Spanish captives languishing on Yucatán, Spaniards who spoke the Indians' language and knew their customs. By native traders he dispatched letters to these captives, sending presents that they might use as ransom. Only one, Jerónimo de Aguilar, a monk, responded to Cortés's invitation and joined him. This was the tale Aguilar told, and thus the fate of Valdivia became known. Eight men survived the shipwreck of the caravel, and they were captured and imprisoned by the chief of the region. When, after a few weeks' rest and feeding, they had regained their health and weight, four were led away, and their horrified friends saw them slaughtered and eaten. Then they understood their own fate: they were being fattened for the table. Faced with such a limited future they tried to escape, but only Aguilar and another lived to reach a distant tribe, where again they were captured. Here, in time, Aguilar won his master's confidence and received a position of trust in his household. The habit of self-denial and an old and worn Book of Hours were Aguilar's only links with his race and his vocation. It was from this master that he obtained his freedom when Cortés's letter was brought him. The monk then hastened to his friend, Gonzalo Guerrero, the only other survivor to take him back to his countrymen. But Guerrero would not go. "Brother Aguilar," he said, "I am married and have three children, and the Indians look on me as a cacique and captain in wartime. I have my face tattooed and my ears pierced; what would the Spaniards say should they see me in this guise?" Guerrero remained with the Indians, with his wife and children; he had accepted their life, among them he was a chief and a man of importance. Alone, Aguilar hastened to join Cortés. He spoke the language of the Mayans, and with the Indian maid, Marina or Malinche, who spoke Mayan and Aztec, he served Cortés in the advance onto the valley of Mexico into the presence of the great Moctezuma.)

Balboa, having dispatched Valdivia to beg for food and supplies, was not content to wait. A little food trickled into Darién,

brought by Indians who traded their produce for Spanish trifles.
This was a help, but the presence of the native traders, whom
the Spaniards knew to be spies, reminded them constantly how
precarious their position was. For many reasons—to obtain food,
to explore the countryside, to subdue near-by enemies, perhaps
to find more treasure—Balboa organized an expedition into the
surrounding territory.

Already rumors had been heard of the great wealth of Dabaibe,
of its goddess whose temple was bursting with golden nuggets
—rumors that persisted for centuries, fata morgana rumors that
led generations of men into the morasses and jungles south of
the Gulf of Urabá. Dabaibe lay up the San Juan or Atrato River,
whose seven mouths—like the Nile, noted Peter Martyr—created
a tangle of water, quagmires, and jungles. Taking about one hundred and sixty men, Balboa divided the group into two parties
and explored widely along the river. The Spaniards penetrated
to villages from which all the natives had fled and which yielded
some pieces of golden jewelry; when the river cut like a dark
tunnel through the enveloping jungle and progress became more
and more difficult, they turned back. They probed into a new
territory, a land of swamps, of shallow lakes, whose inhabitants
lived in commodious homes nesting in the branches of great
spreading trees; in floodtimes they caught the fish that got en-
meshed in the dense branches. The Spaniards had to start chop-
ping down their trees to make them submit. Balboa himself described the trip through this terrain villainously compounded
of water, mud, and trees:

"And the swamps of this land are not such light affairs that we
move through them joyfully, for many times we have to go
naked through marshes and water for one and two and three
leagues, with our clothing collected and placed on the shield on
top of the head; and leaving some marshes we enter into others
and proceed in this manner two and three and ten days."

Forays such as this netted the Spaniards some food and some
gold, but widened the area of hostility and fused many tribes into
a concerted, active opposition.

Unable to find Dabaibe, Balboa returned to Darién. In a village on the river that dominated the region he left thirty men

under his trusted friend, Hurtado. Hurtado spent his time hunting down stray Indians, and when he had collected twenty-four he shipped them back to Darién to be sold as slaves; with them he sent twenty Spaniards who had been wounded or were sick from the fevers that bred in those swamps. The large canoe that carried the captives and Spaniards was ambushed by Cémaco, who, still vigilant and still vengeful, was ready at every favorable occasion to destroy the hated white men who had invaded his country; only two Spaniards escaped the trap of swirling water and concealing jungle and brought the tragic news back to Hurtado. Lonely, threatened by the dark forest and by the unseen Indians, frightened by a report that the implacable Cémaco had joined with four other chiefs to overwhelm Darién, Hurtado and his men left their post to warn Balboa.

Hurtado's news of a native uprising might have been dismissed by the settlers as a prank played by panicked nerves if luck had not still favored Vasco Núñez. He was forewarned not only of the plot but of all its details—the same thing was to happen to Cortés in Cholula—by one of his native sweethearts. Her brother, a warrior close to Cémaco, told her: "Listen to me, my dear sister, and keep to yourself what I tell you. The caciques of the country are resolved to submit no longer to the invader's tyranny. Five caciques"—and he named them—"have combined and collected one hundred canoes. Five thousand warriors on land and water are prepared. Provisions have been collected in Tichiri for their maintenance, and the caciques have already divided among themselves the heads and property of the Spaniards." Then, fearing for her safety, lest she be harmed in the confusion of battle, he urged her to hide on the fateful day. All this, forgetful of her relatives and her people, the trembling girl told Vasco Núñez, her lover.

Balboa struck and struck hard. With seventy men he marched overland to Cémaco's village, where he found that the chief had fled to Dabaibe; at the same time Colmenares with sixty men was paddling up the Atrato River. At Tichiri the two parties met. They captured four ringleaders—again Cémaco had slipped away—and the provisions that had been collected. The four leaders were hanged on the spot. The people were terrified. Not one of them dared raise a finger against the torrent of Spanish wrath. Peace was established, and those chiefs who submitted to the Spaniards were not harmed. Hundreds of frightened Indians carried the great store of foodstuffs from Tichiri to Darién.

At last provisions were plentiful. The country was pacified. But as 1512 drew to a close the colonists realized that something must have happened to Valdivia; disaster had prevented the completion of his mission. The town council met to send representatives to Hispaniola and to Spain. Balboa asked to be allowed to go, to plead for supplies and additional soldiers and colonists, to proclaim the existence of the Southern Sea, and to secure a thousand recruits who would fight their way across the kingdom of Tubanamá to it. But the people would not hear of his leaving them, and instead the council named Rodrigo de Colmenares and Juan de Quecido, an older man, the only settler who had been accompanied by his Spanish wife; like Colmenares, he had been one of Nicuesa's officials. As pledges for their return, Quecido left his wife, Colmenares his properties and slaves— he had spent large sums in planting crops, by the sale of which he hoped to get his hungering companions' gold. The two envoys left at the beginning of November. The journey from Darién to Hispaniola required only eight days with a favorable wind; it took them one hundred brutal days to reach Santo Domingo. So strong were the gales and currents that the vessel seemed to be sailing uphill. The envoys reported fully to Don Diego, answered his many questions, pleaded for supplies and men, and then took passage on a merchant ship that was sailing for Spain. It was May when they finally arrived. When they were received by the King, Peter Martyr noted that "a look at these men is enough to demonstrate the insalubrious climate and temperature of Darién, for they are as yellow as though they suffered from liver complaint, and are puffy." Soon after his arrival in Spain, Quecido died; and alone Colmenares represented Darién. Through Fonseca he met Enciso; he never met Zamudio, for the latter, loyal to Balboa, was disliked by the powerful Fonseca and had gone into hiding. The court and the Council of the Indies, with Fonseca at its head, saw Balboa only through the venomous eyes of Enciso, and Colmenares was too much the courtier to oppose an opinion held by the man who personally directed the affairs of the New World.

Meanwhile, back in Darién, the colony had attained, though

briefly, a peace never before known in the New World. In the year during which he had been the governor of the colony, Balboa by his bravery and diplomacy had conquered the surrounding tribes or won them over as allies; by his generosity each Spaniard had received his share of the spoils. Each colonist had gold, land, and captive slaves. Darién had become a prize that men might aspire to control. Two malcontents, the lawyer Corral and a friend of his, Rua, sought out those who had been friendly to Enciso and Nicuesa and, working on their greed and jealousy, struck at Balboa through charges against his friend Hurtado. Arming themselves, they threw Hurtado into jail. Balboa had him released. Then, accusing Balboa directly, they said he had been unjust in dividing the gold. Balboa met their charges shrewdly. Leaving a sum of gold where the agitators would be certain to find it, he left Darién with some friends to go hunting. News of his departure was brought to the two ringleaders; they immediately found the gold, appropriated and distributed it. Their greed dictated the distribution and they kept so much for themselves that their disgruntled followers turned on them. Messengers sent after Balboa begged him to return at once to Darién. Not even the royal decree naming Balboa governor could have secured him his position more firmly than this invitation from those he led.

The new year had come.   1513 was to be Balboa's year.

7.

The Admiral who first explored this region believes these peaks rise to a height of forty miles, and he says that at the base of the mountains there is a road leading to the South Sea.

PETER MARTYR

With the new year came the help promised by Don Diego. A ship brought what the viceroy could collect on the spot and dispatch at once. Later two more ships arrived loaded with wine, cheese, biscuit, and bacon, badly needed weapons, seeds, plants, cuttings, chickens, and pigs; they carried one hundred and fifty sanguine and energetic new volunteers. The captain of these ships handed Balboa two very important letters. One, which he fell on his knees to accept, was from His Catholic Majesty appointing Vasco Núñez de Balboa temporary governor and captain of the province of Darién. Pride, greater dignity, new-found authority, and joy filled him as he read aloud the royal words. The other letter he opened and read to himself. It came from Zamudio. Dated later than the royal decree, it described the change in the temper and attitude of the court as Enciso lied and falsified and perjured to picture Balboa as a dangerous ruffian who had expelled Enciso and Nicuesa to satisfy his own lust for power, an upstart who, with an ocean between him and his King, had felt free to ignore royal commands and usurp the government in a country where no one was strong enough to challenge his reign of violence. He warned that already they were choosing a successor who would land with many men to destroy the anarchy he had instituted and break this rebellious Balboa to the King's power; he warned that Balboa would be sent back to Spain to be tried for treason. All this Zamudio had learned through friends, for he himself dared not go to court, so thoroughly had Enciso poisoned all against him.

Perhaps, as he read the bad news that Zamudio related, Balboa regretted that he had not, when he had had him in his power, arranged Enciso's death. So well did Enciso mix his frustrations and lies with treacle and law that no one in Spain was aware that Darién was outside Ojeda's province and that thus Enciso had had no authority there, that it was Balboa who had saved all their lives in San Sebastián. Balboa would have loved to return to Spain to confront his enemy. The truth he did not fear. He feared lest a successor arrive before he, Vasco Núñez, should have discovered the Southern Sea, before he could present a new ocean to the King, and by this act win the right to be believed when he told the true story; this alone Balboa feared. He could not afford any delay; he would have to act without any loss of time, using what he had at hand.

It was to vindicate his past and future actions that he wrote his long and famous letter of January 20, 1513, to the King. He told the King fully and with pride and complete obedience how he had worked for two things: to find gold to send to His Majesty, and to be ever vigilant for the well-being and protection of all the men. He spoke of the promise of incalculable treasure that he would find, and made suggestions for the supplying, pacification, and civil rule of the territory; he listed the amounts he had sent the King at various times by different emissaries; and he signed himself "The creature and creation of Your Highness, who kisses your hands and feet." Only once did he slap at the human insects that grew and lived by sucking out his blood:

"I entreat Your Highness to command that no Bachelor of Law nor any other thing, unless it should be of medicine, may pass to these parts of the mainland, for no Bachelor comes here who is not the devil, and they lead the life of devils, and not only are they bad, but they even contrive how to bring about a thousand lawsuits and villainies."

That for Enciso, that for Corral.

He whetted the greed, not only of the King, but of a whole generation when he described the gold that was to be found plentifully, easily.

"The method of collecting this gold is without any labor, in two ways; the one is to wait for the stream to rise in the ravines, and, when the floods pass, the gold remains exposed, washed down from the mountain sides in very large grains. The Indians indicate they are of the size of oranges and like the fist. The other method is to wait until the vegetation on the mountains becomes dry and set it on fire, and, after it is burnt, collect the gold in great quantity and in very beautiful grains."

Peter Martyr, who read Balboa's letter, broadcast to all of Europe:

"Spaniards will not need to mine and dig far into the earth nor to cut asunder mountains in quest of gold; but will find it plentifully on the upper crust of the earth or in the sands of rivers dried up by the heat of summer."

And the gold that was to come from Mexico and Peru, the silver of Potosí and Zacatecas, confirmed him as a prophet.

With Zamudio's news to warn him, Balboa quickly made up his mind. He could not, he dared not, wait for the reenforcements; for with them would come the new governor, the man who was already being chosen to supplant him. He looked over the men of Darién carefully. He passed over the newcomers, for already they were ailing: they could not yet put up with hardships or content their stomachs, accustomed to better food, with the native bread, wild herbs without salt, and river water that was not always wholesome. The veterans of Darién had already been inoculated with doses of the New World; they had become hardened to the insects, the rain and the heat, the foods, the hunger and the thirst, the fighting, and the enemies that they must expect. Carefully he chose his men and armed them well with swords, crossbows, and arquebuses. One hundred and ninety men, a compact, seasoned, greedy group, loyal to him, trusting in his leadership—with their help he would plant the banner of Castile and Aragon on the shore of the unknown Southern Sea.

He did not hide the danger from them or slight the rewards that would be theirs. He told them that Don Carlos had urged him not to try to cross without having one thousand soldiers, so powerful and warlike were the tribes they would meet; but that if each man, with God's help, fought with the fury of five, they would conquer all obstacles and win glory and great riches. Horses they did not have to terrorize the Indians, but they did have bloodhounds. His own dog, Leoncico, tireless and fierce, his russet body scarred with wounds received in many encounters with the Indians, had so proved his worth that no complaints had been made when Balboa gave him a share of booty secured in fighting. Thus Leoncico had accumulated property! The party was increased by natives, some slave and some free, for without Indians the Spaniards could not take a step. Indians supplied and paddled the large canoes dug out of mighty tree-trunks, carried all baggage, built shelters, rafts, or bridges as the occasion demanded, gathered and cooked the food, and by trails known to them opened the New World to the Spaniards. The time would come when these native guides would even have to carry the sick conquerors in native hammocks [1] slung from poles. In a country without draft animals, without land-transport of

---

[1] Both the word (*hámaca*) and the object originated in Central America.

any kind, poor Indians had served their native masters as beasts of burden as they were to serve their new white masters. The pattern was the same; only the burden changed.

On the first day of September 1513 Balboa and his men left Darién. A brigantine and ten canoes carried them to Puerto Careta, the home of his father-in-law and friend. Two pleasant, active days he spent there gathering valuable information about the route to take, collecting supplies, and selecting the men, native and Spanish, who were to accompany him. About half his men were left behind to protect the boats.

In miniature, the expedition of Balboa is a true picture of what Spanish expeditions were to be: the small insecure footing along the coasts, the advance into unknown and hostile territory, the daily problems of food, health, and transportation, the conquest of nature and natives, the inevitability of the triumph of steel and gunpowder, the sad slaughter as two antithetical civilizations met and tested their unequal strengths, the unbelievable energy that drove the invaders, the singleness of purpose, the final victory. Sometimes one element becomes the dominant note in a particular saga, sometimes another; but always all the elements are there. Other conquistadors, Soto and Cabeza de Vaca, were to have longer and more dramatic odysseys; Cortés and Pizarro and Belalcázar were to conquer far greater and richer kingdoms; but all of them came after Vasco Núñez. His was the first, daring step into the unknown interior. As Columbus had been a pioneer in opening the gates of the Atlantic, so Balboa was the pioneer who ventured still farther into the unknown, into the land of the New World. This, then, and not the number of days or miles, or millions, is the measure of his greatness. Unlike Cortés he had no legend of the returning god, Quetzal-coatl,[2] to smooth his path and paralyze his enemies; he had no

---

[2] Among the Mexicans there was a prophecy that their god Quetzalcoatl, the Feathered Serpent, would return in the guise of a white, bearded conqueror from the East. Cortés fitted this ancient prediction so well that Moctezuma was not sure, until too late, whether he should welcome the god or fight an intruder. Cortés, in his conquest of Mexico, certainly the most famous of all the Spanish assaults on the New World, invites comparison with Balboa. My own feeling is that had Balboa escaped execution—as Cortés did—he would have rivaled him in stature and achievement.

long-remembering, nostalgic Bernal Díaz to record his deeds and thoughts and stratagems for posterity. Balboa, the man, rising to greatness and vision, flashed upon the world and vanished in a cloud of blood.

Leaving the steaming, swampy lowlands, Balboa and his men headed for the mountains. Immediately the jungle swallowed them, that massed green that majestically swept almost to the top of the cordilleras. For two days they worked their way over jagged, mountainous country until they arrived at a cluster of leaf-roofed houses, the land and village of Ponca, who, as previously, had fled before the intruders. But this time Balboa, marching away from his base, was not content to leave an enemy between himself and the coast.

Occupying the village, Balboa sent to Ponca messengers promising friendship and offering protection against his enemies. Ponca grabbed at this invitation and quickly returned from his hiding place. The two leaders greeted one another warmly and then exchanged presents: Ponca showered Balboa with gold, knowing the surest way to the white man's heart was by such offerings, and excused its modest amount by reminding Balboa that the Spaniards had taken all his gold on their previous visit. Not to be outdone, Balboa presented him with necklaces of glass beads, mirrors, copper bells, and other trifles that the Indians prized highly, and then secured his friendship firmly with a special gift of iron hatchets, the article most valued by the natives. Until the Europeans brought the Indians iron, stones wrought to a razor edge were laboriously used to fell great trees, to build houses, and to shape canoes. Delighted with this princely present, Ponca offered his new friend guides and bearers. Careta's men, who had served in these capacities, were dismissed with presents and sent home well satisfied with Balboa's generosity. Twelve men who were too ill to proceed were left behind for Ponca to care for and, on their recovery, to be helped back to Puerto Careta.

On September 20, Balboa left his good friend Ponca and pushed on. He faced the sudden, sharp lift of the mountains as they stretched up to their full height. During the next four days the party struggled step by step up slippery cliffs, up tree-tangled slopes; thunderous cascades caused long detours; boiling, foaming streams were perilously crossed on bridges improvised by the natives; they scrambled up and on in the darkness of the matted forest.[3] They spent four sweating, puffing days before they reached the territory ruled by the chief Quarequá, powerful, rich, warlike, and so secure in his remote mountain fastness that no one had thought to warn him of the white men who had newly come to the coast. Quarequá, the invincible, held the key to transit across the Isthmus; here would be decided the outcome of their quest. Balboa first saw the redoubtable chief when the latter, surrounded by his war chiefs and backed by his thousand warriors, advanced, as was his custom, to challenge intruders. "Retrace your steps if you do not wish to be killed to the last man."

So for a moment they faced one another, the small band of Spaniards wearing metal helmets and corselets, their swords drawn, the crossbows fixed, the arquebuses primed; crouched at their feet, their trained dogs waited the signal to jump at the throats of the two-legged game. Their guides and bearers, men of Ponca's tribe, hung back wondering if their powerful new friends could overcome Quarequá, the undisputed master of that region, whose name spelled terror, whose men had never known defeat. The Spaniards looked at the large force opposing them, blocking their path. Quarequá and his war chiefs wore plates of gold on their chests and arms, massive pieces beautifully worked that served as armor and as insignia of rank, resplendent against their copper skins; their breechclouts flaunted golden codpieces or bright seashells to cover their nakedness; they carried shields made of wood and covered with animal skins, heavy two-handed wooden swords, bows and arrows, and fire-hardened, sharp-pointed wooden lances that, hurled from a throwing-stick, could go clean through a naked enemy. They relied on these deadly javelins, on their vast superiority of numbers, on supernatural aid invoked by beaten drums and blown conch shells. For a moment the two sides were poised for battle, the Indians disdainful of this small intrusive party, the Spaniards confident of their firearms. Then the slaughter began.

Shouting their battle cries, seeking to drown the small band under waves of warriors, the Indians, led by Quarequá, threw

---

[3] Prevost in 1853 found the forest so dense that for eleven days he did not see the clear sky.

themselves on the Spaniards, who, not yielding an inch, fired
their weapons. At this point-blank discharge, the natives stopped.
What gods were these that could vomit fire and thunder and kill
and wound men they had not even touched? And as they stood,
the archers loosed their crossbows and killed and wounded more.
Stunned, for a moment the Indians wavered; and, before they
could turn to flee, the Spaniards were among them, wielding
their sharp steel swords, hacking off arms, legs, cutting through
a thigh, severing a head; like butchers cutting up beef and mut-
ton for market, they hacked and cut until Quarequá and six
hundred were slain. The dogs pursued the naked, terror-stricken
natives and brought them down as though they were wild boars
or timid deer. Those who were left alive looked with horror on
the battlefield strewn, not with corpses decently slain, but with
a mass of arms, legs, torsos, and heads, separate and terrible. Not
a Spaniard was killed, and only a few had received slight wounds.

Among the prisoners taken were Quarequá's brother and other
chiefs who, dressed in long cotton skirts, were accused by the
interpreter of wearing women's clothes because they shared the
same passion. To the Spaniards such abnormality was abhorrent
and a sign of the Devil, and Balboa righteously ordered forty of
these perverts to be torn to pieces by the dogs. Peter Martyr
comments approvingly:

"When the natives saw how severely Vasco had treated these
shameless men, they pressed about him as though he were Her-
cules, and spitting upon those whom they suspected of being
guilty of this vice, they begged him to exterminate them, for the
contagion was confined to the courtiers and had not yet spread
to the people. They gave it to be understood that this sin was
the cause of famine and sickness."

When the dogs had finished their terrible task, the bodies
were burned.

Surrounded by the broken, fearful natives, who in a few hours
had seen their chief, all their nobles, and most of their warriors
killed, the Spaniards entered their village. The houses were sys-
tematically searched for loot; the golden breastplates and arm-
bands, the golden, polished, mirrorlike discs, and the fantastic
nose-plugs were stripped from the dead; that was done before

Balboa and his men ate and rested in the village of the dead chief. Night came swiftly, and in this mountain country it was cold.

So thorough had been the defeat of Quarequá that Balboa felt free to leave his sick and wounded men in the village to recuperate. Dismissing the guides and bearers furnished him by Ponca, he sent them back with presents. The stunning news of the great victory traveled back with them.

Early in the morning Balboa would take the trail and, with some newly made captives as guides, would lead his seventy men to the mountain peak from which he had been promised a view of the Southern Sea, that sea which he had staked so much, had struggled and fought so hard, to reach. So near he was, so very near, the promise so imminent, that he forgot that he was tired, forgot the cold that made his weary muscles stiff, and knew only that the cold night was long and never-ending. Doubt haunted him, and he wondered if he had been told legend or lies. Would he find the Sea as the Indian youth had promised; or had he spent his men, his time and strength, in following false words cunningly spoken? Tomorrow he would stand on his peak and feed his eyes on the blue of the distant sea; but until then he must wait in the awful loneliness of his purpose.

A slight wind came with the morning, and with the dawn they were on the trail. That morning, September 25, a guide, pointing to a near-by mountain, told Balboa that from its summit the Southern Sea was visible. Longingly, he looked where the man pointed. He bade his men wait, and taking only his dog, Leoncico, climbed the peak. With each step forward his tension eased. A moment more, a few more steps, he was at the last rise; he would know whether his venture was to be crowned with success. He was at the bare open summit. He looked, and there was the sight never seen before by any man coming out of his world; and the sight he saw brought him to his knees. There was the Sea! a pellucid blue, shot with the gold and silver of the mid-morning sun, a mighty sea that thrust an arm deep into the land. He raised his hand to Heaven and saluted the Southern Sea! And its presence proclaimed his success, his firm reconciliation with the King, his fame, his fortune. From his wildly beating heart he poured forth his boundless gratitude to God—thanking Him and all the heavenly host who had reserved this glory for him, a man of but small wit and knowledge, of little experience and lowly parentage.

When Balboa's first wave of relief and thanksgiving was spent he waved his hand to his companions and when they had come up to him he showed them the great Sea heretofore unknown to the inhabitants of Europe, Africa, and Asia. Prouder than Hannibal showing Italy and the Alps to his soldiers, Balboa promised great riches to them: "Behold the much-desired ocean! Behold, all you men who have shared such efforts, behold the country of which the son of Comogre and all the others told us such wonders!" And the Spaniards knelt and sang a Te Deum, and their song of thankfulness, of success, of praise, filled the thin mountain air.

To mark this spot stones were piled in the form of an altar and on its top a cross was planted into which the letters F and J were carved. In the name of Castile and Aragon, of Ferdinand who was regent for his mad daughter, Juana, they dedicated the peak where Balboa first glimpsed the new sea. Balboa thus gave to Charles, who was soon to reign as King of Spain and Emperor, dominion over the vast Pacific.

As was customary, all this was officially written down and the notary who certified to the discovery of the Sea of the South listed the sixty-seven men who stood beside the altar. One of them was Francisco Pizarro, to whom this was the first step in his twenty-year search for the gold of Peru.

The noon sun stood in the sky as Balboa took a last look and then started down the escarpment, eager to have done with the mountains and forests and stand beside his sea.

His path led straight into the territory of a warlike chief, Chiapes, who, like Quarequá, stood at the head of his warriors and scorned the small, straggling band of tired men who sought passage through his country. Again the arquebuses blazed with supernatural lightning and thunder, again the dogs were unleashed to leap and tear, again the chief and his lieutenants fled while the people fell to the earth too frightened to stand up before such potent mysteries. In a few moments the encounter had been settled, and Balboa commanded his men not to kill: he did not want dead Indians—he wanted friends and allies. As he had won over Ponca so now he won Chiapes. Messengers were sent after the terrified chief and he returned with them; mutually acceptable presents—this time the Spaniards received pearls —were exchanged; Balboa had made another ally.

In Chiapes's pleasant village Balboa decided to rest a few days. He paid off the guides and sent them back with messages for the men he had left in their village, to tell them to rejoin him here where he now awaited them. At the same time he sent out three patrols to search for the nearest way to the new-found sea. Two days later the patrol led by Alonso Martín suddenly came on two canoes. The presence of canoes on dry land arrested their attention. The men stood there, wondering, discussing, trying to decipher the meaning of this riddle, when they heard a far-off whisper; and as they watched, the powerful Pacific tide, many times higher than any they had seen on the Caribbean coast, gobbled up the dry beach and quickly floated the canoes. Martín stepped into one of the canoes and called on his men to witness that he was the first Spaniard to venture on the new sea; one of his men stepped into the remaining canoe and announced that he was the second. Having made these gestures worthy of the greatest explorers, Martín and his patrol quickly returned to the village of Chiapes.

When Balboa heard Martín's jubilant news he quickly collected twenty-six men who had regained their strength and started along Martín's trail to the sea. Through the great forest he marched, through the forest that without a break reached to the very limit of the land. Suddenly the trees stopped and he stepped out into the hot sun. He looked at the dry, tree-ringed bay and then, returning to the shade, lay down to wait for the tide to bring the sea to his feet. He had not long to wait: impetuously the water came in and took possession of the bay.

Balboa unfurled the banner that he had carried with him for this solemn act, a precious banner on which the Virgin and Child smiled above the arms of Castile and Aragon; he drew his sword and fastened his buckler and, conscious of the moment and deed, walked into the sea until his knees were covered.

"Long live the high and mighty monarchs, Don Ferdinand and Dona Juana, sovereigns of Castile, of León, of Aragon, in whose name, and for the royal crown of Castile, I take real and corporal and actual possession of these seas and land and coasts and ports and islands of the south, and all thereunto annexed; and of the kingdoms and provinces which do or may appertain to them, in whatever manner, or by whatever right or title, ancient or modern, in times past, present, or to come, without any contradiction; and if other prince or captain, Christian or infidel, of any law, sect, or condition whatsoever, shall pretend any right to these lands and seas, I am ready and prepared to maintain and defend them, in the name of the Castilian sovereigns present and future, whose is the empire and dominion over these Indian islands, and Tierra Firme, northern and southern, with all their seas, both on the arctic and the antarctic poles, on either side of the equinoctial line, whether within or without the tropics of Cancer and Capricorn, both now and in all times, as long as the world endures, and unto the final day of judgment of all mankind."

As Balboa had spoken his great claim, so the notary wrote it, and to that document the men put their names. Then they waded into the bay and, cupping their hands, lifted its water to their mouths. It was as salty as the waters that beat against their Spanish coast; by this simple test they reassured themselves that it was indeed an ocean they had found; and standing there they bared their heads and thanked God for His great favor to them. Back on shore they cut three great crosses in trees whose roots ran far out into the water, one for the Father, one for the Son, and one for the Holy Ghost. And the forest and the sun and the water witnessed their sacred act of possession. It was September 29, and in honor of the saint's feast day, Balboa called the bay after San Miguel.

Balboa had stood on his peak, and now he gazed at his ocean. Was it, as Columbus had deduced without ever having seen it, a narrow body of water with the River Ganges but ten days' sail from its shore? Did the bits of coral come from Cochin China, the chili pepper from the Spice Islands; was China almost within reach; was he close to the Malay Peninsula, toward which Portugal and Spain were racing? Malacca was known as the Golden Chersonese—"a city of wonderful size with upwards of twenty-five thousand households and most productive of merchandise in India by means of that most famous market where not only abound the different spices and all kinds of perfumes, but also gold and silver, pearls and precious stones." So Columbus had announced and the words of the Indians seemed to promise as much. Conceived out of greed and hope, fed by ignorance, this was the dream-child of the Spanish mind.

Balboa did not know that a short while before this the Portuguese, sailing around Africa, had reached Malacca, the greatest trading post on the crossroads of eastern Asia, or that within two years, in 1511, the great Portuguese viceroy, Albuquerque, had conquered the city for his king. A little later when the *Victoria*, the only surviving ship of those that had started out with Magellan, stumbled home with news of the immensity of the sea Balboa had discovered, Balboa himself would be dead.

8.

Are pearls, as Aristotle states, the heart of the shells, or are they rather, as Pliny says, the product of the intestines and really the excrement of these animals? Do oysters pass their whole life attached to the same rock, or do they move through the sea in numbers, under the leadership of older ones? Does one shell produce one or many pearls? Must one have a rake to detach them? Are pearls in a soft or a hard state when they enter the shell? Is it not really absurd to keep silence about a subject interesting to men and women, which inflames everybody with such immoderate desires? Spain may henceforth satisfy the desires of a Cleopatra for pearls.

PETER MARTYR

Balboa had crossed the jagged central cordillera and tasted the salt of this new sea that without fog or fury quietly filled the deep Gulf of San Miguel. A month had passed since he had started out from Darién, a memorable month crowned with an impressive climax: he had crossed the Isthmus. By destroying Quarequá and securing alliances with Ponca and Chiapes, he had made his line of retreat safe. He had collected much gold. But the party had known terrible days on the trail; eighteen arduous days in which they had hacked out each foot of path through an almost impenetrable forest wall, slipped and stumbled in oozing black mud, inched up water-smooth cliffs—those days of desperate labor, of constant worry, of mounting tension had left them aching with fatigue. They wanted rest, now that at last they could relax. The men were all together again, for those who had been left behind at the village of Quarequá, unable to advance after spending their strength in scaling the mountains, had followed as ordered. As lazy as the blue water he had gazed on, Balboa rested, content and quiet and easy, in the village of Chiapes—a little pause before his restless active spirit again possessed him.

From Chiapes he learned that the pearls he had presented to the Spaniards came from his neighbor and ancient enemy, Cuquera. The pearls had piqued Balboa's curiosity, aroused his greed and hopes. Gold was becoming commonplace, and its weight, the measure of its value, made its transportation a problem. But pearls! Pearls were light and greatly treasured, pearls were associated with silks and spices, pearls bespoke proximity to the longed-for Orient. The delighted Chiapes responded handsomely when Balboa suggested that he would pay a visit to this rich neighbor, and he supplied canoes and paddlers to carry Balboa and fifty men. Hoping to conquer by surprise, they were paddled up the river in the blackness of night, but an alarm was given and when the party reached the village it was deserted. Cuquera, thinking he had an Indian enemy to fight, returned in the morning ready for battle. The mere sight of these strange men with white faces framed by metal headdresses to which plumes were fastened, with flowing beards hiding the lower half of their faces, wearing exotic clothes and carrying unknown weapons, sent Cuquera dashing for the safety of the forest. Again, as with Ponca and with Chiapes, Balboa sent captives and emissaries offering assistance, protection and peace, or promising ruin and death; and again the envoys urged that Cuquera do as their chief had done and told of the supreme authority of this great stranger's magic, of his love for gold and pearls, of his wonderful gifts. And so another Indian chief became his friend. It was Cuquera who pointed seaward and said that from an island not too distant from the shore came the pearls that he had given Balboa in quantity. Loaded with gold and pearls and treasuring the information he had received, Balboa returned to Chiapes's village, which he had made his headquarters.

Balboa could not rest satisfied with his achievement; his curiosity and his ambition demanded that he reach those islands whence the pearls had come. He told Chiapes his intention and asked for canoes and paddlers. But the chief begged him not to attempt a voyage that would be extremely hazardous because of the vicious storms that lashed out suddenly and in full strength during the autumn months, told him that even the amphibious natives, expert and wise in the ways of navigation, did not dare venture far from land. But Balboa, unwilling to recognize obstacles, replied that God and all the heavenly host would assist him because he was laboring for Him to discover treasures that would pay for the wars that must be waged against enemies of the Faith. With such powerful medicine aiding the Spaniards, Chiapes thought that he had nothing to fear and, unwilling to allow the Spaniards to leave his territory under any other escort than his own, insisted on guiding them. Sixty Spaniards went with Balboa, and with Chiapes and his men they embarked in nine great canoes, each hewed out of one mighty tree.

Hardly had the Spaniards reached the open Gulf when a snarling tempest raced down on them. Sheets of rain closed them in and obscured all landmarks, the wind pushed their canoes about, the waves tossed them until, trembling and frightened, the men knew not which way to steer or how to keep afloat. The Indians lashed the canoes together, side by side, to keep them from overturning. Thoroughly alarmed, their quest for pearls forgotten, they hoped only that they might not perish in the storm. Taking refuge on a little islet, they thought themselves safe, and secured their canoes to boulders and small trees. But during the night the tide, that surging deep Pacific tide which they had so far only observed, not coped with, rose foot by foot until its crashing breakers nearly covered the whole islet; foot by foot the men climbed to the highest point and clung there waist-deep in swirling water waiting for morning to come, for the water to recede. Chiapes and his men must have reasoned that the great magic that Balboa had invoked had failed him even as their own sometimes failed them.

Morning came and the growling tide was sucked away. Step by step they descended from their precarious foothold and took account of the damage they had suffered. Their food and equipment were swept away, their canoes split and filled with sand.

The Indians patched and caulked the vessels with moss, pliable bark, and tough marine plants, until they had been made seaworthy enough to carry the men to the nearest shore. Once again they were on the mainland, weak from their terrifying vigil, their wet clothes sticking to their bodies and their skin loose and ribbed from long exposure in the water. They were very hungry and very, very tired.

They were on a part of the coast ruled by a chieftain called Tumaco. Before they could enter his village, before they could eat and rest, with only their swords and courage to rely on, they had to defeat the chief, who with his men denied them entrance. Led by Balboa, the Spaniards threw themselves on the Indians with such fury and skill that soon they had put Tumaco to flight. To the captives and envoys who came in Balboa's behalf, Tumaco listened; but still fearful of the Spaniards' prowess, he sent his son back to act in his place. Balboa presented the naked youth with a Spanish shirt and other presents and returned him to his father—bearing again an offer of friendship. This kindness and generosity won the father's heart and restored his courage. Followed by attendants, Tumaco arrived at his village and, prompted beforehand, offered the Spaniards a sizable amount of gold and two hundred and forty pearls of great size and beauty as well as a quantity of smaller ones. Unfortunately the luster of the pearls was not so luminous as the Spaniards would have liked; the imperfection was traced to the shells' having been cooked before the pearls were extracted. The natives used this method to open the shells and, by steaming, to make the oyster more palatable; cooked oysters were a delicacy reserved for the chief, who valued this royal dish more than he did his pearls. This serious fault was immediately remedied by the Spaniards, who showed the Indians how to open the shell and extract the pearl without using fire. When Tumaco saw that the Spaniards valued only the pearls, he sent out some of his men to dive for more, and in a few days they returned with heaped baskets. Balboa's men hugged one another for joy, their mouths fairly watered with satisfaction, and all they talked about was this great wealth.

The men had heard of more and still greater treasures. Both chiefs, Chiapes and Tumaco, agreed that the finest pearls came from a cluster of islands about twenty miles due west that was ruled by a powerful chief whose navy of canoes controlled the coastal waters and, when the sea was calm, raided the mainland at will. The chief's name was Dites, and to his islands Balboa gave the name Islas de las Perlas. Here were found shells as large as fans holding pearls the size of a bean or an olive. Wouldn't the great and powerful Balboa lead an expedition against Dites's islands and kill him and collect all his pearls? his two allies asked. Because of the storms, it could not be undertaken now; but when the season of the tempests was over, would he not conquer Dites with them? And Balboa promised that he would return soon and sail with them to the Pearl Islands. A few years later Balboa did return and sail to the islands where a treasure had been waiting; but Pizarro, whose instincts and standards were those of a thief, had already, with another companion, sneaked over and reaped the rich harvest. Many of the pearls brought back were of great size and value; they had been easily obtained, a whole basketful having been joyfully given for a few hatchets. The chief of the Pearl Islands explained to Pizarro his pleasure at the transaction: "These hatchets I can turn to useful purposes, but of what value are these pearls to me?"

Balboa, for his part, had still some questions to put to Tumaco and Chiapes, for in his ears were the words that Comogre's son had spoken concerning a great nation that lived far to the south. His allies knew of this nation. It was distant from them, but so great that even they knew of its golden treasure; they knew of its mighty canoes that carried sails, and of animals that, instead of bearers, carried their loads. To illustrate, Tumaco molded a figure out of clay, a quadruped whose body was like that of a sheep but whose neck was grotesquely elongated. Here was more food for speculation and discussion—gold and pearls and now this animal. Some of the Spaniards said the chief lied; that God had made nothing so foolish-looking; others recognized it as a camel, and to them it was proof that Asia was near. It was the llama of Peru, a cameloid ruminant; it has the same stupid haughtiness, the same spitting, nasty temper as its Old World cousin. From Tumaco, Balboa had heard for the second time of the great and wealthy civilization that the Incas ruled in the Andes of Peru. The men talked of these wonderful and new and tempting clues. But only two, Pizarro and Martín, lived to reach Peru and get their hands on its gold.

As Tumaco and Chiapes disclosed the many kingdoms that

rimmed the great Southern Sea, Balboa wanted to make certain
that he had left no legal loophole through which Spain's right to
his discovery might be challenged. Not content with having
made his act of possession in the Gulf of San Miguel, he decided
that he must repeat the ceremony in the great ocean itself. For
this impressive ceremony, Tumaco brought out his state canoe
and Balboa was so amazed by the sight of the royal pearl-studded
paddle handles that he ordered the notary to certify to their
actuality. Again he strapped on his buckler, lifted his banner,
drew his sword, and, wading into the Pacific Ocean, repeated his
inclusive claims.

Another month had passed, a wonderful and rewarding month
spent with his good friends, Chiapes and Tumaco. Balboa had
amassed pounds of gold, bushels of pearls. It was time to turn
back, recross the mountains to Darién, and announce his great
discoveries to the world.

But before Balboa left he wanted to see the oyster beds from
which Tumaco had had his divers fetch pearls. Despite stormy
weather that prevented their working the deep-sea fisheries, they
gathered shells that, churned from their beds by powerful tides,
floated near the surface or were thrown on the beach, enough
shells to fill six small baskets with lustrous pearls, clear and
glowing, the size of dried peas.

When later the royal fifth was sent home, several empty specimen shells were dispatched to convince the King in far-off Spain
of their impressive size, and Peter Martyr examining the whole
fabulous collection rapturously wrote:

"These shells and the gold which has been found pretty much
everywhere are proof that Nature conceals vast treasures in this
country, though thus far the explorations covered the little finger
of a pygmy, since all that is known is in the neighborhood of
Urabá. What will it be when the whole hand of the giant is
known and the Spaniards shall have penetrated into all the profound and mysterious parts of the continent."

9.

*He no longer felt himself a mere soldier of fortune,
at the head of a band of adventurers, but a great
commander conducting an immortal enterprise.*

WASHINGTON IRVING

A lesser man might have made a safe, quick, easy return over
the path he had opened so valiantly on his outward journey, but
Balboa decided to return by another route so that he could expose more of this rich New World. New trails, new tribes, new
treasures beckoned; and to explore and exploit he was ready to
face the unknown with its enemies, its hardships, its dangers.
Chiapes and Tumaco provided him with salt fish and maize and
other foodstuffs, with canoes and paddlers to take him far up the
river that knifed through the forests into the country of the
neighboring chief, Teoca. Tumaco's son and Chiapes accompanied him as guides, and thus supplied, equipped, and directed
by his Indian friends, Balboa started on a roundabout road to his
starting point. It was November 3. He left the sick men safe in
Chiapes's village to be cared for while, with the strong and well,
he faced the hard pull up the vertical, forested wall of the
mountains.

The presence of the Spaniards and their appetite for gold had
spread, and Teoca came out to meet them and receive them with
honors, and as a proof of his affection presented them with a
handsome amount of gold and pearls. The latter, extracted by
the fire process and therefore not very luminous, were eagerly
accepted by Balboa. He offered trinkets in return, and then he
and Teoca greeted each other warmly: the procedure had become a ceremony whose ritual was known to both parties. Here
Balboa said farewell to his good friends, Chiapes and Tumaco's
son; he promised them to return soon, and they, as they turned
homeward after the leave-taking, were in tears. Those genuine
tears were warm and salty with friendship. They are Balboa's
finest memorial, they contrast sharply with the bitter tears,
the despairing, agonized tears that mingled with blood as during the coming centuries the white man dispossessed and slaughtered the Indian.

And so, watched over and provided for by Indian friends, the Spaniards came to the village ruled by Pacra, of whose wealth and abominations they had been warned. Pacra and his people had fled, and the Spaniards at will rifled the houses of gold. Again and again and still again, Balboa sent envoys urging him to return, for though the amount of gold the Spaniards had seized was considerable, native reports had presented Pacra as lord of rich gold mines; Balboa was eager to talk to him. At last Pacra made his appearance with three of his principal nobles. Balboa looked at this man who was reputed master of such fantastic wealth; he looked on a deformed creature, dirty and hideous. As Balboa listened to the natives he felt that this bestial, grotesque body was proper flesh for the brutality and savagery of his deeds; he listened as neighboring chiefs charged Pacra with outrages, oppression, and depravities. Whether it was to satisfy their demands for retribution or because Pacra insisted, despite persuasions, threats, and tortures, that he owned no mines but only the gold handed down from his ancestors; whether it was as an agent of justice or as a frustrated man of greed, Balboa commanded the miserable Pacra to be fed to the sharp-toothed, terrible dogs. Tales of the punishment traveled far and wide; like the streams they flowed north and south from the mountains, and chiefs gauged the power of this stranger who had crushed the monster, Pacra. Near-by rulers hastened to his village, where Balboa remained for the rest of the month, offering more treasure and far-reaching alliances. With all of them Balboa made friends; to all he gave presents.

On December first, the reunited party, still guided by Indian allies, left the village. Before them lay a wide area, empty and desiccated, through which they marched for four days. The river bed they had been following ended as a deep gash in the rocks, and they had to pull themselves out of the rocky canyon. They traversed lonely forests and suffered from the heat and from the torments of thirst and would have perished had the Indians not found a little spring hidden deep under some trees. The dry season had come, and the rivers were caked, dusty channels that tantalized them with the remembrance of flowing water. They plunged into gloomy valleys where quicksand bogs sought to swallow them. Across the jangled face of that deserted region they toiled painfully but unthreatened, wearily, slowly. Carry-

ing more treasure than Europe had yet seen collected, they hungered as they stumbled across the sterile terrain. Many slaves
died. Scarcely able to travel, they arrived at last at the village of
Pocorosa; it was empty of people, but stocked with provisions
and surrounded by gardens. Here they ate and rested; after a few
days and much coaxing the chief returned with his people and he
and Balboa exchanged presents and became allies.

It was Pocorosa who told Balboa that the country of Tubanamá, the great and warlike ruler whom Comogre's son had said
it would take a thousand soldiers to conquer, was but two days'
journey distant. He was powerful and cruel, Pocorosa added,
and had bragged that no one could enter his territory and live.
Balboa, who understood the importance of pacifying and con-
ciliating the native tribes, could not allow this challenge to stand,
especially since Tubanamá was also the feared enemy of Pocorosa, his newest ally. He looked at his men, pale, emaciated,
weary; he wondered if even with their superior organization and
weapons, their careful schooling in conquest, they had the
strength to meet and rout so aggressive an enemy. From his
followers he chose seventy of the strongest and explained the
situation to them: "The chief Tubanamá has often boasted that
he was the enemy of me and my companions. We are obliged to
cross his country, and it is my opinion that we should attack him
while he is not on his guard." He then suggested that by a forced
march they could reach Tubanamá in one day and surprise him
before he had time to collect his warriors.

Aided by Pocorosa's fighters, they fell on their enemy just
after night had fallen, when his subjects and allies had scattered
to their homes. Tubanamá's own village had but two vast grass-
roofed houses: one for himself and his eighty wives; the other,
now empty, to shelter his warriors when they gathered to make
war. The chief and his women were easily captured; and when
the news spread that the dread tiger of the mountains had been
taken, all his allies—whose hatred of him was second only to their
fear—came to Balboa and spat out accusations against the tyrant.
Unlike Balboa's successor, whom the King appointed and who
went through this same country torturing and massacring, Balboa did not kill Tubanamá as he had Pacra. Instead he made a
display of wrath, listening sympathetically to the hostility of
the accusers, and threatened to drown the wretched man even

as the latter had boasted that he would seize the Christians by their hair and drown them in the near-by river.

Tubanamá forgot his dignity, threw himself at Balboa's feet, and begged for mercy. He had never uttered such foolish threats, he said; it was his drunken allies or envious enemies who had put such words in his mouth. "Who other than a fool," he ended his plea, looking straight into Balboa's eyes, "would venture to raise his hand against the sword of a chief like you, who can split a warrior open from head to navel at one stroke and does not hesitate to do it? Let yourself not be persuaded, O bravest of living men, that such speech against you ever proceeded from my mouth."

Allowing his pretended anger to be touched by the Indian's prayers and tears, Balboa pardoned him and set him free. Tubanamá then stripped his women of their golden necklaces, bracelets, and nose-plugs, and dispatched his principal men to bid his subjects bring all their gold to pay the fine the white strangers had imposed. And the golden treasure poured in as, through the forest, Tubanamá's people came bringing whatever of gold they possessed.

While the Spaniards waited there for the fine to be paid, Balboa had his men search the streams and hills to see if gold was as plentiful as had been reported by the son of Comogre. The diggings and washings yielded many golden nuggets and Balboa had his notary record the fact; on the strength of this survey he suggested to the King that settlements be made there to exploit this rich auriferous region.

The day of the nativity of Our Lord was given to rest. December and the year were coming to an end. Balboa began to feel the accumulated fatigue of his labors. Having stripped Tubanamá of his wealth and power, he returned to Pocorosa to rejoin his men and start for home. Tubanamá confided his son to Balboa in order that the boy might live among white men and learn their language and customs; this, he reasoned, would be the best training and preparation the lad could get for dealing with the new masters. The Spaniards piously counted him as a future convert.

Once again at Pocorosa's village, the Spaniards busied themselves for their journey. Eagerly they thought of Darién, where they could rest. And it was then that the tireless Balboa fell ill:

the immense fatigues, the long watches, the great privations, and at last a violent fever, made him yield to his thin, weary body. He joined those too sick to walk, those who were carried by Indians in hammocks suspended from poles; other men, still able to stand upright, were supported under their armpits by Indians; and so, little by little, they slowly traveled the downward trail that led by easy stages to the village of his friend Comogre, where he arrived on the first day of 1514. As Balboa himself described their state: "we have more gold than health."

Comogre was dead, but his son, whom the Spaniards had baptized Carlos, came out joyfully to meet his noble friend. When he saw how thin, how utterly exhausted the white men were, his hospitality grew more lavish, more solicitous; food, fresh from his gardens, and nourishing drinks were set before them; while they rested he waited patiently to hear the great story they had to tell. And then when they had regained a little of their strength he brought them a quantity of gold, hoping thus to speed their recovery. Vasco Núñez, appreciative of his friendship, of the information that had sent him on his immortal discovery of the Southern Sea, returned this generosity with gifts of valuable hatchets and carpenter's tools, a soldier's cloak, and one of his own shirts. His largess made Carlos a hero among his naked neighbors. Four days the Spaniards rested there, for four days they slept and ate and renewed their spent energy. Then they headed for Puerto Careta and the sea.

On the way they were met by four Spaniards whom Careta, Balboa's father-in-law, had sent out to meet him as soon as he had word of his arrival at Comogre's village. The messengers brought the welcome news that four well-laden ships had just reached Darién from Hispaniola. With this to speed his tired steps, Balboa hastened toward the port from which he had started on his overland expedition and reached it on January 17. The next day, with twenty men, he sailed on the brigantine he had left there, and with a fresh breeze and a fair sea reached Darién. Four and a half months after he had started out on a desperate venture, he returned successful, without the loss of a single man, to the seat of his first triumph. To the jubilant colonists he announced the discovery of the Southern Sea.

Balboa immediately sent boats to Puerto Careta to bring back the rest of the men and the treasure they had obtained. A solemn high mass was celebrated on their safe return, and thanks were offered for the splendor of the discoveries, the magnitude of wealth they had amassed. (The actual value of the treasure cannot be safely estimated, for Peter Martyr uses pesos, *castellanos*, crowns, and pounds confusingly, while other historians' estimates vary so markedly that the sums they mention seem to reflect their idea of what a large sum should be rather than what the sum might actually have been.) The booty—gold and pearls, hammocks, robes and other cotton articles, a large number of captives, men and women—was displayed where all could see, examine, and count it; then it was divided. First, the royal fifth was set aside, to which was added two hundred of the finest and largest pearls; then each member of the expedition, including the dogs, received a share commensurate with his rank and service—the notary stood by with his records that listed each man's participation—and lastly the men of Darién who had remained behind were each given some cotton articles or captives. So just and equitable was Balboa's schedule of allotment that all were satisfied; no petty jealousies spoiled their joy; everyone looked forward to new and greater conquests. Even the lawyer Corral and the others who had connived against Balboa were content with the glorious harvest and their share in the fruits of the enterprise. Darién was unanimous in acclaiming the greatness and ability and energy of its leader.

Unknown to anyone in Darién, Ferdinand had sent a trusted observer to get a true picture of conditions in this, his farthest outpost. Ostensibly in charge of the ships that brought food from Hispaniola came Pedro de Arbolancha with secret orders to ascertain the real state of affairs: had Balboa usurped the royal power and would he prevent the landing of a governor appointed to replace him; was he a tyrant and were the colonists fearful of his rule; what had been done to promote the welfare of the colony? Behind Arbolancha's mission lay all these doubts and fears about Balboa. Enciso had calumniated and discredited him, but Ferdinand was too wary a sovereign not to discount personal jealousies and frustrations; he wanted to know for himself what kind of man was this that the colonists had chosen, what qualities they had recognized and rewarded. Arbolancha's arrival found Balboa and all his friends absent on their great venture, yet even Balboa's enemies who remained behind had only praise for what he had accomplished: for the gardens that had been planted, the slaves and women who had been put at their disposal, the harmony that prevailed. Arbolancha saw the spontaneous outpouring of affection that greeted Balboa on his arrival; he watched the division of the spoils, he observed the manner in which Balboa carried himself and attended to the affairs of the colony. Here was no lawless ruffian, no dangerous rebel; Balboa was the truest representative of the vigor and power of Spain, a leader who wielded authority and respected it. Arbolancha, an honest and discerning man, became Balboa's firmest friend, his most zealous partisan. He was ready to return to Spain and report fully and faithfully to the King, urging that Balboa be retained as governor of Darién.

Tragedy and disaster were in the making. Arbolancha delayed his leaving two months—for what reasons it is impossible to tell—until the latter part of March. By the time he arrived with his report and his recommendation, Pedrarias Dávila, newly appointed as governor, had just left the Canaries on his way to the New World. This narrow margin of time was to be fatal.

10.

They praise Balboa now at court.

Peter Martyr

Behold the Spaniards established almost on the equator ready to settle and to found colonies.

Peter Martyr

Steps had already been taken in Spain to replace Balboa. This mission was entrusted to Pedrarias Dávila, whose nickname in Spain was *el Galán*, the Gallant. In the New World he would earn a new name—*Furor Domini*, the Wrath of God. No sooner was this news announced at court than his appointment was challenged on all sides. But Fonseca, the head of the Council of the Indies, who was as assiduous in patronage as he was relentless in persecutions, silenced all complaints. He promptly spoke to the King: "Pedrarias, O Most Catholic King, is a brave man who has often risked his life for Your Majesty and is well adapted to command troops. He distinguished himself in the war against the Moors as a valiant soldier and prudent officer. In my opinion it would be ungracious to withdraw his appointment in response to the representations of envious persons. Let this good man depart under fortunate auspices, let this devoted pupil of Your Majesty, who has lived from infancy in the palace, depart." And the King, heeding this advice, confirmed the appointment and even increased the powers vested in Pedrarias. The accomplishments of the courtier were still the only qualifications recognized. The lesson implicit in the misadventures of Ojeda and Nicuesa—lack of competence, lack of character—had not been learned and never would be.

Pedrarias owed his prominence in public life in large measure to his wife, Doña Isabel de Bobadilla y Peñalosa. A remarkable woman, her influence was derived from another remarkable woman, her aunt, the Marchioness of Moya, who daringly and effectively helped Queen Isabella hold Segovia against the Portuguese. The mother of eight grown children, four sons and four daughters, Doña Isabel left them in Spain and accompanied her husband to Darién after overwhelming him with a long, tender, and dramatic speech in which she insisted that "I would rather die and be eaten by the fish in the sea or devoured on land by cannibals, than consume myself in perpetual mourning and unceasing sorrow awaiting—not my husband—but his letters." Doña Isabel was determined to help her husband collect yellow metal and to prevent his collecting brown women.

This expedition, the last sent out by the aged Ferdinand of Spain and the first organized by the newly created Casa de Contratación, Spain's India House, was impressive and many-purposed. Pedrarias's commission instructed him to challenge any Portuguese ships he might encounter in Spanish waters, to subdue Balboa if necessary, to search for the Southern Sea, to master the natives and seize their lands, their persons, their gold and pearls and other treasures. Darién was given the promising Christian name of Castilla del Oro, Golden Castile. Because of Pedrarias's addiction to elegance and the presence of Doña Isabel, the edict prohibiting the wearing of silks and brocades in the Indies was relaxed, and he and his wife were further indulged by being permitted to take their silver plate with them. Applicants for the glittering adventure—for Balboa had mentioned the need of a thousand men if they were to reach the Southern Sea—swamped the India House. Their number was raised from twelve hundred to two thousand. For most of these men this adventure came at a most opportune moment. Many of them, of noble family, were splendidly dressed, for they had equipped their wardrobes lavishly to serve under *el Gran Capitán*, as Spain's too-popular military chief, Gonzalo de Córdoba, was called; he had been nominated to lead an army to protect Ferdinand's kingdom of Naples against the French. The recruits for Italy were left at loose ends when the King suddenly changed his mind. These men, ripe for danger, and having invested their last cent in rich armor and silken finery to make a magnificent appearance in the Italian campaign, clamored for the chance to serve their king in the New World, where, it was rumored, gold was caught in nets like fish. So intense was the fever to join that to a contemporary it seemed as though all the men would leave Seville, which would become a city of women.

The King had commanded Fonseca to be most liberal in securing personnel and equipment. The ablest pilots were encouraged to enlist; merchants and their agents were given trading privileges; colonists with their wives were offered free passage; skilled artisans were hired; the finest weapons and arms and military supplies were procured; great quantities of staple foodstuffs— flour, wine, oil, vinegar, honey, chickpeas, beans, and biscuit—and basic tools and utensils—axes, shovels, pickaxes, chisels, roasting spits, cooking pans, hammers, nails, saws—were collected for the colony. Officials with impressive titles and high salaries were appointed to Castilla del Oro: in addition to the governor, there were a treasurer, an auditor, a judge, an inspector, a doctor, a surgeon, and an apothecary as part of the civil government; Bishop Quevedo, who was to decide all moral issues, a dean, an archdeacon, a teaching friar, an archpriest, a canon, and three sacristans were to administer the religious life and arrange for the erection of a chapel. All these officers, both civil and religious, all stipends whether for colonization or conquest, were to be paid out of monies made in the newly created metropolitan city of Castilla del Oro, the erstwhile starving, precarious colony of Darién.

In elaborate directions given to Fonseca and translated by him into men, supplies, material, and administrative details, Ferdinand carried out the suggestions Balboa had made in his letter stressing the wealth of Darién and announcing the news of a sea beyond across the cordillera. The King even acted favorably on his plea that no lawyers be permitted in the new colony. But this whole enterprise that gave life to Balboa's proposals was directed against him; because of the fear engendered by Enciso's lies, Balboa was to be deposed immediately, and the newly appointed judge, Gaspar de Espinosa, was ordered to hear the charges Enciso in person was to prefer: only to Balboa was the King stern and severe.

The great, dazzling armada of fifteen ships rode proudly, beckoningly, on the muddy waters of the Guadalquivir. The streets of Seville were filled with richly dressed recruits. This was the period of the Field of the Cloth of Gold, when war was a pageant, a fine procession of gleaming armor and glittering raiment, of meaningless chivalric posturings and gestures. Among those who had managed to join Pedrarias were several who were to make their names immortal and by their explorations and adventures mark the high point of Spanish energy in the New World. On the Isthmus of Panama many men were to serve their hard apprenticeship: Soto, who was sent to Peru with Pizarro, where he amassed a fortune and, on his return, was rewarded with the office of Governor of Cuba and Adelantado of Florida, and who was to discover the Mississippi; Almagro, who was one of the leaders in the conquest of Peru, and who from there penetrated overland to Chile; Belalcázar, who conquered Quito and Popayán; Bernal Díaz, who died as poor as when he first came to the New World, though he marched with Cortés into Mexico and Guatemala, and whose *True Story of the Conquest* is a lively and fascinating first-hand report of one of the most momentous events in history; Serrano, the chief pilot, who later sailed with Magellan and was killed at his side; and Oviedo, the notary and official in charge of smelting and marking gold and branding slaves, who became an early historian of Spain in the New World.

Pedrarias was in no hurry to start. He received his commission in July 1513; the following month he took his oath of fealty and homage before the royal council; and then for the next eight months, though the King regularly sent him notes expressing annoyance at the delays, Pedrarias enjoyed to the fullest the stirring spectacle, the complex hum of activity, the spotlight that the moment and the enterprise threw on him. Month by month the recruits waited and roistered and plagued their creditors for more money to pay for food and lodgings, and still the fleet did not sail; enormous cargoes were loaded on the ships, and yet Colmenares warned that they were ill supplied for so great a number; the year 1513 passed, and still the expedition did not set out. Spring came, and at last Pedrarias and his men, wearing their bravest garments, gay with hope, excited because the long waiting was over, marched splendidly through Seville down to the docks. The armada sailed on April 11, 1514, and, as Bernal Díaz says, "sometimes with good weather and other times with bad weather," arrived off the town of Darién on June 29.

On the way they had passed the ship in which Arbolancha was returning to Spain after his secret mission. It is tempting to imagine what might have happened had Pedrarias delayed long enough for Arbolancha to have arrived *before* the armada sailed: the King, trusting the report of his special investigator and delighted with his gold and pearls, would not have hesitated to be as ungracious to Pedrarias as he had been to *el Gran Capitán*, to change his mind about the armada as he had about the Neapolitan campaign. In his first joy he might have allowed Balboa to remain in office as governor and continue his friendly relations with the Indians. Had Balboa been allowed to live, he would have followed the clues that led to Peru, of which he had twice been told; and, unlike the murderous Pizarro, would not have viciously broken to useless bits the great civilization of the Incas. Had Balboa lived, Bourne said, "the history of the mainland of South America might have been very different." For Arbolancha's report dramatically changed Balboa's position at court. Peter Martyr announced to the world:

"We have received letters from him [Balboa] and from several of his companions [the town council of Darién] written in military style and informing us that he had crossed the mountain chain dividing our ocean from the hitherto unknown South Sea. No letter was ever written in prouder language. Not only is Vasco Núñez reconciled to the Catholic King, who was formerly vexed with him, but he now enjoys the highest favor. For the

King has loaded him with privileges and honors, and has rewarded his daring exploits."

And the Pope, and all his court, who listened as this letter was read aloud while they sat at dinner, listened, and forgot to eat.

While Balboa's name and deeds were becoming known over all Europe, the King, satisfied as to his loyalty and gratified by his present of gold and pearls, issued a decree designating Vasco Núñez as Adelantado of the Coast of the South Sea. Ferdinand thus gave royal recognition to the honors Balboa had already won by his deeds; but he also specified—was this Fonseca's suggestion?—that in Darién he was still under the jurisdiction of Pedrarias. While Balboa's good fortunes were the envy of the whole court of Spain, in the New World, in this town of Darién, he was already tasting the nagging persecutions of the new governor.

Under the thick, syrupy molasses of Pedrarias's fine manners was a sour, irritated conceit. He had expected and been prepared to have to conquer a surly, recalcitrant rebel; instead Balboa, at the head of the town council, knelt and promised for himself and the men of Darién proper obedience, and then graciously offered to Pedrarias and Doña Isabel the use of his own house. Because Balboa's action had deprived him of a martial entrance, Pedrarias had to be satisfied with a solemn, stately procession: holding his wife's hand as for a formal march, and flanked by Bishop Quevedo resplendent in his episcopal robes, the new governor advanced at the head of his fully armed, elegantly clad officials and cavaliers; behind them came chanting, brown-robed friars carrying crosses, swinging censers; and lastly the sailors, artisans, colonists, and men and women who made up the full number of the armada. Wide-eyed, the Indians watched this rich show; pityingly the old colonists, poorly dressed in cotton shirt and drawers and wearing hempen sandals, their lean, sallow faces showing the hardships and fevers of the New World, watched this display of silks and brocades, of fair white skins, and knew that for most of these men and women the New World would prove to be but one step from the next world.

In his hut—it had probably been Cémaco's when the Indians

still possessed the village—Balboa gave a banquet to honor his distinguished guests. And those elegantly dressed cavaliers who since they had joined Pedrarias's expedition had heard nothing but tales of the crude, vainglorious upstart who lolled in oriental ease amid the fabulous riches of Castilla del Oro (had they not been told that the Spaniards found topazes on the beach, but, as they thought only of gold, did not even bother to stoop and gather these precious gems?), sat on the floor while Indian slaves set native roots and fruits, maize and cassava bread before them; they, who had in fancy already tasted the nectar of the New World, were offered river water to drink. To Balboa and his men the goodly amount of food served marked this as a feast. The veterans of Darién, Peter Martyr noted, "were hardened to abide all sorrows, and were exceedingly tolerant of labor, heat, hunger, and watching, insomuch that they merrily make their boast that they have observed a longer and sharper Lent than even your Holiness enjoined, since for the space of four years their food has been herbs and fruits, with now and then fish, and very seldom flesh." Across the food the two groups eyed one another: the new arrivals showed their amazement, their incredulous bewilderment, their disgust; the residents feared what the new regime would mean to themselves, but greater than fear was their pity for these innocents who did not even make a pretense of tasting the food that had been obtained after hard work and against desperate odds. Both groups thought of the gorgeous words "Castilla del Oro." The veterans muttered it profanely: Castilla del Oro! (Bernal Díaz was to deride, applying a bland name to the region of Yucatán: "You had better call it the land where half the soldiers who went there were killed and all those who escaped death were wounded.") The newcomers, too appalled to mutter, looked around at what confronted them. Was this poorly dressed, unassuming man of dignified bearing Vasco Núñez de Balboa? Was this collection of leaf-thatched hovels the metropolitan city of Tierra Firme? Hot, humid, swampy, the valley crowded between steep hills steamed under the fierce tropical sun; the air was heavy with the rank smell of vegetation putrefying in simmering quagmires. An unwholesome, fatal spot it was, where filthy water bubbled into whatever well was dug; a loathsome place where, when the slaves sprinkled the floors of the houses, toads sprang into existence from the drops of water that fell from their hands; a dangerous spot where lightning licked at men sleeping in bed and bats sucked their blood, where alligators seized chickens and swallowed dogs, where fevers walked unchecked through the streets, to take a heavy toll.

Within a month after they had arrived, seven hundred of the gay, exquisitely dressed young men who had marched so splendidly through the streets of Seville were dead. Most were quickly killed by yellow fever, while the rest starved as their provisions were exhausted. Many a fine wardrobe was bartered bit by bit for cassava bread in a vain effort to postpone death. As hidalgos—younger sons or poor aspiring relatives of the nobility—they clung tenaciously to the work they deemed suitable to their rank; they were fitted only for war or conquest—this had been their calling and tradition in Spain; and unable to adjust to the New World, they rotted and perished. Pedrarias sent a boatload back to Cuba, where some enlisted under the governor: a few pitiable remnants returned to Spain, having spent their fortunes, having lost their health and their hopes.

Pedrarias could have overcome his disappointment at the courteous welcome he received; he could reconcile himself to Darién as it was instead of Castilla del Oro as he had imagined it; but he could not forgive Balboa for having already crossed the Isthmus and discovered the Southern Sea. His arrogance, his conceit, his irritability, were transformed into a terrible, unappeasable hate. Balboa had thwarted his highest hopes, and for that he must pay with his life. Had Pedrarias subdued a rebellious Balboa, he might have dealt with him justly. But to face this man who, despite his cotton shirt and drawers, moved with dignity and authority, to hail in him the man who had planted the banner of Castile on the shores of the new sea, who had brought home gold and pearls and had already announced it to the King and the world—so frustrated and infuriated Pedrarias that only Balboa's death would be adequate atonement. And in the governor's murderous hands, Ferdinand had placed the power to destroy the first of the conquistadors.

11.

Man goes as far as he can and not as far as he wishes.

VASCO NÚÑEZ DE BALBOA

The exact date of Balboa's execution is not known; both 1517 and 1519 are mentioned by the historians. The exact date is not important; what matters is that Pedrarias finally satisfied his lacerated pride by a desperate, obscene act. The record of those years leaves a sharp image: Balboa caught and held fast in the silky, sticky meshes of a web that was fashioned out of the frustrations and spewed out of the envy of his enemy, Pedrarias.

The story of those years is the story of the final destruction of a man who had mastered the strange, hostile New World that had broken Nicuesa and had subdued its hostile natives who had defeated the brave Ojeda; who had retained into the years of his vigorous maturity the rare quality of inner growth; who, in the fantastic impact of two civilizations, was strong enough to value and seek peace, was most frugal in blood-letting. When all decent means to cut Balboa down to Pedrarias's own petty level had failed; when a new and greater fortune and glory seemed to await the indomitable explorer; when every man in the New World burned with jealousy at what Balboa had accomplished and was about to undertake—then Pedrarias's need to destroy him was satisfied at last. The mean spirit, like the neurotic, is compelled to eliminate everything bright, anything big.

Balboa's last enterprise is proof of the energy, the fortitude, the vision and purpose of the man. He was the first to build ships in the New World. In them he set sail over the sea he had discovered toward the great kingdom of which he had twice been told. Truly his was a herculean undertaking: he planned to transport the timbers, anchors, rigging, pitch, and tackle across the mountains to the Southern Sea, there to build four small seaworthy ships. His Indian father-in-law had told him that on his land grew trees whose wood was so bitter that even the destructive seaworm would not eat it; near Puerto Careta, Balboa established the town of Acla, where the trees were felled. With a few Spaniards, thirty Negro slaves sent from Hispaniola, and many Indians, he supervised the stupendous task of hauling this heavy, cumbersome equipment through the dense forests, across cascades and torrents, up steep rocky cliffs, over the cordillera. Many Indians died pushing, pulling, hoisting, lifting this staggering load up to the continental divide. There on the summit Balboa had had a rest house built, and there they paused. Then they descended to the sea. Their hearts almost broke when they found that the great timbers they had struggled with were quickly riddled by seaworms; but undismayed they began to cut down likely trees on the Pacific coast. Despite hardships, hunger, and the immensity of the undertaking, they doggedly stuck to their purpose and completed two of the brigantines. As Washington Irving exclaimed: "There are points in the history of these Spanish discoveries of the western hemisphere which make us pause with wonder and admiration at the daring spirit of the men who conducted them and the appalling difficulties surmounted by their courage and perseverance. We know few instances more striking than this piecemeal transportation, across the mountains of Darién, of the first European ships that ploughed the waters of the Pacific." That same undaunted attitude announced to Charles V, in 1529, when it seemed unlikely that an easy, direct water passage connected the two oceans: "We have not found the passage—we must cut it!" A canal from the Caribbean to Panama was started by Spanish engineers whose spirit was willing but whose tools were inadequate.

When the first two ships were ready, Balboa sailed them to the Pearl Islands, where he had decided to make his base; and while the other brigantines were being finished and additional supplies were on their way from Acla, he sailed off in the direction of Peru. The ships had gone about a hundred miles when the men were terrified to find themselves in a sea of spouting whales, monsters as large as their tiny ships, bloodcurdling creatures that churned the sea into foam. No one had ever seen them before, no one had even heard of them; terror-stricken, the mariners threw out their anchors. When at last the sea was empty, the wind had changed and they sailed back to the Pearl Islands.

That was Balboa's farthest. On his return he found that supplies had come from Acla, and with the supplies disturbing news. A new governor, Lope de Sosa, was due to arrive at Darién to succeed Pedrarias. What sort of man was he? Would he interfere with this new venture, which, after so much .abor, should soon yield rewards? A thousand doubts and questions arose to worry and perplex Balboa. After some discussion with his friends he decided to send one of them back to Acla to ascertain how matters stood. Balboa chose for this mission Andrés Garabito, a man who had served him often and well. Unwittingly, he thus put his life in the hands of a man who for very personal reasons wanted his death: Garabito for a long time had coveted Careta's daughter, Balboa's mistress. She had repulsed him in faithfulness to Balboa. Passion coupled with perfidy possessed Garabito, made him cunning and deadly. From Acla he sent a letter to the jealous and ever-suspicious Pedrarias to the effect that Balboa had four ships ready and fitted for a long voyage, three hundred men, and nothing but the sea between him and the fabulous Peru; that Balboa thus planned to escape from Pedrarias's jurisdiction and seek new lands where he would be free of all legal restraints. Garabito chose his poison well. This time Pedrarias determined that Balboa would not escape alive.

Pedrarias sent a letter, friendly and disarming, asking Balboa to meet him in Acla to discuss supplies for the ships, and thither he himself removed with his officials. He ordered Pizarro, with some armed men, to await Balboa at the rest house atop the mountains and bring the leader to him a prisoner. And as Pedrarias planned it, it happened. At the rest house the unsuspecting Balboa met Pizarro and his men. Pizarro demanded his sword of him and told him he was under arrest. "How is this, Francisco?" Balboa asked him. "Is this the way you have been accustomed to receiving me?" And so certain was he of his innocence that he offered no struggle and allowed himself to be taken prisoner.

The trial was swift, secret, and one-sided. The judge was also the prosecutor. Added to the present charge of treason was the old, old resuscitated lie told by Enciso of Balboa's sole responsibility for the expulsion of Nicuesa. Even the judge, warped by his subservience to Pedrarias, shrank from the penalty his master sought. But the unrelenting governor had his way: Balboa was sentenced to be beheaded the next day. Unspoken, unmentioned had been the real case against Balboa: by building and equipping four ships on the Southern Sea, Balboa had doomed himself. Only his death assured Pedrarias of possessing those ships, which could carry him to gold and glory.

The men at Acla awoke to a dark day of dreadfulness. The man who had given them hope and life, had brought success to them all, who had worn his honors and deeds with modest dignity, the man who was the light and life of Darién, was to be executed.

Such were the life and achievements of Vasco Núñez de Balboa, "conqueror of the mountains, pacifier of the Isthmus, and discoverer of the Austral Sea." Such was his brutal, senseless death.

Peter Martyr wrote to the Pope:

"I shall recount what happened in a few words, for the story is not pleasing; in fact it is quite the contrary. There has been nothing but killing and being killed, massacring and being massacred."

After Balboa

BALBOA coincided with that moment in history which marked the shift from the conquest and pacification of the Caribbean islands to the conquest and consolidation of the Valley of Mexico. Balboa, in fact, was the transition between these two phases. Darién is important as the first settlement on the mainland because it was established before Spanish colonial administration had crystalized into its bureaucratic form. On its small stage puppets appear—Ojeda, Enciso, Balboa, Pedrarias; behind the curtain, animating and directing these figures, are historical forces, antagonistic ideologies. Perhaps just because the stage is small and the gestures crude, these forces and these antagonisms are clearly expressed and seen.

From the very beginning Spain assumed a task immense and self-imposed. Self-consciously, gropingly, Spain undertook the inspiring if impossible feat of painting its culture on the American canvas, of transforming all aborigines into peasants, Spanish and Catholic. The scope of such an objective is magnified by the fact that Spain is about the size of Utah and Colorado, and in 1550 numbered under seven million people, while with the rounding out of the conquest Spanish America covered an area about twenty times as large. Spanish authority swept grandly, though in many regions it was spread very thin, over the southern third of the United States, down through Mexico, Central America, the islands of the Caribbean, and South America except for Brazil, Portugal's portion of the New World. The role of Spain in America, the forces that were mobilized, the racial and economic problems that were faced, have aroused controversy, passion, and prejudice. Save for the serious student, most people in the United States think only of Mother England; few know that America was sired by Spain.

The obvious but none the less important fact is that despite all phrases about the decline of Spain, her empire endured, with only minor changes, for three hundred years. The longest-lived of colonial empires, it transplanted to a vast region in the

New World the language, the religion, the culture, and the political institutions of Castile.

Two great currents met and struggled in the ideas and policies of colonial Spain. One of them relied for authority on the papal bull of May 3, 1493, which divided the New World between Spain and Portugal, and explicitly declared the conversion of the natives to be the principal imperial concern. This current, representing what today might be called the national conscience, was in varying degrees and at different times the dominant motive behind the formulation of certain colonial laws. Its most extreme, uncompromising, turbulent manifestation was Bartolomé de las Casas. The other current, which tended to draw Spanish America into the existing social and economic structure, represented the investors in enterprises of exploration: the King and the Spanish soldiers and colonists, who saw in the New World a way to quick riches; banking and trading interests of other European countries, which saw a golden chance for enormous profits. Fonseca, Bishop of Burgos and head of the Casa de Contratación, capable, opportunistic, and politic, is representative of this more worldly current. The struggle between these two forces was clearly drawn in relation to slavery, both Indian and Negro. The struggle affected everyone interested in the New World.

That struggle is part of the American heritage: the transference of feudalism to the New World, the introduction of Negro slavery, and the racial and cultural conflicts. It is amazing that there was a struggle at all, that in the first half of the sixteenth century powerful voices cried out against slavery, against exploitation, against inhumanity, cried out from a Europe in which slavery, exploitation, and cruelty were widespread and time-honored: serfdom in Europe was as degrading as slavery in America; the Inquisition and religious wars were as bloody and merciless as the massacring of Indians. The arguments used in this struggle were religious, the thought expressed was theological, the avowed goal was the establishment of a theocracy—expressions of the time and mental climate that recurred later in a Puritan mutation. Voices of horror and lament were raised over the despoliation of a New World, where the sense of outrage could find a target at which it could safely aim. Blended of these arguments and the blurred picture of savage societies innocent of the ills that plagued Europe, a mighty ferment arose that worked through the ensuing centuries and finally in the eighteenth century found political form and expression.

Columbus, in his letter to the Catholic Sovereigns, which was widely circulated, introduced the inhabitants of the New World to Europe. He wrote sweetly, poetically, of the fairyland he had visited, and dwelt on the gentleness, guilelessness, and generosity of the Indians. To a few these were qualities found only in heaven; to others they promised a heaven-sent chance to satisfy their cupidity without hindrance. Peter Martyr announced that the natives of the New World were living in a golden age; the idea that people might *live* in paradise and not suffer the miseries of the world while waiting for the life hereafter contained within itself the germ of revolutionary hope.

Within twenty years descriptions and attitudes changed. The white man and the red man had met, but without understanding; they had conversed but never communicated. Language barriers had been breached, revealing the insurmountable barriers of alien behaviors, alien goals. Antipathy was mutual, it was articulate: an Indian chief refused baptism because he did not want to go to heaven—heaven was full of Christians. Peter Martyr related this incident as proof of the Indians' obduracy and listed other abominations as the Spaniards spilled them out:

"The Indians are abandoned to drink and gluttony, vice and laziness. They prefer to live in the woods, eating spiders and roots and other filthy things to living with the Spaniards. They have neither shame nor conscience, and take emetics to vomit what they have eaten. They do not wish to be subject to anyone, but to be free to enjoy themselves in idleness. They smoke tobacco. Not one would dig for gold without being driven to it. They have no business sense, as they exchange things of great value for things of no value. The Indians love to go about naked, and they hold money and property of no value, excepting only food and drink. They will not work for wages; they take no interest in commerce, and have no conception of taxes or tithes."

The telling sentence, the gist of the complaints, reads:

"If the Indians were set at liberty they would never become Christians; trade would cease, because they would have nothing

to do with the Spaniards, and the royal rents would cease, as the
Spaniards would all leave the island."

How would the Spanish resolve this problem? How would
they exploit this New World they had found?

The *encomienda* system quickly emerged as the solution to
this problem. The *encomienda*—the word comes from a verb
meaning "to intrust to"—had a dual purpose, a reciprocal intention. By it, settlers were granted the forced labor of Indians
for working mines or cultivating land, and by it they were
obligated to instruct the Indians in matters of faith and to supervise both their physical and their spiritual welfare. Columbus's
petition to the crown to allow colonists the use of Indian labor
"for a year or two until the colony should be on its feet," fore-
shadowed an institution that speedily grew and assumed the
characteristics of feudal landholding in European style. The
crown, as head of both church and state in the New World, was
torn between the antithetical purposes of the *encomienda:* revenues rested firmly on the exploitation of Indian labor, and this
exploitation was at wide variance with the Indians' welfare,
which had been entrusted by the Pope to the crown. Half-
heartedly and in vain the crown tried to break the evil of unending hereditary transmissions; in 1571, Philip II limited such
inheritance to the lifetime of the *encomendero* "and the life of
one heir." The system that had started so desperately, so tenta-
tively in Hispaniola quickly became the institution whereby
Spain's part of the New World became more Spanish than the
mother country. All the evils of huge estates were magnified;
their holdover still cripples Latin America.

Anarchy threatened to destroy Hispaniola at the very start.
Columbus as an administrator had failed, and the two succeeding
governors appointed by their Catholic Majesties—Bobadilla and
Ovando—established a little order by the expedient of giving
legal recognition to the forced labor that the colonists were already exacting from defenseless natives. One early difference
between Hispaniola and Darién is that in the latter the Spaniards
were not afraid to work for their bread. They knew that their
welfare and that of the Indians were of the same tissue. The
"veterans of Darién" worked in the fields with the Indians who
lived near by, and the less drastic exploitation of the natives was

in terms of these Spaniards' own economic backgrounds: they were workmen and soldiers drawn from towns and farms, not nobles and landowners. Unfortunately for Spain in America, Balboa and his veterans were not an advance guard of an anti-authoritarian movement as were the Pilgrims in New England a hundred years later; they were foredoomed by a system that would substitute a Pedrarias for a Balboa. Darién is a slight but significant hint of what might have happened had the nonfeudal elements been permitted to work out their destiny in America. The fate of Darién was decided by the victory of Fonseca. Power politics was already leaving its indelible mark on the New World.

Bartolomé de las Casas, the man of conscience, died in 1566 at the age of ninety-two. He was a young man when Columbus discovered America; he was mature when Magellan's ship circumnavigated the globe and three vast oceans were opened to European trade. His life spanned the Protestant revolution, the publication of the Copernican theory of the solar system, and the establishment of the Spanish empire in the New World, which Bourne considers "events in their novelty and their far-reaching consequences surpassing anything in the history of mankind since the establishment of the Roman Empire and the advent of Christianity." Las Casas was concerned with one aspect of this tremendous and fast-moving panorama: the establishment of the Spanish empire in the New World. The length of his life, with strength undiminished up to the very end, gave impact and continuity to a period of swift transition, the profound shift of gravity that accompanied the change from the age of the conquistador, the initial thrust and discovery, to the colonial period of consolidation and exploitation.

Las Casas grew up in the reign of Ferdinand and Isabella (1474–1516), when adventure marked the political, intellectual, and geographical horizons of Spain and when even its intolerance was touched by excitement and energy, by life and growth. He had the ear and attention of Charles (1516–56), who through his mother, Juana, was the grandson of Ferdinand and Isabella, and through his father, Philip the Fair, was the grandson of Maximilian, a Habsburg emperor, and of Mary of Burgundy. Charles, as the young Archduke of the Low Countries, had Erasmus as his counselor; later he poured enough of the New World's gold into the pockets of the German electors to secure his nomination as emperor against his rivals, Francis I of France and Henry VIII of England; as king and emperor [1] he was, in Madariaga's words, the "mightiest and neediest man in the world." Las Casas dedicated his *Brief Relation of the Destruction of the Indies* to Charles's son, who as Philip II (1556–98) began his reign with a large, ceremonial *auto-da-fé* (burning alive of heretics); whose marriage to Mary Tudor, half sister of Elizabeth of England, was dictated by his political ambitions for the triumph of Catholicism over the Reformation and the maintenance of Spanish hegemony in Europe, and who had as mortal enemies William the Silent and the embattled Netherlanders.

The hatred that William the Silent felt for Philip was, after the former's assassination, bequeathed to the world and translated into folkloristic terms of a bigotry and oppression almost inhuman, always bloody and vindictive. Philip's marriage with Mary threatened the nascent nationalism of England, which was not marked by less intolerance or less bigotry than was Spain, but whose sense of destiny could not brook Spain's Continental ascendency. The Channel enabled the English to resist that domination, and when a gale blew Philip's Invincible Armada to bits, the English felt that God had blessed their side; for the men who had battled against Philip behind anti-Catholic, anti-Spanish banners had been fighting for forces that coveted his dazzling fortune. As Catholics, the English could not challenge the Pope's allotment of the New World to Spain and Portugal; but as Protestants they could thumb their noses at the Pope and send their ships looking for gold: actually the ships came home with furs and fish, whalebone and oil, cargoes that had to satisfy them. As parts of Philip's European domain the Dutch and the English would not have been able to deny the royal will that allocated trade, controlled monopolies, regulated enterprise, and kept both power and profits in the hands of those already established; but independent of his kingdom they could traffic with distant Russia, explore the northern seas, raid Spanish treasure ships, and even stake out colonies in the vast New World. Both Holland and England were jealous of Spain's

---

[1] There is an understandable confusion between his dynastic and imperial names: he was Charles I of Spain but Charles V as Emperor.

overseas wealth; both were struggling to establish the new age of commerce, the era of the great trading companies. In this extended struggle, in the complexities of the clash, no holds were barred. The new age of seaborne trade had no tradition of chivalry to temper its pugnacious spirit; the knightly code never went to sea; pirates and wreckers set the standards and reaped the profits. Toughness was the only guarantee of survival, in nations as in individuals. Social and cultural and religious forms expressed this economic battle. To the English and the Dutch, Spain became a monster, a bloody ogre whose depravity was as great as her wealth, whose cruelty was as apparent as the unending procession of her stately treasure ships, whose infamy, like her colonies, the sun never set on. William of Orange's *Apology*, a warped, scurrilous attack, reduced the struggle against Spain to the low level of a personal vilification of Philip, of whom Trend has justly said that he was "Spanish neither in his vices, which were petty and mean, alien to the Spanish temperament and to the Renascence, nor in his virtues, which were those of a German civil servant."

Las Casas's *Brief Relation* raised the struggle to the high hysteria of a holy war: those who had shuddered at the Inquisition became militant; those who hated Spain now had a cause that justified their enmity; at one stroke righteousness and love of the morbid were satisfied by the bloody butcheries he described. Las Casas published this book in 1552, when he was seventy-eight. During the following hundred and fifty years the book was a bible for those who rationalized their envy and greed, their hopes and ambitions, into a crusade against the enormities practised by Philip's men, against Popish villainy. It established the "black legend" and perpetuated a prejudice; it stigmatized Spanish imperialism. It opened the way for French and Dutch and English attacks on the Spanish and Portuguese empires; it sanctioned the piracy of Drake, whose *Golden Hind* in one raid robbed the Spaniards of valuable ocean charts and over five million dollars in treasure, and in another did such damage to shipping that he could boast he had "singed King Philip's beard." In those hundred and fifty years the book had

"three Italian editions, three Latin, four English, six French, eight German, and eighteen Dutch. The Latin edition of 1664 was suitably illustrated. One cut represents a meat shop. Its armored proprietor is doing a brisk trade in human flesh, while without the door another conqueror superintends the dissection of a luckless savage, and a tender babe is roasting on a grill." [2]

The English edition of 1689 was properly, if somewhat lengthily, entitled:

> *Popery Truly Display'd in its Bloody Colours: Or, a Faithful Narrative of the Horrid and Unexampled Massacres, Butcheries, and all manner of Cruelties, that Hell and Malice could invent, committed by the Popish Spanish Party on the Inhabitants of West-India: Together with the Devastations of several Kingdoms in America by Fire and Sword, for the space of Forty and Two Years, from the time of its First Discovery by Them. Composed first in Spanish by Bartholomew de las Casas, a Bishop there, and an Eye-witness of most of these Barbarous Cruelties; afterwards Translated by him into Latin, then by other hands into High-Dutch, Low-Dutch, French, and now Taught to speak Modern English.*

Who was Las Casas; why had he written this book, and what were its contents?

Las Casas knew the New World at first hand. From the New World came the monies that sent him to the university at Salamanca, where he studied law: his father had accompanied Columbus as a common soldier, and to the New World Las Casas first went in 1502 to supervise the *encomienda* his father had acquired on Hispaniola. As a property owner, Las Casas energetically worked his slaves. Eight years later he took holy orders, the first priest to be ordained in the New World; when he was seventy he was made Bishop of Chiapas. For some years Las Casas did not differ from the other Spaniards who were busy pacifying, exploiting, and settling the islands of the Caribbean. His awakening, when it came, was sudden, violent, dramatic. He immediately renounced his own holding; what mattered much more was that he saw clearly what sort of system the Spanish were loading onto the island Indians whose

---

[2] Lesley Byrd Simpson: *The Encomienda in New Spain. Forced Native Labor in the Spanish Colonies, 1492-1550* (Berkeley, 1929), pp. 2-3.

welfare, physical and spiritual, had been entrusted to them by the Pope. From conquest, disease, and overwork, or merely to escape the white yoke by refusing to live, nine tenths of the Indians had died in a very few years. Soon, if they were not protected, none would be left; the King must be told, laws must be made; the Indians must be guarded.

Cardinal Ximénes, who was regent of Spain between Ferdinand and Charles, gave Las Casas his title and position: for fifty years he was the Protector General of the Indians. To save the Indians from extinction, he advanced the suggestion that Negro slaves, stronger and better able to endure hard work, be allowed into the New World. This was the first and last compromise Las Casas made: "the Spanish language still has no word for compromise, as John Morley understood it." [3] By this expedient, he hoped to save the Indians without interfering with the economic demands of the new colonial enterprises; but when he saw that he had only substituted sin for sin, wrong for wrong, he was the first to cry out his error.

Las Casas could not stop what he had started. The forces set in motion were too strong. It would be naïve to think that Las Casas was responsible for the introduction of Negro slavery: the institution of slavery had antiquity to sanction its existence. The Portuguese, extending their explorations along the African coast, brought back, along with other articles of trade, Negro slaves for the limited markets of Europe—mainly for the galleys, and a few exotic blackamoors for domestic use. Europe had a population sufficient for its needs; but the West Indies, faced with native depopulation and an expanding, profitable sugarcane industry, created an immense need for laborers. Conditions were ripe for the rapid expansion of Negro slavery; Las Casas was at most the agent who suggested the time and place. Las Casas's atonement and repentance reconciled him to himself and to those who see in him one of the great hearts of all time, but the consequences of his action went their own terrible way.

The boom in black flesh was on. The manhunters of the Guinea Coast ruthlessly brought the black ivory out of Africa and loaded it onto ships. The story of the African slave and his fate

---

[3] J. B. Trend: *The Civilization of Spain* (London and New York, 1944), p. 54.

is written in blood. The first slave revolt occurred in 1522 on
Hispaniola. The maritime nations of Europe contended eagerly
for the trade. The Genoese, the Portuguese, and the French
carried thousands of African men and women to slavery in the
Spanish New World; for this monopoly they paid handsomely,
and still the fabulous returns made it one of the prizes of commerce. A mark of England's rise as a European power was her
winning, through the Treaty of Utrecht in 1713, the Spanish
contract for the slave monopoly; and a few years later the
still greedy imperial interests in England publicized the fiendish
practices of the cruel Spaniards, whipped up a war spirit with
an atrocity story, and started the War of Jenkins's Ear in another effort to take a bite out of the Spanish empire. Slavery
persisted long past the time when the ideas for which Las Casas
fought found political expression—that all men were created
free and equal.

It was on religious grounds that Las Casas answered those
who found it expedient to believe the Indians incapable of enjoying the blessing of civilization, a sort of subhuman species
halfway between animals and humans. He admonished the young
Charles, overwhelming him with facts and offering arguments
based on ecclesiastical authorities. He concluded with words
that echo powerfully through the intervening centuries: "The
Christian religion is equal in its operation, and is accommodated
to every nation on the globe. It robs no one of his freedom,
violates none of his inherent rights, on the ground that he is a
slave by nature, as pretended; and it well becomes Your Majesty
to banish so monstrous an oppression from your kingdoms in
the beginning of your reign, that the Almighty may make it
long and glorious." The idea for which Las Casas worked and
argued and fought for fifty tireless years was that no race or
nation was different from or better than any other; in the sight
of God a man was a man, and slavery, which institutionalized
the idea of inequality, was the work of the Devil and merited
extinction.

Some historians say that Las Casas was one-sided, intolerant,
inflexible, antagonistic. They are right. In an intolerant age he
was intolerant of those who disagreed with him. Maybe his
change of heart had been too violent and left, as it were, traces
of angularity and incompleteness; maybe it was the weapon

with which he fought, the uncompromising word and spirit
of the Scriptures, that made him so exasperating and unreason-
able an enemy. He was a man concerned with the ethical concept of justice; he was a brother to Isaiah and Jeremiah and all
the minor prophets whose voices have cried aloud in the wilderness. And like theirs, his was an angry voice, thundering out a
warning: "God will punish Spain and all her people with inevitable severity. So may it be!"

This was the man who wrote the *Brief Relation*. The book is
an indictment of the inhumanity that marked the meeting of the
white and the red men, of the officials who did not choose to stop
the annihilation of a population. In large, passionate figures it
estimates the terrible price paid in human lives for the revenues
collected by the crown, for riches amassed by individuals. Here
as it looked to the conquered is the terrible face of conquest.
Bourne has evaluated Las Casas's position:

"Las Casas was the Lloyd Garrison of Indian rights; [and] it is
as one-sided to depict the Spanish Indian policy primarily from
his pages as it would be to write a history of the American Negro
question exclusively from the files of the *Liberator*. That the
benevolent legislation of the distant mother-country was not, and
probably could not be, wholly enforced will not seem strange
to those familiar with our experience with federal legislation on
the Negro question; but that a lofty ideal was raised and maintained is as true of the Indian laws of Spain as of the Fourteenth
Amendment."

The book was written in 1540, although not published until
twelve years later, for the express purpose that it achieved:
its spirit was incorporated into the New Laws of the Indies
(1542), which prohibited the permanent *encomienda*. The reaction to this law, which struck directly at the economic basis
of colonial Spain, was immediate and violent; and Charles, who
saw his badly needed revenues threatened, was forced to repeal
the prohibition against the inheritance of *encomiendas*. The
ideals and influence of Las Casas, the attempts to break the power
of Spanish landowners over Indian laborers, were unknown or
ignored by those who eagerly read his book. All they asked for
was a picture of infamies and cruelties into which they could

fit their prejudices, a catalyst that would transmute their envy of Spain into a respectable hatred.[4]

Las Casas was not unique in Spain. The warm, fecund current that flowed out of the erudition and reforming ideas of Erasmus found its way across the Pyrenees to stimulate and reassure men who, though few in number, held high positions and great influence. Of them Las Casas was the most forceful and aggressive; but all were distinguished by their sincerity and enthusiasm, their fine education, their clear thinking, their integrity. To these men it was clear that where religious observance had grown most lax was in adhering to the spirit of the Gospels; yet that was the very part which, to them, mattered. "The dangerous doctrine that the Gospels meant what they said—or seemed to say—and meant the same for all men, was held by the Spanish disciples of Erasmus." [5] One of this group, Latin secretary to the Emperor, advocated that those who did not work should not eat, that the poor should share in the income of the rich, and that the income of the crown was public money, not to be squandered on imperialistic and religious wars. A Jesuit historian, discussing the difference between an absolute monarch and a tyrant, concluded that some circumstances warranted regicide, though "with an odd squeamishness about the shedding of royal blood, he recommended poison rather than cold steel"; [6] his book was burned in Paris and eagerly consulted by English revolutionaries. Again, there was Vasco de Quiroga who took with him to Mexico a copy of More's *Utopia*, which he used as a model in framing statutes for the Tarascan Indians of Michoacán.

No, Las Casas was not unique. There was Montesinos, who first cried out publicly in America against slavery and lesser forms of exploitation; Motolinia, another friar, who saw evil eye-to-eye with the turbulent Las Casas, but who protested the publication of the *Brief Relation* because he foresaw how, in enemy hands, it could prove a dangerous weapon against Spain and the Church. There were the men of the *cortes,* or regional

---

[4] In the United States this old, old prejudice about Spain was revived as late as our own Spanish-American War, and the *Brief Relation* was retitled *Horrible Atrocities of Spaniards in Cuba!*

[5] Trend, *op. cit.,* p. 122.

[6] *Ibid.,* p. 107.

parliaments, and the communes who supported Las Casas by petitioning the King to free the Indians. There was also the royal
conscience, in whose safekeeping the Pope had placed the welfare and salvation of the Indians.

Las Casas represents the mobilized Christian zeal of the purest
and best spirits of Spain at a time when the tidal wave of conquest broke upon the coasts of the New World.

If the current represented by Las Casas was unruly, if it was
visionary and impractical, it is, in retrospect, admirable as an ex-
traordinarily quick and sensitive response to the new forces, the
new needs, the new opportunities that were to transform the
world. The other current, represented by Fonseca, flowed on
meanwhile deep and smooth. Its channels had been charted, its
depths plumbed; new winds no more than ruffled its surface. In
it were joined powerful, purposive forces that neither understood change nor welcomed it. Princes of the Church and
grandees of the state stood for the vested interests of feudalism
that now were dependent upon the strong centralized monarchy
for favors and privileges. Ecclesiastical patronage for the New
World was at the disposal of the Spanish King; it was interpreted
so broadly as to allow the King complete power over all church
activities in America. Las Casas and the others who voiced the
radicalism of the Gospel threatened the privileged groups,
focused attention on the injustice of perpetuated inequalities;
the words they spoke were as dangerous as the heresies of
Luther.

Juan Rodríguez de Fonseca, Bishop of Burgos, head and front
of all that Las Casas opposed, came of a noble family; he owed
his political advancement to his ecclesiastical position. Historians
who have been preoccupied with Las Casas, with Columbus, and
with Cortés have usually set off their heroes against the blackened
character of Fonseca, the chief enemy of all three. Other historians, dealing with the larger panorama of Spain in America,
have pictured Fonseca as an able man who served his masters
well. This argument is not important here; here he is viewed not
as a person but as a symbol of the administration of the Indies
during the crucial formative years. As royal chaplain, he had the
complete confidence of Ferdinand and Isabella, and this position and trust were recognized when the Catholic monarchs
named him to assist Columbus in organizing for his second

voyage the imposing armada of 1493. During the next thirty years Fonseca directed colonial affairs—his tenure of office extended into the reign of Charles—and for thirty years he was the bitter, unrelenting, unscrupulous enemy of the three men who were contributing most to Spain: Columbus, Balboa, and Cortés. Columbus, a Genoese, a foreigner, and a mystic, was a combination profoundly irritating to Fonseca, a man eminently practical and intensely nationalistic. Both Balboa and Cortés carved out dominant careers in the vast New World by their own initiative, and thus threatened the foundation on which Fonseca's power rested. Poor, unknown, without powerful connections, they competed with nobles and courtiers for the governorships and captaincies-general. Ojeda was fit to be governor: his uncle was Inquisitor general of Spain; Pedrarias was fit to be governor: he was an accomplished courtier and married to a most influential lady; the governor of Cuba on whose behalf Fonseca fought Cortés with all his power and all his tricks was the husband of Fonseca's niece. . . . In connection with Fonseca such facts lift themselves above the personal level to become matters of policy. Las Casas damned him for defending slavery on the lowest and most corruptive of all grounds: self-interest. Fonseca was a well-endowed absentee landlord (the worst of all *encomenderos*, Las Casas shouted), and stood to lose heavily by the abolition of the system.

Fonseca knew the meaning of power. He had seen Ferdinand and Isabella smash the great nobles to pieces and reassemble them into the more pliable, pleasing pattern of courtiers; he had seen the Moors conquered and the Jews expelled. He had seen the sovereigns' authority grow by absorbing power from those who had previously held it or by breaking the power of those who opposed the royal will. He was close to this supreme authority; the greater it was, the greater security he had in managing a segment of its interests.

Intact as yet was the medieval concept that two things were superior to the King: God and the law—and here the law meant not that created by ruler or legislator, but that known to all and sanctioned by the habitual and customary ways of the community. Equality existed before the law, and in the security of this tradition, Spaniards, through their regional parliaments, co-operated with or criticized the ruler. To them the ruler personified and guaranteed these liberties and rights, and the confidence felt by the people in their government made the Spain of Ferdinand and Isabella an alive and sanguine force. But this tradition threatened those who held and wanted to increase and intended to perpetuate their special privileges.

The centuries-old *cortes* made up of the three estates—nobles, princes of the Church, and bourgeoisie—voiced and guarded this tradition. Widespread familiarity with legal forms, which made Spaniards politically sophisticated, gave form and purpose to the Darién town meeting that ousted the arbitrary Enciso and Nicuesa, and elected Balboa. The trust and understanding between the ruler and the *cortes* held as long as both were Spanish and habit and customs had a common background; conflicts arose when Charles, with his Burgundian and Habsburg blood and background and ambitions, arrived in Spain to assume his inheritance. Suddenly the nobles and bishops and towns-people of Spain found themselves with a king who spoke no Spanish, who was advised by Flemings whom he placed in the most influential and lucrative government positions, who had obligated his Spanish subjects to pay handsomely for his election as emperor, and who wanted to leave them as soon as he decently could. These conditions in part precipitated the revolt of the boroughs of Castile (*communidades*). The revolt was crushed. From that time on, the *cortes* declined. This withering-away was an omen that the trust accorded Ferdinand and Isabella by the people, the trust that had flowered so wonderfully to pro-duce bold, ambitious, tireless conquistadors, would degenerate into lethargy and despair. Men who should have been elected by the people were appointed by the crown, and offices were sold to the highest bidder. It signified the end of this tradition and trust; the *cortes* were dead. In the hands of the King lay the power he had taken from the people; the monarchy of Spain was the law.

When the *cortes* supported Las Casas in his fight against the *encomienda*, petitioning the King for the freedom of the Indians, they were still the organ of public opinion. They, with their living faith in equality before the law, seconded the arguments of those who held that in the eyes of God all men were equal. It was the townspeople, the moneyed middle classes, to whom God and the law were above the King; and it was they with their large, active, and profitable industries who made Spain prosperous. The populous and productive towns were outside of Castile. Segovia had many fine cloth and arms manufactories, Granada and Valencia produced silks and velvets, Toledo's woolen looms were worked by ten thousand skilled weavers, and Barcelona was famous for its cutlery and glass works. Hundreds of skilled workers came to the New World: Balboa asked for and was sent men who could repair weapons damaged by the hot, humid climate of Darién, boatmakers, metalworkers; and later came mining experts, men versed in the sugar-cane industry, silk-growers and weavers. The large urban centers of Spain relied on an intensive agriculture that had been perfected and passed on by the Moors. Their truck gardens along the whole southern coast were able to support the large populations engaged in lucrative industries, in active trade; those masters of irrigation even grew wheat on the high flat Castilian plateau. Unfortunately the Catalan traders, who understood mercantile opportunity and who would have exerted an influence that might have kept Spain abreast of the new commercial age, were barred from the Americas; Barcelona, their great Mediterranean port, "was on the wrong side of Spain," [7] and to Seville passed the monopoly of the American trade—Seville where the Casa de Contratación was established under the rigid control of Fonseca, Seville where the severities of the Inquisition had first fallen.

Distinct from the regions of Spain where wealth flowed from work and where economic progress and social prosperity were found stood Castile. Castile had a pastoral economy to support her aggressive activity. Sheep-raising, during the long centuries in which she fought to dominate the other Spanish kingdoms and drive out the Moors, allowed her people great mobility and the use of most of her man power. During the seven centuries in which Castile led the fight against the Moors, that struggle was an economic pursuit as much as it was a religious crusade. Every Castilian knew he had only to conquer a Moorish village or estate to become rich. The way to earn one's bread was by war and conquest. Courage was the sole prerequisite to wealth, and work was only for those who lacked courage. This attitude, which was to be the mainspring behind

---

[7] *Ibid.*, p. 80.

the New World conquistadors, giving them their incredible driving and holding power, also fostered and featured Castilian pride, which scorned manual labor, industry, and commerce as servile occupations, unworthy of and degrading to a man of birth and breeding.

This pride explains Pedrarias and his elegant followers. They despised Balboa in his cotton shirt and drawers, overseeing his Indian workers; they despised him despite his extraordinary success; they considered him a renegade, a man who had betrayed his class and his country by his behavior. The tradition and pattern of their pride made it impossible for most of them to accept work even as the price of survival. Those who survived, the "veterans of Darién," were those who had managed to forget their training and accept the discipline of work. In the New World they saw to it that work meant supervising Indian and Negro slaves—turning Spanish swords into Indian plowshares. Such a mentality could stand up to conquest because the hardships as well as the rewards lay within the narrow circle of their cultural horizon. And later, in colonization, mining and ranching were permissible to them; the former could be regarded as plundering the earth of its treasure, while the latter was congruent with the Castilian economy. This mentality and this economy were already stunting Spain, where agriculture was now ignored or deplored. Trend has pictured the change that took place: "Sheep grazing, with cheap, unskilled and scanty labor brought easy profits to the landlords at the cost of wide unemployment and a catastrophic fall of the common standard of living. Castilians had never known a general standard of living like that of the Moslem or Roman province of Andalusia. So the rich cultivated lands were covered with sheep, the watercourses disused and choked." In the New World only fragments of an elaborate terracing agriculture survived the arrival of the Spaniards in the Valley of Mexico, and the great irrigation projects of the Incas were destroyed. Sheep and cattle were brought over to the New World, and with them the same economy and social structure that were crystalizing in Spain. In New Spain, as in Spain, Castilian economy and Castilian attitudes damaged what Castilian arms and valor had won. In both, agriculture either was blighted or was cursed with absentee landlordism.

The discovery of the New World dazzled the eyes of Europe after long centuries of having been confined within a cramped subcontinental space. In a political sense the feudal world burst wide open and new elements appeared; in a religious sense Christ was again resurrected to speak out for the masses on whom this feudal pile had rested; in an economic sense towns and cities were growing with new needs, new allegiances. The change that was coming to Europe can be seen in every segment and element of society; and in every aspect of this change the forces of reaction sought to immobilize it. That is the tragedy of Spain; it is also the tragedy of New Spain. Balboa's death is symbolic of Spain's willingness to sacrifice her best to retain her obsolete values. His death gained nothing for Spain or for America: it merely made Pedrarias, the courtier, feel more comfortable. While the rest of Europe was entering on a new era of commerce and trade, Spain affirmed her intention of retaining her pastoral economy and feudal structure by amputating from her body politic the Jews and the Moors. And access to the New World was expressly forbidden to both these groups.

The expulsion of the Jews (1492) robbed the Spanish empire of men who had an international trading and financial tradition —and soon Charles was to beggar himself to obtain monies from the great German banking family, the Fuggers of Augsburg. The expulsion of the Moriscos (1609) changed Spain from a land of abundance to one that has since been chronically hungry —and the silver from the New World went abroad to pay for wheat that had to be imported. Those products that are supposed to have spread over Europe from Spain—rice, cotton, sugar, silk—all were in the hands of the Moors; the expulsion destroyed these Spanish industries for centuries. In vain the great Aragonese landlords protested the decree that robbed them of several hundred thousand skilled Moorish agricultural workers; their uncultivated gardens soon supported vast herds of sheep. The merino, the mainstay of Spanish herds, was famed for its wool, not its meat. This basic shift in the economy largely accounts for the fact that in the seventeenth century, when populations in the rest of Europe were increasing, Spain was the stock example of a depopulated country—a critical situation at a time when European armies were growing in size and significance. In the hundred years after Las Casas raised his voice in horror against the depopulation of Hispaniola, no one protested against the misery and hunger in Spain itself. The same force that countenanced the expulsion of the Jews and the Moriscos operated against all other groups or persons who did not give absolute submission, who deviated in the slightest from a prescribed uniformity.

The instrument used to maintain power in the tight grasp of the monarchy was the concept of homogeneity. This idea, blown up to serve as a national slogan—One King, One Faith, One Law—had proved its use in cementing the separate kingdoms into a united Spain. Much the same was true of any rising nationalism, only in Spain it was expressed in the Castilian theory of racial exclusiveness, of purity of blood, an ideology that then as now is derived from perverted history, pernicious science, and false religion. The tool used to carry out this policy of homogeneity was the Inquisition. Existing outside the law and above the law, it reduced every person and every group to subservience. What had been heresy became treason, and the Inquisition liquidated anyone who was "politically indiscreet or inconvenient to the State." [8] All intellectual inquiry was suspect. The qualities most prized and distinguished in Europe, the dualities that mark the modern era, were scientific curiosity and unhampered investigation; in Spain the Inquisition, distrusting these, demanded docility and credulity. The dynamics of power have never been gentle or just or intelligent, and when terrorism is resorted to, the result is brutal, cruel, and stupid.

The triumph of the Inquisition lay in the complete routing of those two concepts which had been Spain's heritage from the Middle Ages: the belief that God and the law were above the King, and that the King was servant to the law. Before Philip II died, the process begun by his father, Charles, was finished; the King held concentrated in his hands the power that previously had been dispersed. Achieving this demanded the extirpation of those progressive forces which would have made Spain the foremost European power instead of the chief prey of the French, the Dutch, and the English.

The forces symbolized by Fonseca maintained their power over New Spain as well. Viceroys and governors went from

---

[8] *Ibid.*, p. 83.

Spain to administer the American colonies; save for one or two extraordinary exceptions, they were, like the monarchs they represented, men of birth and breeding and huge incompetence. Just as the colonies were held as possessions to enrich the crown, so these officials filled their positions for their own profit. Similarly, the commercial interests of New Spain were subservient to those of the mother country, and any device that could smother colonial economy was allowed. When it was too late, when Spain was about to lose her American colonies, Humboldt summarized the situation:

"Virtuous men have from time to time raised their voices to enlighten the government as to its true interest. . . . These counsels would have been attended to, if the ministry had not sacrificed the interests of the nation of a great continent, to the interest of a few maritime towns of Spain; for the progress of the manufactures in the Colonies has not been impeded by the manufacturers of the Peninsula, a quiet and laborious class of men, but by trading monopolists, whose political influence is favored by great wealth, and kept up by a thorough knowledge of intrigue, and the momentary wants of the court."

The shortsighted, frightened forces of reaction that had impoverished Spain were willing to do the same to New Spain, lest anything interfere with the silver and gold that flowed eastward over the Atlantic to the mother country.

This treasure in itself exerted a force as impersonal as the sun, obeying its own rules in high defiance of all attempts to regulate or coerce it. It produced inflation. The most startling effect of the increase of money in circulation was a rise in prices so swift and so widespread that it effected a price revolution. The vast wealth, flowing into a country whose industry, agriculture, and commerce were declining, found no uses to which it could be profitably put. The crown sent large sums to the Fuggers, who had advanced the monies needed to carry on exhausting continental wars; the wealthy nobles frittered away huge incomes maintaining their elegant positions at court, and thus these incomes were wasted for domestic purposes, often going abroad to pay for finery. With their pennies the common people could buy only one quarter as much in 1601 as a century earlier; their pauperization was complete. The vast wealth flowing into Spain did not tarry there long, but in sums large or small leaked out of the country to buy necessaries that Spain once had been able and eager to produce. The influx of metals, unfortunately, promoted the illusion of riches obtained without the need to work —reenforcing an attitude that had already cost Spain heavily. The dreary, tragic victory of the forces behind Fonseca revealed itself completely. Spain, first of modern European nations to emerge as a centralized state capable of flinging its energies across oceanic spaces, fell limping behind; real power passed to newer, more dynamic nations while Spain remained satisfied and occupied with the outworn forms and ceremony of power.

Balboa was the agent who introduced Spain onto the North American continent. Within fifty years of his death Spain had explored the entire Atlantic coastline from Nova Scotia to Panama, while on the Pacific side Spanish ships had traced the shore from the Strait of Magellan to the present state of Oregon. Esteban Gómez, who coasted along New England in 1524, found these shores reminiscent of his Spanish homeland, where "there was enough of such land and to spare." The idea that these bleak lands were valueless when compared with the lush fertility of the tropics was voiced by Peter Martyr: "What need have we of these things which are common to all the people of Europe? To the South, to the South, for the riches of Aequinoctial they that seek riches must go, not unto the cold and frozen North." Spain, spreading her sparse population thinly up into the continent, was looking for more gold, not for more land. For a hundred years New England was scorned by European enterprise.

The impulse that motivated the coastal explorations of the continent was the same from the last voyage of Columbus on: the search for a waterway that would lead through the New World barrier. Only such a strait would afford ships direct access to the fabulous wealth of the East; to find it Dutch, French, and English explorers went northward along the Atlantic coast, deep into all the great rivers and bays; the need for this transcontinental water route continued until one was built—the Panama Canal. A different hope animated the inland journeys of the Spaniards. Cortés had conquered Mexico, its treasures, its mines; and other conquistadors dreamed of other marvelous cities that would yield gold and silver and glory. The gold rush was on. During the following centuries it jumped from Mexico to California to Alaska; always it led into the interior; it was inspired by dreams and it was beckoned on by rumors of cities paved with precious metals, of palaces studded with turquoise. It occasioned three especially famous explorations.

In 1534 Cabeza de Vaca, with three companions, returned to Mexico—all that remained of a sizable expedition sent to seek the treasure that had eluded Ponce de León in Florida. In their long wanderings they had touched at the edge of the great plains and there heard rumors of the wonder cities of Cíbola to the north, rumors that drew out first Friar Marcos and then Coronado (1540). While Coronado searched the vast southwest of the present United States, Hernando de Soto explored the southeast on a similar quest; an Indian woman who escaped from Coronado's expedition in Kansas met De Soto's party only nine days later. De Soto discovered and crossed the Mississippi River; there he died, and in "the middest of the River" was secretly buried. These two expeditions were the most impressive and energetic of the efforts made by the Spaniards to explore the interior of North America; in certain respects they have never been surpassed. Between them Soto and Coronado nearly bridged the continent from Georgia to the Gulf of California. Two hundred and fifty years later Lewis and Clark were to start westward across the plains, beginning at Coronado's farthest north.

The need for a passageway to the East and the hope of gold in the interior were dramatically fused by Balboa. Gold, and pearls too, he found, though he was killed before he had a chance to seek either Mexico or Peru; but his westward crossing, his path across the Isthmus, gave Spain a short direct overland passage from the Atlantic to the Pacific. The transisthmian road, "the path of empire, the most valuable asset of Spanish commerce, [was the] artery sought after by all other nations." [9]

---

[9] Victor Wolfgang von Hagen: *South America Called Them* (New York, 1945), p. 21.

To the city of Panama on the Pacific, where Pedrarias established his capital—leaving Darién, the first stable settlement on the mainland, to go back to the Indians and the jungle—came the gold and silver mined in Peru and Bolivia and exotic Eastern treasures from the Philippines, which had been conquered and colonized from Mexico, beginning in 1527. From Panama City a cobblestoned path led back across the cordillera, and it was worn smooth by countless pack trains of mules carrying the assorted treasures of the empire to the Chagres River, where it was floated to the Caribbean and thence to the port of Nombre de Dios. This settlement became increasingly significant as the eastern terminus of the overland route.

It was Balboa's good fortune to find himself at the narrowest part of the New World; it was Spain's good fortune that he had the imagination to understand the value of a transcontinental route when he first learned of it, the imagination and the towering courage and ability to cross the interior. The first crossing of the Isthmus was Balboa's gift to Spain.

Coronado and Soto, despite their impressive journeys and their heroic courage, both symbolize heartbreaking disillusionment, long and obstinate refusal to accept reality as they faced it deep in the continent. And yet they added an essential element of its civilization to the American scene: horses. Both these explorers started out with hundreds of horses, some of which, too poor or crippled to be of further use, were abandoned, and some of which may have escaped. As romantic and amazing as the story of the conquistadors is the saga of these horses and of the part they have played in the life of our country; for these horses survived and, multiplying, spread over the plains west of the Mississippi. Not just any type of horse would have fitted so exquisitely into this very special region.

"The horses of Spain were the horses of Arabia, of northern Africa, of the Moors; in short they were the horses of the desert. This meant they were hardy and tough, could live on scant food, on forage and grass, and did not depend entirely on grain. This Asiatic, Arabian, African-bred horse (and cattle of equal hardihood) flourished in semi-arid America. Had the north-European breed of grain-fed stock first struck the Plains, history might have been very different. The Spanish mustang, the

Indian pony, became the cow horse of the cattle kingdom, and the longhorn of Spanish descent travelled from the valley of the Rio Grande to [Lewis and Clark's] Milk River, gaining flesh on the road." [10]

These horses made the Plains Indians mobile, elusive, a fierce and living barrier to our westward expansion; they were to make the cowboy on his pony a very different man from his eastern brother who walked.

If the horse was a fortuitous gift of Spain to the New World, not so were the plants and animals with which it enriched the Americas. Plants, cuttings, seeds, and animals were brought over in the very first wave of exploration and conquest. Columbus carried them on his second voyage to Hispaniola; Ojeda and Nicuesa carried them to the mainland, where Balboa planted them; Cortés carried them to the Valley of Mexico; the Casa de Contratación had an official who supervised the careful transmission of plants and animals to the New World. Sugar cane, established in Spain just before the discovery of America, was immediately brought over to the islands of the Caribbean; machinery for sugar mills was sent, and experts from the Canaries to guide the new industry; within a century sugar had entrenched itself as insular gold. Sugar, not the gold of Hispaniola, paid for the great palaces Charles built at Madrid and Toledo. From Africa the Spaniards obtained cultivated bananas; to the Philippines they took sugar cane, and from there they brought back to Mexico mangoes and the *lukban*, or dry grapefruit.

Most of the great staple foodstuffs of mankind, domesticated and cultivated in the Old World, were quickly transmitted to the New: wheat, barley, rice, rye, lentils, and chickpeas. Wheat was most reluctant to cross the ocean. Hundreds of bushels of wheat spoiled before reaching America; more was lost when it was planted in the warm lowlands. But still the Spaniards persisted, and finally on the cool highlands it grew. The legend of the struggle to acclimatize wheat in the New World tells the fate of three stray grains found in a bag of rice. Two grains sprouted and grew, and from this casual, precarious beginning successive plantings gave enough seed to insure a supply of

---

[10] Walter Prescott Webb: *The Great Plains* (Boston, 1931), p. 97.

wheat. Flour mills were subsidized, and soon each Spanish town in the Americas had fine brown, fragrant loaves of bread regularly, plentifully.

Seeds for fodder for horses and cattle came early: alfalfa, which the Moors had brought into Europe, red clover, timothy, and a bluegrass that spread as the land was cleared and found a home waiting for it in the yet unnamed Kentucky and Canada. As early as 1531 the results of such experimentation were recognized by an official decree. An endless variety of small trees, bedded down in the earth-filled barrels, rode the decks of Spanish ships coming to America. Oranges, both the sour of Seville and the sweet of China, had arrived with Columbus; and when Oviedo came with Pedrarias he found orange groves in Hispaniola, a few young trees in Darién, and local marmalade that was properly pungent and sweet. With orange trees came lemons, citrons, and limes, apples, pears, apricots, plums, and other pitted fruits. By 1531 the olive and fig were growing in Mexico—had not the great Cortés insisted that no ships should arrive without seeds and plants?—and from there they went, two hundred years later, with the missions, into California. Almonds, chestnuts, and "English" walnuts made the crossing; mulberries came, and later silkworms from the famous centers in southern Spain. Flax was planted; its growing was later to be made compulsory in many of the English colonies. All the ordinary vegetables found in truck gardens in Europe grew with such speed and to such size that many times Peter Martyr remarked on this fecundity to His Holiness.

Today the picture of America includes vast stretches of golden wheat, of sugar-cane plantations, of orderly groves of citrus trees, of flat fields striped with rows of beets, lettuce, cabbages, and carrots, of ranches across which great herds of cattle graze, of orchards heavy with apples and pears and plums; it also takes in cherished flowers. The Spaniards brought over flowers as lovingly as other plants. Carnations spiced the air of Mexico, and marigolds and lilies ran wild there. When the first rose seeds came to Lima in 1552, the event was celebrated; one of the seeds was placed on the altar when mass was sung. Geraniums grew into small trees, and rosemary was planted for remembrance of distant Spanish homes.

The romance of the transmission of plants also includes the use of American foods in Europe. The tomato, scarcely regarded as a food until the nineteenth century, was grown as an ornamental shrub—the loveapple—in seventeeth-century England. The potato, which was brought back by Columbus, was long regarded as a delicacy to be made into preserves, to be spiced or steeped in wine; from Spain it spread over the continent. One story gives Drake the credit for taking it to Ireland, from which, as the Irish potato, it came westward to New England. Tobacco, a plant closely related to both the potato and the tomato, was introduced into Spain in the sixteenth century.

North America, which had domesticated only the turkey, received from Spain not only horses, which ran wild and multiplied into thundering herds, but mules and cattle, hogs and sheep. In 1531 twelve jack mules and three jennies arrived; as mules became more numerous the Indians "blessed the beasts which relieved them from burden-bearing." [11] Like the horses, the hogs and cattle increased so rapidly that soon, on Hispaniola and other West Indian islands, it was easy and profitable to kill them for their meat and hides.

The dissemination of trees, grains, vegetables, and flowers, of horses, mules, hogs, sheep, and cattle, which scientifically brought the treasures of Old World husbandry to the New, is a forcible reminder that the Spaniard was a farmer and colonizer as well as a conquistador: New Spain celebrated a thanksgiving many, many times before the Plymouth Pilgrims did. Today it seems very fair to agree with Father Bernabé Cobo, who, three hundred years ago, argued that the plants and animals brought to the New World more than paid for all the gold and silver that had here been mined and shipped back to Spain.

The gold and silver that Spain had found in the New World enriched all Europe, which for centuries had been gold-hungry. It speeded up the change from a barter economy to a money economy and flowed to those groups and nations who understood its purposes and use, whose industry and commerce were waiting for capital to enlarge and launch out on great enterprises.

---

[11] Herbert Ingram Priestley: *The Coming of the White Man* (New York, 1930), p. 27.

Surely and naturally it flowed to France, to the Low Countries, to England, and made them strong enough to compete with Spain in and for the New World. By prosaic transactions this gold seeped into northern Europe. Men of those countries too had hopefully looked for gold, but the New World had only one Mexico, one Peru, one Panama: they returned, their ships carrying unromantic cargoes smelling of fish and furs.

PART II
Furs for the Company
(*Mackenzie*)

HISTORIA GENERAL
DE LOS HECHOS
DE LOS CASTELLANOS
EN LAS ISLAS Y TIERRA FIRME
DEL MAR OCEANO
Escrita por Antonio de Herrera
Coronista
Mayor de SU MAGESTAD
de las Yndias y Coronista de Castilla
y Leon
DECADA SEGUNDA
AL REY Nuestro Señor

En MADRID
en la Officina Real de Nicolas Rodriguez Franco. 1726.
Con Privilegio de su Magestad

Title page of the second decade of Herrera's General History. The upper right-hand picture shows Balboa and his taking possession of the Sea of the South; the middle picture on the right is an idealization of Santa Maria de la Antigua del Darien.

A land of swamps whose inhabitants lived in the branches of great spreading trees. To conquer them, the Spaniards had to chop down the trees.

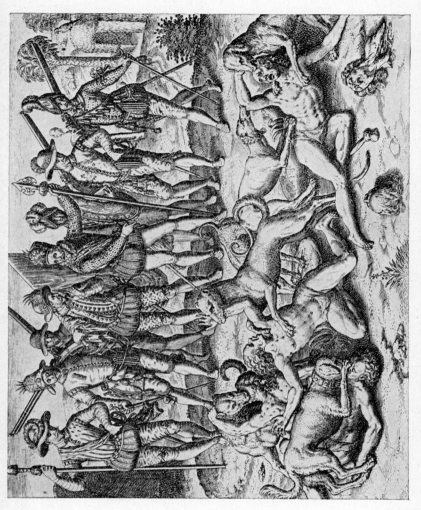

The bloodhounds brought down the naked, terror-stricken natives as though they were wild boars or timid deer.

As the eldest son of Comogre struck the scales with his fist he told Balboa of the Pacific Ocean and the treasure to be found there.

VERAGVA PARS.

Balboa was the first European to build ships in the New World.

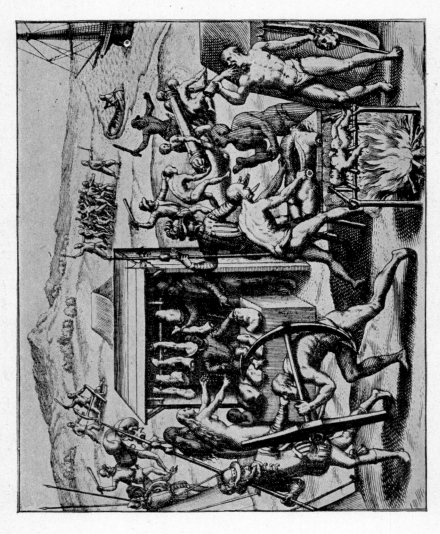

An example of the "Butcheries, and all manner of Cruelties . . . committed by the Popish Spanish Party on the inhabitants of West-India." (See p. 89)

Sir Alexander Mackenzie.

The Canadian voyageur *was the bone and sinew of the fur trade.*

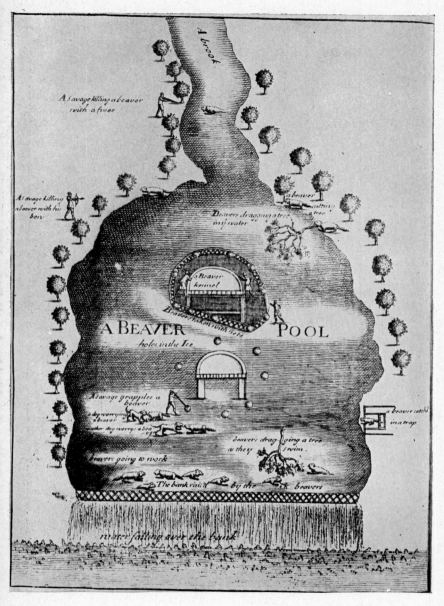

A diagram illustrating a beaver pool, its formation and its fate.

A birch canoe poled among rocks and stones against a rapid stream.

A Chinook house. Large, weather-tight, and strong, it was put together and secured by intricate cedar lashings.

Spanish insult to the British flag at Nootka Sound, 1789.

Beavers, Indians, and the French

> *In a certain sense, the French were not really the builders of the northern commercial empire: they were its first owners, its first occupants. They read the meaning of the region, they invoked its spirit, and they first dreamed the dream which the [St. Lawrence River] inspired in the minds of all those who came to live upon its banks.*
>
> CREIGHTON

FRENCHMEN, like Spaniards and other men from the Atlantic countries of Europe, from the early sixteenth century on searched the New World for cities of gold and silver or the longed-for passageway to the East. French and Dutch and English navigators sailed the northerly latitudes—Spain, strong and powerful, jealously dominated the southern routes—exploring, questioning, hoping. Eagerly they coasted from Florida to Newfoundland looking for treasure, for a waterway, unaware that the farther north they sailed, the farther the shore bowed out eastward to give the continent its greatest breadth. Just behind the protecting wedge of Newfoundland, Jacques Cartier, an experienced navigator of Saint-Malo, found a waterway that led, the Indians told him, a long, long way toward the south and west. And so little, so very little, was understood of the depth and breadth and length of this New World that the sanguine Frenchmen who heard the Indians that summer's day in 1534 grasped at a new and stimulating hope: if this great waterway would not lead to treasures or to China, perhaps it would open a back door through which the French could take Cortés and the Spaniards by surprise. For many decades, as gold and silver and pearls and precious stones eluded the itching hands of French and English explorers and settlers, as the fabulous East receded halfway around the world, this third hope remained; and as the inland system of rivers was deciphered, it became their goal—an interior approach to the glories of Mexico, to the incredible silver riches of San Luis Potosí. Chance had opened the St. Lawrence to the French; furs provided the incentive and the profits for generations of *voyageurs* to penetrate ever deeper into the Great Lakes and from there northward to Lake Winnipeg and southward down the Mississippi.

As Cortés had heard of Mexico, so Cartier was told of Stadacona, the Montagnais fortress perched on a rock, and Hochelaga, the palisaded Huron-Iroquois village set on an island in the river. Stadacona, the germ of Quebec, and Hochelaga, that of Montreal, gave no promise of their future greatness, and Cartier saw only simple aboriginal villages dominating the river that sustained them. Furs from the north, the west, and the south, furs carried for hundreds of miles or traded from tribe to tribe, came out of the wilderness in loaded canoes. On this trade that linked the civilization of Europe to the savagery of America and tied the economic destiny of the one to the everyday necessity of the other, the first great fortunes of Montreal were built.

Unlike the discovery of a silver mine or a pearl fishery, the beginnings of the fur trade were casual, undramatic, haphazard, and unrecorded. Compared with the quick, directed entrenchment of the Spanish in the south, the northern European enterprises in the New World were scattered and slow and barely remunerative; nothing contrasts more strikingly with the luck of the Spaniards in finding spectacular sources of wealth in the south than the disappointed French and English searches for them in the north. John Cabot in 1497 had announced that the sea off Newfoundland was "swarming with fish, which can be taken not only with the net, but in baskets let down with a stone." But, cried the English merchant adventurers bitterly, the Spaniards come back with baskets of pearls! And yet these fishing banks were to be called the "silver mines of the Atlantic"; on the staple they yielded, Catholic Europe was to depend, and cod, together with the resources of the forest, was to provide the foundation for the commercial energy of New England. In Virginia the colonists led by John Smith looked for precious metals and a way through the mountains to the sea which, King James hoped, they would find just beyond. Gold of a different kind there was in Virginia, where fortunes were made in rich tidewater tobacco plantations, but while the colonists were struggling and starving in the effort to establish their commercial enterprises soundly, John Smith could honestly write that "Fishes and Furres was then our refuge." From Virginia north along the Atlantic coast, the survival and security of settlers—Pilgrims included—lay in fish and furs. Without any of the applause and the spotlight given to the discoverer of a silver mine, the first fur trader is shrouded in anonymity; yet it was the fur traders who had the incentive to explore and infiltrate the continent.

Fish and furs! Peter Martyr was told by Cabot "of a certain kind of great fish like tunnies . . . that at times even stayed the passage of his ships," but those who read his book did not appreciate the significance of his observation. It was by word of mouth that knowledge of this great bounty of the sea spread among illiterate Europeans. Sturdy deep-sea fishermen from Biscay to Normandy set their little boats for the distant banks, lifted tons of slippery, silvery cod into their holds, and raced back to waiting markets. These fishermen were also the first fur traders; by tradition and vocation they thought wholly in terms of fishing, and the furs they brought back meant no more to them than souvenirs, casually, capriciously procured in barter at the price of a knife, a nail, an iron pot. Wherever the Indians could find and communicate with the fishermen, this formless rudimentary trade was transacted. From many small centers of activity—so small that contemporary observers narrated their doings as amusing or quaint without perceiving their larger import—markets developed on both continents. In retrospect the forces that pressed this formless trade into a definite pattern to answer the needs of Europe, the urgent needs of America, fall into order and sequence; slowly, imperceptibly, it outgrew its curio stage and evolved its own economic structure.

In Europe, the fur trade was a luxury trade. It grew as the wealth of Europe grew; at first it merely satisfied the demands for courtly elegance, with precious marten skins to flatter princely robes, but with the use of beaver for felt it supplied among the rising middle classes a mark of prestige as well. Imperative and capricious as are all fashions, that of the hat assumed a political cast. Millinery mirrored every major political upheaval. In England styles changed with the kings: one kind of hat bowed the Stuarts onto the throne, another condemned

Charles I to execution; from the Puritan Commonwealth through the Restoration and the Glorious Revolution to the French Revolution each political readjustment wore its distinguishing headgear. The techniques for making felt hats, including beaver felt—like those of many other industries in England —were introduced by artisans who found the air of Spain and the Low Countries bad for their political health. In 1604 the Worshipful Company of the Art or Mistery of Feltmakers of London was incorporated, and English hats began to compete with the older and more skilled French industry. At the end of that century France expelled the Huguenots, in whose deft hands the fine secrets of the trade had rested, and the French hat industry was destroyed; and England, welcoming numerous refugees, added another item to her growing commercial supremacy. From that time on, the hat industry was the largest consumer of furs brought back from America, and of the fur imports two thirds were beaver skins.

In America the fur trade shook and forever altered the Indians' life. It brought them iron. In the inhabitants of the New World, who depended on elaborately worked stone for hatchets and arrow tips, on bone patiently processed into needles and awls, on cooking utensils fashioned out of bark, wood, or pottery, the uses to which iron could be put aroused a desperate hunger. Iron kettles, iron knives, iron hatchets, even iron nails, were things so incalculably precious that to obtain them they would travel for miles, for weeks, to seek out the fair-skinned men and offer whatever they asked. Furs were the one item the Indian could bring that the European was always willing to take. All winter long the Indian hunted and trapped and collected furs to have them ready for the returning fishing boats; all winter the hunter and his family wore robes of beaver skins, fur side to their bodies, to impart the greasy patina (*castor gras*) desired by hatmakers. The focus of the Indian's economy changed. No longer did he live, the master of his destiny, in his northern woods, able to manufacture whatever artifacts he needed for his existence; now he worked to procure the objects of iron, of wool, the firearms, the beads, the constantly expanding list of articles that had ceased being luxuries and had become necessaries. The old skills were lost, and with them independence. Firearms made the Indian a more efficient, the need for trade goods made him a more ruthless hunter; with firearms he was suddenly superior to those who still used the bow and arrow—power depended on European goods, not on personal or cultural attainments. To the native of North America, European manufactures produced a change that was transmitted far inland, a revolution that was profound, continuous, and fatal: no longer could he live without the things his furs bought. For better for worse, for life for death, the fates of the Indian and of the beaver were linked. The beaver frontier and the Indian frontier paced one another. The extinction of the beaver was the bell that tolled the doom of the Indian.

The beaver is a fascinating animal, and not only for his fur, which is luscious and possesses very special qualities that make it sought after for felt, or for his powerful teeth that can and do fell large trees, but are otherwise dedicated to gentleness: he is also delightfully, vulnerably, human. Were he elusive like the deer or fugitive like the fox, fearsome like the bear or prolific like the rabbit, his near-extermination would not have been so easy or quick. He is none of these. He is a monogamist, a domesticated family man, a husbandman, a good provider, the Caspar Milquetoast of the wild. His dams, marvelously built of trees and wattle and mud, provide safe living quarters for his mate and offspring; but they are easily discovered and, with iron hatchets, very easily broken into. Mild, charming, and respectable, the beaver might have survived the coming of iron to the New World had his fur not had a spicated, downy layer that was unrivaled for the making of felt. Beaver felt was so tough and resilient that the master Huguenot hatmakers of La Rochelle reblocked discarded French hats and sold them in Spain, and after this second wearing reworked them for the Portuguese in Brazil, who later sold them profitably in Africa—their final destination. Yearly, thousands upon thousands of beaver skins found their way to the traders' storerooms; yearly, as the beaver frontier receded, the Indian possessed more and more assorted trade goods and was increasingly dependent on them; yearly the demands of fashion and commerce increased until the financial rewards of the fur trade became the goal for which England and France, the colonists and their far-flung Indian allies, would fight a long, relentless war; yearly, as the maze of forests and rivers and plains was invaded in the search for beaver, the secrets of the inner continent were revealed.

Quite soon a point had been reached at which the desire of the European to make money was greater than the aboriginal's need for trade goods, and fur-trade profits engaged the attention of merchant adventurers. Late in the sixteenth century, some enterprising merchants of Saint-Malo sent vessels up the St. Lawrence River in search of Indians still unsophisticated. Not only to seek a passageway to China or to New Spain, but also to follow the retreating line of the doomed beaver and to meet in the interior new tribes who would gladly beggar themselves for a kettle, a knife, or a nail—these were the tasks the French set themselves. As early as 1603, Champlain decided that "With the canoes of the savages one may travel freely and quickly throughout the country." With the simplicity of genius he recognized that Europeans could not penetrate the New World—its forests and rivers, rapids and portages—unless they stripped themselves of encumbrances and adopted the Indian style of travel, dress, food, and shelter. Some young Frenchmen lived as Indians among the Indians, learned their languages and customs, the trails they used, the neighbors with whom they traded. Thus early arose the *voyageur*, who knew the forests and later the plains beyond. Such simple men, who fell in love with the American wilderness and learned its contour and moods from the aboriginal inhabitants—passing this knowledge on to other white men and thus steadily increasing the awareness of streams and portages and lakes and how they were connected or separated into different drainage systems—were the pioneers who laid the groundwork for the great pathfinders who followed and co-ordinated and extended their trails. And as these young men fanned out from the great river where the French had established themselves, they carried precious presents, they made friends; the Indian was gently wooed into dependence on the French and reliance on their trade goods.

A distinct class of men, the *voyageurs* with their canoes linked Lachine—the settlement above the Montreal rapids where the traders maintained outfitting stores—with the upper posts and deeper Indian country. Into the wilderness they carried trade goods, and from it they returned loaded with fur packs; during the winter, when ice covered their highways, they scattered into small bands to trap and trade with the Indians. These wintering huts were always the trade centers of large regions: there the Indians found clothing, guns, ammunition, and brandy, and there they brought their furs in payment. Often a *voyageur* who spent several years among the Indians established a relationship with them, as Balboa had by taking a chief's daughter who combined perfectly the roles of wife, servant, and chief lady of the fort. And though many such unions were temporary, some were permanent and happy and persisted even after the men returned to civilization. Gradually, as the trade spread deeper into the interior and transportation and provisioning required a larger organization and trade goods involved greater sums, the *voyageurs* began to work for men who commanded greater credits. Thus the *voyageur* became an *engagé*, under contract to an employer, the contract clearly stipulating where he was to go, how long he was to stay, the equipment to be furnished him, and his wages. As the trade became more highly organized, the services and skills of the *voyageur* became more specific: he might be merely the middle man in the canoe; he might, if more skilful, occupy a key position in bow or stern; if he had leadership as well as dexterity, he might become the *guide*, in charge of a brigade of canoes. To this life these men of the American wilderness brought color and dash, songs and legends and gay clothes, bravado and hair-trigger temperaments. They lived hard, lonely, violent lives; they subsisted on fish—unrelieved by salt or cereal or vegetable—and brandy. They were the bone and sinew of the fur trade—the *engagé* and the canoe! The buoyant birchbark canoe carried loads swiftly, easily, and safely; weightless, it was lifted past falls or rapids or from stream to stream; it could be quickly repaired with fresh bark and gum, found everywhere in the forests. The canoe and the *engagé*, wedded happily together by the French, were ready and waiting to carry British traders through the staggering difficulties of the river systems. British merchants found these bilingual Frenchmen the perfect guides to lead the expanding, accelerating fur trade into the recesses of the continent.

Since the time of Champlain's young men, the two races had met, steadily, subtly, intimately, and the meeting had marked them both. The Indian had lost his pristine self-dependence; the

European, ironically, had had to forfeit his traditional culture. To both, the vast wilderness was home, and the Indian, dressed in imported trade cloth and using European arms and utensils, was brother to the Frenchman who had learned his language, followed his trails, lived in his camps, adopted his canoe, and found happiness with Indian women. With the fur trader, the Indian had an equality of sorts; contemporary Europeans bathed both in the same romantic light. But, like the beaver, they and their short adventurous life were doomed. Another man representing another economy, antagonistic to the wilderness, was to take their place; the settler would push westward, ever westward, spilling over the Appalachians, across the great rivers, filling the land, driving the frontier before him. By the time the British came, the Indian trails scratched on the surface of the wilderness were discernible paths trod hard and flat and clear by generations of French *voyageurs;* they would become the wide mud roads over which settlers' wagons lurched. But this was far in a future when only strange aboriginal names placed on the maps side by side with familiar French names would recall the early beginning: the Abitibi River, the St. Pierre, the Ottawa, the St. Lawrence, the Saskatchewan, the Athabaska, the Qu'Appelle . . . or the lakes—Timiskaming, Winnipeg, Nipigon, Manitoba, Winnipegosis, Lac des Pluies, Lac Dauphin, Lac Seul. . . . Every map shows in this mingling of languages the commingling of men, the bond that united the two races as they hunted for furs in the great forest belt north of the Laurentians, the amply watered wilderness that was the happy home of the beaver.

Seventeen-sixty-three is one of those rare dates that delight the heart of the historian of North America: it ends one volume and starts another. Seventeen-sixty-three officially marks the end of France as a power in the New World. The volume that had begun more than two hundred years before, with Cartier piercing the northern mists to search for treasures to match those that Spain had found far to the south, the volume that recorded the stirring work of Champlain and La Salle, of the Jesuits and the *voyageurs,* the volume that bit by bit extended the system of lakes and rivers—a silver filigree set in the lazy gloom of northern forests—westward toward the great plains and the

Rockies, the volume that had for its climax the beginning of the struggle to control the West, the Mississippi and its trade—that volume was finished. A handful of intrepid Frenchmen—traders, explorers, and fighters—had with audacious, oversized imagination almost knitted together an empire stretching in the south from New Spain eastward to the Atlantic colonies of England, in the north from the Great Lakes westward to Russian trading posts on the Pacific. But neither the vision of France's empire-builders nor the zeal of her missionaries, not even the amazing plasticity of her *voyageurs* as they adapted themselves to the New World and its natives, could long postpone the inevitable end. Many factors influencing the drift of Great Britain's economic life gave to her alone of all European nations a surplus of strong, energetic men and women who, habituated to farm drudgery and dispossessed from the soil, were available to a growing labor market as wageworkers or as colonists to overseas settlements. In large part, New France was broken by the commercial genius and imperialistic ambitions of Great Britain, which produced more desirable and cheaper trade goods and had mothered far more populous colonies.

Seventeen-sixty-three is a date of convenient coincidences. That year saw the birth of Alexander Mackenzie in Scotland and of John Jacob Astor in Germany, two men who were to make their fortunes in the New World—two very different men whose careers, started and shaped by a continental hunt for furred wealth, enter into the early pages of our western history. The story of early western exploration is contained in the story of the fur trade; it centers on the beaver population that lived in the streams and ponds veining North America. In 1763 the Hudson's Bay Company had just celebrated its centennial; for a hundred years it had held a monopoly of furs caught within its vast preserve—the Hudson Bay drainage basin. The shrewdness and enterprise that had understood the strategic importance of the Bay's oceanic bite deep into the breadth of North America and had formed the Company of Adventurers of England Trading into Hudson's Bay, the heroic resolution that had defended the Bay against the French, declined into foppish and complacent management. With French encroachment and competition eliminated, the directors of the company thought their factors need only wait in their trading posts for the

Indians to bring in valuable furs to exchange for blankets, cotton cloth, kettles, knives, trinkets, mirrors, and beads—items manufactured cheaply and profitably in Great Britain. But the company was to learn from Alexander Mackenzie and other Montreal fur traders that the struggle lay deeper than a conflict between the British of the Hudson's Bay Company and the French of the St. Lawrence. The struggle lay between the Bay which relied on coastal trading, and the river, which had evolved a continental trade system; between special privilege and monopoly entrenched in the Old World and the daring and energy and initiative evoked and rewarded by the New World. Mackenzie and his friends inherited the trained men and the perfected methods, the system and the strategy, of their French predecessors who first followd Indian trails and water routes deeper and deeper into North America in search of the beaver.

Seventeen-sixty-three saw the military occupation of the St. Lawrence by the British, and with it the transference of commercial power, for such was the meaning of the capture of the far-flung river system. Quebec, the capital, remained upon her rock, proud and alien and sullen, paralyzed by conflicting emotions. Bitter at having been abandoned by her motherland, but nostalgic, Quebec still clung tenaciously to her customs, language, and allegiances, her gaze riveted on a France that was to perish in the Revolution. Quite different was Montreal, a small provincial river town looking westward to her fur trade. Montreal's colossal purpose and concentration were to win her an avenue across the continent, to help her become a city of consequence and authority. Her men who spoke French and newcomers who spoke English worked together freely and profitably in business. Here French Canadians and British Canadians were fused together by a dream that transcended Old World ties and suspicions. Together they created a cosmopolitan, tolerant, worldly society, which, amid hard living and heavy drinking, was pleased to favor a gusty magnificence, a grim formality; its symbol was the famous Beaver Club, to which only the great men of Montreal's western empire belonged.

One of the greatest of these was Alexander Mackenzie, who almost single-handed gave Montreal her western empire. Just after Great Britain lost her thirteen colonies, Mackenzie in two historic journeys plumbed Canada's deep hinterland. Starting from Fort Chipewyan, the post he established almost mid-way along the Mackenzie River system, he first explored the great highway down to its mouth at the Arctic Ocean and then westward, up to its headwaters in the Rocky Mountains. Mackenzie's name, that of a giant in North American exploration, has been rightly given to the river he traced—the second largest river on the continent.

Mackenzie

PETER POND died in 1807, when Sir Alexander Mackenzie—knighted for his great deeds—was being fêted and hailed as the greatest of living explorers, was enjoying the comfortable elegance of a fortune founded on furs, and was moving easily in the assorted company that surrounded the Prince of Wales. There is a sad irony in this contrast. Peter Pond deserved a better fate, a more lasting name.

Pond went to Montreal for the first time while following the fife and drum and colors he had joined when the land exploded into the French and Indian War. He was twenty when, as a soldier under Amherst, he stood before Montreal in 1760. His home town of Milford, Connecticut, was, for him, a place to be born in, poor and obscure, and a place to end his days in, in poverty and obscurity. Between his two sojourns there he enjoyed his fill of hard and strange adventure: he blazed a trail to the Athabaska country over an ironlike expanse of snow; he lived and worked and achieved renown in a remote, savage wilderness. He was a man who had to find the country for which he was born. Rootless and restless, he followed the fife and drums out of Milford, for, as he noted long after in his misspelt journal, "It is well known that from fifth gineration downward we ware all waryers ither by sea or land."

Pond had learned much, and had much to tell Mackenzie during the long winter they spent together on Lake Athabaska in 1788–9. The American was already old. The strenuous life of the north woods with its appalling privations counted any trader past thirty as old, and Pond was close to fifty.

What happened during his long, intimate wintering with Mackenzie is not recorded. The picture, though clear enough, is static. Pond, his uncouthness in tune with the primitive surroundings, his words casting a spell that swallowed up his illiteracy as he revealed the mysteries of the unknown northwest, which he had labored to decipher and note on his curious map, imparted bit by bit the shape and color and urgency of the dream he had dreamed to a man young enough to translate his dream into action—Mackenzie, shrewd, ambitious, untried, listening, learning, and accepting fully his legacy. From that wintering, Mackenzie went forward to his two great explorations, which in large part vindicated Pond's plan, while Pond merely jotted down that he had left instructions "to another man by the name of McKenzie with orders to go down the river and from thence to Unalaska and so to Kamchatka and thence to England through Russia"!—and left the wilderness forever.

Thus laconically Pond detailed his dream to the world. It was, as all dreams are, a fascinating brew of reality, hopes, and needs; it reveals much of the dreamer and his world. For Pond is at once an individual and the representative of a handful of named but little-known men who discovered and delineated the vast half-continent in which they had chosen to work.

Frenchmen, Britishers, and American colonists in small groups probed the wide belt of rock and lake and forest and made tentative thrusts into the great plains; they advanced from one Indian tribe to another—with a subdued excitement and apprehension—and learned to respect and rely on maps drawn by aborigines or on information given by Indian prisoners who were native to regions still farther west. They had to map out their own domain, control the slightest action of their *voyageurs*, and serve as their own emissaries to the ever-strange tribes to the west. There, in the unknown and savage societies of the interior, they were immediately and completely free of every traditional restraint; there, in an untrod world, man and nature were adept at treachery, primed for violence; there the balance swung dangerously between measureless chances for success and failure, calamity, and sudden death. They were traders who moved through the tenseness of adventure, and adventurers whose mission was subordinated to the normal pursuits of commerce. Interspersed with notations of numbers of fur packs and amounts of trade goods and wages paid canoemen are words that tell of murder, of scalping parties, of the triumph and fortune met with on finding a way past jealous Indian middlemen to new tribes beyond.

This was the world for which they had been born; beauty they found in "the way of the Indians, the tangled portages as spring broke in the woods around them, the day dawning in fear and sorrow over one of the vast northern lakes and the unbroken, flowing desolation of the winter prairie." [1]

To this type Pond belonged, and to this group of traders he gave his own special qualities of initiative, indomitableness, of violence and vision. His apprenticeship in the fur trade had been spent near Detroit in the rich triangle formed by the Ohio and the Mississippi. That he could leave this still rewarding region for the virgin Canadian Northwest reveals him as an intrepid trader who had accepted the inexorable law of his trade: the greatest returns were to be found far behind the beaver frontier. From that time (1775) onward he moved with purpose and courage deeper and farther into the wilderness, making contacts and trading with Indians who had not yet fully exploited the local beaver population, learning the simple, basic, grand articulation of the north country, hazarding a dream that was a mixture of his knowledge and his hopes.

Pond knew, for this was part of his long apprenticeship, how the St. Lawrence magnificently and proudly drained the immense cluster of the Great Lakes, the turbulent, untamed Ottawa, the St. Maurice and the Saguenay, into the Atlantic; how just north of the lakes and thence in a line eastward connecting the sources of those rivers a gradual, easily traversed height of land led to streams and lakes that, like wrinkles around a puckered mouth, emptied into the enormous circumference of Hudson Bay. Pond himself had crossed the facile low portages that separated the drainage basin of the St. Lawrence from the Mohawk, the Ohio, and the Mississippi. He thought of the St. Lawrence as a long corridor off which numerous doors opened in many directions. Those to the south he had tried and rejected, for already the settlements along the Atlantic were reaching westward, driving into the wilderness; also he knew that northern furs were finer. To the north all doors led to the vast preserve of the Hudson's Bay Company. He must try the far western door—the nine-mile-long Grand Portage—that by stream and

---

[1] D. G. Creighton: *The Commercial Empire of the St. Lawrence* (Toronto, 1937), p. 202.

pond and river connected Lake Superior with Lake Winnipeg. The strategic importance of Lake Winnipeg had already been perceived: it stood at the continental crossroads; from the Rockies the forked Saskatchewan flowed into it; through the Nelson it drained into Hudson Bay. To the south, Portage la Prairie crossed the line dividing the source of the Red River, emptying into Lake Winnipeg, from the Mississippi system, and separated the forests of the north from the treeless plain to the south. North of the lake, Pond knew that an intricate series of portages, streams, and ponds led "to Athabaska, country hitherto unknown but from Indian report."

Into this unknown territory Pond went in 1778–9. He was the first man to cross the height of land—the Methye Portage—that separated the waters draining into Hudson Bay from those that were part of the great northward-flowing highway that lost itself at last in the Arctic Ocean. The thirteen-mile portage was, unlike the others he knew, a dramatic, vehement line of demarcation. Mackenzie, who followed in Pond's steps, described it:

"The Portage is of a level surface, in some parts abounding with stones, but in general it is an entire sand, and covered with the cypress, the pine, the spruce fir, and other trees natural to the soil. Within three miles of the North-West termination, there is a small round lake . . . which affords a trifling respite to the labour of carrying. Within a mile of the termination of the Portage a very steep precipice, whose ascent and descent appears to be equally impracticable in any way, as it consists of a succession of eight hills, some of which are almost perpendicular. . . . This precipice, which rises upwards of a thousand feet of the plains beneath it, commands a most extensive, romantic, and ravishing prospect. From thence the eye looks down on the course of a *little* river . . . beautifully meandering for upwards of thirty miles."

This little river, which Pond saw from the Portage, led him into the Athabaska River, on which he built his post. There he passed the winter.

Pond's boldness in pushing out into the unknown was dazzlingly successful. In the spring he met with great numbers of Cree and Chipewyans, "who used to carry their furs annually to Churchill [to the Hudson's Bay Company]; the latter by the barren grounds, where they suffered innumerable hardships, and were sometimes even starved to death. The former followed the course of the lakes and rivers, through a country that abounded in animals, and where there was plenty of fish: but though they did not suffer from want of food, the intolerable fatigue of such a journey could not be easily repaid to an Indian: they were, therefore, highly gratified by seeing people come to their country to relieve them from such long, toilsome, and dangerous journeys; and were immediately reconciled to give an advanced price for the articles necessary for their comfort and convenience. Mr. Pond's reception and success was accordingly beyond his expectation; and he procured twice as many furs as his canoes would carry [an indication that he paid only half as much as he had expected to]. They also supplied him with as much provision as he required during his residence among them, and sufficient for his homeward voyage. Such of the furs as he could not embark, he secured in one of his winter huts, and they were found the following season, in the same state in which he left them."

Many of Pond's rewards and some of his problems are alluded to in this account. The birchbark-rind canoe, while answering admirably the needs of the *voyageur*, had definite limitations when fur trading swelled into big business: it simply could not contain all the men, trade goods, and food for a protracted trip. Two full strenuous traveling seasons were spent reaching this distant region, two seasons more passed before the furs reached Montreal; and this delay raised problems of supplying food, of longer credits, of maintaining the extended two-way flow of goods. These increasing complexities, too great for any single trader, as well as the wastefulness, bitterness, and bloodiness of cutthroat competition among the independent Montreal traders, forced them to form a copartnership, which gave them protection while supporting their far-flung enterprises. The formation of the North West Company, as they called themselves, showed that these highly individualistic men—traders and merchants— meant to survive; it also served notice on the Hudson's Bay Company that the men of the St. Lawrence, in their alliance, were once again ready, eager, and able to dance rings around the lethargic older group. "To dance rings" is no figure of speech. For the strategy of the Montrealers—the Pedlars, as the Hudson's Bay Company contemptuously called them—continued where the French had left off: swinging deep inland, in a clockwise motion, they proposed, as Pond had already done, to ring the rivers leading to the bay and thus drain off the flow of furs. And Pond, with the united Pedlars behind him, established food depots, which were kept stocked by distant buffalo-hunting Indians, organized the shuttle that carried the trade goods in and the furs out, and, having surmounted those problems, proposed the Athabaska country as the jumping-off place for further exploration. From some of the Indians Pond learned of pemmican, "which is dry'd meat, pounded to a powder and mixed up with buffeloes greese." On the use of this nutritious compressed food the invasion of the far northwest was largely sustained.

Somewhere, in the four canoes that Pond led into the distant northwest, a bit of frightful freight had stowed away, and horror and tragedy slipped along in Pond's tracks. Smallpox, like an evil spirit, tried to extirpate the Indian. It

"spread its destructive and desolating power, as the fire consumes the dry grass of the field. . . . [It] spread around with a baneful rapidity which no flight could escape, and with a fatal effect that nothing could resist. It destroyed with its pestilential breath whole families and tribes. . . . To aggravate the picture, if aggravation were possible, may be added, the putrid carcases which the wolves, with a furious voracity, dragged forth from the huts. . . . The consequences of this melancholy event to the traders must be self-evident; the means of disposing of their goods were cut off; and no furs were obtained, but such as could be gathered from the habitations of the deceased Indians."

Yet when the traders returned the following year (1782–3), they "found the inhabitants in some sort of tranquillity, and more numerous than they had reason to expect, so their success was proportionately better."

Pond and the Pedlars! Courage and endurance they had; business acumen and the genius to organize the enormous continental venture into a functioning, profitable system they achieved;

it is their driving ambition that distinguishes them, that points up the difference between traders and empire-builders. For the next task to which the Pedlars put their strength and mind had a truly grandiose quality—using their wilderness as the highway between the oceans.

At just this time a book was published that galvanized the commercial world and sent echoes and impulses deep into the Northwest. In 1784 there appeared in London the account of Captain James Cook's last voyage—the voyage that took him along the Northern Pacific beyond Bering Strait and from there to his tragic death on Hawaii. The volume included, neither haphazardly nor foolishly, though belatedly, the first account of Samuel Hearne's discoveries in North America (1769–72); the Bishop of Salisbury, as editor, juxtaposed the two narratives for the purpose of wiping out the hypothetical, mythical, desired strait that had been supposed to cut through the continent from Hudson Bay to the Pacific. Hearne, sent out by the Company when it had been pricked into exploration and goaded by competition and critics into enlarging its trade, was an extraordinary leader able to hold together a motley collection of Indians for almost nineteen months. He explored the forest and tundra from Hudson Bay to where the Coppermine joins the Arctic Ocean. His findings exploded the hope of an Indian copper mine that had figured handsomely in many schemes; his journal indicated that "the Continent of America is much wider than people imagine"; and finally by walking across the supposed site of the Northwest Passage, he almost stilled the shrill diehards who kept insisting that such a passage opened out from Hudson Bay. Captain Cook, the greatest navigator of his day, established that the strait was nonexistent on the Pacific side. The good bishop achieved his end, and the strait disappeared from the maps. But the furor the book created was touched off by its incidental picture of Russian traders' looting the North Pacific of sea otter and Alaska seal. There in the dangerous, fog-bound, tempest-swept waters around the Aleutians were immense kelp beds, the breeding ground for those sociable animals. There daring Russian fur traders hunted them, driving them inland where they were clubbed to death by the clumsy defenseless hundreds—a shot would have waked the sleeping animals and sent them instantly plunging to safety. The Russians had already established a fur station on Kodiak Island; near by Cook had marked his inlet into which emptied Cook's River, the river Pond hoped to reach. This marine wealth the Russian traders marketed in China, where the furs fetched fantastic prices; for a generation, undisturbed until Captain Cook peered into their part of the globe, the traders from Kamchatka had plied their profitable plundering. Instantly the North Pacific and especially the northwest coast of America commanded the cupidity of the world. Every country that had ships sent them there; ships flying the colors of Spain, Holland, Great Britain, France, and the young United States hurried to map and hunt in those waters. It drew, as later the discovery of gold in California was to draw, men from all countries to a single spot.

The good news of great riches quickly crossed the Atlantic and reached Montreal. The Pedlars, with immense daring and a bold, imaginative response—here Pond's hand showed—proposed nothing less than a mighty stride across the continent to that very region. They argued that, though their way might be lengthy, it was shorter and quicker than the long voyage around the Cape and up the extended length of the Americas. Their plan rested on information already collected from some wandering Indians about a river "called the Peace, which descended from the Stony or Rocky Mountains, and from which mountains the distance to the *salt lake*, meaning the Pacific Ocean, was not great." This river, the Indians said, emptied into Lake Athabaska, which emptied in turn into a river flowing northward into another lake. Here was the first reference to the Slave River and Great Slave Lake. "But whether this lake was or was not the sea they were unable to say." From such scraps of Indian lore Pond himself had pieced together a fairly true picture of the nature and extent of the Rockies and the assumption that the Peace in some unique manner actually pierced this western barrier and that its source lay close to other rivers that flowed *westward*. His most impressive evidence of the Pacific's proximity to these parts, he asserted, was that "he has had possitive information from the natives who have been on the coast of the North Pacific Ocean that there is a trading Post already established by the Russians."

Such were the clues with which Pond had to work—and he knew that the right answer would lead straight to the incalculable riches of the Russians. He had a strange assortment of facts to reconcile: the spot where Cook had located his river—Pond could not picture the sweeping western arc that Alaska makes—did not tally with the Indians' statement that the Pacific Ocean was not distant from the Rockies; the estuary where Hearne had seen the Arctic tides rise and fall seemed too far from the river that would drain the Great Slave Lake. And where did the Peace fit in? Quickly he must find the proper solution. Already "ships are now fitting out from the United States of America, under the command of Experienced sea-men (who accompanied Captain Cook in his last Voyage) in order to establish a Furr trade upon the North-West Coast of America." News had reached Montreal that energetic Yankee merchants from New York and Massachusetts, hoping for multiplied profits—sending trade goods to the Pacific Indians, exchanging them advantageously for oriental goods, bringing tea and silks and spices back to the home ports, where they would fetch handsome prices—had immediately dispatched two boats there in 1784. The proper conclusions—and time: those two matters bedeviled Pond. He was not oblivious of the South Sea Company's monopoly, which barred Britishers from the Pacific, or of the East India Company's monopoly, which further barred them from China; but, like the Hudson's Bay Company, whose monopoly it had been his great pleasure to circumvent, those were comparatively easy problems. To find the right geographical conclusions Pond returned to his Athabaska country.

The last three years that Pond spent in the northern country (1785–8) were devoted to active exploring. He was possessed of the energy needed to fill in some of the geographical gaps. He pushed on as far as Great Slave Lake and, seeing that its outlet flowed southwest, as the Mackenzie River does for a short distance, knew that it must be distinct from the river Hearne had found; he assumed that this was, instead, the source of Cook's River and the back door to the North Pacific. Somewhere, hope told him, that river passed through the mountains and reached the western sea; this certainly was the final step connecting Montreal with Unalaska that would bring the Pedlars face to face with the Kamchatkan traders. The other river, the Peace, would lead too far to the south. He did not forget the Peace and the knowledge that it had forced its way through the Rocky Mountains from its western birthplace.

Time was against Pond. He was close to fifty, too old to follow the rivers he had marked out on his famous map. Also word
had leaked back to Montreal that a rival trader had been killed
"in a scuffle with Mr. Pond's men"; it was not the first time that
his name had been tied to violence and murder. Old, imperious,
violent, but with a glorious vision of the shape and size and contour of the northwest, of the direction and alignment of the
flowing highways that traversed the forests and tundra and
mountains—this was Peter Pond when he heard that another man
was coming out to carry on his work.

Would his successor respond to Pond's ambition? Would he
find his way to Unalaska and so to Kamchatka and so across the
breadth of Asia and Europe to England? Three quarters of the
way across the American continent had been blazed for this
unknown young man. The remaining step was indicated. Eagerly, in his fort on the Athabaska, Pond awaited his successor.

2.

. . . we concluded this voyage, which had occu-
pied the considerable space of one hundred and
two days.
                                        MACKENZIE

Thus laconically Mackenzie notes the swift conclusion of his
first great journey of discovery. He had explored three thousand
miles, descending and ascending the Mackenzie River; he had
proved the qualities of cool judgment and quiet control, of
muscle and discernment, that mark the born explorer. He was
just twenty-six. Yet the river, named to honor its young and
brilliant discoverer, was called by him the river Disappointment. This described not the river but his own state of mind.
The sweep and vast extent of the river, dominating a country
that abounded in beaver and other fur-bearing animals, and the
new Indian tribes—Slaves and Dogribs and Quarrelers—whose
trust and trade he had enlisted must have made him mindful of
the magnificence of his accomplishment. But he was a Pedlar, a
fur trader; he was heir to Pond's dream and had himself become
possessed of the hope of completing a transcontinental crossing.
For him at that crucial time to follow a river debouching into

the Arctic was a miscalculation, a mistake, an effort wasted, a failure. On July 14, 1789—the day the Bastille was razed by the people of Paris—he had seen not the Russian factory at Kodiak but a school of whales sporting happily in the Arctic Ocean.

No huzzahs, no firing of salvos, not a syllable of satisfaction, mark the conclusion of this first trip. Rather, a grimness, a tightening of lip and resolve, an iron acceptance of a first failure, a steely determination that a second attempt must succeed. And so there is a haste about this terse entry, as if the young man who had so perfectly fitted into Pond's shoes was in a hurry to do what he had to do so that he might the more quickly set foot on his second trail. Only to his cousin Roderic Mackenzie, who had taken over his duties at Fort Chipewyan on Lake Athabaska —the trading post built to replace Pond's Old Establishment there—does he hint at his true feelings. In a letter describing the meeting at which he made his report to the Pedlars, Mackenzie says: "My expedition was hardly spoken of, but that is what I expected."

Whatever Mackenzie called his river and however he may have felt, he was primarily a practical man out to secure the best pelts at bargain prices. The reaction of the Pedlars to his effort had forcibly reminded him that additional profits were the only justification for further exploration; the latter was servant to the former. A second venture must wait while he proved the economic worth of his first. In the next two years (1789–91) he rapidly extended the North West Company's trade in the Mackenzie basin to Indians who until then had possessed no iron. Only when heavy packs of furs had been dispatched back to Montreal did he feel free to prepare himself for his second voyage of discovery.

No longer was Mackenzie a simple fur trader opening up and exploiting new territories. He had become a man with a destiny, a collected, aware young man who wanted to prepare himself properly for the great task ahead. He had already felt the lack of mathematics and astronomy, navigation and geography; these he must know if his work was to win acclaim and scientific standing. Leaving his cousin Roderic in charge of Fort Chipewyan, Mackenzie went to Montreal and thence to England. The winter of 1791–2 he spent in London studying. There, his work unknown, unnoticed, he passed busy, eager months.

Always his heart and mind were dedicated to his great project. He bought books indispensable to his studies and the best new instruments, whose use and application he was mastering. He visited the great London fur-trading firms where portly merchants blustered out their fury at the French for their Revolution, which was ruining exports and overseas trade. In coffee shops he listened to men who had sailed with Cook tell and retell the thrill of selling otter skins, picked up for the merest trifle, for one hundred and twenty dollars apiece at Macao near Canton. With an eye on the calendar he wrote detailed instructions to Roderic to send men up to the Peace to start cutting lumber for a new fort, and hard on the heels of those letters he himself followed. With the fall of 1792 Mackenzie was back at Fort Chipewyan.

The energy of the man! There was no respite, no lessening in his prodigious vitality. Between his two exhausting and exacting historic ventures he made a 3700-mile round trip between Grand Portage and Fort Chipewyan, worked two years in the harsh new wilderness, hurried all the way to London to spend feverish months in serious and unaccustomed study, and then hurried all the long way back to trade and, on the side, to prepare for his next ambitious venture. There was about Mackenzie a stir and ardor, a haste that gathered momentum and became velocity; there was a prodigal spending of self. And yet his words are as calm and ordered as was his demeanor; his constant understatement matches his unruffled mien. It is almost as though he set the style, in his energy and reticence, for the young explorers who came after him and extended and refined the two great paths—northward, along the Mackenzie, and westward, along its tributary, the Peace—that he pioneered.

Only in the preface to his *Voyages* does Mackenzie for a moment drop his reserve and objectivity. Excusing his lack of time and training, which precluded extensive scientific investigations, he writes:

"I could not stop to dig into the earth, over whose surface I was compelled to pass with rapid steps; nor could I turn aside to collect the plants when my thoughts were anxiously employed in making provision for the day that was passing over me. I had to encounter perils by land and perils by water; to watch the savage who was our guide, or to guard against those of his tribe who might meditate our destruction. I had, also, the passions and fears of others to control and subdue. Today, I had to assuage the rising discontents, and on the morrow, to cheer the fainting spirits of the people who accompanied me. The toil of our navigation was incessant, and oftentimes extreme; and in our progress over land, we had no protection from the severity of the elements, and possessed no accommodations or conveniences but such as could be contained in the burden on our shoulders, which aggravated the toils of our march, and added to the wearisomeness of our way."

From Mackenzie himself there are detailed small pictures of the more prosaic aspects of the fur trade; vignettes from a forgotten world, they give it color and substance.

"The articles necessary for this trade, are coarse woollen blankets of different sizes; arms and ammunition; twist and carrot tobacco; Manchester goods; linens and coarse sheetings; thread, lines, and twine; common hardware; cutlery and ironmongery of several descriptions; kettles of brass and copper, and sheet-iron; silk and cotton handkerchiefs, hats, shoes, and hose; calicoes and printed cottons; and so forth."

Or he lists the number of men employed by the Pedlars:

"viz., fifty clerks, seventy-one interpreters and clerks, 1120 canoe-men, and thirty-five guides. Of these, five clerks, eighteen guides, and three hundred and fifty canoe-men were employed for the summer season in going from Montreal to the Grand Portage, and are called Porkeaters. The canoe-men had what is called an equipment, consisting of two blankets, two shirts, two pair of trowsers, two handkerchiefs, fourteen pounds of carrot tobacco, and some trifling articles. . . .
"The necessary number of canoes being purchased, the goods formed into packages [weighing between ninety and one hundred pounds each and containing an assortment of merchandise], the rivers and lakes free of ice, which they usually are the beginning of May, they are dispatched from La Chine, eight miles above Montreal, with eight or ten men in each canoe, and their

baggage; and sixty-five packages of goods, six hundred weight of biscuit, two hundred weight of pork, three bushels of pease, for the men's provision; two oil-cloths to cover the goods, a sail, etc., an axe, a towing-line, a kettle, and a sponge to bail out the water, with a quantity of gum, bark, and watape, to repair the vessel."

Watape, he noted elsewhere,

"is the name given to the divided roots of the spruce fir, which the natives weave into a degree of compactness that renders it capable of containing a fluid. The different parts of the bark canoes are also sewed together with this kind of filament. . . . An European on seeing one of these slender vessels thus laden, heaped up, and sunk with her gunwale within six inches of the water, would think his fate inevitable in such a boat, but the Canadians are so expert that few accidents happen."

The hundreds of miles from Lachine to Grand Portage are then described: the name of each lake, its size and special quality; each stream and river, its current and channel, its rapids and hidden snags; the number of paces to each portage, where the canoe can be towed or where it and its contents must be unloaded, carried, and reloaded. Precisely, meticulously, each step of the route is catalogued :

"Over this portage, which is six hundred and forty-three paces long, the canoe and all the lading are carried. The rock is so steep and difficult of access, that it requires twelve men to take the canoe out of the water. . . . Though the river is increased in this part, some care is necessary to avoid rocks and stumps of trees. . . . Lake Superior is the largest and most magnificent body of fresh water in the world. This vast collection of water is often covered with fog, which driving against the high barren rocks dissolves in torrents of rain."

At the end of this lake was Grand Portage, the gateway of the trail to the northwest. In an amphitheater, cleared and enclosed, stood "the fort, picketed in with cedar pallisadoes, and inclosing houses built with wood and covered with shingles. They are calculated for every convenience of trade, as well as to accommodate the proprietors and clerks during their short residence there. The north men live under tents: but the more frugal pork-eater lodges beneath his canoe. . . . When they are arrived at Grande Portage, which is near nine miles over, each of them has to carry eight packages of such goods and provisions as are necessary for the interior country. . . . If more goods are to be carried over, they are allowed a Spanish dollar for each package; and so inured are they to this kind of labour, that I have known some of them to set off with two packages of ninety pounds each, and return with two others of the same weight, in the course of six hours, being a distance of eighteen miles over hills and mountains."

This same labor, reversed, ferried the furs across the portage and started them on their way back to Montreal.

Business transactions, regulated by contract and agreement, took little time. Rather, Grand Portage stands out for the short space of its activity vividly, excitedly, noisily as a place where a thousand men from Montreal and others who had been working months or years in solitude gorged on talk, food, and drink. These men of the north ate prodigiously and drank stupendously and stupefyingly. Like camels storing water in every cell of their bodies, they filled themselves with gossip, banter, news, songs, experiences and exploits, with which to face the lonely wilderness for another year or two or three. Fights and friendships were renewed, appetites assuaged; eyes and ears and voices had their fill of sociable function. Grand Portage was lusty and lively, hugely satisfying; it was active, animated, strenuous. And through the clamor and movement of canoemen and guides, northmen and clerks, moved the employers, partners in the North West Company, the Pedlars; respect and obedience attended them as they moved about, masters of many men and half a continent. Here Pond had commanded the attention of the Pedlars, and now Mackenzie filled their ears with talk of the Pacific.

From Grand Portage northward canoes only half as large, holding half as much, traveled the 1850 miles to Fort Chipewyan.

Over lakes stocked with whitefish "which are exquisite"; past
rivers winding sluggishly through swamps rich with wild rice,
through sun-flecked groves of oak and maple, pine and birch,
the trail led to Lake Winnipeg. Here was the perfect country
for "uncivilized men, [offering] everything necessary to the
wants and comforts of such a people. Fish, venison, and fowl,
with wild rice, are in great plenty; while at the same time, their
subsistence requires that bodily exercise so necessary to health
and vigour." Along the Saskatchewan they met and traded with
Indians who had horses stolen "from the Spanish settlements in
Mexico; and many of them have been seen even in the back parts
of this country, branded with initials of their original owners'
names." They crossed Frog Portage, named by Indians to com-
memorate the ignorance of a tribe who, unskilled in hunting the
beaver and preparing its skin, were derisively thrown the
stretched skin of a frog. At Lake of the Hills they paddled past
petroleum pools whose thick liquid they mixed with resin from
the spruce fir to gum their canoes. They passed the place where
Pond's Old Establishment had stood, where Mackenzie had spent
that memorable winter, and where the old trader had grown
parsnips, turnips, and carrots in "as fine a kitchen garden as I
ever saw in Canada." September gone, their long journey was
over, and they had reached Fort Chipewyan. "This," wrote
Mackenzie, "was the place which I made my headquarters for
eight years, and from whence I took my departure, on both my
expeditions."

On October 10, 1792, with no bold line, no sharp color to catch
the casual eye, Mackenzie writes:

"I left Fort Chipewyan, to proceed up the Peace River. I had
resolved to go as far as our most distant settlement, which would
occupy the remaining part of the season, it being the route by
which I proposed to attempt my next discovery, across the
mountains from the source of that river; for whatever distance
I would reach this fall, would be a proportionate advancement
of my voyage. . . . I left accompanied by two canoes laden
with the necessary articles for trade. . . .

"We entered the Peace River at seven in the morning of the
12th, taking a Westerly course. Peace Point, from which the
river derives it name, was the spot where the Knisteneaux [Cree]

and Beaver Indians settled their dispute; the real name of the river
and the point being that of the land which was the object of
contention. I did not find the current so strong in this river as
I had been induced to believe."

But his first taste of the Peace's current came in the late fall
months before spring thaws added volume and authority, miles
away from the fury of the canyon where the irresistible power
of the current had overcome the immovable might of the Rockies
and drilled a passageway through.

The weather was cold and raw, and soon snow fell. The first
hard frost came in less than a week, and Mackenzie, fearing lest
the ice stop them, began their hard day at three o'clock in the
morning. Putting every ounce of strength into every moment of
travel, they reached—at six o'clock in the morning of the twentieth—the outpost on the Peace. "We landed before the house
amidst the rejoicing and firing of the people, who were animated
with the prospect of again indulging themselves in the luxury of
rum, of which they had been deprived since the beginning of
May." To the three hundred Indians belonging to the fort,
Mackenzie gave advice—"equally advantageous to them and to
us"—which, to insure its proper reception, was followed by a gift
of a nine-gallon cask of reduced rum and a quantity of tobacco.
Here he stayed only over night; "the thickness of the ice in the
morning was a sufficient notice" to proceed. Hurrying against
the onrushing winter, exposed day and night, working or resting,
to cold disagreeable weather, they arrived on the first of November, quite exhausted, at the place picked for their winter's residence. Nor was their ordeal at an end: there was not a single
hut to shelter them. Before they could rest and relax they had
to build their houses; before they could start building they had to
exchange formalities—rum and tobacco—with the Indian hunters
and equip and ready them for the winter's serious occupation of
beaver hunting.

But by the seventh Mackenzie was able to "set all hands at
work to construct the fort, build the house, and form the store
houses." The two men who had been sent on ahead had worked
hard and well; they had cut a "sufficient quantity of pallisades
eighteen feet long and seven inches in diameter, to enclose a
square of an hundred and twenty feet; they had also dug a ditch

three feet deep to receive them; and had prepared timber and
planks, for the erection of a house." On the twenty-second the
river was firmly frozen over, and five days later "the frost was
so severe that the axes of the workmen became almost as brittle
as glass." Yet another six weeks passed before the men had finished their houses. Mackenzie counted on the northmen's acceptance of toil under brutal conditions when he undertook this
enterprise, which promised sustained drudgery and unmitigated
hardships heightened by an unrelenting fear as they went into
the unknown. Inured to such a life and trained to complete
obedience, the *voyageurs* were the perfect instrument ready and
waiting for an explorer with a fixed goal.

"It is necessary to describe in some measure the hardships which
they undergo without a murmur, in order to convey a general
notion of them. The men who were now with me, left this place
[Fort Chipewyan] in the beginning of last May, and went to the
Rainy Lake [at the western end of Grand Portage] in canoes,
laden with packs of fur, which is a most severe trial of patience
and perseverance: there they do not remain a sufficient time for
ordinary repose, when they take a load of goods in exchange,
and proceed on their return, in a great measure, day and night.
They had been arrived near two months and had been continuously engaged in very toilsome labour, with nothing more than
a common shed to protect them from frost and snow. Such is the
life these people lead; and is continued with unremitting exertion,
till their strength is lost in premature old age."

The winter passed. During April the Indians returned laden
with the skins they had secured; Mackenzie was still the fur
trader, busy with bargaining, arranging, recording.

"I ordered our old canoes to be repaired with bark, and added
four new ones to them, when, with the furs and provisions I had
purchased, six canoes were loaded and dispatched on the 8th of
May for Fort Chipewyan. I had, however, retained six of the
men, who agreed to accompany me on my projected voyage of
discovery. I also engaged my hunters, and closed the business
of the year for the company by writing my public and private
dispatches."

So Mackenzie the fur trader closed his business books for the season. Now he could concentrate all his energy and attention on the dream in his heart. It was Mackenzie the explorer who wrote to his cousin: "I send you a couple of guineas; the rest I take with me to traffic with the Russians." This time he would succeed. No matter what lay between him and the Pacific, this time he would reach it. Surely this was the meaning behind his words.

3.

. . . the river above us, as far as we could see, was one white sheet of foaming water.

MACKENZIE

(9 May–24 May)

Evening had almost fallen when, on May 9, 1793, the canoe was put in the water.

"Her dimensions were twenty-five feet long within, exclusive of the curves of stem and stern, twenty-six inches hold, and four feet nine inches beam. At the same time she was so light, that two men could carry her on a good road three or four miles without resting. In this slender vessel, we shipped provisions, goods for presents, arms, ammunition, and baggage to the weight of three thousand pounds, and an equipage of ten people."

Accompanying Mackenzie were Joseph Landry and Charles Ducette, who had been with him down the Mackenzie River to the Arctic, and four other French Canadians, two Indians as hunters, guides, and interpreters, and Alexander Mackay, a Scotch clerk in the North West Company.

"With these people I embarked at seven in the evening. My winter interpreter, with another person, whom I left here to take care of the fort, shed tears on the reflection of those dangers which we might encounter in our expedition, while my own people offered up their prayers that we might return in safety from it."

A late afternoon departure, making a few miles and pitching camp, was a custom that served to separate two activities, two moods. Feverish, yet deliberate and meticulous preparations were finished, excitement was left behind, last partings shouted, and the fort, cozy and familiar, slipped out of sight. Now they faced the unknown. Now they must be ever alert for the dangers of an untried river; steady, driving, unending work lay ahead; no palisades protected them from a stealthy approach; they would meet with Indians whose language they did not speak, to whom they would be suspect, as were all things strange; now they were completely, finally, terrifyingly on their own. It is possible to understand why Mackenzie, who understood the goal and would share handsomely in the profits, went; it is not so simple to know why the canoemen and Indians accompanied him. They did not possess his dream, nor were they by nature eager and curious. Having been asked, and being obedient, they acquiesced.

Mackenzie was proud of his canoe, so capacious and so light. And never was pride more misplaced. Carrying their persons and all they possessed, the canoe immediately and continuously proved itself too delicate for its load, too flimsy for the Peace, swollen with spring floods. From the first mention on their first day out: "The canoe being strained from its having been very heavily laden, became so leaky, that we were obliged to land, unload, and gum it," until they finally had to abandon it two months later, the tale of the canoe is one of querulous leaking, of minor and major accident. The river tore at it, pierced and broke it with rocks, racked and flattened it in powerful rapids; it was regummed and patched, mended and rebuilt, and, like a chronic invalid who shakily survives into old age, it carried them and was carried by them until they left the river to walk to the sea. A crazy, charmed, exasperating, but extraordinary little craft, this canoe, with its precious state of health, seems almost like a member of the expedition.

Mackenzie's party worked hard to make headway against the strong, still-rising current. Cutting through the foothills, the river opened on

"the most beautiful scenery I had ever beheld. The ground rises at intervals to a considerable height, and stretching inwards to a considerable distance; at every pause in the rise, there is a very gently-ascending space or lawn, which is alternate with abrupt precipices to the summit of the whole. The magnificent theatre of nature has all the decorations which the trees and animals of the country can afford it: groves of poplars in every shape vary the scene; and their intervals are enlivened with vast herds of elk and buffaloes; the former choosing the steeps and uplands, the latter preferring the plains. At this time the buffaloes were attended by their young ones who were frisking about them: and it appeared that the elks would soon exhibit the same enlivening aspect. The whole country displayed an exuberant verdure."

Through this natural park with its vast herds of game, the canoe slowly made its way upstream. They ate well, enjoyed the bounty of the countryside, and after an especially strenuous day were fortified with a "regale" of rum.

An Indian group pestered them with demands to be ferried across the river. Mackenzie, who feared to lose his hunters by offending their tribesmen, but was unwilling to lose time, shrewdly used his knowledge of the many taboos imposed on their women in order to give them an excuse they would accept; and he kept going. "I stated to him [the Chief] that, as the canoe was intended for a voyage of such consequence, no woman could be permitted to embark in it." Among these parties of wandering Indians he looked in vain for an old man who had previously given him an account of the country beyond the limits of his tribe. "This man had been at war on another large river beyond the Rocky Mountains, and described to me a fork of it between the mountains; *the southern branch of which he directed me to take* [italics mine]; from thence, he said, there was a carrying-place of about a day's march for a young man to get to the river." But none of the Indians he now met knew that region, none could add to this precious scrap of information which had been handed him. They merely expressed surprise that he had managed to paddle so far up the river and voiced doubts that he would master the cascades and rapids at the first mountains.

Rain and strong north winds made their progress hard and slow, but by the sixteenth they reached the confluence of the Pine and the Peace.

"This spot would be an excellent situation for a fort or factory, as there is every reason to believe that the country abounds in beaver. As for the other animals, the elk and the buffalo are seen in possession of the hills and the plain. . . . The country is so crowded with animals as to have the appearance, in some places, of a stall-yard, from the state of the ground and the quantity of dung which is scattered over it. The soil is black and light. We this day saw two grisly and hideous bears." Previously they had only seen their enormous tracks, "nine inches wide and of a proportionate length."

They also saw a *watee* or den wherein the huge animals hibernated.

The next day "at two in the afternoon the rocky mountains appeared in sight, with their summits covered with snow: they formed a very agreeable object to every person in the canoe, as we attained the view of them much sooner than we expected." Maybe it was this view that dazzled Mackenzie and robbed him of his usual caution. When he brushed aside the Indians' doubts that he would get past the rapids and falls he showed courage and perseverance. He remembered how on his first journey his exploration of the Mackenzie River had been made in disregard of Indian prophecies of monsters and numbing terrors, of insurmountable obstacles; like the Europeans before Columbus, the Indians ringed their known world with every danger, natural and supernatural, that the imagination could create—stories to be listened to lightly and quickly dismissed. But when, on the nineteenth, his trained eye saw signs unmistakable and meaningful, he should have paused, considered, examined.

"About noon we had landed on an island where there were about eight lodges of last year. The natives had prepared bark here for five canoes [how precisely the signs speak out!], and there is a road along the hills where they passed. Branches were cut and broken along it. . . . The current was very strong through the whole of the day, and the coming up along some of the banks was rendered very dangerous, from the continual falling of large stones, from the upper parts of them. This place appears to be a particular pass for animals across the river, as there are paths leading to it on both sides, every ten yards."

That spot marked the eastern end of the canyon. Mackenzie was brave, not foolhardy; yet by ignoring those significant warnings he imperiled their lives.

No, Mackenzie was not foolhardy; he could not have imagined what lay just ahead of him.

The Peace River Canyon is a compromise between the static strength of the Rockies and the ramming power of the Peace: the mountains have yielded a narrow passage, while the river, forfeiting its nature, has become an elemental fury. Shaped like two sides of an isosceles triangle with its angle pointing southward, the canyon narrows into a funnel through which the mighty Peace, which elsewhere spreads out a mile or so in width, pours through the mountain barrier onto the great north central plain. The zigzagging path covers almost twenty-five miles, and in that savage space the river, in a succession of falls and rapids, drops 270 feet to the foothills below. Up-ended banks of bare rock seven to eleven hundred feet high contain the snarling, swirling water; in places a precarious footing is found between water and bank, in other places the undercut banks tremble as the thunderous mass of water stampedes from side to side. Such was the canyon, and such the river—a river swollen and still mounting—that Mackenzie tried to ascend.

Paddling was futile. Against that current they pitted their strength and skill: they poled, portaged, and tracked their canoe and baggage. For three exhausting days they fought the Peace. The struggle to overcome their first major obstacle is well described by Mackenzie. His style—with its clarity, precision, and muted vivacity—has a contemporary flavor.

"*Sunday, 19:* The account which had been given me of the rapids, was perfectly correct: though by crossing to the other side, the river appeared to me to be practicable as far as we could see: the traverse, therefore, was attempted and proved successful. . . . We continued our course for about three quarters of a mile. We could now proceed no further on this side of the water, and the traverse was rendered extremely dangerous, not only from the strength of the current, but by the cascades just below us, which, if we had got among them, would have involved us and the canoe in one common destruction. . . . When we had effected our passage, the current on the West side was almost

equally violent with that from whence we had just escaped, but
the craggy bank being somewhat lower, we were enabled, with
a line of sixty fathoms [360 feet], to tow the canoe, till we came
to the foot of the most rapid cascade we had hitherto seen. Here
we unloaded, and carried everything over a rocky point of an
hundred and twenty paces. When the canoe was reloaded, I,
with those of my people who were not immediately employed,
ascended the bank. My present situation was so elevated, that
the men who were coming up a strong point, could not hear me,
though I called to them with the utmost strength of my voice,
to lighten the canoe of part of its lading. And here I could not
but reflect, with infinite anxiety, on the hazard of my enterprise;
one false step of those who were attached to the line, or the
breaking of the line itself, would have at once consigned the
canoe, and everything it contained, to instant destruction: it,
however, ascended the rapid in perfect security, but new dangers
immediately presented themselves, for stones, both small and
great, were continually rolling from the bank, so as to render
the situation of those who were dragging the canoe beneath it
extremely perilous; besides, they were at every step in danger,
from the steepness of the ground, of falling into the water; nor
was my solicitude diminished by my being necessarily removed
at times from the sight of them. . . .

"We proceeded with the line as far as I had already been, when
we crossed over and encamped on the opposite beach. I now
dispatched a man with an Indian to visit the rapids above. . . .
Just as the obscurity of night drew on, the man returned with
an account that it would be impracticable to pass several points,
as well as the other super-impending promontories.

"*Monday, 20.*—The weather was clear with a sharp air. We
now, with infinite difficulty passed along the foot of a rock,
which fortunately, was not an hard stone, so that we were enabled to cut steps in it for the distance of twenty feet; from
which, at the hazard of my life, I leaped on a small rock below,
where I received those who followed me on my shoulders. In
this manner four of us passed and dragged up the canoe, in which
attempt we broke her. . . . We again resumed our course with
the assistance of poles, with which we pushed onwards till we
came beneath a precipice, where we could not find any bottom;
so that we were again obliged to have recourse to the line, the

management of which was rendered not only difficult but dangerous, as the men employed in towing were under the necessity of passing on the outside of trees that grew on the edge of the precipice. We, however, surmounted this difficulty, as we had done many others. . . . We now continued our toilsome and perilous progress with the line, and as we proceeded the rapidity of the current increased, so that in the distance of two miles we were obliged to unload four times and carry everything but the canoe. . . .

"At five we had proceeded to where the river was one continued rapid. Here we again took everything out of the canoe, in order to tow her with the line. At length, however, the agitation of the water was so great, that a wave striking on the bow of the canoe broke the line, and filled us with inexpressible dismay, as it appeared impossible that the vessel could escape from being dashed to pieces, and those who were in her from perishing. Another wave, more propitious than the former, drove her out of the tumbling water, so that the men were enabled to bring her ashore, and though she had been carried over rocks by these swells which left them naked a moment after, the canoe received no material injury. The men were, however, in such a state from their late alarm, that it would not only have been unavailing but imprudent to have proposed any further progress. . . . Indeed, it began to be muttered on all sides that there was no alternative but to return. Instead of paying any attention to these murmurs, I desired those who had uttered them to exert themselves in gaining ascent of the hill, and encamp there for the night.

"In the mean time I set off with one of the Indians, and though I continued my examination of the river as long as there was any light to assist me, I could see no end of the rapids and cascades: I was, therefore, perfectly satisfied, that it would be impracticable to proceed any further by water. We returned from this reconnoitring excursion very much fatigued, with our shoes worn out and wounded feet; when I found that, by felling trees on the declivity of the first hill, my people had contrived to ascend it. At the place where we made our landing, the river is not more than fifty yards wide, and flows between stupendous rocks, from whence huge fragments sometimes tumble down, and falling from such a height, dash into small stones, with sharp points, and form the beach between the rocky projections.

"*Tuesday, 21.*—It rained in the morning, and did not cease till eight, and as the men had been very fatigued and disheartened, I suffered them to continue their rest until that hour. Such was the state of the river that no alternative was left us: nor did any means of proceeding present themselves to us, but the passage of the mountain over which we were to carry the canoe as well as the baggage. I dispatched Mr. Mackay with three men and the two Indians to proceed in a strait course from the top of the mountain, and to keep the line of the river till they should find it navigable. . . . At sun set they returned. They had penetrated thick woods, ascended hills and sunk into vallies till they got beyond the rapid. . . . They agreed, that with all its difficulties, and they were of a very alarming nature, the outward course was that which must be preferred. Unpromising, however, as the account of their expedition appeared, it did not sink them into a state of discouragement; and a kettle of wild rice sweetened with sugar, with their usual regale of rum, soon renewed that courage which disdained all obstacles that threatened our progress: and they went to rest, with a full determination to surmount them on the morrow. I sat up in the hope of getting an observation of Jupiter. . . .

"*Wednesday, 22.*—At break of day we entered on the extraordinary journey which was to occupy the remaining part of it. The men began, without delay, to cut a road up the mountain, and as the trees were but of small growth, I ordered them to fell them in such a manner that they might fall parallel with the road, but, at the same time, not separate them entirely from the stumps, so that they might form a kind of railing on either side. The baggage was now brought from the waterside to our encampment. When this was attained, the whole party proceeded with no small degree of apprehension, to fetch the canoe; and, as soon as we had recovered from our fatigue, we advanced with it up the mountain, having the line doubled and fastened successively as we went on to the stumps; while a man at the end of it, hauled it around a tree, holding it on and shifting as we proceeded; so that we may be said, with strict truth, to have warped the canoe up the mountain; indeed by a general and most laborious exertion, we got everything up to the summit by two in the afternoon. At five I sent the men to cut the road onwards, which they effected for about a mile, when they returned. . . . At about ten, I observed an emersion of Jupiter's second satellite. . . .

"*Thursday, 23.*—The weather was clear at four this morning when the men began to carry. I joined [some of the men] in the labour of cutting the road. In the afternoon the ground became very uneven; hills and deep defiles alternately presented themselves to us. Our progress exceeded my expectation, and it was not till four in the afternoon that the carriers overtook us. At five, in a state of fatigue that may be more readily conceived than expressed, we encamped near a rivulet or spring that issued from beneath a large mass of snow and ice. Our toilsome journey of this day I compute at about three miles. . . . We found the country overspread with the trunks of trees, laid low by fire some years ago; among which large copses had sprung up of a close growth, and intermixed with briars, so as to render the passage through them painful and tedious.

"*Friday, 24.*—We continued our very laborious journey, which led us down some steep hills, and through a wood of tall pines. After much toil and trouble, at four in the afternoon we arrived at the river, some hundred yards above the rapids of falls, with all our baggage. I compute the distance of this day's progress to be about four miles. But after all, the Indian carrying-way, whatever may be its length, and I think it cannot exceed ten miles, will always be found more safe and expeditious than the passage which our toil and perseverance formed and surmounted. . . . About two hundred yards below us, the stream rushed with an astonishing but silent velocity, between perpendicular rocks, which are not more than thirty-five yards asunder."

Weary but victorious, the party camped on the far side of their first great obstacle.

4.

*Rivers are highways that move on, and bear us
whither we wish to go.*

　　　　　　　PASCAL: *Pensées*, Chap. IX, 38

(*24 May–12 June*)

Mackenzie and his men had climbed into the midst of the snow-covered Rockies, yet all around them were traces—felled trees and snare enclosures—of Indians who used and hunted along this ancient east-west highway. For a day they rested. Their triumph over Peace Canyon was a tonic to their tired muscles, and songs and smiles festooned their easy, simple tasks. They cut and smoothed poles of various lengths for use against the current; they patched and strengthened the canoe. Here, as a gesture of friendship and an invitation to trade, Mackenzie left a trader's visiting card: a small packet containing a knife, a steel and flint, beads, and other trifles, placed where it would attract attention. One of the Indians added a "small round piece of green wood, chewed at one end in the form of a brush, which the Indians use to pick the marrow out of the bones. This he informed me was an emblem of a country abounding in animals." The success of the fur trade was based on friendship; the trader's advance was opened and cleared by tokens of amity.

Progressing up the Peace, they forced their way onto the high plateau where the bitter cold numbed those hardy northmen. The month of May was ending, and Mackenzie was impatient. Already he had spent thirteen days in advancing only 250 miles, and he was worried by a chain of mountains ahead that barred their westward passage. Running north and south as far as the eye could see, the ridge indicated the approaching forks where the Parsnip flowing from the south joined the Finley flowing from the north: together these formed the Peace. Mackenzie had been told of the juncture of the two rivers, and with the description had gone a warning. Until then he had had no choice but to be guided by the river; now he was to acknowledge the advice of the old Indian who had spoken authoritatively of this country, known to him from many war parties. The Finley, coming from the direction in which Mackenzie wanted to penetrate, with its broad, smooth expanse, did seem the more inviting, the more logical river to follow.

"But the old man . . . had warned me not, on any account, to follow it, as it was soon lost in various branches among the mountains, and that there was no great river that ran in any direction near it; *but by following the latter* [the Parsnip], *he said, we should arrive at a carrying-place to another large river, that did not exceed a day's march* [italics mine], where the inhabitants build houses, and live upon islands."

Despite his theoretical inclinations, despite the rapids that made the Parsnip repellent, despite the tired desire of his men that he should choose the more promising Finley, Mackenzie ordered the canoe steered into the powerful, rushing current of the Parsnip. Wisely he obeyed the old Indian's advice. He had chosen the true path.

A very personal note in Mackenzie's journal offers an apology and insight. As one reads the daily entries—the mere writing of which took precious time—Mackenzie emerges as a tireless leader. He shared in all the heavy work; he directed, planned, and encouraged; he made the observations and calculations that showed them where they were, where they were to go, and how far they had gone; and it was he who remained alert and on guard at night. The personal note explains how he could work day and night, week after strenuous week. "I was in the habit of sometimes indulging myself with a short doze in the canoe," he writes to account for the loss of a notebook that held a week's data, "and I imagine that the branches of the trees brushed my book from me, when I was in such a situation." He must literally have been asleep to have overlooked the mouth of the Pack River, which would have opened to him an easy and direct way into the Fraser; such at least is the suggestion of Simon Fraser, who followed Mackenzie a few years later and for whom the river was named.

Having missed the Pack, the canoe continued up the Parsnip and reached at last a region of bogs and morasses, a hodge-podge of mountain streams distorted and dispersed by myriads of beaver dams into shallow, snag-infested lakes. Physical misery aggravated the men's confusion as rain and thaw, increasing the rivers' burden, made them overflow their banks. Sometimes the men wearily paddled until late into the night before they found a space large enough to camp and eat and sleep. Often the fast-rising water soaked them and their baggage during the night. Desperately, carefully, they clung to the channel of the Parsnip, fearful lest without it to guide them they become lost in that tangle of water and obscuring forests and enclosing mountains. The current, which had been strong, gradually slackened, the river became shallower; anxiously they wondered where they would find the carrying-place. Mackenzie himself confessed that "Our only hope was in such information as we should be able to procure from the natives. All that remained for us to do, was to push forwards till the river should no longer be navigable." And again that night, tired and hungry, they searched the flooded land until eight o'clock before they discovered a place to encamp. Having found plenty of wild parsnips, they gathered the tops and boiled them with pemmican for supper.

The very next day, June ninth, they met some Indians.

Suddenly they caught the smell of fire. Like a whisper it told of people. Alert, they moved cautiously forward. But they had been seen. Soon the woods cracked with the sound of headlong running, of wild confusion. Who were the unseen people about them? Until they found out, their heartbeats were as wild, as startling, as the sounds they heard. Their guns were not primed. How large a party had they surprised? Mackenzie ordered his men to paddle across the river that the alarmed Indians might see they were not being pursued. They were halfway across when out of the woods on a bank rising above them two warriors appeared, "brandishing their spears, displaying their bows and arrows, and accompanying their hostile gestures with loud vociferations." Mackenzie's Indian interpreter called out that here were white men, friends; but the warriors stood their ground, still threatening, unconvinced. For a long time, reassuring them through his Indian, Mackenzie sat motionless in his canoe until the Indians, their first shock dissipated, consented to his landing. "I stepped forward and took each of them by the hand, one of them, but with a very tremulous action, drew his knife from his sleeve, and presented it to me as a mark of his submission to my will and pleasure." He had stilled their fear,

disarmed their hostility. With the same placidity he satisfied
their curiosity. "They examined us, and everything about us,
with a minute and suspicious attention. They had heard of white
men, but this was the first time they had ever seen a human being
of a complexion different from their own. . . . One of them I
sent to recall his people, and the other, for very obvious reasons,
we kept with us." Mackenzie knew how badly he needed them
to guide him across this scrambled height of land, to the river
that, only a day's march beyond, flowed westward. This information he must get from them, and to them he must convey his
own peaceful motive; he could not leave hostility and suspicion
to endanger his return.

With the patience of a diplomat and the skill of a surgeon
Mackenzie sought to establish friendly relations and probe the
Indians' knowledge of their terrain. He had the canoe unloaded,
the baggage brought up onto the bank, the tents pitched; here
he would stay until he had achieved his end. In a few hours
the whole Indian party—three men, three women, and seven or
eight children, scratched, disheveled, frightened—had reassem-
bled. Beads and other pleasing trifles were given, pemmican was
shared with them; at last their terror relaxed, and they seemed
sufficiently composed to be questioned. Where had they obtained their iron objects? These were proof of contact with the
Pacific, for as yet the Atlantic trading sphere had not been
extended to them. But though he was adroit and skilful, the
information he hoped for was not given. Instead they described
how dressed beaver and moose skins passed from the interior
through a series of tribes toward the coast, while from the coast
iron progressed into the interior, its price in skins rising with
each transaction. They knew that at the end of the long chain of
Indian barters of furs and skins was the sea, "or, to use their
expression, the Stinking Lake, where [the coastal Indians] trade
with people like us, that come there in vessels as big as islands."
Mackenzie promised them arms and ammunition to make them
as strong as their most aggressive and feared neighbors; he offered cloth and kettles, knives and axes, tobacco and rum—
"everything they might want," if only they would tell him of
this other river for which he was looking; but they only repeated stubbornly the details of the lengthy overland trade
route. And so eager was he to reach the Pacific and so bewil-

dered by not knowing which way to go that he flirted with the idea of following the tedious path they had described. But he lacked the food and the time for such a prolonged trip.

His hope still rested on the words of the old Indian who had told him to follow the Parsnip—on which he now was—from which a day's march would bring him to another large river. This portage over the height of land and this second river he must find. Against the studied reticence of the Indians he tried more patience, more gifts, more questions. Night came; white men and red men slept. Only Mackenzie, perplexed and disappointed, wondered if there on that high plateau, which they had attained by following the Peace to its farthermost reach, where the water-soaked earth, the trees, and the mountains conspired to confuse and confound him—if there the barren silence of the Indians was to end his expedition and his hope. A tragic, ugly spot, this, should it mark the grave of Pond's vision and the Pedlars' plans. The bitterness of a doomed dream haunted the night, and alone as he had been in his determination, so he was alone in his despair. At last morning came: he had been awaiting it a long, long while.

Again Mackenzie questioned the Indians and again. And then, when the morning was still young, unexpectedly a word and a gesture rewarded his waiting. He had listened while one of the Indians, remaining by his fire, talked with his interpreter. "I understood enough of his language to know that he mentioned something about a great river, at the same time pointing significantly up that which was before us." For this he had been patient; here was his answer at last. Yes, the Indian knew of a large river that flowed toward the midday sun. It had a branch that reached out toward the Parsnip, and the intervening distance was easily bridged by three small lakes with as many carrying-places. A map drawn with charcoal on a piece of birchbark satisfied Mackenzie. He asked the Indians for a guide, and as soon as one of them volunteered, Mackenzie, elated and eager for his party to be on their way, parted from the other Indians. Confidently he told them to expect his party back in two moons and encouraged them to watch for his return.

Two days' paddling brought them close to the source of the Parsnip. A short distance before that their new guide steered them into a small branch that snaked forward by twists and turns

into a lake. To Mackenzie this was no ordinary flooded mountain lake. It was, he recognized, one of the headwaters of the
great Mackenzie River: "I consider [it] as the highest and South-
ernmost source of the Unjigah, or Peace River . . . [which]
after a winding course through a vast extent of country, receiving many large rivers in its progress, and passing through the
Slave Lake, empties itself into the Frozen Ocean." Mackenzie
and his men crossed the lake, landed, unloaded, and followed a
beaten path over a low ridge of land—"eight hundred and seventeen paces in length"—to another small lake.

This low height of land was endowed with the grace of a
revelation. As in a magical setting two streams gushed from the
rocks on the right and found their way into the lake they had
just crossed, while two other streams poured from the opposite
side into the lake they were approaching. For a moment Mackenzie stood on the continental divide. Exultingly, trenchantly,
he noted: "We are now going with the stream."

5.

*Out of this nettle, danger, we pluck this flower,
safety.*
SHAKESPEARE: King Henry IV, Part I, Act I, Sc. 3

(*12 June–21 June*)

The continental divide over which Mackenzie had stepped
separated more than the flow of waters, momentous though that
was. The northern world he had known and explored from
Montreal to the Arctic was behind him, a vast world caught close
by common characteristics: an endless forest belt broken everywhere by rivers and lakes and streams. There man and beast,
alike native to the forest, wandered in small family groups; the
forest determined the mode of life of both. The moose, the caribou of the woods, the bear, and the beaver, unlike the buffalo
of the plains and the caribou of the tundra, never formed herds;
they were elusive, solitary, and hard to come by, and inexorably
they limited the total population as well as the size of the human
groups whose main subsistence they were. The fish—whitefish,

pike, trout, and sturgeon—were hooked singly. Thus life in the forest belt was precarious, fishing was sporadic, and hunting hazardous; the existence of the Indians, dependent entirely upon meat and fish, swung dizzily between a deceptive abundance and real starvation: their whole life was a desperate struggle to satisfy their appetite. Few in number, frightened by the harsh, unremitting environment, they welcomed the trader and indeed respected him as a veritable *deus ex machina*. For the trader brought arms and ammunition, iron axes, rum that warmed and numbed; he established posts and forts where relief could be found when famine stalked the land.

Across the continental divide lay a very different world. The path that Mackenzie traced to the Pacific disclosed a country as varied as the other was uniform. To the watered forest that he knew, there was added a rugged upland region, comparatively dry and open and mild, another range of mountains, and finally a moisture-laden, densely wooded, thickly berried coast. The great fundamental and pervasive difference was in the effect the Pacific Ocean exerted over the whole country west of the Rockies. Here the sea water teemed with life. Here the great marine mammals sported offshore—whales spouted fountains high into the air and schools of porpoises slowly arched upward and as slowly dived; along the indented coast, sea lions, sea otters, and seals frisked and flipped and barked and slid playfully down rocky chutes. Herring, cod, and halibut patterned the water, and to that abundance the migratory salmon added its blessing.

Here, in brief, was one of the earth's rare regions of natural plenty. Salmon, fresh or cured, was the staple provided in profusion. Myriads of huge silver-scaled salmon, following an age-old compulsion, moved up the turbulent rivers; swimming against powerful currents, leaping high over cascades and rapids, they found their way into all the inland streams and lakes; in fantastic numbers they solidly packed the surface of pools. They moved at a rate of two to seven miles a day until they reached the farthest limits of waters to which there was access from the Pacific; there they spawned and there they died, and their smolts, born to seek the ocean, returned to it to grow large and fat and strong enough to fight their long way back to the waters of their birth. The annual upstream rush supplied abundant food to a large population. Mackenzie, who had known only the scattered, wandering, insecure Indians to the east, suddenly found himself in a region of permanent villages consisting of commodious communal houses built of wood, where wealth and property and classes were concepts recognized and rooted in the society, where the people were openly aggressive in their trespassing and menacingly suspicious of strangers. Here the Indians, copying the courage and cunning of the salmon, maneuvered canoes up and down river highways and maintained intervillage communication and transport, while well-beaten paths carried intertribal trade from the coast deep into the interior. From village to village, from tribe to tribe, up the rivers and over the trails, were carried tales of struggle and death, which already had marked the meeting of white men and red men along the coast. Here was a populous world, self-possessed and self-sufficient, sensing in the trader an intruder to be met with circumspection and condescension.

If the story of Mackenzie's journey to the Pacific were only an account of his reading rightly the riddle of mountains and rivers and of his adamantine ardor, then it were quickly told. But when on the twelfth of June he and his small party crossed the continental divide they stepped into an alien world. From that day until they were once again safely back across the divide, their fear mounted to terror, their terror to panic, as the party, small and lost, encountered unfriendliness, animosity, hostility. Mackenzie's success as an explorer lay in his ability to achieve his goal while by his calm, open manner he ingratiated himself with the natives and controlled his men. He had a talent for knowing the word, the gesture, the attitude, to dispel each crisis; he sensed when to yield and when to remain firm, when to withdraw and when to push on. His reactions seemed spontaneous; always they were superlatively right.

Until Mackenzie reached the Fraser, his problems remained relatively simple and equally strenuous. The party crossed the second and third small lakes and then followed a rapid stream. Spring freshets had built up hurdles of gravel beds and uprooted trees; again and again they had to jump into the water to lighten the canoe so that it would not ground, or had to lift it over an obstacle. The water, cold as the ice from which it had just issued, numbed them. As far as they had gone the stream was tormented, and yet it was but a taste of worse to come: two men sent ahead

to scout brought back "a fearful detail of rapid currents, fallen
trees, and large stones." The Bad River fully earned its name.
After portaging around a rapid, the canoe was reloaded and set
back in the mountain torrent. Mackenzie himself wanted to walk
with some of the men in order to lighten the canoe as much as
possible, but those in the boat begged him to go with them so
that they would not perish alone. They knew what might happen. Expert canoemen, they used their skill and strength to control their craft, but the powerful current pushed her sideways
down the river and banged her on a sandy bar. Immediately
everyone jumped overboard, seeking to stop her, to straighten
her, but the current whirled the canoe into deeper water, and
the men piled back in. A second later the canoe was driven onto
a rock that shattered the stern; she caromed onto another rock
that stove the bow in and then bounced over a cascade that
punched large holes in the bottom. The stricken craft, held together by her loosened frame and her own rugged assertiveness,
lay flat on the water, flooded, but still bearing her precious cargo.
Again the men jumped overboard. By holding fast to the water-
logged canoe they saved themselves from being churned and
broken by the murderous power of water and rock. Grimly,
through several hundred yards, they held on until at last they
felt ground under their feet. Only the weighted canoe anchored
them there; no longer had they strength left to fight the river.
Their struggle had been short, terrifying, critical: in those few
minutes the swirling, icy current had almost attained its violent,
evil goal.

The canoemen were dragging themselves and their belongings
out of the water as the land party reached them. The Indians
took one look, sat down, and burst into tears, abandoning themselves to their fears instead of helping the canoemen, who were
almost too benumbed to stand. When finally the latter were on
shore, safe, sound, and reunited with their companions, they
unloaded the crippled canoe. Their whole stock of bullets and
some of their equipment were gone, but their supply of powder
and shot remained, and Mackenzie's precious instruments and
books were intact. The men's joy at being safe matched the
frantic peril from which they had only just escaped; hysterically
they poured out a mixture of happiness and horror, of death and
deliverance. They had had enough, they had gone far enough;

surely now they could return to Fort Chipewyan. To this outburst of fear and hope Mackenzie listened; only later, when they
were warm and fortified by a hearty meal and soothed by a regale
of rum, did he talk. He reassured them, reminded them that all
were alive and well, scolded them for faltering at the first danger—had he not promised them difficulties and dangers?—scoffed
at their softness, exhorted them to live up to the valiant tradition of the northmen and return home only in triumph. "In short,
my harangue produced the desired effect, and a very general
assent appeared to go wherever I should lead the way."

Rehabilitating the wrecked canoe was their first task. With
bark, some pieces of oilcloth, and plenty of gum the shattered
vessel was made ready. Doggedly they continued their forward
march. And a march it was as they carried the weakened canoe
past an endless succession of shoals and rapids, rafts of jammed
driftwood, and fallen trees. Fourteen hours' hard work, and
they made only three miles! The next day was even worse. A
portage around a high waterfall lay through swampy low country. Deep mud, the constant hazard of slippery roots and fallen
trees, an impenetrable forest through which they had to cut a
road, the canoe so weighted down by repeated gummings that
two men exhausted themselves in carrying her only a hundred
yards, a heavy cargo to be transported, clouds of tormenting
mosquitoes and sand flies—and at the end of another terrible
day they had covered only two miles. That night their Indian
guide deserted. Undeterred, they continued their dreadful way,
wading thigh-deep through a dismal morass, until at last, after
all their toil and anxiety, they had the inexpressible satisfaction
of reaching on the west side of the first great range of mountains
a navigable river. Six strained, wearisome, plagued days had
passed.

The strong, swift current of the Herrick carried them mile
after mile. Soon the river broadened into a lake, the current
slackened; this was the forks their guide had spoken of where
another stream joined theirs to form the McGregor River, the
north branch of the Fraser. Everywhere, smoke rising in the
woods told of the presence of Indians, but the Indians themselves they did not see. The next day (*June 19*) hours and miles
flew by; at noon the river passed through banks "of high white
cliffs, crowned with pinnacles in very grotesque shapes. . . .

[Soon] the rocks contracted in such a manner on both sides of the river, as to afford the appearance of the upper part of a fall or cataract." Prudently they landed to look for a portage, and found a faintly traced footpath, worn by the Indians in carrying their canoes. To use the portage they had first to widen the trail. The canoe now weighed so much from the frequent repairs and patchings that she cracked and broke on the shoulders of the men who bore her. "The labour and fatigue of this undertaking, from eight until twelve, beggars all description"—a telling phrase from the unwearied, indomitable Mackenzie.

The next day (*June 20*) the country changed: the rugged, towering banks that enclosed the river widened out, and they could look away to distant hills. A heavy covering of poplars and cypresses, an absence of underbrush, gave the scene a trim, noble, parklike quality. In this setting, close to the water, stood a deserted house, so novel and arresting, so clearly announcing a completely different region, that it was like an important sign that they must stop and read. It was "the only Indian habitation of this kind that I had seen this side of Mechilimakina," Mackenzie noted, remembering the impressive long houses of the Huron-Iroquois villages twenty-five hundred miles away near the Great Lakes. Thirty feet long and twenty wide, it had three low doors; within were three fireplaces with beds ranged on either side—obviously to house three families. The house was built of very straight spruce timbers; a ridgepole resting on two upright forks ten feet high supported the roof. The whole structure, weather-tight and strong, was put together and secured by intricate cedar lashings. Under the roof were long rods on which fish could be hung and dried. But the most extraordinary thing was a machine so large that it filled most of the house—it would have been necessary to take the roof off to get it out! Cylindrical in shape, the huge contraption consisted of long pieces of split wood rounded to the size of a finger, and placed an inch apart, and ingeniously designed as a fish snare. From the presence of the weir and the ordered state of the house, they decided that it was a summer habitation whose owners would soon return. This house was the outpost of a highly developed, rich culture-area that Mackenzie was soon to touch.

A short distance beyond, they passed a river that flowed in from the right through land that was high and rocky and thickly covered with larch. This was the Blackwater—Mackenzie's West-Road River—the end of a much-traveled Indian trail that led to the coast. To this river and to this trail Mackenzie would retrace his steps when the ferocity and length of the Fraser and the hostility of its Indians made it advisable for him to walk overland from there to the Pacific.

At the moment these dangers had not yet appeared. The men were concerned about their canoe, which had become so crazy that a new one was urgently needed. Whenever they saw likely birch trees, they landed to collect bark. They prepared enough altogether for a canoe thirty feet long and four and a half feet high, but they were still too short of material to start building. Their wretched old canoe would still have to carry them through terrible moments before they could let her rest. So heavy and infirm was she that at one place the men chose to run a rapid rather than carry her half a mile overland; Mackenzie, tense and anxious, awaited them at the foot of the rapid, which they reached half-drowned but safe. Again they patched and gummed her and went on.

Game had become increasingly scarce. As a precaution against starvation on their return, they cached a ninety-pound package of pemmican. They buried it in a hole deep enough to allow them to build a fire over it without damage to the food; this method insured their treasure from being stolen by natives or pillaged by animals. Several times they made similar caches as they advanced, spacing them so that they would be assured of some food on their homeward path; it lightened their cargo and lessened the amount of goods to be loaded and unloaded; and it was reassuring to look ahead thus to their return and to the pleasant thought of food.

A few miles farther on, suddenly and dramatically they met the Indians of the upper Fraser. They saw a small new empty canoe drawn up by the bank; soon another appeared with a man in it. He looked at the unusual canoe with its strange crew and gave a whoop of alarm that brought his friends, armed with bows and arrows and spears, to his side. With fierce frenzy they broadcast their intention to kill the strangers instantly if they landed; they shouted threats and warnings; they discharged volleys of arrows to point up their words and pantomime. Mackenzie's reaction to this frantic outburst was that here and now he must

establish amicable relations with these new Indians. Since they
would not even listen to his interpreters, who shouted out reassuring words to pacify them, he realized the extreme folly of
making any approaches until their fury and fear had abated. As
he saw two Indians paddle furiously away down river to sound
the alarm and summon help, he knew that the meeting must
terminate in friendship: he could not fight both the river and the
natives; he could conquer the former only if he had the help of
the latter. Everything—the expedition and the lives of his party—
depended on his securing the Indians' confidence, and this must
be done before their reinforcements arrived. Since his interpreter's words had made no impression—was it only the shouting the
red men heard, not the words?—he sensed that only a simple,
large, clear gesture would carry his message far enough and quick
enough to forestall trouble on a large scale. He ordered his men
to paddle to the opposite shore, to move easily without showing
the slightest confusion.

He had resolved on a daring scheme.

He walked alone away from the canoe, along the bank, hoping
that when the natives saw that he was too far away for his men
to protect him, their natural curiosity would embolden them to
risk investigating his solitary person. At the same time, to secure
his own safety, he told one of his armed Indians to keep him carefully in sight but to stay hidden in the woods and to join him
only if the natives landed and approached; he impressed on the
man that he was not to fire unless Mackenzie did so first. Meanwhile the other Indian interpreter kept calling out to the natives
that here were men who wanted peace. Mackenzie, sitting quite
alone, quickly baited the natives' inquisitiveness. Two of them
began bravely paddling toward him, but stopped far short; he
encouraged them by making signs to land and, as added inducement, held up mirrors, beads, and other trinkets. Nervously, ap-
prehensively, their canoe approached the shore, stern first; but
they would not land. Quietly he came over to them, offering
bright beads. Their courage, tried to its limit, urged them to push
off; but Mackenzie's calm was contagious and they listened to
him. His phrases were meaningless, unintelligible, to them; his
attitude of ease and good will they understood. Just then his
Indian, who had watched over him from ambush, joined him;
now his words were translated; he soothed the fears and won

the trust of the native emissaries. They paddled back to their waiting friends, reported all that had happened—they had examined everything about the white man—displayed their trinkets, held a short consultation, and invited their astonishing visitors to join them. Mackenzie accepted, acting on the invitation so quickly that, had the emissaries not reassured their friends, they would have fled in panic. Mackenzie had gained his objective, his calm had inspired confidence, his consummate mastery had unobtrusively asserted itself; the two groups sat side by side, and by words and signs they became acquainted, friendly.

In the Pacific West, which boasts many independent languages, Mackenzie was lucky to have met with the Carriers, a tribe whose Athapascan language was widespread in the vast forest belt of the East. A common language was a common bond; it made it possible for these two groups, so different, so fearful of one another, to converse freely, precisely, fully. The Carriers—whom the French Canadians had called Porteurs because of their custom of having widows carry the bones of their cremated spouses in a sack during their mourning period—lived in villages along the upper Fraser; and these comparatively populous groups acted as a unit, maintaining a village solidarity for peace or war. Having become friendly with the first group he met led, as he soon learned, to the goodwill of the entire village. From that village, as from a sensitive nerve ganglion, impulses of peace and amity would be transmitted to the other Carrier villages farther down the river.

From these new friends, who knew their own country and the regions beyond, Mackenzie received explicit answers to the many questions he asked. He learned that the river was very long, that it flowed to the south, and that at its mouth—so they had been told—white men were building houses. The current of the Fraser was everywhere powerful and strong, and in three places it was altogether impassable; but besides the dangers and difficulties of navigation, the intruders would be in danger from the malignancy of some neighboring Indians, the Shuswaps. While the report, as Mackenzie viewed it, was alarming, the prospect was not impossible. He would continue; his original plan was unaltered; he was concerned only about how to arrange the immediate details to serve his purpose best.

Mackenzie was ready to proceed to the village when a small

canoe with three men in it appeared. And though they saw the strangers in a group with their relatives, they had come prepared for hostilities, and it took them some time to quiet down, to realize that it was peace, not war, they were expected to participate in. One of the three, a middle-aged man who was treated with particular respect by all, asked who the strangers were, whence they came, whither they were going, and what motive brought them to this region. When his questions had been satisfied, he instantly advised Mackenzie not to proceed that night, because the villagers below, thoroughly alarmed by the messengers who had been sent to warn them, were ready to fight and would fight even if some of these friendly Indians accompanied the strangers. He added that by sunset the men of the village would arrive, and that they would be convinced, as he had been, that here were good people whom they need not fear. Mackenzie followed his advice and gave orders to camp.

The rest of the day he spent conversing with his new friends.

6.

Fear is sharp-sighted, and can see things under-ground and much more in the skies.
CERVANTES: *Don Quixote,* Book iii, Chap. VI

(21 June–4 July)

The Fraser is named for Simon Fraser, who first negotiated all its turbulent, twisting length; Mackenzie was not to have that honor, though this was the river he had heard of and it supplied the route he had planned to follow. Therefore he quickly dismissed the misgivings of the Carriers about it; the warning, like one spoken in a fairy tale, would have to be thrice repeated before he would heed it and alter his itinerary. His unswerving fidelity to his great project, which had survived the river Disappointment and the period of waiting before his second attempt, stopped just short of blind obstinacy. A whole generation of Englishmen who later traced the Arctic mazes of North America were to be his equals in heroism, energy, and dedication to a preconceived idea. In the truest sense many of them were not explorers, for exploration implies the ability to learn, not the ability at cost of life to push a few miles farther; the reward of learning is to find that a problem has many solutions, that one must be flexible enough to choose the solution that best answers the existing conditions. This is the essence of the great explorer; and in this sense, Mackenzie ranks high in North America. His story for the period from the twenty-second of June to the fourth of July, though almost drowned out by its crashing accompaniment of flight, bewilderment, and panic, is that of his inner struggle and momentary confusion on giving up the Fraser River for a more promising route to the Pacific Coast.

Two Carriers accompanied Mackenzie's party as they continued down the Fraser. One of them, in a small, pointed, kayak-like canoe, went ahead to announce their coming, while the other traveled with them. Twice within a few hours these Carriers, less guides than ambassadors, had to vouch for the strangers' goodwill, to turn enmity into fellowship, desertion into hospitality. At the first village women who had fled into hiding rejoined their men once their apprehensions had been stilled; then presents were distributed, and their friendliness and the peaceful nature of the white men's journey explained. The second group, wilder and more ferocious than any natives yet seen, were harder to conciliate; when finally they advanced to meet the strangers, Mackenzie shook hands ceremonially with each man and woman and explained that this salutation was a ritual of friendship. The natives reciprocated with an invitation to spend the night at their lodges and the promise to send two of their own men along to introduce the newcomers to the neighboring nation, a people very numerous and badly disposed toward strangers. On the basis of the information obtained in the lodges of this village Mackenzie changed his plans. By doing so he unwittingly precipitated a crisis.

An elderly Carrier whose intelligent, responsive face had impressed Mackenzie was questioned closely. When he was asked to make a sketch of the country on a large piece of bark, he was so eager to be accurate and comprehensive that he consulted his relatives for criticisms or corrections.

"He described the river as running to the East of South, receiving many rivers, and every six or eight leagues [18 to 24 miles] en-

cumbered with falls and rapids, some of which were very
dangerous, and six of them impracticable. The carrying-places
he represented as of great length, and passing over hills and
mountains. He depicted the lands of the three other tribes, in
succession, who spoke different languages. Beyond that he knew
nothing of the river or country, only that it was still a long way
to the sea."

He added that few Indians were on the river now, but they
would arrive soon for the fishing season; that iron, brass, copper, and trinkets that used to come up the river now came more
easily overland. A very old man joined in to remark that as long
as he could remember he had heard of white men far to the
south; one wonders if these were not the Spanish in Northern
California, word of whose coming had spread over so long a distance. As compared with the long river route, the mapmaker
urged the shortness of the trail across the country to the west;
he reaffirmed that the road, which avoided the mountains and
kept to the low land between, was not difficult. His people used
that trail often; the path skirting small lakes and rivers was plainly
visible; it took no more than six nights to reach the coastal
tribes, who gave them iron and trinkets for their dressed leather
and pelts, and who had told them that a journey of another three
days or two nights would reach the region visited by white men.
Mackenzie was impressed with the contrast the Indians drew
between the two approaches to the western sea. A choice had
to be made between them. His problem as he states it with its
many ramifications, his profound and intricate distress, must, if
his agitation is to be shared, be set against his long-held determination.

"My people listened with great attention to the relation which
had been given me, and it seemed to be their opinion, that it
would be absolute madness to attempt a passage through so many
savage and barbarous nations. My situation may indeed, be more
easily conceived than expressed: I had no more than thirty days
provision remaining . . . besides, our ammunition would soon be
exhausted. . . . The more I thought of the river, the more I
was convinced [that] the distance was very great. Such being
the discouraging circumstances of my situation, which were now

heightened by the discontent of my people, I could not but be alarmed at the idea of attempting to get to the discharge of such a rapid river. . . . Even if I should meet with no obstructions from the natives. . . . I must give up every expectation of returning this season to Athabaska. At the same time I suffered myself to nourish the hope that I might be able to penetrate with more safety, and in a shorter period, to the ocean by the inland western communication. To carry this project into execution I must return a considerable distance up the river, which would necessarily be attended with very serious inconvenience: as in a voyage of this kind, a retrograde motion could not fail to cool the ardour, slacken the zeal, and weaken the confidence of those, who have no greater inducement to the undertaking, than to follow the conductor of it."

That night he wrestled with his problem.

The next morning Mackenzie questioned the villagers again, to test the truth of their previous statements, and in search of additional details to weight his decision. Their facts were repeated exactly as they had first reported them. The decision had to be made, and he made it: he chose the comparative shortness and security of the overland trail. Then he spoke to his men, in full explanation of the reasons why he had changed his plan; he praised their fortitude, patience, and perseverance; he told them that he would consider returning to the spot whence the overland trail started only if they would follow him by either route until they reached the sea. He declared solemnly that he would not abandon his purpose even if it meant going on alone. He added, as though to make this last statement less grim, that he had every hope, every intention, of returning safely to his friends. The response to his plea was warm, enthusiastic, complete: they would follow him wherever he led. They made ready to go back to the trail, and at Mackenzie's request Mackay engraved his name and the year on a tree. A Carrier who had volunteered to lead them over the western trail and was told that they would shortly be leaving decided to go by land to his lodge so that he could make the necessary preparations for the journey. To make certain of the man's services, Mackenzie had Mackay and the two Indian guides accompany him. He set the rendezvous at a "subterranean" house they had passed the previous

day; such houses, with their floors set more or less underground
for the sake of warmth, were common in that region.

The faintest whisper of a warning passed unnoticed: when
Mackenzie told the villagers of his intention to go back up the
river, several of them took an abrupt leave; since he had impressed them with his firm resolution to voyage down the river,
his sudden change disturbed them. If he could change his plan—
they must have argued from a latent base of fear and suspicion—
he might change his motive; he who had talked openly of peace
might be plotting some devious treachery. Their reasoning was
perverse and distorted. Mackenzie could not know this, was too
preoccupied to sense it; he was to suffer its wild nightmarish
effects.

They went upstream much faster than he had expected in such
a crazy canoe and soon caught up with Mackay's party at the
rendezvous. The Carrier still insisted on going on by land, and,
still escorted, he continued. They were to meet again at the
trail's beginning. A short time after leaving the subterranean
house they spied a canoe with three natives who, as soon as they
saw the strangers, made for the shore and hurried into the woods;
the canoe was recognized as belonging to the lodges where the
party had passed such a pleasant night. Another canoe, drawn
stern foremost on the shore—as though poised for instant flight—
was the only sign of life they encountered as they continued
on against the rain and wind and current. That night they
camped near two families, and while his tent was being pitched,
Mackenzie sat down with the natives. The younger of the two
men quit the shed and did not return, and Mackenzie tried by
signs to explain to the other, who had been with him a full day
and night on his way down, the reason for his sudden unexpected return. That night Mackenzie's men still slept in a state
of perfect security, nor had they the slightest fear for the
safety of those who had gone on by land.

The next morning they passed an Indian house where everything appeared to be tranquil, and by eight o'clock had reached
the point where they had first made friends with the Carriers.
Here they were delighted to see Mackay and their two Indians:
delight became alarm when Mackenzie looked at the haggard,
frightened faces of Mackay and his Indians and heard their
harrowing story.

Mackay reported that the three of them had sought refuge in a near-by ruined house in the determination "to sell their lives, which they considered in the most iminent danger, as dear as possible"; that when they did not find Mackenzie at the appointed place, they concluded that the river party had been destroyed; and that they had already formed their plan to take to the woods and cross as directly as they could to the waters of the Peace River, "a scheme which could only have been suggested by despair." The three men had been through an ordeal; they had been subjected to a series of intangible crises that mounted in intensity and were monstrously intensified by fatigue and hunger. Reassured by Mackenzie's presence, Mackay told what had happened. Shortly after leaving the canoe, they met some Indians—probably the same who had left their canoe and fled to the woods when they saw Mackenzie—who were in a great rage and had their bows bent and their arrows ready. The guide questioned the group in an unknown language, and suddenly dashed off as fast as he could, Mackay following until exhaustion brought him to a pause. The Carrier told him that he thought some treachery was planned.

"The guide then conducted them through very bad ways, as fast as they could run; and when he was desired to slacken his pace, he answered they might follow him in any manner they pleased, but that he was impatient to get to his family, in order to prepare shoes, and other necessaries, for his journey. They did not, however, think it prudent to quit him, and he would not stop till ten at night. On passing a track that was but lately made, they began to be seriously alarmed, and on inquiring of the guide where they were, he pretended not to understand them. They then all laid down, spent with fatigue, and without any kind of covering; they were cold, wet, and hungry, but dared not light a fire, from the apprehension of an enemy. This comfortless spot they left at dawn and, on their arrival at the lodges, found them deserted; the property of the Indians being scattered about as if abandoned forever. The guide then made two or three trips into the woods, calling aloud, and bellowing like a madman. At length he had set off in the same direction as they came, and had not since appeared."

Mackenzie sensed how this panic among the Carriers might explode at any moment and from the most unlikely cause; not knowing its origin, he was powerless to combat it. His men, who only yesterday had been resolute and willing, were now filled with fear under the conviction that the voyage was hopeless. Disregarding their opinions and surmises, he ordered them to empty the canoe, and while some were left to guard the loading, he returned with others to where they and the two families had camped the previous night. From them he would find the solution to the mystery that seeped ominously about them. When he arrived, he was disappointed and more perplexed than ever: the families, in the silence of the night, had stolen away from their sheds and abandoned all their small possessions. He did not fear an attack—even if they all combined against them —but this invisible terror threatened his overland journey. "I could not reflect on the possibility of such a disappointment but with sensations little short of agony." His men sensed his bitter frustration, his bewilderment, and their only reaction was to cry out: "Let us re-embark, and be gone." Brusquely he told them he had no intention of giving up. There they would spend the night.

Obedient, they arranged their camp so that it became a fort, put their weapons in order, filled their flasks with powder, and distributed the remaining bullets. They were afraid to light a fire lest it serve as a target for hostile arrows, and only made a smoke to keep off the tormenting flies. Mackenzie and Mackay, with three men, kept alternate watches. Uneasily they settled down, alert for what the night might bring. The silence that surrounded them was more ominous and monstrous because it was a silence.

Nothing happened. They spent the next day prepared for the attack they felt must come. Still nothing happened. Their only visitor was a young woman who, though she told them she had come to fetch something—they received her with kindness and treated her to food and presents—left without taking a single article of her own! She must be a spy, the men agreed, and they kept their guns ready, their sentinels posted. While Mackenzie thought only of how he might re-establish his friendly relations with the Carriers, lest without their aid his "darling project

. . . end in disappointment," his men were equally decided to get away before they were trapped and killed. For the first time they made a gesture of complete defiance: without orders, on their own initiative, they loaded the canoe. Mackenzie, certain that this was done according to a prearranged plan, took no notice of it, but waited for further developments. Although the men were desperate with their desire to depart, they had been so trained to obedience that they could not act decisively; they could only splutter and grumble and hope. So the long day passed, and again they faced the menace of night.

At midnight a rustling noise woke them to tense expectancy. The noise ceased. Two hours later their sentinel reported seeing something like a human figure creeping on all fours quite near them.

When light came, they searched and found an old, gray-haired blind native who, too old to follow his relatives in flight, had been hidden by them. Hunger had driven him out. His fear was so acute that when Mackenzie touched him he almost had convulsions; yet here in "this object of decaying nature" Mackenzie had someone who might explain the mad terror that had possessed everyone for the last two days. The blind man told them that soon after they had left on their way downstream some natives arrived who insisted that the white men were enemies; when in direct contradiction to the statements Mackenzie had made about descending the full length of the river, the white men had suddenly returned, this opinion about them had gained credence. Fear had caused the Indians to scatter widely; it would be a long time before the white men would meet them again. Mackenzie explained to the old man why he had changed his plan and, having fed him, kept him with them that he might by his presence and treatment demonstrate to his people that there was nothing to fear from the white strangers. Now at last Mackenzie understood the mystery in which they had been steeped; now there was nothing to prevent their starting for the river where their guide had promised to meet them. With the old man accompanying them, their living credential to natives they might meet up the river, Mackenzie felt that he could safely continue.

By this time the canoe had become so leaky that one man had to bail constantly. Before they could start overland they

must have a new canoe. They headed for a spot where, the old
man assured them, they would find the bark and cedar they
needed for a new vessel. The appalling condition of the canoe
and a river totally deserted, though everywhere there were
signs of Indians, combined to make that day's progress so difficult and nerve-racking that the men expressed their ill humor,
their fatigue, their unresolved fears, in querulous complaining
and quarreling. By afternoon they had come to the place described by the old man. A grassy island, separated only by a
small channel from all the wood they required, suited their requirements perfectly.

The very next morning (*June 28*) they started to make another canoe: different parties went out looking for wood,
watape, and gum, and except for the last item they returned
with sufficient supplies. By the following day the work was
well advanced, and when their guide suddenly showed up,
everything began to look brighter and more hopeful. He apolo-
gized for his behavior, but assured Mackenzie that all his time
had been spent looking for his family, which had fled in the
general panic. The blind man related how good the white
strangers had been to him, and once again a mixed group sat
easily and pleasantly together. The tension that had made the
days endless and the nights unbearable was dissipated; the canoe
was taking shape and they were able to salvage enough gum
from the old canoe to make the new one strong and watertight.
Even the tormenting flies and a regimen of only two meals a
day—a regulation peculiarly offensive to a Canadian *voyageur*
—had not provoked complaints. June had been a harrowing
month: they had looked on death, they had almost admitted
failure; but, as the days slipped by, their problems had been
faced and settled. And when on the first day of July they put
the new canoe in the water and found her stronger and better
than the old one, they felt as willing and buoyant as their new
little vessel. For a few hours, the first relaxation since they had
started, they cleaned and refreshed themselves, they lay about
smoking, talking, singing. Into a few hours they crammed a
carefree holiday mood.

Their Carrier guide again went on ahead; again Mackenzie
wondered if they would meet him when and where he had
said he would be waiting. The old blind Indian told them firmly

that he would not go farther with them, and they left him, as he desired, there on Canoe Island with a few pounds of pemmican at his side until his relatives should fetch him.

Up the river they went. They were plagued by flies and soaked by a hard rain, but their advance against the current was fast, and on the afternoon of the third they arrived at the Blackwater, the small river that marked the beginning of the trail to the sea. Here, where they had expected to meet their guide, they experienced a few hours of worry and bewilderment when they did not find him. But he soon arrived resplendent in a painted beaver robe, and Mackenzie was so relieved and delighted to see him, to hear him proclaim his steadfast intention to act as their guide, that he gave him "a jacket, a pair of trowsers, and a handkerchief, as a reward for his honourable conduct."

7.

A decent boldness ever meets with friends.
POPE: *The Odyssey of Homer*

(4 July– 17 July)

Into the day-by-day account of hardship, of strength and endurance pushed to their limits, of being wet and cold, hungry and weary—into this heroic saga, a worried, very human, slightly grotesque, but congruous preoccupation with etiquette is injected. During his walk to the Pacific, Mackenzie's chief concern centered on his meeting with strangers. Each day he met new families, new groups, new tribes; each encounter was clouded with uncertainty; each encounter—and repetition did not dull it—became a small but crucial climax; each was aimed at turning the stranger into a friend. Mackenzie knew that there are many ways to meet a stranger. Society has prescribed ways, but he was outside any familiar social structure. As they passed from one alien society to another, traversing a region where a stranger was an enemy unless known to be a friend, the formalities, the importance of proper and authoritative introductions, became a weight thrown decisively on scales fluttering between life and death, success and failure. It was a bizarre business, but it was neither neurotic nor finical. Mackenzie knew that some explorers had had their men strike up a tune and dance a jig so that their loud, explicit gestures should mark them as friends. He also knew how some arrogant, short-sighted captains had confused their superiority in arms with belief in their own superiority, and had greeted the natives with the bitter, ineradicable salutation of blood and strife. And so, as Mackenzie advanced, his major care was to secure proper and adequate introductions; the social art of how to meet a stranger was his main concern.

Coaxing, bribing, subordinating his plan to the natives' wishes —anything rather than that his party be left unchaperoned— he forged a chain of guides and interpreters from the Fraser to the Pacific. With but one frightening break he maintained that fragile, fortuitous lifeline, extended it, and with it safeguarded his men and achieved his goal.

The early morning hours of the fourth of July were spent preparing for the overland march. In two caches they hid a ninety-pound bag of pemmican, two bags each of wild rice and Indian corn, a gallon keg of gunpowder, and a bale of assorted merchandise. They left their canoe, bottom up on a rack, shaded from the sun by a covering of small trees and branches; and within a shelter made of green timbers and covered with larger pieces they placed everything not needed for the trip. They took about three hundred and fifty pounds of pemmican, the case containing Mackenzie's instruments, a parcel of goods for presents, and ammunition. The Canadians carried about ninety pounds each, while their two Indians grumbled at being burdened with half that weight: hauling was squaw's work and not proper for a warrior and hunter. The two Scotsmen had assorted packs of seventy pounds each, and Mackenzie was burdened, in addition, with his long, awkward telescope. Every man carried a gun and ammunition.

At noon they began their journey. Immediately they faced a steep ascent through a leafy forest. Soon it began raining, and though the rain ceased around evening, the underwood continued to drip on them. That night they caught up with their Carrier guide, who had pushed on ahead and was awaiting them at an Indian camp where they met an elderly native and three younger men who were returning from the seacoast. There

Mackenzie saw how poorly the Indians lived just before the great fishing season—all they had to offer was a few small dried fish. Weary from the hard march and spent from the worries and doubts that had fallen heavily on them when they left their canoe and started on their long foot journey, they were lulled into a deep, secure sleep by the natives' singing. In an intimate, unaccustomed style, unaccompanied by drum, rattle, or dancing, the Indians hummed soft, plaintive tones in "a modulation that was rather agreeable: it had somewhat the air of church music."

As the party was about to start the next morning, the guide announced that he could go no farther with them and would let the young men whom they had met the previous night take his place. Mackenzie, knowing it would be useless to remonstrate with him, submitted to his caprice and without a trace of sarcasm solicited his help in recovering a lost dagger. He offered a small knife as a reward. The dagger was returned to its owner after an impressive conjuring scene. And as they took the trail, without urging or shame their guide resumed his place! A little farther on they came to a small lake where three families were encamped. There Mackenzie was astonished and delighted to find, hanging as ornaments from the ears of a child, two half-pence, "one of his present Majesty, and the other of the State of Massachusett's Bay, coined in 1787." For those two coins, which eloquently and surely pointed to recent trade with the coast, he exchanged two coins of his own. On and on the well-beaten track led them, past small lakes, across creeks, through open country, past many well-built Indian houses; and always the rain poured down, rain that was so copious, so cold, that in some places it turned into hail and whitened the ground.

The first night with the additional young guides, Mackenzie made certain of not being abandoned by inviting the youngest to sleep with him.

"These people have no covering but their beaver garments, and that of my companions was a nest of vermin. I, however, spread it under us, and having laid down upon it, we covered ourselves with my camblet cloak. My companion's hair being greased with fish-oil, and his body smeared with red earth, my sense of smelling as well as that of feeling, threatened to interrupt my rest; but these inconveniences yielded to my fatigue, and I passed a night of sound repose."

Quite simply Mackenzie had guaranteed the presence of these evasive, capricious guides by guarding against their desertion in the night; by day he made it his practice to see that the guides were always visible. Thus when, on the second day, the young Carriers told him that, because the road was clear and well marked, they would go ahead and announce them to the next tribe, he was apprehensive lest, using that as an excuse, they go ahead, duck off the road, and return home after the party had passed. No sooner had they uttered their intentions than they walked quickly ahead and were soon out of sight. Immediately Mackenzie told one of his interpreters to throw down his pack and catch up with the disappearing guides. He too pushed on ahead and told his men to follow as quickly as possible; he would stop to wait for them as soon as he had met with the first new natives ahead. Mackenzie and his Indian, walking as fast as they could, finally overtook the guides whom they found chatting with a native family—a man, two women and six children.

Having been properly apprised of its visitors, the family showed no fear of the strangers; the husband was very willing to talk, and when he was told of their destination, he pointed to

"one of his wives, who was a native of the sea-coast. . . . This woman was more inclined to corpulency than any we had yet seen, was of low stature, with an oblong face, grey eyes, and a flattish nose. . . . She had learned the language of her husband's tribe, and confirmed his account, that we were at no great distance from the sea."

The speed with which the Indians traveled—he had been hard put to it to overtake his guides though he had followed them "with all the expedition in our power"—forced Mackenzie to make drastic allowances for a difference in rate of travel; if the Indians calculated the journey at six days, his party would take double that time.

The days passed, each like the one before: they walked and walked along rivers and lakes, they passed houses, rain fell; the terrain varied between hilly, swampy country into which they sank knee-deep and dry, stony valleys. The days passed, and at each new meeting they were reassured that the seacoast was not far off. Their journey has monotony, and yet scattered through Mackenzie's account are the vivid sensations, the shifting worries, the novel impressions each day brought. On the tenth of July their trail led along the side of a lake—bordered in mustard and mint—under a range of beautiful verdant hills. This region was occupied by the Red-fish Men, a new group belonging to the widespread Carrier tribe.

"They were much more cleanly, healthy, and agreeable in their appearance than any of the natives whom we had passed. . . . These people appeared to live in a state of comparative comfort; they take a greater share in the labour of the women, than is common among the savage tribes, and are content with one wife. Though this circumstance may proceed rather from the difficulty of procuring subsistence, than any habitual aversion to polygamy."

The next day (*July 11*) is one long lament:

"I passed a most uncomfortable night: the first part of it I was tormented with flies and in the later deluged with rain. . . . At five in the afternoon we were so wet and cold that we were compelled to stop for the night. . . . Our conductors now began to complain of our mode of travelling, and mentioned their intention of leaving us. . . . Besides these circumstances, and the apprehension that the distance from the sea might be greater than I had imagined it, it became a matter of real necessity that we should begin to diminish the consumption of our provisions, and to subsist upon two-thirds of our allowance."

It was the night of July 12 that the long, tenuous, ever-changing line of guides and interpreters to which they had clung as they advanced deeper and deeper into the countryside broke, leaving them to face the fears they had tried to avoid. In the afternoon "our conductors renewed their menace of leaving us, and I was obliged to give them several articles, and promise more, in order to induce them to continue till we could procure other natives to succeed them." A few hours later the guides pushed on ahead, solely, they said, for the purpose of preventing the natives from shooting arrows at the white strangers. Mackenzie and his men walked as fast as they could, but by evening

"we were so fatigued, that we encamped without them; the mountains covered with snow appeared to be directly before us. As we were collecting wood for our fire, we discovered a cross-road. . . . In short, our situation was such as to afford a just cause for alarm, and that of the people with me was of a nature to defy immediate alleviation. . . . Surrounded, as we were, with snow-clad mountains, the air became so cold, that the violence of our exercise, was not sufficient to produce a comfortable degree of warmth. Our course today was from West to South and at least thirty-six miles. The land in general was very barren and stony."

At five the next morning, after warming themselves at a large fire, they started on their dubious journey. An hour later they came to the edge of a wood, and there, on a green spot by the side of a small river, was a house. Smoke drifting out into the still, cold morning air spoke of people.

"I immediately pushed forward towards this mansion, while my people were in such a state of alarm, that they followed me with the greatest reluctance. . . . I was close upon the house before the inhabitants perceived us, when the women and children uttered the most horrid shrieks, and the only man who appeared to be with them, escaped out of the back door which I reached just in time to prevent the women and children from following him. The man fled with all his speed into the woods. . . . It is impossible to describe the distress and alarm of these poor people, who believing they were attacked by enemies, expected an immediate massacre. . . . Our prisoners consisted of three women and seven children. At length by our demeanor, and our presents, we contrived to dissipate their apprehensions. One of the women then informed us . . . that from the mountains before us, which were covered with snow, the sea was visible; and accompanied her information with a present of dried fish."

Mackenzie suggested that if the man would return—he could be seen dimly, cautiously lurking in the woods—they would like to engage him as their guide; and though the women called out to him that this was not a war party but strangers who came as friends, he still remained, frightened, at a distance, ready to fly for his life. Only after a long time and much jittery maneuvering did the man edge toward the house. They were arranging with him to be their guide when another man suddenly appeared. As he advanced he talked aloud; they made out his words: he threw himself on their mercy, they might kill him if that was their pleasure, but from what he had heard and seen he hoped for friendship rather than enmity.

"He was an elderly person, of a decent appearance, and I gave him some articles to conciliate him to us . . . he gave me several half dried fish, which I considered as a peace offering. After some conversation with these people, respecting the country, and our future progress through it, we retired to rest, with sensations very different from those with which we had risen in the morning."

Mackenzie had restored the vital continuity of guides and guarantors.

He had need to re-establish his security, for, as the woman had said, just beyond the mountains was the sea; they were approaching the end of the trail and with it a world totally different from anything any of them—white or Indian—had known. The next morning (*July 14*) the elderly man and two of his sons accompanied them. Mackenzie did not want the younger one along, for to him, with an eye on rapidly diminishing provisions, it was another and unnecessary mouth to feed. The elderly man assured him that none of them would encroach on the food supplies, "as they were used to sustain themselves on their journeys on herbs, and the inner tegument of the bark of the trees, for the stripping of which he had a thin piece of bone, then hanging by his side. The latter is of glutinous quality, of a clammy, sweet taste, and is generally considered by the more interior Indians as a delicacy." All day they walked, ascending hill after hill, with their horizon always ending in the line of snow-covered mountains; at nine that night, thoroughly exhausted, they camped. "Our guides encouraged us with the hope, that in two days of similar exertion, we should arrive among people of the other nation!"

The last days on the trail had almost a holiday mood. The new guides proved not only reliable, but happy to be in the company of the white strangers; what was an even greater and rarer pleasure was the luxury of their solicitude. A large group of natives, camped along the trail, welcomed them with kindness and examined them with the most minute attention. "They must, however, have been told that we were white, as our faces no longer indicated that distinguishing complexion." Here Mackenzie's guides asked to keep the party company for another day. The new group were attractive-looking:

"The hair of the women was tied in large loose knots over the ears, and plaited with great neatness. . . . Some of them had adorned their tresses with beads, with a very pretty effect. The men were clothed in leather, their hair was nicely combed, and their complexion was fairer, or perhaps it may be said with more propriety, that they were more cleanly, than any of the natives we had yet seen. Their eyes . . . were of a grey hue with a tinge of red. There was one man amongst them of at least six feet four inches in height . . . he was about twenty-eight years of age, and was treated with particular respect by his party. Every man, woman, and child carried a proportionate burden, consisting of beaver coating, and parchment, as well as skins of the otter, the marten, the bear, the lynx, and dressed moose-skins. . . . Such an escort was the most fortunate that could happen in our favour. They told us, that as the women and children could not travel fast, we shall be three days getting to the end of our journey; which [was] very agreeable information to people in our exhausted condition."

No longer did Mackenzie and his men have to gallop to keep pace with the fast-disappearing backs of their guides; even this leisurely pace netted them twenty miles during the day.

The next afternoon (*July 16*) the large, comfortable group whose company they had enjoyed halted to await friends, people of another tribe who had heard of the white men and wanted to see and examine such curious beings. His Indian companions told Mackenzie that they would let the new group lead him over the mountain, because they "had changed their minds, and intended to follow a small river which . . . went in a direction very different from the line of our journey." This was the Salmon River, which led directly to the head of Dean Channel, an inlet of the sea; and Mackenzie thus missed the quickest way to his objective. One can only assume that there was some misunderstanding: his mentioning the overland trail or crossing the mountain from which the sea was visible or reaching *the* village from which trade goods came must have misled them as to his ultimate objective; they mistook the synonyms he used for his goal for the goal itself. The news of the Indians' intention was very disappointing to Mackenzie.

"It was my wish to continue with these people whatever way they went; but neither my promises or entreaties would avail . . . and when I represented the low state of our provisions, one of them answered that if we would stay with them all night, he would boil a kettle of fish-roes for us. Accordingly, without receiving any answer, he began to make preparations to fulfil his engagement. He took the roes out of a bag, and having bruised them between two stones, put them in water to soak. His wife then took a handful of dry grass in her hand, with which she squeezed them through her fingers; in the mean time her husband [made] a fire for the purpose of heating stones. When she had finished her operation, she filled a water kettle nearly full of water, and poured the roes into it. When the stones were sufficiently heated, some of them were put into the kettle, and others were thrown in from time to time, till the water was boiling, the woman also continued stirring the contents of the kettle, till they were rough to a thick consistency; the stones were then taken out, and the whole was seasoned with a pint of strong rancid oil. The smell of this curious dish was sufficient to sicken me without tasting it, but the hunger of my people surmounted the nauseous meal. When unadulterated by the stinking oil, these boiled roes are not an unpalatable dish."

The men had just finished this novel meal when the expected newcomers arrived, and they parted from their pleasant fellow travelers. That afternoon they forded the Salmon River and, led by their new guides, cut across the hills that stood between them and the Bella Coola River. Up and up their path lay. They climbed over hard, packed snow-drifts; they were pelted by hail, snow, and rain; a raging mountain wind tore at them and icy mountain air numbed them; and there, walking, as it seemed to them, on the top of the world, a stupendous mountain whose snowy summit was lost in the clouds suddenly appeared. Between it and their immediate course flowed the river to which they were going. The storm past, they found wood with which to make a fire and cook the venison their hunters had secured for them. They ate as they had not eaten in a long, long time; at last they had the pleasant satisfying feeling that comes from an appeased appetite. "To the comfort which I have just mentioned, I added that of taking off my beard, as well as changing my linen, and my people followed the humanizing example." They had come almost to the edge of the fabulous world that they had traveled so long, had worked so hard, to reach. On the promised coast they must make their appearance as white men. They were conscious of the niceties they must maintain.

Now they moved forward with greater speed; as they advanced, the mountain seemed to withdraw. The country between opened up to their view, and, towering up from its base, the awful elevation was wholly revealed. The path led downward. At the very edge of a precipice their guides pointed out the river and a village on its banks. The heavily timbered western slope dropped in a wild series of sharp breaks. Here they were told there were mountain goats, here they passed through mighty stands of pine, spruce, and hemlock, and here were the largest and loftiest elder and cedar trees these men from the Atlantic had ever seen.

Everywhere the berries were ripe, the air was warm and moist; here was a pervadingly strange and different world.

8.

ALEXANDER MACKENZIE, FROM CANADA, BY LAND, THE TWENTY-SECOND OF JULY, ONE THOUSAND SEVEN HUNDRED AND NINETY-THREE. *Mackenzie's inscription on a rock in Dean Channel, British Columbia*

(*17 July–22 July*)

Steadily, as Mackenzie had advanced from the Fraser to the coast, he had noticed that the houses were more closely spaced, better built and more elaborately decorated; that the people were more numerous, less poverty-stricken, more self-assured; even so he was not prepared for the wealth, the secure plenty, the intricate social structure that he was to find among the natives of the Pacific West. Until now his main problem had been to allay fear; now he would have to contend with arrogance. Previously he had had to disclaim hostile intentions; now he would have to dispel them. He was not a Balboa finding gold and pearls among Pacific tribes, nor a Cortés conquering the mighty capital of an extended empire; he saw here merely the heyday of a rich, complex world whose symbols of wealth were non-European, fantastic; and though he was not the first to discover the furs and salmon there, his exploration in large measure secured that region and that wealth for Canada and Great Britain—and who shall say, as between pearls and salmon, gold and furs, which were the greater treasures?

The Japan Current swings eastward across the Pacific to bathe the northwest American coast and bless it with warmth; its moisture, striking the high snow-capped mountains that tower above the ocean, is precipitated into an abundant rain. Those western slopes were the home of gigantic trees that provided the natives with wood for their impressive houses and large dugout canoes, with bark cloth, and even with food to supplement the salmon. The cedar was to them all that the fabulous coconut palm is to the South Sea Islander. The men used its outer bark to make their ropes and lines; with it they shingled their houses; and they twisted it into "traveling fire," or slow-burning matches. Their wives wove soft garments from its inner bark for themselves and their children, made it into bedding, and fashioned it into the soft, firm rolls with which they bound their infants' heads into what was to them a properly human shape. From its wood the men built their commodious communal dwellings and all the furniture and utensils they needed: tubs, pots, kettles, platters, bowls, and dishes; their graceful, seaworthy fishing and war canoes were constructed out of cedar planks, and so too their strong treasure chests and their coffins. From it they carved their ceremonial masks, their heraldic emblems, and their extraordinary totem poles. The branches of the younger trees made ideal withes and ties, and from the split roots the women wove beautiful watertight baskets.

Endowed with a plentiful food supply, these villages and tribes were scattered along an immense coastline, among the sheltered channels and large islands from Vancouver to Alaska. The sea running between the mainland and the steep, large islands paralleling the shore was their Mediterranean, containing their world. Here a common environment had set its exotic, fruitful stamp on tribes of different languages; common traits were either emphasized or muted to present surface contrasts, but they all shared an independent nature, an arrogant spirit, an opulent world. Haughty, proud, brazen, aggressive, they were men of property and men of war; among themselves they vied for superiority, using weapons, taunting, shaming songs, a reckless competitive destruction of property. If they addressed their fellow men with insolence, they addressed their supernatural beings with shrill reminders of what was due to this humanity—like cheated, irate tenants, not like suppliants begging grace.

Their villages were large, their wooden houses sheltered many families. The cohesion and stability of this large group was evident in impressive communal enterprises—in their remarkable houses, in their elaborate and ingenious salmon weirs. Each village had its chief, who with his relatives formed the noble class. Under them was a rich middle class, then a class of dependents, and at bottom a slave class—war prisoners. The territory belonging to each village was defined and known, and within this larger unit each family had its fishing grounds, its woods, its berry patches, its springs—its security. They had leisure, the time to create artistic artifacts—the men built and carved and painted their houses, canoes, boxes, and totem poles; the women lavished skill and beauty on their weaving; their imaginations created a rich, supernatural, totemic world from which they claimed descent, and their lineages, magnificently and strangely carved and painted, stood straight and high and visible, proclaiming to all the world the pretensions and pride of the village chief. Their names—Tsimshian, Haida, Kwakiutl, Nootka, Bella Bella, and Bella Coola—have an alien lost sound, a savage distant sound. These were the tribes, populous and property-conscious, who, seeing the white men trespass on the land and in the waters that had been theirs (as they maintained) since the world was formed, turned on these traders to plunder and massacre.

This was the world into which Mackenzie groped his way after the sun had set and twilight, creeping out of the thick, dark, enclosing forest, claimed the Bella Coola River. Only the branches of the trees, broken by their guides to mark the trail, led him toward the village glimpsed from the cliff. Tired, hungry, fearful, the men wanted to stop where they were, but Mackenzie insisted that they follow him into the village.

There is something profoundly heroic in the way that, alone, Mackenzie entered the first house he came to, threw down his pack, and shook hands with the people. He was received without surprise—his guides had done their work well—but by signs he was urged to go to a larger house that, set high above the ground on upright posts, was reached by a native ladder, a broad piece of timber with steps notched in it.

"I entered the house at one end; and having passed three fires, at equal distances in the middle of the building, I was received by several people, sitting upon a very wide board, at the upper end of it. I shook hands with them, and seated myself beside a man, the dignity of whose countenance induced me to give him that preference. I soon discovered one of my guides seated a little above me. . . . In a short time my people arrived, and placed themselves near me, when the man by whom I sat immediately rose and fetched . . . a quantity of roasted salmon. He then directed a mat to be placed before me and Mr. Mackay, who was now sitting by me. When this ceremony was performed, he brought a salmon for each of us, and half an one to each of my men."

After this ceremonial reception, the chief invited them, by signs, to sleep in his house. Here, in the face of an utterly alien language, Mackenzie's interpreters were of no more use to him than his own quick ears and alert mind; and rather than act without being absolutely certain of the chief's intentions—lest unwittingly he offend—Mackenzie told his men they would sleep outside.

"When [the chief] observed our design, he placed boards for us, that we might not take our repose on the bare ground, and ordered a fire to be prepared for us. We had not been long seated around it, when we received a large dish of salmon roes, pounded fine and beat up with water, so as to give it the appearance of cream. . . . Another dish soon followed, the principal article of which was also salmon roes, with a large proportion of goose-berries, and an herb that appeared to be sorrel. Its acidity rendered it more agreeable to my taste than the former preparation. Having been regaled with these delicacies . . . we laid ourselves down to rest, with no other canopy than the sky; but I never enjoyed a more sound and refreshing rest, though I had a board for my bed, and a billet for my pillow."

Was it luck that led Mackenzie to this "Friendly Village," as he called it, whose chief accorded him a hospitable welcome, gave him food and canoes, and in a very real sense made his final triumph possible and secured his safe return? How rare was the treatment shown him he was to realize when, as he made his short, quick dash to the Pacific, he was met with suspicion and distrust and finally with overt hostility. That first night on the Pacific coast he slept, almost at rest now that he was about to realize after so long a time his dream; and if he dreamed, it was to enjoy in his sleep the comfort and reassurance of having looked on the face of a friend.

Mackenzie awoke the next morning (*July 18*) to find that the natives had already lighted a fire and were ready with break-fast—more salmon and a profusion of gooseberries, huckleberries, and raspberries, "the finest I ever saw or tasted." Then he was shown—but from a distance, so superstitious were the Indians about the river and the salmon—the impressive engineering used in the construction of their weirs, which rose four feet above the surface and dammed two thirds of the river's turbulent width. Traps cunningly placed caught the salmon as they fell back, unable to surmount the artificial obstacle; passageways on either side led the fish directly into ponds whence they were scooped up at pleasure with dipping nets. "The water of this river is the colour of asses' milk, which I attribute in part to the limestone!" Mackenzie continually encountered the superstitions with which the Indians surrounded the salmon: it was the only animal food allowed them: meat was forbidden, and even the handling of meat was polluting. When he asked the friendly chief for a canoe and for people to take them to the sea, which was about thirty miles distant, and was put off with excuses and evasive replies, his intuition and understanding told him to look further for the chief's real objection: his refusal was directed against the venison they still had with them. Had they taken this with them in the canoe, they were solemnly told, the fish would have instantly smelled it and abandoned them so that they would all starve. To ease the chief's mind of this monstrous threat, Mackenzie did as he suggested and gave the meat to a stranger who belonged to a tribe that was not bound by strict taboos.

That afternoon, in two borrowed canoes with seven natives to guide them, the party started down the river.

"The stream was rapid and ran upwards of six miles an hour. We came to a weir . . . where the natives landed us, and shot over it without taking a drop of water. They then received us on board again. I had imagined that the Canadians who accompanied me were the most expert canoe-men in the world, but they were inferior to these people, as they themselves acknowledge. . . . We proceeded at a very great rate for about two hours and a half, when we were informed that we must land, as the Great Village was only a short distance."

Some of the Indians ran ahead to announce the strangers' arrival, and Mackenzie and his men followed them along a path through a small thicket. As they approached, they heard loud and confused shouting, and on coming out of the woods they were aghast to see the alarmed natives running from house to house, armed with bows and arrows, spears, and axes. To Mackenzie, there was only one way to face such a frightening scene—to "walk resolutely up to them, without manifesting any signs of apprehension at their hostile appearance." His behavior induced most of the people to lay down their arms and surge toward him. He was busy shaking hands with those nearest him when an elderly man broke through the crowd and took him in his arms; then came another, who, almost shoving the older man away, repeated the same hug. This embrace, the Bella Coola equivalent of a handshake, was a sign of respect and friendship; it was emphasized by the present of a magnificent sea-otter robe. The chief of the village and his sons led the party to their house. In this village of about two hundred persons Mackenzie counted four elevated houses, seven built on the ground, and a large number of kitchens and sheds for curing fish; the raised houses were over a hundred feet long by forty feet wide and were divided into three, four, or five apartments arranged so as to give each family privacy. Indoors they were served a fascinating banquet. In addition to the customary roast salmon they were offered a special delicacy: a large cake made of the inner rind of the hemlock bark, dried and compressed, was served after it had been soaked in water, pulled to pieces like oakum, piled into a special long, shallow, troughlike dish, and liberally sprinkled with clear, sweet salmon oil. To the young chief who had presented him with the fur robe Mackenzie gave a woolen blanket; to the older chief, his father, he offered a pair of scissors, "whose use I explained to him, for clipping his beard, which was of great length; and to that purpose he immediately applied it."

Everywhere Mackenzie saw the amazing abundance of salmon with which these people were dowered. In front of the chief's house were four sprawling heaps, each containing from three to four hundred fish; sixteen women were busy cleaning and preparing them. He saw thousands more salmon strung on cords and fastened to stakes in the river, waiting to be cleaned, roasted, and stored away for the year's supply. And hovering over these riches were the supernatural safeguards with which the Indians surrounded this staple that mysteriously appeared every year to fill their storage racks and then as mysteriously ceased crowding the river. Salmon disliked the smell of iron, Mackenzie was told here as they took away his kettle—a precaution lest he dip it in the river; they substituted for it watertight wooden boxes. Before the salmon, source and sustainer of life, they walked humbly; delicately they arranged their ideas that they might not give offense to the salmon.

The next morning (*July 19*) the chief paid the white men a visit and complained of a pain in his breast. Mackenzie poured a few drops of Turlington's Balsam, a well-known pharmaceutical preparation consisting of compound tincture of benzoin, on a piece of sugar and was gratified to see him take it without fear or hesitation. Then the chief led him to a shed, where, surrounded by people, lay another of his sons, who was very ill. "They immediately uncovered him, and showed me a violent ulcer in the small of his back, in the foulest state that can be imagined. . . . This unhappy man was reduced to a skeleton, and . . . drawing near to an end of his pains." The people wanted Mackenzie to touch him; the father begged him to give him some medicine; again Mackenzie doctored with the balsam, which he knew could do no harm. Then he watched as the native doctors worked on the dying man.

"They blew on him, and then whistled, at times they pressed their extended fingers, with all their strength on his stomach; they also put their forefingers doubled up into his mouth, and spouted water from their own with great violence into his face. . . . I had observed that his belly and breast were covered with scars . . . caused by a custom prevalent among them, of applying pieces of lighted touch-wood to their flesh, in order to relieve pain or demonstrate their courage. He was now placed on a broad plank, and carried by six men into the woods. . . . When they had advanced a short distance, they laid him upon a clear spot, and kindled a fire against his back, when the physician began to scarify the ulcer with a very blunt instrument, the cruel pain of which operation the patient bore with incredible resolution. The scene afflicted me, and I left it."

The diabolical energy of these native physicians in tormenting the patient's last days—killing him with their ministrations?—is

proof that they were primitive medicine men; yet a casual reading of eighteenth-century medical practices makes one wonder
whether the treatment was not as characteristic of the century
as of a backward culture.

On returning to the village from this frightful operation Mackenzie visited the chief, who showed him

"a garment of blue cloth, decorated with brass buttons; and
another of flowered cotton, which I supposed were Spanish.
. . . Copper and brass are in great estimation among them, and
of the former they have a great plenty: they point their arrows
and spears with it, and work it up into personal ornaments; such
as collars, ear-rings, and bracelets which they wear on their
wrists, arms, and legs. . . . The brass is in thin squares; their
copper is in larger pieces, and some of it appeared to be old stills
cut up. They also abound in iron [which they make into] poign-
ards and daggers."

With understandable emotion Mackenzie examined the chief's
large canoe, in which years before he had paddled a considerable
distance with forty of his people, "when he saw two large vessels
full of such men as myself, by whom he was kindly received."
These ships carrying the first white people ever seen by the Bella
Coola were those commanded by Captain Cook. The forty-five-
foot canoe was built of cedar, painted black and decorated with
white figures of different kinds of fish; its gunwales were inlaid
with sea-otter teeth. Cook mistook these for human teeth, which
they greatly resemble; to his eyes, the mistake probably added
a cruel ferocity to the natives' self-assurance and daring. Perhaps
Mackenzie felt that in the hospitality and trust shown him he
was reaping the reward of the kind cordiality that Captain Cook
had set as a pattern long years before; the sight of the canoe and
the history it evoked seemed a subtle justification for the years
he had devoted to following, not the wake of the great navigator, but the example he had set in extending the good name and
trade of Great Britain.

Pleasant and cordial though the chief was, it almost seemed
that he was unwilling to let the white men proceed. Several times
during the morning Mackenzie had asked for canoes and guides,
but it was not until he produced his instruments and was about

to take an altitude—which he was asked not to do lest such an operation frighten the salmon from that part of the river—that his request was quickly acted upon. A canoe and four natives were put at his disposal, and the young chief who had presented him with the fine fur robe was singled out to accompany him to the sea. Everything was made ready and they were about to embark when Mackenzie was told that one of their axes was missing.

"I immediately applied to the chief, and requested its restoration; but he would not understand me till I sat myself down on a stone . . . and made it appear that I should not depart till the stolen article was restored. The village was immediately in an uproar, and some danger was apprehended from the confusion that prevailed in it. The axe, however, which was hidden under the chief's canoe, was soon returned. Though this instrument was not, in itself, of sufficient value to justify a dispute with these people, I apprehended that the suffering them to keep it, after we had declared its loss, might have occasioned the loss of everything we carried with us, and of our lives also."

Mackenzie knew that if he allowed the pilfering of an axe, blackmail and appeasement could arrest their forward march, could result in their complete destitution and death. This was his reasoning, and on this he acted even though "my people were dissatisfied with me at the moment."

The river was almost one continuous rapid. They flew downstream past settlements until they reached two large houses whose owner was a person of importance. Here they were received and regaled in the best Bella Coola manner, while their host, to establish his wealth and standing, showed them many European articles, including about forty pounds of old copper stills. Putting in at different villages, they saw many new sights: a woman "with two pieces of copper in her under lip, as described by Captain Cook"; they watched the different steps in the making of bark cloth; they saw women beating the inner rind of the cedar bark until it looked like flax, while others spun it with distaff and spindles, and one actually weaving it into a robe, working in stripes of sea-otter skin.

Navigation became more difficult as the current, losing none of its force, rushed seaward through many constricted channels. On they went,

"with great velocity, till we came to a fall, where we left our canoe, and carried our luggage along a road through a wood for some hundred yards, when we came to a village, consisting of six very large houses, erected on pallisades, rising twenty-five feet from the ground. . . . From these houses I could perceive the termination of the river, and its discharge into a narrow arm of the sea."

There was the sea, whose narrow arm, Dean Channel, extending landward as if in greeting, ended quietly, satisfyingly, a long day crowded with a disorderly procession of new impressions, new faces, new tensions, old fears, and still older hopes. It was half-past six in the evening. Mackenzie did not know—he would not know until long after—that by the slim margin of a few weeks he had missed meeting the ships' boats of Captain George Vancouver, who was that summer making his detailed survey of the British Columbia coast; it was on the third of June that the latter had explored Dean Channel, where the Bella Coola River empties!

Mackenzie was up early the next morning (*July 20*), eager to reach the mouth of the river, but when he proposed to the Indians to continue "they turned a deaf ear, as they imagined that I should be satisfied with having come in sight of the sea." Two of the Indians absolutely refused to go with him and turned back with their canoe. He was given a larger canoe in which to go on, and though it leaked badly, he was glad to have it. "At about eight we got out of the river which discharges itself by various channels into an arm of the sea. The tide was out and had left a large space covered with sea-weed. The surrounding hills were involved in fog." He had no need to taste the water, he knew it was salty. As they paddled close to land, into a strong wind, they saw a great number of sea otters, many porpoises, a white-headed eagle, small gulls, and ducks. By afternoon the swell was so high and their canoe so leaky that they were forced to put in to a cove. When they had landed, their remaining Bella Coola Indians hurriedly left them; and they had resigned themselves to being without a guide when the young chief returned, carrying a large porcupine that he had killed and that he now proceeded to clean and cook. This episode, which gave their camp site the name Porcupine Cove, added to their reduced food stock a porcupine too large to be held by their kettle; it must have loomed large in the eyes and minds of "ten half-starved men, in a leaky vessel, on a barbarous coast."

The food situation was very serious, but to Mackenzie even that was dwarfed by his urgent problem: he must stay in one place long enough to get a day and a night observation for latitude and longitude. The fog that hugged the land, the clouded atmosphere that hid the sun, the fear felt by the young chief, his men's impatience, seemed to mock at this modest need. If the Indians had not been able to understand why he had to paddle to the ocean after he had seen it, his own simple, illiterate men could hardly be expected to appreciate why he had to call on the sun and stars to tell him where he was. It seemed far-fetched; they could not share his devotion to science, his passion for a series of abstract figures. They knew where they were, they could have found the way back there blindfolded; they were realists enough to know that their food was running low and that the region was hourly becoming more dangerous, more ominous. To Mackenzie, acutely aware of these perils, aware no less keenly of the scientific obligations imposed on exploration, the next few days were taut and nerve-racking.

It was while they were coasting along (*July 21*), looking for a proper place to take an observation, that they first experienced the less ceremonial behavior of the Pacific coast Indians. They met three canoes with fifteen men in them who spoke to the young chief and

"examined everything we had in our canoe with an air of indifference and disdain. One of them in particular made me understand, with an air of insolence, that a large canoe had lately been in this bay, with people in her like me, and that one of them, whom he called *Macubah* had fired on him and his friends. . . . He also produced several European articles, which could not have been long in his possession. From his conduct and appearance, I wished very much to be rid of him. . . . However, when I prepared to part from them, they turned their canoes about, and persuaded my young man to leave me, which I could not prevent."

The young man who had exasperated Macubah (Vancouver) so that he had fired his guns to frighten him and quiet his insolence saw in Mackenzie's small party a safe target for his revenge, a proper victim of indignities such as he himself had sustained. He soon returned, forced himself into their canoe, and, pointing to a narrow channel on the opposite shore, requested that they steer toward it. Mackenzie could not very well refuse him.

"His importunities now became very irksome, and he wanted to see everything we had. . . . He asked for my hat, my handkerchief, and, in short, everything that he saw about me. At the same time he frequently repeated the unpleasant intelligence that he had been shot at by people of my colour. . . . When we were in mid-channel I perceived some sheds . . . and as I thought it probable that some Europeans might have been there I directed my steersman to make for that spot. . . . We landed, and found the ruins of a village, in a situation well calculated for defence."

Quickly ten Indian canoes, carrying three to six men each, assembled there. The men told Mackenzie he was expected at their village, but from their attitude he feared "that some hostile design was meditated against us, and for the first time I acknowledged my apprehensions to my people. I accordingly desired them to be very much on their guard, and to be prepared if any violence was offered to defend themselves to the last." The most troublesome Indians, after being as irritating as they knew how, left; the others stayed on, urging again and again that the white men accompany them to their village. Only the setting sun and the unshaken refusals finally induced their departure, and when Mackenzie's people were finally alone, they counted up the many articles stolen. Another canoe then arrived with seven stout, prosperous native traders who offered Mackenzie a very fine sea-otter skin and an exquisitely dressed wild goatskin.

"For the former they demanded my hanger [a short sword], which . . . could not be spared in our present situation, and they actually refused to take a yard and a half of common broad cloth, with some other articles . . . which proves the unreflecting improvidence of our European traders. The goat-skin was so bulky that I did not offer to purchase it. . . . When I offered them what they did not choose to accept for the otter-skin, they shook their heads, and very distinctly answered, 'No, no.' And to mark their refusal of anything we asked from them, they emphatically employed the same British monosyllable."

They must have heard "No, no" from all sides as they poked and snooped and impudently tried the patience of Vancouver.

At last all the natives had gone. The exploring party made a fire for warmth, and after a pitifully small meal prepared to sleep. That night a watch was kept.

Mackenzie was busy the next morning (*July 23*) taking five altitudes for time, when two canoes arrived, bringing back the young chief who had left them the previous day. He

"was now very anxious to persuade our people to depart, as the natives, he said, were as numerous as mosquitoes, and of a very malignant character. This information produced some very earnest remonstrances to me to hasten our departure, but as I was determined not to leave this place, except I was absolutely compelled to it, till I had ascertained its situation, these solicitations were not repeated."

But even as Mackenzie was intent on his measurements, two larger canoes, well manned, appeared from the channel. To the frightened Canadians they seemed to be a vanguard of an approaching hostile force. The young chief again besought Mackenzie to leave, with the warning that the latest comers were prepared to hurl spears and clouds of arrows at the party.

"In relating our danger, his agitation was so violent, that he foamed at the mouth. . . . The two canoes now approached . . . and in a short time five men, with their families, landed very quietly from them. My instruments being exposed, they examined them with much apparent admiration and astonishment. My altitude . . . gave me 52° 20′ 48″ North Latitude. . . .

"I now mixed up some vermillion in melted grease, and in-

scribed, in large characters, on the South-East face of the rock
on which we had slept last night, this brief memorial—'Alexander
Mackenzie, from Canada, by land, the twenty-second of July,
one thousand seven hundred and ninety-three'. . . . I had now
determined my situation, which is the most fortunate circumstance of my long, painful, and perilous journey, as a few cloudy
days would have prevented me."

At last! breathed his men—Mackenzie was ready, eager, and
intent, for the homeward journey.

9.

History hath triumphed over time . . .
      SIR WALTER RALEGH: Historie of the World,
                                              Preface

(*22 July–24 Aug.*)

Now they could go home.

Latitude had been determined. Mackenzie was taking his last
observations to establish their longitude, the canoe was ready,
loaded, awaiting him. At ten that night he had finished. Immediately the canoe started along the homeward trail. So eager were
the men to get beyond the reach of the Dean Channel natives
that they paddled without a rest until, in the early morning, they
came to the mouth of the river. They landed as near the village
as the ebb tide permitted. Here real trouble awaited them.

Mackenzie, following the young chief closely, was out in
front, away from the others on the path leading to the village;
well behind him in a long line straggled his men, stumbling
through the thick underbrush. He was within sight of the houses
when suddenly he was electrified to see two men running toward
him. Drawn daggers, vicious looks—instantly he was on guard.
Dropping his pack, he faced them squarely, his gun ready,
pointed at them. Luckily for him, they knew the dreadful power
of firearms. They dropped their daggers, which were fastened
by string to their wrists, and slowed down. As they retarded
their advance, he relaxed his defense and rested his gun in his

left hand while he fingered his small cutlass. Now several others with dangling daggers joined them—he recognized the obnoxious Indian who had exasperated Vancouver, persecuted him, and frightened his men; this was, Mackenzie knew, the evil agent, the cause, of his present peril. Now the natives were close: they seemed to flow around him; from behind one grabbed him. Quickly Mackenzie threw the Indian off, freed his arm—wondering why in that moment the man had not stabbed him—and braced himself for a fight that would be bloody but hopeless. As he waited, tense and expectant, one of his men walked out of the woods. Instantly the natives, the young chief with them, fled to the high shelter of their houses.

"It was, however, upwards of ten minutes before all my people joined me; and as they came one after the other, [he reflected that] these people might have successively dispatched every one of us. If they had killed me in the first instance, this consequence would certainly have followed, and not one of us would have returned home to tell the horrid fate of his companions."

Immediately Mackenzie told his men what had happened. Their safety demanded the punishment of such an unprovoked attack; such irresponsible insolence must be curbed. He would compel the Indians to return his hat and cloak, stolen in the scuffle, and other articles sneaked away at other times. The men primed their guns afresh and prepared to enforce his orders. Ready to fight, they stood beneath the houses. The young chief hurried down the ladder and explained that the malicious Indian had inflamed the villagers with stories of how the white strangers had abused him and killed four of his friends. Mackenzie denied this indignantly, and as evidence of their belief in him, his goodwill and friendship, demanded that all the loot be restored and some fish sold them. The terms were met and a dubious reconciliation was effected, but the young chief, terrified by the whole scene, insisted on taking his canoe and hurrying home by himself. This village, the one from which Mackenzie had first seen the ocean, was to be remembered as the Rascal's Village.

Mackenzie had won through, but even he was to question the value of his victory. The current of the river was very swift.

The men all were suffering with colds, and one of their Indians was so weak that he could hardly walk. The young chief had left them and would probably influence his father against them. Terrifying and ill-omened was the threat implied in the sight of their obnoxious and envenomed Indian opponent paddling upstream with four companions, overtaking them and going on ahead. The hard current, their fears, their sick fatigue—even a sudden thought of the distance they must travel before they would see home—combined insidiously to unbalance Mackenzie's men. A wave of hysteria engulfed them. They swore they would *not* go up that river—somehow they would find their way over the mountains; they would not go up *that* river. And in an uncontrolled frenzy they threw everything but their blankets into the water. It took all of Mackenzie's patience, all his logic, all his leadership, to bring them out of their frantic terror. Quite simply he told them over and over again that he too wanted to go home. For seventy-five days they had followed him out of obedience and, as they pushed into the unknown, out of a feeling that he was their only safety in a lost and terrible world; for seventy-five days they had had constantly to deny their impulse to return to the familiar, and now, suddenly, they no longer had to disown their instinct for self-preservation. In a subtle spiritual sense Mackenzie and his men were at last united, unreservedly, completely; their efforts, their thoughts, their hopes, their goals, were identical. The basic conflict that had so long possessed them was resolved, and the men could wholeheartedly rejoice that in Mackenzie they had a magnificent leader. It seemed almost as if this unanimity gave them the astonishing burst of energy that speeded them along the homeward trail.

Their dismay lest poison spread by the malicious Indian who had preceded them upstream cause more trouble was dispelled as in each village they were politely met and supplied with food.

"The Indians who had caused us so much alarm, we now discovered to be inhabitants of the islands, and traders in various articles, such as cedar-bark, prepared to be woven into mats, fish-spawn, copper, iron, and beads. . . . For these they receive in exchange roasted salmon, hemlock bark cakes, and the other kind made of salmon roes, sorrel, and bitter berries."

Up the swift river they forced their way, stopping to rest at each house, where they were supplied with fish and luscious berries, canoes, and sometimes native paddlers. And so on the twenty-fifth they approached the Great Village where Mackenzie had given Turlington's Balsam to the dying man—was he dead and would they be blamed for it? Also the young chief from this place had unpleasantly, precipitately parted from them at the Rascal's Village.

The villagers hurried out to them, but Mackenzie was disconcerted and suspicious when in the crowd he saw no member of the chief's family. By signs he was urged to go to the chief's house. "I signified to them not to crowd about us, and indeed drew a line, beyond which I made them understand they must not pass. I directed Mr. Mackay and the men to remain there, with their arms in readiness, and to keep the natives at a distance, as I was determined to go alone to the chief's house." If his men heard his pistol—which he would use only as a last desperate measure—they were to get away as best they could, "as it would be equally fruitless and dangerous to attempt giving me any assistance." Prepared for the worst, for instability flowing from outraged grief, for ideas dangerously distorted by the young chief's panic, Mackenzie advanced slowly, alone, toward the chief's house. Everything seemed quiet and calm: the chief's wife motioned that her husband was at another house; women invited him to share their supper of salmon roes and berries; only the absence of men fed his suspicions. Mackay, unable to bear leaving his leader all alone, hurried to his side. "At length the chief appeared, and his son, who had been our guide, following him; displeasure was painted in the old man's countenance, and he held in his hand a bead tobacco pouch which belonged to Mr. Mackay, [which] the young chief had purloined from him. When he had approached . . . he threw it at me with great indignation, and walked away." So *that* was the cause of his discontent: that he should be forced to return stolen articles! Quickly Mackenzie caught up with the chief, took his hand in friendship. The old man was in mourning for his son—"he had cut off his hair and blackened his face on the melancholy occasion"; he spoke of his fears for the son who had gone seaward with Mackenzie and whom he had imagined killed by the white men—or perhaps they had all perished. When the chief revealed his sorrow and his misgivings, Mackenzie took both him and his son by the hand and with them returned to where his men were anxiously awaiting him. To the two men he gave many gifts, paying for the services of the young chief, repaying the old man's hospitality. "The presents had the desired effect of restoring us to their favor; but these people are of so changeable a nature, that there is no security with them."

When Mackenzie and his men had been entertained with a meal and provided with additional roasted salmon for their journey, the chief, his son, and most of the villagers accompanied them as far as the last house; there they said farewell. And yet Mackenzie was not completely reassured about the natives' attitude. He was distrustful of a people in whom a constancy of emotion was lacking. His suspicions seemed only too well founded when soon he heard loud, confused noises coming from the village; then natives came running after him. Some made signs for him to stop, others rushed by ahead of him, one made gestures warning that they had taken the wrong trail.

"I immediately called out to Mr. Mackay [who was at the head of the line] to stop. This was naturally enough taken for an alarm, and threw my people into great disorder. When I was understood . . . our Indian informed us that the noise we had heard was occasioned by a debate among the natives, whether they should stop us or not."

At last Mackenzie and his men were on the right road, but still so panicky and fearful that they imagined that the friends who had guided them might suddenly become enemies who would ambush them. Their tense mood persisted, and when night came, they did not dare to light a fire. "Every man took his tree, and laid down in his clothes. . . . We had removed a short distance from the path; no sentinel was now appointed, and every one was left to watch for his own safety." The night was restless but undisturbed.

Starting at the first light and walking quickly, they soon reached the first village they had entered—was it only a little more than a week before?—on the Bella Coola River; they now comfortingly called it Friendly Village. As before, the chief extended a cordial hospitality, and Mackenzie was so relieved and delighted at this continued friendship that "I did not withhold anything in my power to give, which might afford him satisfaction. I presented him with two yards of blue cloth, an axe, knives, and various other articles." He was given many presents—"curious articles"—in return, but the thought of the three-hundred-mile hike over mountainous country that lay ahead prevented his accepting them. Their entry had not disturbed the natives or interrupted their activities. He saw women boiling a thick mixture of sorrel and various berries with salmon roes in large square cedar tubs, and watched them as they ladled it into sizable shallow frames where the sun dried it into cakes. "From the quantity of this kind of provision, it must be a principal article of food, and probably of traffic. . . . At eleven in the morning . . . we took a cordial leave of them; and if we might judge from appearances, they parted from us with regret."

Each man carried about twenty pounds of fish for his own use; beyond this, only a bit of flour and some pemmican were left. The river was behind them, the climbing path cleared the woods, and there before them was the towering mountain up whose steep, wild cliffs they had to lift themselves.

"The fatigue of ascending these precipices I shall not attempt to describe, and it was past five when we arrived at a spot where we could get water, and in such an extremity of weariness, that it was with great pain any of us could crawl about to gather wood. . . . We consoled ourselves by sitting around a blazing fire, talking of past dangers, and indulging the delightful reflection that we were thus far advanced on our homeward journey. . . . At this place, which is the first step towards gaining the summit of the mountains, the climate was very sensibly changed. The air that fanned the village which we left at noon was mild and cheering; the grass was verdant, and the wild fruits ripe around it. But here the snow was not yet dissolved, the ground was still bound by frost, the herbage had scarce begun to spring, and the crowberry bushes were just beginning to blossom."

From midsummer they had turned back to early spring.

Fine weather made the going pleasant. The regularly spaced caches in which they had stored food were untouched, and the pemmican was in good condition; they traveled alone: the natives whom they had met coming and going before were now absent, "being all gone, as we supposed to the Great River." Their packs held a minimum of supplies and equipment; their hearts were light; mile after mile was put behind them. On the fourth of August, one month after they had left, they were back at the overland trail's end, by the Fraser River. Their canoe and property were found in perfect condition, untouched; not even the print of a foot came near the spot.

"We now pitched our tent, and made a blazing fire [enjoying a fire seems a small but certain index of their feeling of security] and I treated myself, as well as the people, with a dram; but we had been so long without tasting any spirituous liquor, that we had lost all relish for it. The Indians now arrived from above, and were rewarded for the care they had taken of our property."

Mackenzie sent the canoe to pick up the pemmican that had been cached along the river, and while the men were gone he traded, purchasing fine beaver skins for large knives. During this activity, the natives, who had not bothered their unprotected property, began stealing various utensils from the camp. This gave Mackenzie an opportunity to show that he had learned well the respect and fear with which the salmon is surrounded. He did not want to start a quarrel to regain the articles; instead he sadly remarked to some Indians that their relatives had imperiled them all by their thefts. Gravely he announced that the salmon came from the sea, the property of the white man who had the power of preventing the salmon from entering the rivers; the white man might get angry and use this power unless all stolen objects were returned. So exquisitely did this argument fit in with the Indians' pattern of life and beliefs that the quietly spoken warning went up and down the river and brought back groups eager to return what they had taken and to ask pity for their children and forgiveness for themselves.

Soon (*August 16*) Mackenzie and his men recrossed the divide. Now they had only to go with the current of the Parsnip and the Peace to be soon home; now they found plenty of whitefish, trout, "jub," and carp—the fish they had always caught and eaten. Two months before, Mackenzie had forced open the door of the unknown and led them by river and trail to the western edge of the continent, into a new, a strange, a terrifying world; and now here they stood once again. Only now they had done with exploration and danger, with the strange and the new; and before them was the sweet comfort of a familiar world. But having forced that door, led them through, and brought them safely back, Mackenzie was stricken. His ankles were so swollen that he could walk only with pain and difficulty. "Had I been able to exert myself . . . it was my intention to have taken some salmon alive, and colonized them in the Peace River." The next day he could not even hobble and had to submit to being carried over a miserable portage, a field flooded with icy water and badly snared with driftwood.

A great ease and contentment came when on the morrow they began to glide along with the current of the Peace. In one day they covered a distance that on the outward journey had taken seven. But their provisions were getting so low—they had only sufficient for two meals—that Mackenzie sent Mackay out with the hunters to secure some game. They had come to the head of the Peace River Canyon. While five of the men went forward with the baggage, Mackenzie and another took the canoe apart to clean her and, by drying out her lining and timbers, to lighten her. At sunset the hunters returned, carrying as much buffalo meat as they could stagger under; the carriers had transferred most of the lading, the canoe was cleaned and dried and ready to be carried; a hearty meal brought the day to an end, and every fear of future want was removed. The portage was exhausting; the men found it as hard to lower the canoe down the mountain as it had been to haul her up.

On August 23 they were on the water before daylight, and when the sun rose they passed through the beautiful parklike foothills, the home of great herds of buffalo and deer. They who so lately had been cold and numb now found the warm weather oppressive. That night they made an early camp and prepared themselves for their arrival. They washed and shaved, tidied their clothes, put on their brightest handkerchiefs.

Next day, the twenty-fourth of August, in clear, warm weather they came to the end of their great journey.

"At length, as we rounded a point, and came in view of the Fort, we threw out a flag, and accompanied it with a general discharge of our fire-arms; while the men were in such spirits, and made such an active use of their paddles, that we arrived before the two men whom we left here in the spring, could recover their senses to answer us. Thus we landed at four in the afternoon, at the place which we left on the ninth of May.—Here my voyages of discovery terminate. Their toils and their dangers, their solicitudes and sufferings, have not been exaggerated. . . . I received, however, the reward of my labours, for they were crowned with success.

". . . I have now resumed the character of a trader. . . ."

At thirty Mackenzie had finished with exploration. He had not reached a Russian factory, but, except for this small detail, he had brilliantly, energetically, realized Pond's great dream. Truly and majestically he had also realized an older dream: following the inland trail of lakes and rivers, his canoe, crossing the continent at its greatest width, had linked the Atlantic to the Pacific. He had made an overland Northwest Passage.

And Russians from the West

THE explosion that ripped Europe open at the close of the fifteenth century and sent out great impulses of westward exploration had, within three generations, slowed down. In those heroic years, Spanish ships traced the long coastline of America from Newfoundland through the Strait of Magellan and as far north as Oregon; the islands of the Caribbean were discovered, pacified, settled, and planted; and, through the narrow funnel of Central America, Spanish explorers spilled out into the interior, northward and southward, reaching at their high-water mark in the north deep into the southern half of what is now the United States. Then, their energy spent, the Spaniards rested, consolidated, exploited mines and plantations, built great cities with churches, universities, and hospitals, and created out of their blood and sperm and sweat that unstable but shining amalgam which today is Mexico and Central America. As the Spaniards rested and as their powerful church and monarchy dedicated themselves to the morbid task of stemming the life-giving current of growth and change, other nations, not so dedicated, studied, used, and were served by the new sciences and technologies; in turn they explored and exploited and colonized along the Atlantic, north of the Spanish outposts that guarded glorious, golden New Spain. Compared with this first sustained thrust of Spain, the efforts of the Dutch, the French, and the English were late, small, limited, straggling, separate. Only from the vantage point of elapsed centuries do dispersed and individual efforts achieve continuity and coherence: the insecure footholds of the Dutch yield to the grand strategy of the French, to the irresistible, complex destiny of the English.

From the day when Balboa waded into the Pacific and claimed it for his king against all princes until the Day of Doom, through Cortés and later explorers who wandered north from Mexico by sea and land—over the long decades when Spanish galleons ferried between Manila and Mexico—Spain assumed proudly, confidently, that the Pacific and its American coast belonged to her.

But empire and possession rest on the humbler but more pertinent bases of settlement and trade; along the western coast, north
of Mexico, Spain had neither.

It was not laziness or accident that had left California untouched. Had the Spaniards found evidence of the gold that was
there, they would have conquered the burning deserts, the arid
rugged mountains, the unbroken narrow coastal shelf that offered no protection from wind and wave. They knew only that
the country was poor: its natives were poor, and water was so
scarce that it was as precious as the treasure they sought. Such
a country—which offered nothing to the colonist, the miner, the
rancher—did invite Jesuit missionaries. The more unprepossessing the outlook, the greater their zeal; the more frightful, the
more dangerous the hazards, the surer their everlasting reward.
Along the Great Lakes, the bodies of French Jesuits, tortured
and scalped by deadly, desperate Hurons and Iroquois, paved a
path over which traders and explorers passed. Hysterically,
eagerly, these missionaries hurried into the wilderness to seek in
a swift and terrible death their certain way to Heaven. In Lower
California, a succession of undiscouraged, dedicated Jesuits labored to establish posts; from these pitiful missions Spain was
able to advance into Upper California and toward the Northwest.

The leisurely, pious extension of New Spain had almost come
to a standstill in the bitter, sterile terrain of Lower California
when a combination of events made it clear that Spain could
continue neither the slow pace of her expansion nor its religious
character. The empire was vulnerable unless the Pacific was
made safe for Spanish shipping. Already, during the War of
Jenkins's Ear (1742), a British fleet had raided Spanish ships in
the Pacific and actually captured the Manila galleon off Mexico.
Disastrous though this was, it was but one of a series of ominous
signs demonstrating that Europe was aggressively interested in
the Pacific and its American coast. By 1750, numerous reports
of the Russian expedition to the New World appeared in Western Europe, and eight years later Müller published his Russian
history—a collection, like Hakluyt's, of voyages of discovery—
which presented a systematic summary of Russian explorations
in Siberia and along the Pacific coast. Even a book as innocuous
as a Spanish Jesuit's detailed account of the missions around the
Gulf of California was avidly read by the Jesuit-hating British

and Dutch. Europe was hungry for any fact or fancy connected with the North Pacific and its littoral.

The Peace of Paris in 1763 provided a pause, a new direction for energies that had been tied up in war, a new arrangement of Europe in America; and in Spain a new, vigorous, ambitious king ruled. Of the house of Bourbon, he replaced the defunct Habsburg line. By a secret treaty in 1762, Louis XV of France placed in his Spanish cousin's hands for safekeeping the island of New Orleans and France's trans-Mississippi territory—that much the French king salvaged from the British. Forty years later, the Louisiana Purchase was to add this western empire to the United States.

Charles III of Spain was a surprisingly able king to find on the Catholic throne. By sweeping reforms he tried to bring Spain abreast of the age she was in, to have her catch up with the hundred and fifty years she had passed in what John Stuart Mill called the "deep slumber of a decided opinion." Charles tried to pump oxygen into lungs that for almost two centuries had been inhaling the ether of a rigid power politics. What he and his able assistants accomplished was amazing, almost miraculous; his reign stands out brightly from the dust and decay of modern Spanish history; but he could only patch and mend and try to cover with a coat of glossy paint the sagging structure that still presented an imposing façade to the world. For a time Spain seemed young again; but she was not rejuvenated, she had only had her face lifted. Under Charles, the far-flung borders of the Spanish empire received careful attention from intelligent, efficient administrators, replacing inept nobles and ecclesiastics whose management had faithfully mirrored the incompetence at home. This tardy revival of imperial power was as spectacular as it was unexpected. Had Charles come earlier, or had his successors not deliberately sought to undo what he created, the story of Spain in America might have been very different. He almost succeeded in forcing Spain to catch up with the centuries she had missed, but he was utterly unable to understand or prepare her for the revolutions that were soon to destroy her empire.

Spain had not lost the stern stuff of which explorers and hardy settlers are made. The second and last extension of New Spain, though not so widely known as the earlier epic, was carried on in the invincible classic tradition. The people of the United

States, who with pleasurable pride hail the lusty, resolute competence of Daniel Boone, carving the Wilderness Road to open Kentucky to settlers, would appreciate his Spanish brother, Juan Bautista de Anza, whose "Yankee" qualities—he was a third-generation Sonora frontier Indian fighter—make him a very familiar, appealing type. The *soldados de cuera* (Leather-Jackets), named for their leather jackets thick enough to stop Indian arrows, also wore leather aprons to protect their legs from the wicked brush through which they rode, and used long bull-hide shields for defense—the Leather-Jackets were the mounted counterpart of the more easterly buckskin-clad, 'coon-hatted frontiersmen. The country they opened and crisscrossed with their trails was the pitilessly hot, desperately arid Southwest, a region of salt dune and desert, of broken, tortured mountains that were to become the luckless grave of many forty-niners. Theirs was not an exploratory sortie, an advance and an immediate return when once the goal was reached; it was a rapid extension of New Spain, complex and cultured, as far north as San Francisco, with contact and communication maintained between Mexico City and her distant outposts. If the birchbark canoe and the picturesque *voyageur* were the symbols of French exploration, the Spanish idiom was an impressive, colorful, varied procession: the plumed elegance of the leaders, the omnipresent brown-robed friars—who marched along to conquer, convert, and cultivate—squads of toughened Leather-Jackets, dozens of Christian Indians who cleared a way and cared for the hundreds of horses and mules, the droves of cattle.

Out of Mexico, out of Lower California, by land, by sea, the Spaniards advanced up the coast; at the same time (1769) from their settlements along the Río Grande they sought out the mobile Plains Indians and, for a while, brought even the fierce Comanche into their sphere of influence. These far-flung measures were their strategic defense in depth against the threat of Russian encroachment from the north and British infiltration from the east. The design thus made was grandiose and truly imperial in scope; brilliantly the Spaniards used their scanty frontier resources to secure possession of western Louisiana. From the Mississippi to the Pacific, Spain was on the march, ready to save her empire from her old enemy, Great Britain, and from her new one, Russia. The famous Camino Real, the main road to San Francisco, was protected and policed by four large military outposts—San Diego, established in 1769, Monterey in 1770, San Francisco in 1776, and Santa Barbara in 1782—while strung between, spaced a day's march apart, were twenty-one missions, started by the marvelous and mild Father Junípero Serra. Here officials and travelers and traders rested and refreshed themselves: here was introduced the California mission style, loved for its thick, cool adobe walls, for its friendly red-tiled roof, which from afar spelled welcome, for its lazy, shaded arcade. Within half a century these missions were settled and rich: the seeds and slips brought in, the cattle and sheep and hogs and horses, multiplied amazingly; orchards and gardens and flowers flourished; four hundred thousand horned cattle—half were annually killed for their hides—three hundred thousand sheep and hogs, sixty thousand horses, were the visible sign of their prosperity. Over a hundred thousand bushels of cereal crops were produced each year, as well as an abundance of wine, oil, cotton, tobacco, fruits, hemp, and soap. Thirty thousand serf-like Indians clustered around the missions, did all the work. Here was an indolent, feudal, pastoral life, so rich, so ripe, so unprotected, once the empire fell apart, that it was swallowed not by the Russians, not by the British—whom the Spanish had so feared —but by the United States, which was being born even as the Leather-Jackets and the friars took possession of the great bay and Golden Gate of San Francisco.

"I proceeded to erect a fort to occupy and defend the port from the atrocities of the Russians, who were about to invade us," said Portolá, the first governor of Upper California, in building his administrative seat at Monterey. This was an expression of his fears, not of the facts: the Russians were far away, as Spanish sea expeditions were to find. In 1774, the viceroy of New Spain sent out a ship with instructions to go north to the sixtieth degree of latitude, where its commander was to take formal possession of the land; it was ordered to coast along the shore on its return. These precise directions prove that the Spaniards knew the idiosyncrasies of obdurate, persistent winds and obscuring fogs that sailing vessels contended with along the North Pacific coast.

Of that first voyage on which Spain staked her claim, it may be said that the commander was timid and the elements capricious: as the ship was blown about or becalmed, the coast was sighted at a few places and the expedition sailed back, having fulfilled none of the prerequisites for formal possession. For one day only the commander put in at Nootka Sound, a small C-shaped roadstead on the western side of Vancouver Island, where the natives paddled out in their large seaworthy canoes and in a brief moment stole two silver spoons belonging to the pilot, Martínez—a trifling loss, which was to be telling evidence of that first Spanish visit. The next year two ships went north with the same instructions. Separated by a storm, both captains took possession at various points; both reported their men sick with scurvy: "their gums quite putrid and legs as big round as their bodies quite numb." One of the ships noted the strong current suggestive of a river—the Columbia—and named the bay at its mouth Assumption Bay. A third expedition, in 1779, touched at Prince William Sound, near the sixtieth parallel, the northing the first expedition had been ordered to make.

These three voyages satisfied Spain that she had established priority and sovereignty over the coast north of San Francisco; she set up no forts or trading posts, and no further explorations were made. Knowledge of the expeditions was kept in Spain, yet as early as 1776 the fact—nothing but the fact that a Spanish ship had sailed northward along that coast—was known in Great Britain, and instantly the British were agog. What had been discovered? They were aware of the Russian explorations. Was it to meet a Russian challenge that Spanish ships had sailed north?

Gradually, tardily, the countries of Western Europe realized that while they had been engrossed in pushing westward into the New World, the Russians, in a wave as extraordinary and expansive, had flowed eastward across the breadth of Siberia. About 1580, when the Spanish empire began to suffer from hardening of the arteries, and in much the same manner as the freedom-loving, space-happy frontiersmen of the United States two centuries later spilled over the Alleghanies into the continent beyond, there to build homes and settlements or to follow the reckless, unregulated life of trader or trapper—so Russian Cossacks fought their way eastward across Siberia and occupied the enormous sweep of frozen tundra and taiga forest; making their epic way eastward, deeper and deeper, they stood at last at the edge of the

continent, the Pacific Ocean at their feet. Furs paid the way of
the Cossacks as they infiltrated the vast Siberian hinterland; skins
of the fox and reindeer, ermine and sable (and mammoth ivory
fantastically preserved in Arctic ice cliffs), were sent back to
Russia. The completion of this striding extension—Kamchatka
on the Pacific was occupied in 1697—was the prelude to overseas
Russian exploration, expansion still farther eastward. The impulse that had started under Ivan the Terrible reached its continental limits at the time of Peter the Great.

The Russians reached the Pacific as the seventeenth century
was ending, the same year that Peter the Great toured Western
Europe to find out the decisive factors that, by contrast, made
his a backward country. While his vigorous and eager mind
grappled with profound facts, his eyes were delighted with an
assortment of small ingenious inventions: he saw city streets
paved and lighted; he used a fork, newly designed, when he
dined, and he enjoyed the novelty of cooled drinks, ices, cham-
pagnes; the advantages of cork as a bottle-stopper were explained
to him; he admired the new-fangled speaking trumpet, the effi-
ciency of the fire-hose, the increased skill of calico printing, the
artistry lavished on decorative glassware. He marveled at the
precision instruments for which England was already famous,
and prophetically he might have sensed that the humble clock
would one day be mankind's despot demanding punctuality and
exactness when the bourgeois virtue of respectability conclu-
sively replaced chivalry and piety. Journalism, the newest of the
arts, had already reached a robust maturity, while the youngest
of the sciences, statistics, had been born to serve the political
theorists of the next century. From a mass of evidence his sharp
eyes picked out signs of Europe's increasing wealth and the
growing scale of economic life. He studied Dutch methods of
business organization—they employed the lowest rate of interest, and their ships were the cheapest to build—which gained
them control of the money-market and enabled them to be the
common carriers of the world.

In London, at the Royal Society, Czar Peter was honored to
meet Sir Isaac Newton, who examined the mysteries of a sun-
centered universe and gave order and meaning to a world that
had outgrown the Catholic mythology. The seventeenth century
had great men: John Milton spoke out passionately for freedom,

and John Locke lucidly expounded his system of natural rights;
Harvey proved the circulation of the blood, and Leeuwenhoek
in his microscope saw it move inside the minute capillaries; Hal-
ley studied the heavens and by predicting his comet scotched the
calamitous superstitions that had accompanied celestial phenom-
ena; Leibniz and Galileo lived and worked and questioned the
mysteries of nature and answered a few basic questions; Cervantes, Racine, Molière, wrote their masterpieces; Rembrandt
and Rubens and El Greco painted in the color and image of
their genius.

The seventeenth was a wonderful century, and its enduring
and special glory was its systematic questioning of the fundamental nature of the physical world and a searching examination
of religion, philosophy, and politics. Experiment had challenged
and was superseding authority. Among the forerunners of this
new age were the geographers and navigators whose voyages
established basic truths. Exploration did more than enlarge
Europe's horizon—exploration was experimentation on a global
scale.

An overbold but essentially sound contrast may be drawn
between Spain and Russia at this time—those extremes of Europe
that were soon to meet on the other side of the world. In Spain,
a witless, dying dynasty had sealed off the Iberian peninsula and
her empire from the rest of Europe, from the ferment of ideas
and inventions and techniques that characterized the seventeenth
century and changed the world; in Russia, Peter, with a passion
for science, an understanding of its vital role in the superiority of
the West, and an energy superhuman enough to achieve a one-
man revolution, abolished beards—as symbolic a step as discard-
ing the veil or cutting off the pigtail—and forced Russia into the
main current of European thought and activity. Even if Charles
III of Spain had matched Peter the Great in genius and stature,
the inexorable logic of events would have made the former's a
hopeless task: Peter achieved his westernization when Russia
could still partake currently of the scientific advances made in
the seventeenth century; he reoriented the country sufficiently
so that a group of "intellectuals"—pupils of imported scholars
and technicians—shared in subsequent European movements.
Herzen describes these Europeanized Russians as "foreigners at
home, foreigners in other lands, idle spectators, spoilt for Russia

by Western prejudices and for the West by Russian habits." Because Peter the Great began his country's westernization, Russia, in her coming contacts with the strong forces of the West, could hold her own. One cause of Western supremacy Peter recognized in the growing importance of sea power. And Europe, accustomed to royal eccentricities, gasped at the news of a king shipping as a common sailor on English and Dutch ships and gaped at him as he worked in Dutch shipyards. But such training enabled him to build and launch a ship on the White Sea and start the Russian navy; because of what he learned he envisioned Russia's need for ice-free ports. He also appraised the value Europe put on trade with the Far East and so, when his Cossacks occupied Kamchatka and there found a shipwrecked Japanese sailor, Peter ordered him to Moscow to teach Japanese to selected Russian children; embassies were dispatched to establish relations with Japan and China. To Peter the Great, Kamchatka was an ideal port, a year-round open port, a logical base for Pacific exploration, for Pacific trade.

Siberia, Western science, shipbuilding, geographical problems agitating scholars, eastward exploration—many separate elements to which Peter responded enthusiastically were magnificently fused into a dynamic unit when he drew up the memorandum that inspired the Great Northern Expedition. From Kamchatka he commissioned boats to sail north and east, to determine—for the problem was a lively one to his learned friends in Europe— whether Asia and America were joined or distinct. He named Vitus Bering, a Dane who had been with the Russian navy for many years, to head the expedition. Bering's first voyage in 1728 was inconclusive: he sailed north, rounded East Cape (Cape Dezhnev), and returned, reporting that Asia turned westward and that, in his *opinion*, Asia and America must therefore be separate. And though Peter died (1725) soon after outlining this great scheme, and his hopes were mocked by Bering's indecisive conclusion, the great project conceived by Peter was not abandoned. Vast new sums were added, and the Academy of Sciences, another of Peter's innovations, was entrusted with supervising the gigantic undertaking. The Great Northern Expedition of 1729–41 was enlarged to embrace the delineation of the entire Arctic coastline of Siberia; it offered Bering another opportunity to place America in relation to Asia.

This expedition, the child of Peter's rich and curious mind, was not only the most important single piece of concerted scientific effort that Europe had as yet witnessed; it was almost the first such undertaking to be officially sponsored and paid for, and it has remained an outstanding enterprise in the history of science.

In 1741 Bering again sailed from Kamchatka, and this time he touched—just brushed against—the Alaskan coast near Sitka, and then hurried home lest his scurvy-stricken crew die and their great news die with them. Past the rocky, barren, fog-bound string of the Aleutian Islands the haunted ship sailed until the sick men and their dying commander took refuge on a small island. There Bering died. The next spring a few survivors in a makeshift boat crept back to Petropavlovsk (St. Peter and St. Paul), the harbor on Kamchatka. The tale they told was tragic, and yet, mixed into the recital of ambush and massacre, of sickness, of fog and inhospitable islands girt with cliffs, of a jungle sea thick with kelp, were details of packs of tormenting, bold blue foxes, of men keeping themselves alive on sea otters. Magnificent pelts substantiated their stories. Starvation, scurvy, and death were instantly forgotten at the promise of riches to be had for the daring. The next year Russian traders, clumsy sailors, sought out those islands and returned with precious furs. Along the long curved arm of the Aleutian archipelago they hunted and sailed; by 1763 they reached Kodiak Island and started a fur station. Trade relations between China and Russia had been established—traffic was confined to one spot on the Siberian-Mongolian border—and for fabulous prices Russian traders poured a stream of luscious skins into China.

Russia had reached America from the west, but even this important fact was overshadowed by her discovery of the marine mine that yielded golden returns. The north that Peter Martyr had despised became the lodestone that attracted Spain and France, Great Britain and the new United States.

Spain's sensitive response to the energy and luck of the Russians in the North Pacific was immediate. By land she occupied the coast as far as San Francisco, but her three seaborne gestures, intended to establish sovereignty farther north, were outmoded. Possession, not priority, was the new principle underlying ownership; it provided an opening for other nations into that region, and it galvanized Great Britain and the United States into extraordinary action.

Great Britain knew only vaguely what was happening in the North Pacific: some British East India Company agents in China reported evidence of Russian activity; accounts of Russian explorations had been published; and then came the bare news that Spain had sent a ship into those waters. The keen mercantile noses of the British smelled trade and profits. So aroused was their curiosity, so feverish their impatience, that they hurriedly sent Captain Cook, who had just returned from his extended and historic South Pacific discoveries, back halfway around the world to explore the North Pacific. Sailing in 1776, ostensibly to determine the relationship of Asia and America—Bering's results were felt to be inconclusive—and to locate along the western coast the strait that some still maintained cut across the continent, Cook was secretly instructed to ascertain what Spain and Russia were doing along the northwest coast.

And Captain James Cook on his last voyage served his country well. The men who trained under him—Portlock, Dixon, Colnett, Vancouver—initiated and saved the fur trade for Great Britain in the waters he explored. On his way north, Cook stayed awhile at Friendly Cove in Nootka Sound, trading informally with the natives, winning their friendship, observing their customs. The sea-otter skins obtained here were taken as curios until his men found they could sell them for fabulous prices at Macao. Toward the end of his stay he bought the two silver spoons that had been stolen from the Spaniards. Thus casually he discovered that he had been preceded there, and, abiding by his instructions forbidding him to intrude on the domain of any European prince or state, he left. From Nootka, north through Bering Strait, he examined the coast vainly for a passage to Hudson Bay. His persistent probings along the American side can be followed by the names he gave to capes and inlets, to mountains and coves and islands, from Cape Foulweather on the Oregon coast to his northernmost point, Icy Cape.

A Northwest Passage did not exist, Cook had said. But there was no thought of discouragement at his report; as soon as conditions permitted—Great Britain was trying to subdue her rebellious colonies—every merchant who could equip a ship and find a captain scurried around to trade with the natives, form contacts with the Russians, sell in China, and make his fortune. The rush was on. British captains—who were doubly hamstrung by the monopolies of the East India and the South Sea companies—flew foreign flags as an artifice to circumvent those restrictive companies. Each year more and more ships slipped into quiet harbors to traffic for skins. Clashes occurred, and both white men and red men died; but the trade, the continuous commerce that looped Europe, America, and Asia in profitable exchange, kept growing. With it developed a situation that held all the ingredients of strife: wealth to tempt, a confusion of nationalities and languages, a welter of conflicting claims. Would British traders give greater recognition to a formal possession, an untenanted occupation by Spain—the giant that had preempted so much of the world and its treasure, that old and still unbeaten enemy—than they did to their own powerful prohibitive monopolies? Russia, utterly alien, of untested strength, had home ports relatively close by, and might resent intrusion in her waters. In that vast empty region, remote, wild, unpoliced, who was master other than the man with the gun? Who was owner other than the man on the spot? Interlopers and freebooters trafficked boldly; trespassing was not a sin, for property had not yet been canonized there. Brisk winds carried ships; currents scattered them; fogs hid them one from another. Each ship was a small kingdom, ready to fight for its sovereignty, and resolved to nip off, whether by force or by devious devices, any attempted interruption of its trade.

Nootka Sound, with its protected inner Friendly Cove, its mild climate and open water, its availability to numerous Indian groups, became the base from which many ships operated. There Spain's last bold imperial stand in North America was made. Of the Nootka Sound controversy, it is the outcome that is here important.

In 1786 the governor of Upper California was warned of Russian activities—a Russian was supposed to have said that Catherine the Great was planning to occupy the Sound the very next year in order to oust British fur traders. Suspicious and apprehensive, the Spanish governor decided to check the Russians; instead he precipitated a clash with the British. The whole episode—begun with a resolute but gallant finesse, and terminating in diplomatic exchanges and an adjusted settlement—rose to a feverish, distorted climax, which, but for British fatigue and Spanish impotence, would have led to war.

Martínez, from whom the silver spoons had been stolen, was ordered to build and maintain a fort in Nootka Sound and to request all traders who put in there to acknowledge Spanish sovereignty. Behind this gloved civility, this suave formality, lurked the threat of the Spanish colonial system, which excluded all foreign traders from her colonies and domains. Martínez had achieved an urbane victory over a number of greedy captains sailing under foreign flags when Captain Colnett, who had first seen those waters with Cook, sailed into Nootka Sound flying the Union Jack. Colnett understood that acquiescence would jeopardize future rights. Politely he maintained that he had sailed those waters many times in the past, that he was a servant of the crown, sent to establish a colony. The inevitable clash followed, and Martínez seized both man and ship. Each of the leaders had acted honestly, fully conscious of the rights, the needs, the hopes of his country. As the news of the encounter traveled back to Europe it was smeared with outrage and inflated large enough to precipitate war.

Yet war was decidedly what neither Spain nor Great Britain wanted. Wild new forces rising in Europe made old alignments unpredictable. France had burst into revolution. A high wind was blowing, a wind that had carried a few burning sparks from the New World to set the French Bourbon house aflame. Where next might the sparks light? Energies long suppressed now declared themselves with frightening effect. With a great show of strength, but governed by caution, Spain and Great Britain settled their difference, a difference dwarfed by the mighty upheaval that was convulsing France and threatening Europe. The Nootka Sound Convention was finally signed in 1794. The claim that mere discovery gave the vast Northwest Pacific exclusively to Spain was forever ended. Great Britain had won for herself and for all nations the right to trade and settle in this spacious region—the resounding words and inclusive gesture made by Balboa and his heirs had spent their force centuries before they reached those northern coasts and waters.

The Nootka Sound Convention clarified some issues; new ones were in the making. Squatter sovereignty, the principle recognized and honored by the convention, the principle that

replaced exclusive ownership derived from discovery, lay behind the agreement of 1818: Oregon, the immense territory between Spanish California and Russian Alaska, was placed under
the joint ownership of the United States and Great Britain. This
compromise clearly recognized that while the Columbia River
had been discovered by the United States, it was the Pedlars
from Montreal who had there maintained forts and trading posts.

Charles III had died in 1788. No longer did Spain have the
will or the energy to extend her distant trading frontiers. She
withdrew from the North Pacific and never returned. Russia,
Great Britain, and the United States remained.

As the eighteenth century drew to a close, the Pacific coast
of North America—the newest treasure-house in the New World
—had been breached from the west, the south, and, more slowly,
from the east. Furs joined Kamchatka, Mexico, and Montreal in
a common bond; furs provided the motive and paid the piper.

Surely Mackenzie, during the winter he spent in London before starting his trip to the Pacific, followed the international
situation. What he heard sharpened his impatience to get started,
and strengthened his determination to break an overland trail
to that desirable region. The ultimate agreement reached was
an old story to a Pedlar. Mackenzie knew that exploration did
not secure territorial sovereignty; exploration was only an introduction; possession depended on forts and trading factories.
With his eyes on the Northwest—and they were the penetrating
eyes of the true explorer, eager and ready to break new paths—
Mackenzie, the Scotsman, viewed objectively the empire Great
Britain had amassed and saw how artificial and inefficient, how
cramping and contradictory, the British mercantile structure
was as it affected Canadian fur traders. The true estimation of
him as an explorer must include not only his superb success in
the field, but his subsequent untiring—and bitter—organizational
struggles. Rich and famous and knighted, he used his money, his
experience, his ideas, to argue against the inertia of complacent
habits, both regional and economic.

To Mackenzie it was obvious that the shortest and cheapest
route across Canada lay via Hudson Bay. His solution was
equally obvious: a union of the North West Company and the
Hudson's Bay Company to make British fur-trading interests

so powerful, so incisive, that they would dominate the crafty traders in New York and St. Louis, and control the industry in North America. Furthermore, this shorter transcontinental crossing he saw as the most direct route between Great Britain and the East; to that commerce, a world commerce that fused three continents in profitable enterprise, the entrenched monopolies—the Hudson's Bay, the East India, and the South Sea companies—were crippling impediments. He argued that by subordinating all monopoly interests to the imperial ones of Great Britain, all involved would "succeed equally to their own proper & to the public advantage."

As the first major step in securing this global flow of trade Mackenzie advocated the merger of the two Canadian fur-trading companies. Both sides opposed the rashness of the young man who urged it: the Hudson's Bay Company felt so secure in its territorial advantage that it spurned a chance to avail itself of the matchless personnel of the Pedlars; and the latter, happily wedded to Montreal, could not find it in their hearts to abandon their city to what must be a secondary role in this proposed transcontinental trade.

At the time Mackenzie spoke out, he was, in the eyes of the controlling powers of both groups, a visionary, a radical. And so he was indeed. For those epithets are used in derogation of anyone who appreciates the dynamic quality of all institutions, all situations, and, looking ahead, seeks to be prepared for change. Twenty years of violent rivalry—of ruinous transportation costs for the Pedlars and diminishing dividends for the Company— were needed to teach both sets of directors the rightness, the soundness, of his proposal. In 1821 the two great fur-trading companies saved themselves from bankruptcy by uniting; the ancient struggle between Hudson Bay and the St. Lawrence River ended. But by that time Mackenzie had been dead a year.

By that time Yankee traders, combining the maritime skill of Boston and the commercial system of New York, and unhampered by restricting British monopolies, had almost succeeded in realizing Mackenzie's dream of global commerce. It took nothing less than a war—the War of 1812, in which British sea power supported the aggressive Pedlars—to dislodge Yankee traders, agents of John Jacob Astor, from their key position at Astoria on the Pacific.

A beginning to that tale was made by Robert Gray, captain of the *Columbia Rediviva* out of Boston, who on his second voyage to the Northwest sailed his ship through a screen of mighty breakers into the estuary of an unknown river even as Mackenzie was making his way down the Bella Coola. This was the Columbia River—named for Gray's ship—which Lewis and Clark were sent up the Missouri River and over the Rockies to find and to secure for the United States.

PART III
Commerce for the Nation
(*Lewis and Clark*)

John Ledyard, the American Traveler

> *Hospitality I have found as universal as the face of man.*
> LEDYARD in a letter to Jefferson

SOMEWHERE on an unknown wall, unrecognized, there may hang the portrait of a young man named John Ledyard, dressed in the fashion of the 1780s. In a period of gorgeous fripperies the dress worn by the sitter must have been sober; in an age distinguished by men's devotion to reason the painter would impart to this subject the grain of fanaticism that is usually essential to success—for fanaticism acts on people's nerves and carries them away. Time and neglect may have dulled the colors and blurred the features; yet the essential qualities may still emerge: the active, concentrated intelligence of the man blazoned in the melancholy set of his eyes, a steadfast persistence and strength of will giving lines to the brow, an aura to the face. This lost likeness of John Ledyard of Connecticut was commissioned by an English country squire who had taken a wonderful fancy to the American and "begs to hang me in his hall"; it was executed by a boy "who is as deaf and dumb as the portrait itself," but whose talent had secured for him the patronage of Sir Joshua Reynolds, "the English Raphael." England was celebrating her greatest painters, and on canvas after canvas the patrician face and form and scene was being recorded with grace and color, lightness and delicacy; only famous actors and writers, "aristocrats and their apes," commanded the brushes of Gainsborough, Reynolds, and Romney, when a forgotten squire hired an anonymous apprentice to paint the poor and unknown young American. It is proof —if more were needed than selections from Ledyard's journals and letters recounting his fabulous adventures, his impact on

223

the famous men of his day—that he was an extraordinary and arresting character, a strange, compelling, lonely personality.

John Ledyard is as forgotten as a bright arrow that has missed its mark. His short life was extremely eventful; he was born in Groton, Connecticut, in 1751, and died of a fever in Cairo thirty-eight years later. He was that rare thing, a man serving an idea, and his idea should give him a place in history. It disciplined his harum-scarum nature into daring, strength, and purpose, it made him a wanderer in far-off places and a petitioner in important circles and gained him entrée and attention from many famous men. Ledyard was the first, the very first, to urge the trading possibilities of the northwest coast of America; he hailed its enormous profits and plotted its ramifications; but, more than that, he hoped and attempted—before Mackenzie— to cross North America from the Pacific coast to the Mississippi valley. Three years after Ledyard tried in vain to convince the merchants of Boston of the worthiness of his trading plan, they dispatched Captain Robert Gray on his first profitable voyage; less than twenty years after Ledyard found in Jefferson, then United States Minister to France, an understanding ear and helping hand, Lewis and Clark were commissioned to explore the region he had hoped to traverse. By no very great measure he missed the immortality he deserved.

Unlike Peter Pond—Mackenzie's direct precursor—whose junior he was by eleven years, Ledyard had family connections that somewhat offset his poverty. The Reverend Eleazar Wheelock, a friend of his grandfather, invited him to attend his school, named for its patron the Earl of Dartmouth. The pious clergyman had only just cut away the trees and erected his building when Ledyard arrived in 1772. The college had been strategically placed near the frontier in the New Hampshire wilderness to serve Wheelock's dual purpose: to train young men for the missionary field and to teach young Indians to take their place in the white man's world. Very soon Ledyard renounced his intention of becoming a missionary and left the college after only a year; yet his stay there is a proper preface to his life. On his own initiative, without permission, he disappeared from college and spent almost four months among the Six Nations, learning Indian ways and customs and language—a curriculum certainly not intended by the good Dr. Wheelock. His departure from that institution smacked of theatricalism and romanticism; in a fifty-foot canoe hollowed out of a noble tree, with sufficient provisions to sustain him and only a bearskin to cover him, he floated down the Connecticut River from Dartmouth to his home in Hartford, alone, immensely pleased with himself, delighted with the scenery, engaged in reading the Greek Testament and Ovid. The fact that the river was swollen and sullen with spring thaws, that he had to seek help to carry his canoe around Bellows Falls, were small matters, subordinate to his scheme and mood. Here was a hero whom Rousseau might have created; here were real adventures that rivaled those invented by James Fenimore Cooper, here was a man cast in the image of the romantic age that was soon to dawn.

Neither Connecticut nor the snug security of the ministry could hold a spirit so unconventional as Ledyard's. Poverty, which was his faithful companion, and adventure, to whose siren call his ears were always attuned, were the incompatible forces that ruled his life. Not politically minded, he missed the cues that announced the greatest adventure of all—the rebellion of the colonies—and worked his way to England on a gay, bootless search for rich relatives. Such was the indirect path that brought him to London at the very time when Captain Cook was preparing for his last voyage around the world. Here at last were a captain and a venture that could value and use the qualities Ledyard possessed; here was a shining adventure harnessed to the mundane interests of men. This was the college he had been looking for, whose curriculum fitted his talents and ambitions. As a corporal in the British marines he sailed with the expedition on July 12, 1776.

Of that great voyage around the world little escaped the keen eye, the alert mind, of Ledyard. He noted the lands they stopped at, the peoples they encountered; his picture of the Tasmanians, those dead-end children off the avenues of civilization, who knew not clothes, shelter, weapons, fire, or any of the basic inventions, is as true and telling as his account of the penguins, which, never having looked on man, knew him not as an enemy and, unconcerned and composed, allowed themselves to be bludgeoned to death. A leisurely trip across the Pacific introduced Ledyard to many islands and their fascinating inhabitants. He speculated on the unhappy case of Omai, a Samoan, whom

Cook had taken to London with him on his previous trip and who was now returned to his native island. It was hoped to transform him into an English countryman: a house was built for him, a garden planted with various European seeds, and live animals created a perfect rural setting. Yet it was a dejected Omai who watched the ships sail off. Forever would he be an alien in the land of his birth, unsatisfied with a fate that had changed his home into a prison immobilizing his adventuresome spirit.

And so, crossing the wide Pacific eastward, Ledyard came to Nootka Sound.

"I had no sooner beheld these Americans, than I set them down for the same kind of people that inhabit the opposite side of the continent. They are rather above the middle stature, copper-colored, and of an athletic make. They have long black hair, which they generally wear in a club on the top of the head; they fill it, when dressed, with oil, paint, and the down of birds. They also paint their faces with red, blue, and white colors. . . . Their language is very guttural. . . . They are bold and ferocious, sly and reserved, not easily provoked, but revengeful."

This was interesting to Ledyard, who knew the Indians along the Atlantic coast; but to him the real meaning of Nootka Sound —and it was not anthropological, linguistic, or speculative— was the way in which the Pacific Northwest fitted into the world's growing trade.

"The light in which this country will appear most to advantage respects the variety of its animals, and the richness of their furs. They have foxes, sables, hares, marmosets, ermines, weazles, bears, wolves, deer, moose, dogs, otters, beavers, and a species of weazle called the glutton. The skin of this animal was sold at Kamchatka, a Russian factory on the Asiatic coast, for sixty rubles, which is near twelve guineas, and had it been sold in China, it would have been worth thirty guineas. We purchased while here about fifteen hundred beaver, besides other skins, but took none but the best, having no thoughts at that time of using them to any other advantage, than converting them to the purposes of clothing; but it afterwards happened that skins,

which did not cost the purchaser sixpence sterling, sold in China
for one hundred dollars. Neither did we purchase a quarter part
of the beaver and other fur skins we might have done, and most
certainly should have done, had we known of meeting the opportunity of disposing of them to such an astonishing profit."

Of all the people on Cook's two ships, only Ledyard met the
Russians and saw their settlement on Unalaska Island. As Cook
had sailed northward through Bering Strait, his curiosity had
been piqued by the sight of many European articles: tobacco,
rum, and snuff, and blue linen shirts and drawers. And then
when an Aleut offered him a salmon baked in rye meal and seasoned with salt and pepper, and by motions offered to lead them
to where he had obtained the foreign items, the invitation could
not be refused. Because Cook was unwilling to risk sending a
large party—a group traveled slower than an individual, and
should they be killed, he could ill afford so sizable a loss to his
ships' personnel—either it was a gamble for one man to take or
the invitation must be declined. Ledyard offered to go. He went
alone, carrying only some useful presents, some bread and
brandy. Two days' hard travel over land and water brought
him late one night to his destination. As the door opened, to his
joy and surprise the lamplight revealed "Europeans, fair and
comely, and [I] concluded from their appearance they were
Russians." The hut was long, with a sleeping platform running
along the sides. He was led between rows of Indians, bowing
from the waist in a civilized manner, to a platform at the far
end of the house.

Dry clothes were given him—"a blue silk shirt and drawers,
a fur cap, boots, and gown"—and he was fed and made warm
and comfortable. In the name of Captain Cook he offered his
presents, at which the leader "rose and kissed my hand, the rest
uncovering their heads," and thanked him in the name of the
Empress Catherine of Russia, whose subjects they were. In the
few days he spent in this village he learned to admire the warmth
of their half-sunken, earth-covered houses; he was hospitably
offered a Russian bath—he fainted when he entered the steaming
room—and a festive breakfast of "whale, seahorse, and bear,
which though smoked, dried, and boiled, produced a composition of smells very offensive at nine or ten in the morning."

When he left, "well satisfied with the happy issue of a tour, which was now as agreeable as it was at first undesirable," he was courteously escorted halfway back by three of the Russians.

The first meeting between American and Russian in the Northwest had taken place. Despite a language barrier, they had met; curiosity had yielded to cordiality; neither fear nor distrust had poisoned this initial encounter, and the first picture given to the new United States of her great neighbor was penned by Ledyard, describing the small, lonely Aleutian outpost where he had spent three cozy days as a guest of Russian traders.

Ledyard could hardly wait to announce to the world his stunning, exciting, golden news. Surely from the time his ship left Macao—where he himself had seen the eager bidding, the fantastic prices willingly paid for furs—he was aflame with a single idea: to pioneer the new Pacific trade. It would be interesting to read his own words written at that time, to see with what force the idea, complete and radiant, took possession of him; but all private diaries kept by officers and men on that voyage had to be given up when the ships returned to England. This procedure was adopted by the Admiralty to insure a proper reception for the official account of Cook's last voyage and to prevent a premature private publication such as Ledyard actually made, refreshing his memory from a report that already had been hurriedly brought out by someone else in London in 1781.

Long months passed before the ships reached London, and, when they arrived, Ledyard found that the rebellion at home had attained the stature and scope of a revolution. For two years he sat around London, unable in time of war to get a discharge from the marines. He had no taste for fighting against his fellow Americans. But as the war persisted—with neither side able to claim victory and neither side willing to concede defeat—he asked to be transferred to the American service and was sent back across the Atlantic in 1782. Immediately he deserted ship, returned to his home, and hid until, with the declaration of peace, he was once again a free man.

Ledyard's *Journal of Captain Cook's Last Voyage to the Pacific Ocean* was published the following year, and with it he launched a campaign to find some person or some group who would listen to his fabulous scheme for trade with the northwest coast and China. The merchants of New London and Boston turned him down. Not only were ships few and expensive; shrewd men were too smart to be taken in by the romantic dreams of a young man who, it was plain to see, was wild and unsteady. Had he not run away from Dr. Wheelock's estimable institution? Had he not given up the ministry to be a common sailor? Harum-scarum, they called him, and devil-may-care—not the kind to entrust with good money, they said, and went their own sensible, sober ways. And therein lay the quiet grave of Ledyard's hopes, of his golden dream. These realistic men of trade could not understand that Ledyard was talking dollars and more dollars and could have piled them into profits such as the merchants had never known; they heard "Nootka" and "China," "Una-laska" and "Russia," names of unsubstantial heathen places not yet fit for Christian money. Another generation, and Yankee merchants were to be the most daring, the most romantic and successful on the high seas. They would cut ice in New England ponds and ship it in sawdust halfway around the world to chill the drinks of Indian princes; they would piously reap fortunes from the dark agony of opium and slavery—but that generation had not yet been born, and Ledyard talked and talked and pleaded in vain with men who were not ready for the strange cargoes and exotic ports that the clipper ships were to weave into a pattern of profits and high adventure.

A few brilliant minds understood that Ledyard was no hare-brained adventurer but a portent of the new day when romance and commerce would wed and engender solid fortunes. Robert Morris of Philadelphia tried to help him—"Morris is wrapt up in the idea of Yankee sailors!"—and when Ledyard had exhausted the limited shipping resources of the United States, Morris gave him letters of introduction and recommendation to French merchants in a Brittany port where the adventurous aspect of the fur trade was understood and respected. Somewhere Ledyard hoped to find men who believed in his idea, who would back it, who would allow him to shower them with wealth. Alternately he was dazzled with his own imminent good fortune—a French syndicate was going to send him out—and tasted the bitter, hope-less brew of frustration as when again and again the plans fizzled out. After months of waiting and planning, the Brittany project fell through. Paris was obviously his next hope.

In Paris the story was the same; only the details differed.

Thomas Jefferson, then minister to France, proved an attentive listener, and because he was aware of the political implications of the Louisiana Territory, so vast, so unknown, that stretched between the United States and the Pacific, he enlarged on Ledyard's plans. Who made the initial suggestion that western America should be traversed is obscure; it is sufficient that Ledyard did everything humanly possible to be the one to make the important journey of discovery, and that Jefferson persisted in the purpose and, well after Ledyard's death, dispatched Lewis and Clark on their historic mission.

Without a cent in his pocket, Ledyard was forced to rely on his friends, and accepted a precarious existence and an unenviable dependence while promoting his great idea. Everywhere he was welcome; everyone responded to his unique qualities and experiences: his forthright poverty, his burning zeal and strange ambition, his pure and candid nature, gave him a romantic aura. In a letter he tells how the aged Dr. Franklin received him with "the kindness of a friendly countryman," and how his cause was forwarded by the Marquis de La Fayette, "one of the most growing characters in this kingdom. He has planted a tree in America, and sits under its shade at Versailles." John Paul Jones, who had been "crowned with laurels at the great Opera House in Paris, after the action between the *Bon Homme Richard* and the *Serapis*," was the next who wanted to join Ledyard in his proposed trading venture; but after several months Jones had to withdraw to devote himself to claiming the prize monies due for the captured ships he had sent to French ports. An eccentric wealthy Englishman, Sir James Hall, sought Ledyard out and sent him scurrying to London to catch a ship about to sail that would land him on the northwest coast. "Sir James Hall presented me with twenty guineas *pro bono publico*. I bought two great dogs, an Indian pipe, and a hatchet." With this scanty equipment, hastily assembled, Ledyard planned to cross the continent: the dogs would serve him as companions and hunters, the pipe would declare his mission of peace, and the hatchet would be his all-around tool. His faith, his courage, his determination, his philosophy that declared "all uncivilized men are hospitable," would also serve his needs. The sight of such a lonely figure, so equipped and so sustained, setting out to walk across the wide waist of North America, stirs the imagination. But it was not to be. The vessel was "unfortunately seized by the customhouse," and he was left—to what?

Between the trading venture to be undertaken with Jones and the solitary expedition to be financed by Hall there is a sharp distinction. The former still adhered to Ledyard's brilliant idea of initiating a lucrative commerce with the northwest coast and China; he still had hopes then that reasonable men would find his proposals reasonable and act on them. Time would prove his plan sound and himself precociously astute. But time was against him. He would have been understood by Balboa and the Spaniards of that day; his spirit had the lusty daring of Elizabethan England, and the Merchant Adventurers would certainly have financed him; the rakish Restoration courtiers who had seen the value of Hudson Bay and formed their company would have grabbed at the plan he outlined. Against his fondest hopes he was forced to accept the romantic character that was thrust upon him, to give up his commercial scheme and acknowledge "the irregularity of my genius." The Hall episode confirmed him in the role of explorer. "I die with anxiety to be on the back of the American States, after having come from or penetrated to the Pacific Ocean." Ledyard the Yankee merchant had yielded to Ledyard the American traveler.

Ledyard's plan, as he had formulated it, was amazingly simple. He would go to Kamchatka, where he would secure passage on a Russian sloop bound for the northwest coast, and, having thus reached North America, he would then proceed on foot to the Mississippi. As Jefferson explained it at a later date, the unique plan had its own unique method, for "having no money, they kick him from place to place, and thus he expects to be kicked around the globe." Only two things he lacked: the permission of the Empress of Russia to cross her vast territory, and a little money, just enough to get him started. Money was a minor consideration: he was headed for regions where its use was unknown and its lack would not be felt. Official permission was necessary, and Jefferson tried every avenue of approach to procure it for him. Russia had withheld recognition of the United States as a government founded in revolution, and Jefferson had to work through oblique diplomatic channels. Ledyard resigned himself to a long wait, for added to the time it took to communicate with St. Petersburg was the usual pace at which

crowned heads worked on such matters; it was during his patient inactivity that Hall almost secured his passage to the
northwest coast. This last disappointment decided Ledyard
that quick action was imperative if he was to achieve his daring
purpose. Aided by Hall and Sir Joseph Banks, the naturalist
and patron of exploration, he raised a small amount of money
and started on his fantastic journey.

Unless one had one's own coach and horses, like the wealthy
English lords who made the Grand Tour, travel in Europe was
a heroic undertaking. People without funds did not move around
much. A twenty-mile trip took planning, courage, and ingenuity.
And not even the richest or most eccentric Englishman would
lightly start across northern Europe in wintertime; yet in the
month of December 1786 Ledyard set out on just such a trip.
St. Petersburg was his destination, Catherine's permission his
immediate goal.

"I am here," he wrote from Hamburg, "with ten guineas exactly and in perfect health. One of my dogs is no more. I lost
him on my passage up the river Elbe . . . in a snow storm. I
was out in it forty hours in an open boat." From there he went
to Copenhagen and thence to Stockholm, where he expected
to cut across the Gulf of Bothnia to St. Petersburg. But now it
seemed as though even the elements conspired against him.
Usually winter laid down a highway of thick ice over the gulf,
but not that season; contrarily there was too much ice to permit
a boat to sail and too much open water for a sledge. Ledyard's
alternative was a twelve-hundred-mile walk over deep, trackless
snows, through a sparsely populated region, at a season when
the nights are long and the cold intense. His purse would not
afford his waiting until spring, even if his impetuous nature had
allowed it. It took him seven weeks—an average of almost
twenty-five miles a day!—to reach the Russian capital. So delighted was he with the progress he had made that he could
write: "I find the little French I have, of infinite service to me.
I could not do without it. It is a most extraordinary language.
I believe wolves, rocks, woods, and snow understand it, for I
have addressed them all in it, and they have all been very com-
plaisant to me." French also served him in conversing with men:
the eminent Professor Pallas undertook, for want of a minister
from the United States, to procure for Ledyard a "Royal Pass-

port, without which I cannot stir." Again there was a delay, again Ledyard had to wait, for Catherine was on her famous trip to the Crimea, and it would be months before she returned. Spring came, increasing Ledyard's impatience. Through a Russian officer who belonged to the royal household he received a passport just in time for it to benefit him. By a stroke of luck—unusual for him—he was thus able to accept the invitation to share the coach of a Scottish physician who was traveling eastward in the service of the Empress; in speed and luxury he was carried across Russia, across the Urals and well into Siberia, as far as Barnaul, the doctor's destination.

"I am a curiosity here myself. Those who have heard of America flock around to see me. . . . I anticipate my fate with the most lively ardor. Pity it is, that in such a career, one should be subjected, like a horse, to the beggarly impediments of sleep and hunger." Thus gaily he wrote from Barnaul. At last he was embarked on a venture that would bring him "honest fame." Despair and denials and vexations were far behind him; his heart was very happy. Interesting exiles added spice to the poor, lonely towns strung out along his route; the officials were honored to have him as their guest and eager to expedite his forward journey. They arranged for him to accompany the mail courier as far as Irkutsk, and the few fragments saved from his Siberian journals and letters reveal how, free from the dreary daily need to provide against sleep and hunger, he responded to his changing and novel surroundings. To Pallas he forwarded fossil bones found imbedded in the banks of the Ob, and for Jefferson he drew comparisons between Siberian aborigines and their American cousins; he remarked on the enormous variation between the heat of the day and the cold of the night, a characteristic of continental temperatures; he marveled at the great rivers—he counted twenty-five that he had already crossed—that were the natural highways of that vast, thinly populated land. August was almost at an end when he reached the headwaters of one of the mightiest, the Lena River. In company with a Swedish officer he had met at Irkutsk, the administrative seat for eastern Siberia, he floated fourteen hundred miles to Yakutsk—using a simple native river boat, shooting wild fowl or catching fish as they went along, stopping at villages on the way for additional provisions and supplies. Here surely was a country for an impecunious traveler. A few cents bought them a whole sheep, three quarts of milk, two loaves of bread, cakes with carrots and radishes baked in them, onions, one dozen fresh and two dozen salted fish, and straw and bark to mend the covering of the boat! The current was brisk, and in twenty-two days they reached their destination. And none too soon. The final week was punctuated by snow and gales; the river had carried them northeastward from the lush weather of late summer into the iron rule of winter.

There at Yakutsk Ledyard was advised against further travel that season. A mere six or seven hundred miles separated him from Ohkotsk and the boats that would have taken him to the northwest coast.

Yakutsk was as far as Ledyard was to go, and a premonition of his returning luckless destiny possessed him. Fear for his fate, his future, fills his journal:

"What, alas, shall I do, for I am miserably prepared for this unlooked-for delay. . . . I cannot expect to resume my march until May, which will be eight months. My funds! (only a guinea and one fourth in my purse; and in a place where the necessaries of life are dearer than in Europe . . . to leave Yakutsk with respectability and reach Ohkotsk alive, will be to pass a Scylla and Charybdis, which I have never yet encountered). I have but two long frozen stages more, and I shall be beyond the want, or aid of money, until, emerging from the deep deserts [the trans-Mississippi country!], I gain the American Atlantic States. . . . Poverty has travelled with me hand in hand over half the globe. . . . This is the third time that I have been overtaken and arrested by winter; and both the others, by giving time for my evil genius to rally his hosts about me, have defeated the enterprise. . . . I am the slave of cowardly solicitude, lest in the heart of this dread winter, there lurk the seeds of disappointment to my ardent desire. . . . The only consolation I have . . . is to reflect, that he who travels for information must be supposed to want it. By being here eight months, I shall be able to make my observations much more extensive. . . ."

And then follows page after page of description, commentary, speculation. He was enraptured by the beauty of the prehistoric mammoth ivory to be found everywhere, preserved in the frozen earth and commonly used for handles of knives and spoons; the Tongusians, the Kalmuks, the Yakuti, the Chukchi, the Kuriles —their location, their dress, their economy, their customs—are explained and compared. He was awed by the extraordinary cold of the region (he was very near the cold pole of the earth): wells were useless in ground solidly frozen to great depths, and instead large cakes of ice, stacked in yards, were thawed out as needed; milk was sold in icy chunks, and the cold frosted the air into a thick fog. When to this frightful cold a wind was added, none stirred abroad; the "animals submit themselves to hunger and security, and so does man. All nature groans beneath the rigorous winter."

Two months had thus passed when a most unexpected meeting took place. To Yakutsk came Joseph Billings, whom Ledyard knew well from the years when both had served under Cook, and who had lately been hired by Catherine to direct the survey of the coast of the Chukchi peninsula, most northeasterly part of Siberia. This survey, had it been carried out, would have linked the Russian discoveries with Cook's voyage and would have completed the delineation of the Arctic coast. There was an irony in the meeting. Billings, incompetent and fearful, let slip through his trembling hands an opportunity offered by a lavishly equipped and imperially maintained expedition; Ledyard, superbly endowed by nature with all the requisites for great discoveries, was a poor, insecure free-lance, ready and eager for magnificent accomplishments. The irony bit deeper than mere juxtaposition: Siberia scared the life out of Billings, who was too timid to try anything—he just kept making elaborate preparations and then equally elaborate excuses—while Ledyard, to whom Siberia was only the prelude to a really hazardous venture, was ordered out of Siberia on pain of death.

It is hard to say which of the two was happier for their chance meeting—Ledyard for the material assistance that Billings gave, or Billings for the resolution and strength that Ledyard exuded. Certain it is that when Catherine's police arrested Ledyard and proceeded to take him back to Russia, she picked on the wrong man. Captain Burney, another alumnus of Cook's last voyage and brother of Fanny Burney, knew both men well. His reaction was: "If the Empress had understood the character of the two men, the commander of the expedition would probably have been ordered to Moscow, and Ledyard . . . appointed to supply his place." Sadness tinges the perversity of that situation. Two small details complete the scene: the guards arrested Ledyard on February 24, 1788, and he left, according to an eyewitness, with "his linen quite wet from the wash-tub . . . and astonishing composure."

Retracing the route by which he had so happily come, Ledyard was escorted back as fast as horses and sledge could fly; he who had been the honored guest of the officials on his outward journey was once again their guest, lodged for security in "vile, dirty, gloomy, damp rooms"—an endless succession of miserable prisons; he who had sought to obtain as much information as he could about the little-known regions through which he was advancing had only "the mysterious wisdom in the face of" his sergeant to help him decipher his own fate. Of that long-drawn-out, pathetic anticlimax a letter of Ledyard's tells all that is known:

"I had penetrated through Europe and Asia, almost to the Pacific Ocean, but, in the midst of my career, was arrested a prisoner to the Empress of Russia, by an express sent after me for that purpose. I passed under a guard part of last winter and spring; was banished the empire, and conveyed to the frontiers of Poland, six thousand versts [four thousand miles] . . . in six weeks. . . . I know not how I passed through the kingdoms of Poland and Prussia, or from thence to London, where I arrived in the beginning of May, disappointed, ragged, penniless; and yet so accustomed am I to such things, that I declare my heart was whole. My health for the first time had suffered from confinement. . . . But my liberty regained, and a few days' rest among the beautiful daughters of Israel in Poland, re-established it. . . . Jarvis says I look much older than when he saw me three summers ago at Paris, which I can readily believe. An American face does not wear well, like an American heart."

Thus Ledyard said farewell to the dazzling idea that for ten years had been his whole life; the shifting fortune of his hopes had ended on a closing chord, poignant but brief as befits the pathos of a man's complete and final frustration.

Ledyard's courage was of the same heroic proportions as his hopes. Arrived in London, he presented himself to his good friend Sir Joseph Banks, who immediately offered him, as proof of undiminished faith, an opportunity to explore for the African Association. When he was asked when he could be ready to start on a three-year trek across Africa—a perilous assignment —Ledyard answered, "Tomorrow morning!" As soon as he was certain of his new goal, he sent his Siberian equipment back to his family in Hartford with a long explanatory letter. Included in the package was his traveling cloak, for which he would have no need.

"The cloak was made in London. I travelled on foot with it in Denmark, Sweden, Lapland, Finland, and the Lord knows where. I have slept in it, ate in it, drank in it, fought in it, negotiated in it. Through every scene it has been my constant and hardy servant. . . . And now to give it an asylum (for I have none) I send it to you. Lay it up; as soon as I can, I will call and lay myself up with it."

The cloak went home to rest while Ledyard set out on his new mission. For the first time in his short career he had ample funds, rich and powerful sponsors, and letters of introduction that magically opened all doors to him. At Cairo, while in the midst of preparing for his penetration of Africa, he died of a sudden fever. It had taken the Empress of Russia to stop him on his first journey; it took death itself to end his African travels.

There is a rare and heart-warming quality about John Ledyard. By his knowledge and hopes and inexhaustible courage he gave urgency and shape to the western dreams of Thomas Jefferson. It was the latter who characterized him as "a man of genius, of some science, and of fearless courage, & enterprise." Time has not impaired this estimate. Across the years he still retains the startling brilliance of a shooting star, and in the too brief light he cast he pointed the way for Lewis and Clark.

Lewis and Clark

THERE is a mighty unhappiness about the Missouri. Still mindful of the defeat it suffered in the glacial age, still fretting at the irreparable injury then inflicted, the Grandfather of Waters is a crazed, irresponsible Titan, the victim of one of the "brutal catastrophes of geological history." Before the invading icecap smothered the eastern half of Canada, the river ran straight and strong and clear from the Rocky Mountains north and east to the Atlantic Ocean, into Hudson Bay or the basin now filled by the Great Lakes. Wrenched out of its course by ice masses, its ancient right of way barred by half a continent of boulder clay, the river desperately sought the sea. The straight line of its flow was bent; south the river went, south through the soft soil that the ice sheet had scraped and pushed off the ravaged rocks to the north; south to where, unopposed, it could again turn east and pour its waters, wild and wilful and dirty, into the Mississippi. It is almost as though the river remembered its former channel and, with a determined unwillingness ever to find rest in its new surroundings, had tossed and turned fretfully, vindictively, using its mighty force to dominate, to scar, to assert its thwarted will on the vast, yielding alluvial plain.

The Missouri is the longest river on the continent; and its closest rivals, the Mackenzie and the Mississippi, are each almost five hundred miles shy of its sprawling, twisting length; its far-flung watershed constituted the heart of the empire known as the Louisiana Territory. Of vague but admittedly vast proportions, the Louisiana Territory stretched from New Orleans —the vital port that controlled all Mississippi commerce—to the crest of the Rockies, since, by definition, the Territory included those lands drained by the Mississippi and its tributaries. The Missouri was the highway to the west. From 1700 on, it was the preferred road of the fur traders, the men engaged in America's biggest business—and soon the men of the Missouri would

238

(*Lewis and Clark*)

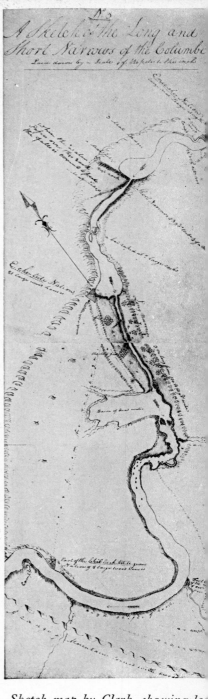

Sketch map by Lewis, showing falls and portage on the Missouri River.

Sketch map by Clark, showing long and short narrows on the Columbia River.

A Mandan village in summer. Squaws using bull-boats, capacious and safe.

A Mandan village in winter. The large round houses were well covered with grass and ... *were mud-plastered ... villages of the Great Plains.*

The elk and the buffalo are seen in possession of the hills and the plains.

They approached the Gates of the Rocky Mountains.

Junction of the Yellowstone River and the Missouri.

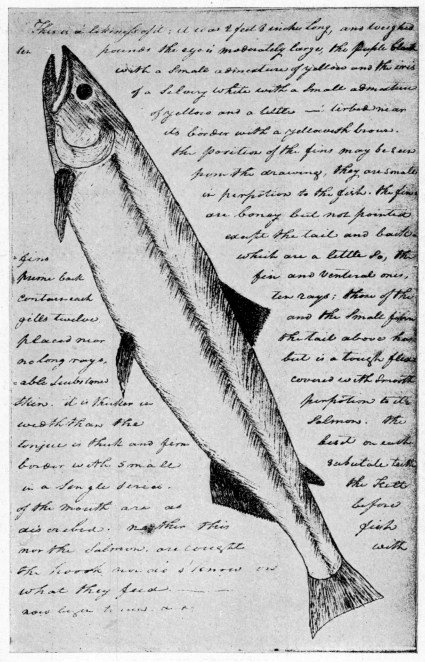

A page from Clark's diary—drawing and description of a white salmon trout.

challenge the men of the St. Lawrence for the use of the still unknown Columbia. In the great epic of the United States, the westward-moving settlers, whether they were headed for the Santa Fe or the Oregon trail, went up the river from St. Louis to Independence. West and north and west again the river beckoned, and as French and Spanish and British and Americans filtered into the territory, a man's nationality was a matter of no more concern than the color of his eyes; Daniel Boone, the symbol of the American frontiersman, owed allegiance to the King of Spain [1] for his vast grant of land. In those days red men and white men, for a brief moment in history, stood in equilibrium, when numerical superiority balanced superiority in arms, when hunting was a common way of life, before the advent of men whose hunger for land brought them long, long miles from Europe to feast on the endless acres of unplowed America.

The size and importance of the Missouri were matched only by its wickedness. Père Marquette, who, with Louis Joliet, the first Europeans to see the mouth of the river (1673), must have crossed himself at the sight of a force so blatantly Satanic:

"As we were gently sailing down the still clear water [the Mississippi], we heard a noise of a rapid into which we were about to fall. I have seen nothing more frightful, a mass of large trees entire with branches, real floating islands came from the Pekittanoui [one of the Missouri's many names], so impetuous that we could not without danger expose ourselves to pass across. The agitation was so great that the water was all muddy, and could not get clear."

Big Muddy is the English translation of one of the Indian names for the Missouri. But no name can describe its cussedness, the variety of its tricks and traps. Constantly the level of the

---

[1] When in 1762 Louis XV of France saw that New France was doomed, he ceded the Louisiana Territory to his Bourbon cousin, the King of Spain, thus preventing it from falling into British hands. From that date until Napoleon (between 1800 and 1802) coerced Charles IV, the stupid Spanish king, into retroceding the Territory back to France, Spain held sovereignty over most of North America.

water is changing: rising, the river floats its grim massive cargo of debris, sending huge logs and matted driftwood careening downstream; jabbing viciously at its banks, it carries off bushes, stumps, living trees—roots, branches, and festooning vines— replenishing the trophies of its terrible might; the falling river strands its frightful freight, dumping it on bars where sand and silt quickly transform it into bogus masses that have every feature of an island except stability, every attribute of a raft except usefulness. Millions of snags cunningly concealed under the muddy surface are lethal weapons that can tear the heart out of a boat, and quicksand slimes the bars and banks. The Missouri has unique terrors. There is the diabolic "sawyer," a snag endowed with murderous motion, which is fastened securely but not immovably and seesaws sickeningly as the weight of the current bears it down, down, until its buoyancy jerks it up. The smack of a surging sawyer strikes with sudden doom. Or the river is weirdly waggish, and huge rocks are seen bobbing along its surface; that the rocks are pumice and as light as corks only explains, but does not modify, the impact of the spectacle. All these tricks are surface manifestations of a spirit that refuses to be tamed. The river has a colossal inconstancy. As it moves it changes; there is no stability in the location of its snags and sawyers, no fixity in its bars and banks, no permanence to its channels and currents.

How to master such a fluid demon? A canoe was like an eggshell standing up to a battering-ram. Quickly the *voyageurs* learned that to survive they must forsake their beloved birch-bark vessel and adopt the pirogue used by the Indians whose villages dotted the banks of the Big Muddy. A pirogue was a canoe hollowed from a solid log; flat-bottomed, without keel or rudder, it floated on the water like the large wooden chip it was. Being of solid wood, it had strength; its shallow draft permitted it to pass over snags and gravel bars thinly veiled with water; but it was awkward to handle and dangerously tipsy. To guard against upsetting, the *voyageurs* used two pirogues as pontoons, stretched a deck between, and achieved both steadiness and additional space for their cargo. Such were the rafts Lewis and Clark found in use along the lower stretches of that western highway.

The Missouri was always known as the way to the West. Marquette and Joliet told of the Indian tradition that placed its headwaters near a portage that led to a river flowing into Balboa's sea; and this Indian report was incorporated in European maps published not long after, at the beginning of the eighteenth century. Then French explorers pushed their way a few hundred miles up the river and into some of its tributaries. After them came French fur trappers and traders, and they ranged along the Platte and the Kansas as far as the Rockies. Men like them, and like them interested in fur trapping, gravitated there from Kentucky. To the north, down from Lake Winnipeg, traders serving the Montreal Pedlars came often to the Mandan villages scattered along the great bend of the Missouri. Yes, the Big Muddy was known, by legend and report, by explorer and trapper, by Frenchmen and Britishers and Spaniards and Americans hunting and trading for furs. A handful of men thinly spaced over the years knew part of the river that led to the West.

And yet it is fair to say that the river was unknown. Its lower half had been visited, but the news brought back was of furs and freedom, not of the river. Traders went in ones and twos, and were indistinguishable from the Indians; they were not pioneers, because pioneers plant their civilization along the frontier and herald the end of the wilderness. Yes, the Missouri was unknown. Its majesty and malevolence were to be finally revealed by Lewis and Clark's journey up its meandering miles.

Never forget the infernal nature of the Big Muddy, which snakes its vast length three thousand miles across the western half of the United States, easily swallowing mighty tributaries —the Grand, Kansas, Platte, Dakota, Niobrara, White, Big Cheyenne, Yellowstone, Milk, Marias, and Musselshell. Like an imperious stallion that has never felt the weight of a saddle nor tasted a bit, the river runs terrible and strong, unwilling to be mastered. Part of the Lewis and Clark epic is their victory over the Missouri.

For twenty years before Thomas Jefferson dispatched Lewis and Clark, he had been aware of the imperial designs of Europe on the American West. In 1783 he wrote to George Rogers

Clark, the hero of Kaskaskia and Vincennes, and made to him his first hesitant suggestion for western exploration.

"I find they had subscribed a very large sum of money in England for exploring the country from the Missisipi to California. they pretend it is only to promote knolege. I am afraid they had thoughts of colonizing into that quarter. some of us have been talking here in a feeble way of making the attempt to search that country. but I doubt whether we have enough of that kind of spirit to raise the money. how would you like to lead such a party? tho I am afraid our prospect is not worth asking the question."

This suggestion was too early, too feeble, and died as soon as it was made. Then followed the intense, hopeful, purposeful years in which Jefferson and Ledyard shared their dreams of western exploration, when he wrote from Paris: "It [Ledyard] returns [from Africa], he has promised me to go to America and penetrate from Kentucke to the western side of the continent." Only in Ledyard did he find another who independently was possessed of the same vision—the high promise of the West with its vast resources and incalculable commerce, where, clear and bold, their ultimate destiny awaited the States that fringed the Atlantic.

Jefferson, whose friendships and correspondence were as wide as his interests, whose versatility made him a clearinghouse for new ideas and old disciplines, watched the feverish activity that followed the publication of the narrative of Cook's last voyage; he knew of Peter Pond's geographical deductions and his dream of a transcontinental route. This is evident from his efforts in 1793, as vice-president of the American Philosophical Society, to solicit subscriptions "to enable Andrew Michaux to make discoveries in the Western Country." The amount so raised was one hundred and twenty-eight dollars and twenty-five cents, and Michaux, a Frenchman, a brilliant botanist and dauntless traveler, was ready to start! In part Jefferson's instructions to him stated: "the chief objects of your journey are to find the shortest and most convenient route of communication between the United States and the Pacific ocean" and suggested the Missouri

as the logical route, since "it would seem by the latest maps as
if a river called the Oregon [Columbia], interlocked with the
Missouri for a considerable distance, and entered the Pacific
ocean not far southward of Nootka Sound." Because of foreign
political complications, the Michaux project fell through. But it
was a significant step in the growth of the idea that culminated
ten years later in the United States military expedition headed
by Lewis and Clark. The apologetic note that had marked Jefferson's first suggestion to George Rogers Clark, the enthusiastic
response he had given to Ledyard's hopes and plans, had settled
into quiet determination. Perhaps he had learned from those
earlier schemes the futility of trying to finance his dream of
western exploration through private patrons. Pure science, to
the realm of which this expedition belonged, could not yet command the purses of the rich. Perhaps Jefferson recalled the impressive results achieved by the Great Northern Expedition,
started and sustained by funds from an imperial treasury, and
how by such a governmental undertaking Russia had succeeded
in the vast task of delineating her Siberian Arctic coast. Surely
he could never forget how vainly Ledyard had sought and
begged for paltry sums to enable him to try his magnificent plans.
One can almost sense how Jefferson had decided that his dream
of western exploration must be a public venture, of a proper
size and with sure and suitable backing.

Jefferson was aware—because he made it his concern to know
—of the many factors converging on the American West. He
knew of the commercial and territorial race whose beginnings
were marked by the Nootka Sound episode; he understood the
meaning of Mackenzie's voyages and of his subsequent proposals for concerted British exploitation and settlement. Jefferson's anxiety grew as he saw more and more of the western coast
being pre-empted by foreign powers—Russia to the north, Spain
to the south, and now Great Britain establishing her rights between those two. At last a note of urgency entered into his
dreams of western exploration. Before it was too late—those
were the accelerating propulsive words—before it was too late,
the United States must stake out her Pacific claims: the nation
he had done so much to found must not be deprived of her
proper growth; the United States must have a transcontinental

route, traversing a moderate climate, ready for the vast enriching commerce that would flow through her from Europe to Asia—before it was too late.

Jefferson's next step was taken when in January 1803, as President of the United States, he sent a secret message to Congress, asking for the appropriation of twenty-five hundred dollars for exploration west of the Mississippi. The message was confidential for the very good reason that the region he proposed crossing belonged to France. The pretext he used to cover his real objective was the continuance of an act establishing trading posts among the Indians; the argument he advanced was the need to combat British traders who were siphoning off "great supplies of furs and peltries"; the diplomatic device he suggested was that this be termed "a literary pursuit," which would satisfy French prestige and still allow passage through her territory. Congress appropriated the sum asked "for the purpose of extending the external commerce of the United States," and Jefferson immediately went ahead with the plans he had already started. His private secretary and young friend, Captain Meriwether Lewis, had long since been fired by Jefferson with the importance and adventure of such a journey, and many, many times the two men had talked over and planned such an expedition. Six months before his message to Congress, Jefferson had offered Lewis the command, and, in order that he might be better prepared for an undertaking so important, privately sent him to Philadelphia—then the scientific center—to learn the "technical language of the natural sciences, and readiness in the astronomical observations." Like Mackenzie before him, Lewis had to study so that the expedition up the Missouri to the western sea would have scientific validity and be as comprehensive as possible.

For the leader of such a venture Jefferson had envisioned an ideal composite of frontiersman and scientist. He thought of a Condamine, a Humboldt, a Michaux—but had to admit that "We cannot in the U.S. find a person who to courage, prudence, habits & health adapted to the woods, & some familiarity with the Indian character, joins a perfect knowledge of botany, natural history, mineralogy & astronomy, all of which would be desirable." Lewis possessed the first half of these requirements, and Jefferson hoped that intensive tutoring by the ablest men in

America would give him, if not a perfect knowledge, at least a certain familiarity with the others. At Jefferson's request, Benjamin Rush and Caspar Wistar, both eminent physicians, scientists, and vice-presidents of the American Philosophical Society; Robert Patterson, professor of mathematics; and Benjamin Smith Barton, professor of botany and natural science, gave Lewis the basic concepts of their various sciences. Andrew Ellicott, who surveyed the Niagara, laid out the city of Washington, and was surveyor general of the United States, instructed him in scientific surveying and the use of mathematical instruments. Lewis made his own sketches of the lower Columbia from Vancouver's survey of the northwest coast, for the work itself, as he wrote Jefferson, was "both too costly, and too weighty, for me either to purchase or carry."

With Jefferson's permission Lewis wrote his friend Captain William Clark, whose older and famous brother had been the recipient of Jefferson's first proposal twenty years before, asking him to share the command, "it's fatiegues, it's dangers and it's honors [because] there is no man on earth with whom I should feel equal pleasure in sharing them as with yourself." So the red-headed Clark entered the expedition. Never has a command been more perfectly shared. Whether this ideal merger, which endured throughout the hazardous years of the expedition, was due to a background Clark and Lewis shared, or whether it was their natures, so different that there was no common ground for friction, but only an awareness that each complemented the other, or whether it was a combination of these factors—one can only guess and, having guessed, marvel that together they shared dangers and despair, fatigue and illness and hunger, and emerged from their great journey together and still fast friends. Their partnership is a thing so unusual, so excellent, that it stands out like a lesson or a fable.

Among the many papers concerned with preparations for the expedition, one catches the eye and goes straight to the heart. The paper lists items and amounts; yet it has an aura of high innocence, for there in Lewis's own handwriting is the neat result of many hours' worry and cogitation, of effort and endeavor; it is the "Recapitulation of an estimate of the sum necessary to carry into effect the Missie. expedicion." Herein a precise mind and a frugal nature figure to the very last dollar the cost of a journey—how far he knew not, nor for how long, not even the shape of the unknown toward which he was traveling:

Mathematical Instruments	$ 217
Arms & Accoutrements extraordinary	81
Camp Ecquipage	255
Medecine & packing	55
Means of transportation	430
Indian presents	696
Provisions extraordinary	224
Materials for making up the various articles into portable packs	55
For the pay of hunters guides & Interpreters	300
In silver coin to defray the expenses of the party from Nashville to the last white settlement on the Missisourie	100
Contingencies	87
	$2,500

It is the last sum, the leeway allowed, that shows the precise mind and the frugal nature. However naïve this list may seem, the equipment and supplies actually bought and taken show careful, comprehensive planning.

Jefferson's instructions to Lewis were most elaborately and thoroughly thought out. The purpose of the expedition was clearly stated: "The object of your mission is to explore the Missouri river & such principal stream of it, as, by it's course & communication with the waters of the Pacific Ocean, may offer the most direct & practicable water communication across this continent, for the purposes of commerce." As though in answer to Mackenzie's excuse, speed was subordinated to thoroughness and time spent in all kinds of observations "to be taken with great pains & accuracy." Point by point the instructions reminded Lewis of the variety of questions that it was hoped his journey would answer. And then a new note, a novel emphasis, comes in. Safety. "We value too much the lives of our citizens" is still a powerful reminder that this expedition is dispatched not for gain, not for personal success, but to benefit a nation; that the leaders are enjoined "to err on the side of safety" since the life of a single man is more precious than gold mines or pearl fisheries or the most fabulous furs in the world. Man at last is more precious than treasures. Ferdinand and Jefferson belong to different geological formations, to different ages of mankind; the private venture of Mackenzie with its merciless need for success is replaced by a cautioned hope for success.

The Lewis and Clark expedition has very different overtones from those of their predecessors. In part it was that neither Lewis nor Clark was the original dreamer of the dream. Where Mackenzie, and Balboa before him, had felt the terrible compulsion that had sent them forth on their great journeys, in this one Jefferson was the creative agent, the propelling factor, and Lewis and Clark were but agents serving his vision. Capable they were, but they lack the glamour that glitters around the other two. The agonized urgency, the lonely unshared vigils, are gone; their place is taken by conscientiousness, by a meticulous adherence to the full spirit of instructions. These men are carrying out a job capably; they are not giving form to a vision. Their journey has an earnest, plodding pedestrian quality, and the whir of winged horses is gone. And yet this difference implies not less than the other two, but more. Glamour is replaced by safety; for the creative, compulsive note there is a harmonious co-ordination, a care for scientific inquiry; for the hope of personal glory and immediate return there is substituted the impersonal destiny of the nation whose sons Lewis and Clark were. And because they were servants of their country they could afford a larger group, a better equipment; they could afford to take the time they needed for the observations they were asked to make. The expedition was as new and different as the century it ushered in.

2.

Unlike the transcontinental crossings of Balboa and Mackenzie, it is difficult to say at what particular point the Lewis and Clark expedition stepped into wilderness. It is almost a matter of personal preference, for by their time the sharp edge of the unknown had been softened and dissolved. The earlier stages of the enterprise were a series of small but significant severings, a gentle, long-drawn-out parting from friends, from settlements, from known trails, a testing of equipment, a training of personnel, a careful, comprehensive preparation.

The first of the farewells was spoken on July 4, 1803, when Lewis spent the night at the White House and had his final talk with Jefferson. The details had all been discussed, and what passed between those two at the end must have been not so much words as emotion: Lewis eager and grave and trembling with the importance of the trust committed to him, ready to serve his country and still readier to be the humble instrument of his very great friend's hope; and Jefferson, at this moment when a twenty years' dream was to be clothed in flesh and action, sensing the impatience and ardor of his neighbor's son and praying that he had left nothing undone that might keep them from success. His tender, brooding worry can still be felt in the letter of credit he wrote that very night:

"In the journey which you are about to undertake . . . your party being small, it is to be expected that you will encounter considerable dangers from the Indian inhabitants. should you escape those dangers and reach the Pacific ocean, you may find it imprudent to hazard a return the same way, and be forced to seek a passage round by sea . . . but you will be without money, without clothes, & other necessaries. . . . your resource in that case can only be in the credit of the U.S. . . . and I solemnly pledge the faith of the United States that these draughts shall be paid punctually at the date they are made payable. . . . And to give more entire satisfaction & confidence to those who may be disposed to aid you, I Thomas Jefferson, President of the United States of America, have written this letter of general credit for you with my own hand, and signed it with my name."

Before dawn of the fifth, Lewis left the White House and its sleeping host and hastened to Harpers Ferry, where he loaded a wagon with rifles, pipe-tomahawks, and knives made for his use, and then headed for Pittsburg on the Ohio. As he passed through Charlestown, Frankfort, Uniontown, and Redstone Old Fort on his way west, the farmers and townspeople who saw him did not know the strange adventure, the high destiny, to which he was so steadfastly committed. A minimum of publicity had been given to the "innocent literary" venture; the purchase of the Louisiana Territory had not yet been publicly confirmed. So it was just another quiet, sober rider, another wagonload of goods, that passed. At Pittsburg the long summer days slipped by; the Ohio sank lower and lower until navigation was declared impossible, and Lewis "was moste shamefully detained" by a boatmaker who dawdled and drowsed and got drunk while he was supposed to be constructing a specially designed iron frame that, covered with buffalo skins, was expected to provide the party with a tough and capacious forty-foot canoe of shallow draft suitable for the upper Missouri. On the last day of August the work was finished, and, sending part of the baggage ahead by wagon, Lewis with some recruits floated his great river boat down an Ohio so shrunken that "on many bars the water in the deepest part dose not exceed six inches." When even this trickle failed him, he cut a canal through gravel bars, proud that the crew could shovel through fifty yards in one hour: "This method is impracticable when driftwood or clay in any quantity is intermixed with the gravel; in such cases Horses or oxen are the last resort; I find them the most efficient sailors in the present state of the navigation of this river. . . ."

Past Wheeling, Marietta, Cincinnati—where he had to let his men rest, they were so "fatiegued with the labour to which they had been subjected in descending the river"—down the Ohio he went, and then up the Mississippi to St. Louis, where he beheld the Missouri. At Louisville they had taken aboard Clark, his powerful tall black slave York, and a handful of volunteers— "robust helthy hardy young men," Clark called them, who were as wild as their Kentucky country, impatient of restraint, spunky, and nimble, schooled in hunting, fishing, and the many arts a man must know who lives far from stores and settlements.

"Capts. Lewis & Clark wintered at the enterance of a Small river opposit the Mouth of Missouri Called Wood River [Dubois River] where they formed their party." Thus Clark mildly summarizes the process that changed the unlicked Kentucky boys into a military group. Personal initiative and private desire had to be subordinated to commands and the common welfare; the lusty individualism of the frontier had to yield to the mightier power of a directed and co-ordinated group; each man had to learn obedience without relinquishing his own hardy assertiveness. Survival was no longer a personal affair depending on quick wits and quicker reactions: it was a social necessity, for each member was part of an organic whole. If Lewis and Clark were to conquer the wilful Missouri, they had to have a disciplined group with which to fight. From December, when they went into camp, until their departure on May 14, 1804, sergeants were appointed and the men were trained, tested, and taught, the rough human metal tempered; headstrong foolishness was admonished and punished:

"The Court are of the oppinion that the Prisoners Warner & Hall are Both Guilty of being absent from camp without leave, it being a breach of the Rules and articles of War and do Sentence them each to receive twenty-five *lashes* on their naked back."

Slowly and skilfully the commanders created a group to which each man added his special talent—whether skill in hunting, or fluency in the Indian sign language, or a gay readiness with a fiddle—a cohesive group that would and could follow them to the edge of the continent and back.

At each stop that far Lewis had written fully to Jefferson, and at each stop letters awaited him. As long as they were within reach of a courier, Jefferson was with them, directing, advising, reassuring, keeping them posted on official news as it affected them. On July 15, 1803, Jefferson dashed off a note: ". . . last night also we received the treaty from Paris ceding [the] Louisiana [Territory] according to the bounds to which France had a right. price 11 1/4 millions of Dollars, besides paying certain debts of France to our citizens which will be from 1, to 4, millions." This was the unexpected climax to negotiations which had begun merely with the hope of buying New Orleans. The speed and size of the actual transaction had frightened both James Monroe, who had been hurriedly dispatched to Paris, and Robert Livingston, minister to France; on May 2, 1803, the treaty was signed. Later Jefferson continued:

"I enclose you also copies of the treaties . . . orders went from hence signed by the King of Spain & the first Consul of France, so as to arrive at Natchez yesterday evening and we expect the delivery of the province at New Orleans will take place about the close of the ensuing week . . . the boundaries of interior

Louisiana are *the high lands enclosing all the waters which run
into the Missipi or Missouri directly or indirectly.*"

Lewis was called to St. Louis for March 9 and 10, to be the
chief official witness of the ceremony by which interior (or
upper) Louisiana was transferred first from Spain to France and
then from France to the United States.

Two letters sent in January 1804 caught Lewis before the
expedition left.

"I now enclose you a map of the Missouri as far as the Mendans,
12 or 1500 miles I presume above it's [the Missouri's] mouth. it
is said to be very accurate having been done by a mr Evans [2]
by order of the Spanish government. . . . the acquisition of the
country through which you are to pass has inspired the public
generally with a great deal of interest in your enterprise. the
enquiries are perpetual as to your progress. The Fed. [eralists]
alone still treat it as a philosophism and would rejoice in it's
failure. their bitterness increases with the diminution of their
numbers and despair of a resurrection. I hope you will take care
of yourself, and be the living witness of their malice and folly."

The other letter received at the same time—and this was the
final severing from Jefferson—authorized him to announce to all
the Indians "whom you may meet . . . that henceforward we
become their fathers and friends, and that we shall endeavor that
they shall have no cause to lament the change." No longer were
Lewis and Clark mere explorers—even explorers faithfully trying
to live up to Jefferson's formidable definition of that work: they
were ambassadors announcing to the princes of the wilderness
the existence of their new father in the village on the Potomac.
Toward any parties belonging to the Siouan nation "we wish
most particularly to make a friendly impression, because of their
immense power, and because we learn they are very desirous of
being on the most friendly terms with us."

This was to be no carefree jaunt through the unknown. It was

---

[2] He was "a Welshman," Jefferson wrote, "employed by the Spanish
government for that purpose, but whose original object I believe had been
to go in search of the Welsh Indians said to be up the Missouri."

a deliberate national advance, planned to promote varied and important interests. Geography, trade, a western empire, assorted sciences, diplomacy—all were tied together into a serious mission; all were comprehended in Jefferson's vast curiosity and concern. So conscious of these overtones was the group making the historic journey that sergeants as well as leaders kept diaries. No matter how tired or cold or hungry they might be, no matter what the weather—rain or snow or sun—the day's events were set down as each man saw them. In their desire to satisfy, to give answers to the lists of questions submitted by scientists, they were completely stumped only by one in "Inquiries relitive to the *Indians* of Louisiana": "What is the State of the pulse in both Sexes, Children, grown persons, and in old age, by feeling the Pulse, Morning, Noon, & Night &c?"

Compared with Mackenzie's account of his voyages and Peter Martyr's record of the news from the New World as he received it, these diaries have a misleading quality. They drone on and on, occupied with each pinprick of time in the making; there is a repetitious, almost tedious quality to the entries; there is a matter-of-factness, a preoccupation with soil and game, with humdrum minutiae, that obscures the continuity and the heroic mission. Affectation, restraint, perspective, all are absent from these diaries; the temporary calamities of storm and flood, the obstreperousness of the river, the hunters' luck, fill much of the page; tumors, bilious attacks, remedies, plague both writer and reader—and yet after plodding through the long pages adding up to eight volumes, the armchair explorer finds that he has been somehow a party to the great journey. It is like following some wooded trail as it climbs up and ever up—logs and brooks have to be crossed, foliage and ferns admired, lichens examined, as the path leads wearily up through a green world, until of a sudden timberline is reached, the universe becomes all sky, and from a bare rocky summit a sweeping, dazzling, rewarding panorama lies below with sky and forest related and defined in a vast and true design. No résumé can capture the flavor or the scope of the diaries; it can only hope to hint at the originals' manifold variety.

"I," wrote Clark, "Set out at 4 oClock P.M, in the presence of many of the neighboring inhabitents, and proceeded under a jentle brease up the Missourie"—so quietly they started up the river. The day was Monday, May 14, 1804. A "jentle brease" breathes even in the spelling of the diaries, a spicy mixture of schooling and phonetics, a mixture that fills the ear with the sound of the words as spoken. Americans of that day, it has been remarked, "not only had freedom of speech but freedom of spelling." [3]

Clark had personally supervised every step of the preparation. Their stores were divided equally and packed so that each unit held a complete assortment, to minimize loss in case of accident; in addition there were boxes of ammunition for hunting and defense and kegs of liquor to cheer the men and win the tribes they were to meet along the river. For the Indians they carried laced coats and ruffled calico skirts, striped silk ribbons, scarlet cloth, and gaudy handkerchiefs, medals and beads, small bells, mirrors, knives, pipe-tomahawks, rings, brooches, brass kettles, and paints—a trader's complete stock. The party, augmented by an escort of six soldiers under a corporal and nine experienced boatmen who were to accompany them as far as the Mandan villages, where the first winter was to be spent, embarked in two pirogues, one of seven oars and the other of six, and a boat, with their supplies. The boat, the largest craft that had ever attempted the Missouri, was fifty-five feet long, drew three feet of water, and was fitted with sails and twenty-two oars; two decks, each ten feet long, covered the bow and stern and carried cabins; the mid-section was inclosed by lockers, which could be opened up to form a protective breastwork in case of attack. Two hunting horses paced the boats along the bank.

Clark's first objective was St. Charles, a French village about seven leagues up the river, where Lewis, who was finishing his business in St. Louis, was to join them by land. Before they could make even that distance they had to learn a little about the Missouri. The very first day the

"barge run foul three times on logs, and in one instance it was with much difficulty they could get her off. . . . Persons accustomed to navigation of the Missouri . . . uniformly take the precaution to load their vessels heavyest in the bow when they ascend the river in order to avoid the danger incedent to run-

---

[3] Stanley Vestal: *The Missouri* (New York, 1945), p. 248.

ing foul of the concealed timber . . . the water excessively rapid, & Banks falling in."

At St. Charles, a village of about one hundred houses, "most of them small and indefferent," time was taken to reload the boat and the pirogues with greater weight in the bows. During this time and under the stress of leaving civilization three of the men forgot their "true respect for their own Dignity . . . behaveing in an unbecoming manner at the Ball," and were duly punished. The little harbor was crowded when two keelboats arrived from Kentucky, loaded with whiskey and hats to trade for furs. On the twenty-first, "under three cheers from the gentlemen on the bank," the expedition left St. Charles and sailed into a hard wind and a hard rain.

At once the Missouri snarled and tore and tricked and bedeviled them. The swift current wheeled the boat around, broke their towline, drove her on deadly sandbars, tried to catch them under caving banks. On the twenty-fifth they passed a "Small french Village of 7 houses and as many families, settled at this place to be convt. to hunt, & trade with the Indians. . . . The people at this Village is pore, houses Small, they sent us milk & eggs to eat." This was the last white settlement they would pass, but traders, men who used that western highway, the great avenue of the fur trade, were met with constantly as loaded pirogues and rafts floated downstream to the market at St. Louis. Rain and more rain, thunder and lightning, cloudy days and drenching squalls, filled the month of May. Steadily the boats went up the river, pausing to note each small creek, a hill reported to have lead ore, a projecting rock on which Indians had painted a figure. Hunters ranging the countryside brought in fat deer, and fat bear added proof—if any were needed—"that the Countrey thro: which they passed . . . is fine, rich land, & well watered."

Furs and land—trapping and farming—were the values and ways of living they knew, understood, and loved. Day after day they met men coming down with heavy packs of pelts: "This day we met 3 men on a Cajaux [raft] from the River of the Soux above the Mahar Nation [Omaha] those men had been hunting 12 mo: & made about 900$ in pelts & furs"—quite a fortune, to recruits whose wages were five and eight dollars a month. Mile

after mile revealed a varied landscape. They distinguished between the low, flooded bottomland where cotton trees and willows grew and the high bottomland "of rich furtile Soile" covered with walnut, ash, hackberry and mulberry, linden and
sycamore; beyond, higher land rolled gently away, land crowned
by different kinds of oak and blue ash, always a lover of rich
earth. On the plain they found a kind of "Grass resembling
Timothey which appeared well Calculated for Hay" and also
"Hasel Grapes & a wild plumb of a Superior quallity, called the
Osages Plumb Grows on a bush the hight of a Hasel and hang
in great quantities on the bushes." The sky, a dramatic prairie
firmament, and even the air were commented on: "at Sunset the
atmespier presented every appearance of wind, Blue & White
Streeks centiring at the Sun as She disappeared and the Clouds
Situated to the S. W. Guilded in the most butifull manner." How
those men must have smiled at the foolishness of Napoleon, who
had sold this vast wonderful country that he might have monies
for war; those men who used both gun and plow were filled with
joy that this great bounty was now theirs to enter and use: "Our
party in high Sperrits!"

But the river was mean, as mean as the land was fair. Like
some ill-assorted pair the land and the water sing their different
tunes. The river is a succession of savage, tearing, frightening
chords seeking to drown out a sweet pastoral melody:

"Set out early and had not proceeded far e'er we wheeled on a
Sawyer which was near injuring us verry much . . . the river
riseing, water verry swift . . . passed between two Islands, a
verry bad place, moveing Sands, we were nearly being swallowed up by the rolling Sands over which the Current was so
Strong that we could not Stem it with our Sales under a Stiff
breese in addition to our ores, we were compelled to pass under
a bank which was falling in, and use the Toe rope occasionally
. . . the Mosquitoes & Ticks are noumerous & bad."

In contrast the land has scenes of innocence and ease, of deer
nibbling on the "young willows and earbage in the Banks and on
the Sand bars"; of a large lazy snake peacefully sunning itself;
of the noise and gay color of great numbers of parroquets. In
the evening they would feast on raspberries, gooseberries, wild

apples. No, the Missouri with all its meanness and malice would never keep these men from responding to the beauty of the country.

"(I will only remark that dureing the time I lay on the sand waiting for the boat, a large Snake Swam to the bank imediately under the Deer which was hanging over the water, and no great distance from it, I threw chunks and drove this snake off Several times. I found that he was so determined on getting to the meet, I was compell'd to kill him, the part of the Deer which attracted this Snake I think was the Milk from the bag of the Doe.)"

Thus, parentheses and all, Clark records the conclusion of an early morning hunt.

June had almost passed, the days were getting hot—"the Thermometer at 3 oClock stood at 96° above o"—and under the merciless sun "the men becom verry feeble." So now the note of heat is added to the beauties of the country, the ferocity of the river. "I observe that the men Swet more than is common from Some cause, I think the Missouris Water is the principal Cause." And the next day: "one man verry sick, Struck with the Sun, Capt. Lewis bled him & gave Niter which has revived him much." The diaries run on and on with their daily conglomeration of routine observations, hunting, description, and reaction to their surroundings and their flowing antagonist: "fish and Gees & Goslings and young swans . . . great quantity of Summer & fall Grapes, Berries & Wild roases," burial mounds and abandoned Indian villages, side excursions over a land that always was rich, endlessly "butifull."

On July 19 the party approached the mouth of the Platte. Rising in the Rockies, it flows almost a thousand miles through broad bottomlands across the Great Plains to add its water and silt to the Missouri. This river—whose name in French means "calm"—spewed sandbars and quicksand as far as twenty-five miles below its mouth.

"This Great river being much more rapid than the Missourie forces its Current against the opposit Shore. The Current of this river comes with great velosity roleing its Sands into the Missouri, filling up its Bead & Compelling it to incroach on the [north] Shore. we found great dificuelty in passing around the Sand at the Mouth of this River."

But the Platte was more than a tributary; it was the beginning of Indian country. Until then they had been passing through a land emptied of its native inhabitants; near Independence (named because they had made camp there on the Fourth of July) "the Kanzas Indians formerly lived, this Town appears to have covd: a large Space, the Nation must have been noumerous at the time they lived here, the Cause of their moveing to the Kanzas River, I have never heard, nor can I learn; . . . on the tops of those hills in every direction, I observed artificial Mounds which to me is strong evidence of this Country being once thickly settled."

Now there were no people, only the mounds on high ground separated by glades small, quiet, lush with wild timothy, the succulent green called lamb's-quarters, "Cuckle burs & rich weed. Sumr: Grapes, Plum's, & Goose berries."

Up the Platte and above the Platte were Indian tribes. Ten miles past the mouth they found a good place to camp and

"Concluded to delay at this place a fiew days and Send for Some of the Chiefs of that nation [Oto], to let them know of the Change in Government the wishes of our government to Cultivate friendship with them, the Objects of our journy and to present them with a flag and Some Small presents."

The Oto village was quite near, and a day's march beyond was the village of the Pawnee. Messengers sent to these villages found them empty, for these were the active midsummer weeks when the Plains Indians left their semipermanent villages for the annual buffalo hunt. One of the men brought back a Missouri Indian whom he had met while looking for game: "This Indian is one of the fiew remaining of that nation, & lives with the Otteauz [Oto] . . . he informs that the 'great gangue' of the Nation were hunting the Buffalow in the Plains. his party was Small Consisting only of about 20 Lodges." Knowing that it was useless to wait where they were, they went on; they saw where huge timbers—trees four feet in diameter—had been sheared close to the ground, eloquent witnesses to "the ravages of a Dreddful harican which had passed oblequely across the river." The spot where they had camped to make contact with the Indians was called Camp White Catfish to mark a place where "in a fiew minits [they] Cought three verry large *Cat fish* one nearly white, those fish are in great plenty on the Sides of the river and verry fat, a quart of Oile Came out of the surpolous fat of one of those fish."

On August second a party of Oto and Missouri Indians approached.

"Among those Indians 6 were Chiefs, (not the principal Chiefs) Capt. Lewis & myself met those Indians & informed them we were glad to see them, and would speak to them tomorrow, Sent them Some rosted meat, Pork flour & meal, in return they sent us Water *millions*. every man on his Guard & ready for any thing."

In this first official meeting between the Plains Indians and the envoys of the United States, there is a reminder of Balboa's impressing his Indian father-in-law by parading before him the power and wealth of the white intruder:

"Mad up a Small preasent for those people in perpotion to their Consiquence . . . our Party paraded & [we] Delivered a long speech to them expressive of our journey the wishes of our Government, Some advice to them and Directions how they were to conduct themselves. the principal Chief for the Nation being absent, we Sent him the Speech flag Meadel & Some Cloathes. after hering what they had to say Delivered a Medal of Second Grade to one for the Ottos & one for the Missourie and presented 4 Medals of a third Grade to the inferior chiefs two for each tribe."

In reply each chief answered with a speech, promised to follow the advice given, and declared himself happy to know that his new fathers were men who could be depended on. "We gave them a Cannister of Powder and a Bottle of Whiskey [the traditional symbols of trade and friendship] and delivered a few presents to the whole."

The place where this first formal meeting had taken place they called

"*Councile Bluff* or Handsom Prarie, [and] appears to be a verry proper place for a Tradeing establishment & fortification The Soil of the Bluff well adapted for Brick, Great deel of timber above . . . and I am told Senteral to Several nations viz. one Days march from the Ottoe Town, one Day & a half from the great Pania [Pawnee] village, 2 days from the Mahar [Omaha] Towns, two 1/4 Days from the *Loups* village, & convenient to the Countrey thro: which Bands of the Soux hunt,"

and only twenty-five days from the Spanish settlement at Santa Fe.

Having successfully concluded their first Indian conference, Lewis and Clark looked forward to the Omaha, whose village they were soon to reach. Once a populous tribe, most of the Omaha had succumbed to a smallpox epidemic that four years before had swept up the river and across the plains; once part of a proud and warlike group, the pitiful remnants were "left to the insults of their weaker neighbors." While the expedition waited near the Omaha village, Clark found a creek dammed by beaver, which he dragged by means of a seine improvised out of willow and bark; he

"Cought 318 fish of different kind i.e. Pike, Bass, Salmon, perch, red horse, small cat, and a kind of perch Called Silver fish, on the Ohio. I cought a Srimp prosisely of Shape Size & flavour of those about N. Orleans . . . this Creek is Crouded with large Musstles verry fat, Ducks, Plover of different kinds."

A second day they waited for the tribe, and on that day, using the same method, Lewis "Cought upwards of 800 fine fish." Everywhere the country was spreading a rich feast for them. "Set the Praries on fire to bring the Mahars & Soues if any were near, this being the useal Signal." Visible from afar, the finger of fire beckoned to the Omaha. The same formal ceremony, the same speeches, gifts and medals, tobacco and whiskey, the contract delivered that sealed the formal treaty of friendship. An extra dram of whiskey was passed around, and they feasted and danced late into the night. "those People are all naked, Covered only with Breech Clouts Blankets or Buffalow Roabes, the flesh Side Painted of Different colours and figures."

Up to this time (*August 19*) the men had had colds, sunstroke, boils, tumors, and felons; now tragedy struck, and struck suddenly. The only death in the course of the long expedition occurred soon after they left the Omaha village. Clark tells the brief pitiful events:

"Serjeant Floyd is taken verry bad all at once with a Biliose Chorlick we attempt to relieve him without success as yet, he gets worst and we are much allarmed at his Situation, all attention to him . . . Sergeant Floyd much weaker and no better. [The entry resumes on the next day] . . . We Set out under a gentle breeze. . . . Serjeant Floyd as bad as he can be no pulse & nothing will Stay a moment on his Stomach or bowels. . . . Serj. Floyd Died with a great deal of Composure, before his death he Said to me, 'I am going away I want you to write me a letter.' We buried him on the top of the bluff to which we Gave his name. . . . after paying all the honor to our Decesed brother we camped in the Mouth of floyds River about 30 yards wide, a butifull evening."

Floyd's Bluff and Floyd's River still carry the name of this young man who died far from home amid alien lands that were soon to be home to hundreds and thousands of his own kind. The diary notes that the breeze was gentle and the night was beautiful when young Floyd died. The country of the Omaha lay behind; that of the Sioux, whom Jefferson had specially commended to them, lay just ahead. "We Set the Praries on fire as a signal for the Soues to Come to the River," and they kept advancing deeper into Sioux territory. Two days later they sent two men with an interpreter to the main Sioux camp to invite the chiefs to meet them "at a Bluff above Called the Calumet." On a beautiful plain near the bluff they made their camp, prepared their presents, and rehearsed the speech they would make. On August 30, five days after they had announced their arrival by the fire signal, Lewis and Clark hoisted the flag and with carefully chosen words welcomed the Sioux chiefs and warriors. Medals (first class) stamped with Jefferson's serene profile and gaudy printed handkerchiefs were presented to each of three great chiefs; to the Grand Chief went a flag, the printed contract of friendship, wampum, and "a richly laced uniform of the

United States artillery corps, with a cocked hat and read feather"; the pipe of peace was solemnly passed around, and then both parties retired to eat. The Sioux

"are a Stout bold looking people, (the young men handsom) & well made, the greater part of them use Bows & arrows . . . the Warriers are Verry much deckerated with Paint Porcupine quils & feathers, large leagins and mockersons, all with buffalow roabs of Different Colours. the Squars wore Peticoats & a White Buffalow roabe with the black hare turned back over their necks and Sholders."

The Sioux chiefs complained to Lewis and Clark of their poverty and distress because of their "not haveing traders, & wished us to take pity on them, they wanted Powder Ball & a *little Milk*" —their name for rum, for by a rhetorical logic they called hard liquor the milk of the Great Father. To this Lewis and Clark replied that the Sioux would receive all the help they needed if they would but ask the Great Father themselves. It was arranged with the interpreter that next spring they should go to Washington and ask Jefferson for the things they wanted.

September came. Soon there was a chill in the air, the rain was heavy, and the wind blew hard from the north, making progress slower. Flannel shirts were issued to the men. On the nineteenth they reached "the Commencement of what is Called & Known by the *Grand de Tortu* [Detour] or *Big Bend* of the Missourie . . . we Sent a man to Measure [step off] the Distance across the gouge, he made it 2,000 yds., The distance arround is 30 Mls." As their beautifully drawn chart shows, it is an almost perfect loop inscribed by a river in the heart of a continent. Six days later they reached the mouth of the Teton River, named for the Teton branch of the Sioux tribe, whom they met there. Five tense days were spent with the Tetons, days when they were prepared for an attack they feared might come at any moment, nights made sleepless by the shrill noise and savage ritual of the scalp dance. The Teton Sioux were bullies charged with fresh arrogance from a recent raid on an Omaha camp; they were celebrating a victory in which they had killed seventy-five men and boys and captured forty-eight women and children, pitiful captives: "a retched and Dejected looking people the Squars appear low

& Corse but this is an unfavourable time to judge of them." It was at this camp that the explorers first tasted pemmican. Here they saw the strict policing of the camp by soldier-warriors who carried whips of authority and maintained both order and guard; for four nights they watched women decorated with feathers and paint dance and sing of the warrior's prowess that had procured the scalp they waved on the end of a stock; they noticed how the Tetons' arms were scarred by arrows that the Indians had driven deep into their own flesh during orgies of grief. This savage medley was exhausting; and, lacking a good translator, the speeches, the formal ceremonies, and the proffer of presents were difficult and endless, for each warrior demanded individual recognition. When at last the boat started up the river again, Clark's fatigue, confusion, and anxiety find oblique expression: "a verry Cold evening, all on guard. Sand bars are So noumerous, that it is impossible to describe them, & think it unnecessary to mention them."

Frost came with October; the days grew cloudy and cold. Daily now, Indians hailed them from the banks, but they did not stop to deal with these isolated groups, because the Mandan village where they were to winter was still many miles distant. Near the foot of some high, bald, uneven hills was a large island where the Arikara villages and fields were located. Two French traders were living there, men who knew the language and the customs and were of great assistance during the few days spent among this tribe. It was not the guns that were fired for the astonishment of the Arikara, nor the goods bestowed for their pleasure and good will, nor the boat—so unusually large and different that it was called "big medicine," a term applied to anything impressive and mysterious—that made the greatest stir among these Indians, but York, Clark's servant—the first Negro ever seen by them. Certainly he added to their legends by telling them that he was a wild animal that had been caught and tamed by his master, and this gorgeous lie made his strong-man acts and strange looks wonderful and terrible.

In many ways these village-dwelling Arikara were different from the Indians previously met: they had well-tended gardens that supplied them with corn, beans, squash, and tobacco; their pride was evident in the gifts of food they sent their guests in return for the presents they had received; their hospitality amazed the white men, because sex was offered to the honored visitor as well as shelter and food. A settled people, they built large round houses and covered them well with grass and earth for warmth—a sort of huge mud igloo. Their special quality stands out as vividly as a small light glowing in a wide gloom; the small incidents Lewis and Clark tell fasten the attention on this meeting of savage and civilized man. The Arikara, Clark says, "are not fond of Spiritous liquers, nor do they apper to be fond of Receiveing any or thankfull for it. (they say we are no friends or we would not give them what makes them fools)." And their reaction to punishment meted out to one of the white men who had been tried and convicted was such that at the first bite of the lash a chief protested against wanton shaming and cruelty: "his nation never whiped even their Children, from their burth."

As the expedition left the village, an Arikara chief went with them to establish peace between his people and the Mandans who lived above them on the river. Half of October passed. The fast-falling leaves were an omen of winter; the north wind blew so hard that on some days it was impossible to move against it. Soon the party passed the large ruins of former Mandan villages, and twice they saw Sioux warriors naked save for breech-clouts and moccasins—a war party bent on revenge or plunder. As the boats pushed on, groups of Mandans appeared along the banks and visited them when they camped at night. "Several Indians came to see us this evening, amongst others the Sun of the late Great Chief . . . this man has his two little fingers cut off; on inquireing the cause, was told it was customary for this nation to Show their greaf by some testimony of pain." The country they were approaching announced itself in tales of bloodshed and violence: "We are told that the Seaux has latterly fallen in with & Stole the horses of the *Big bellies* [Gros Ventres], on their way home they fell in with the Ossiniboin who killed them and took the horses. a frenchman has latterly been killed." That night (*October 26*) they reached the Mandan village. The first person they met there was an agent of the North West Company, a Pedlar, who had come from the north to seek horses and buffalo robes.

Five and a half months they had taken to reach the Mandan village. So far they had been successful in getting their large boat up the Missouri. Without haste, without major mishap, they had negotiated sixteen hundred miles; they had examined the region as thoroughly as they could and had an acquaintance-ship with its inhabitants, its animals, its vegetation. Impressively and happily they had conducted their meetings with the Indi-ans; conscientiously they had written of the land and the river so that all the world might learn what lay in the heartland of North America. There is, in their simple recital of the vastness and richness of the river and its valley, the pure strain of a lyric poem. Thus far they had precise Spanish charts and the tech-niques of the French rivermen to guide them; from this point on, they would be in wholly uncharted country.

3.

The night before leaving the Mandan village to explore the upper Missouri and beyond, Lewis wrote Jefferson of his prepa-rations and his prospects. A few men, unsound and unhappy, had been weeded out and were being sent back to St. Louis with the extra boatmen, "able-bodied men well armed and provided with sufficient stock of provision." To the safekeeping of the corporal who commanded the guard of soldiers Lewis entrusted this group and his precious dispatches, the surplus supplies, and boxes, trunks, and cages that held a fascinating miscellany—min-eral, animal, and vegetable—precisely labeled, chosen for their oddity, importance, originality, and interest. The collection sent to Jefferson (whose curiosity embraced all categories) included animal skins and skeletons; "Specimens of earths, Salts, and min-erals, numbered from 1 to 67"; some sixty plants and seeds; Indian clothing, utensils and art ("1 Buffalow robe painted by a Mandan man representing a battle which was fought 8 years since, by the Sioux & Ricaras, against the Mandans, Minitarras & Ahwah-harways"); a "parsel of roots, highly prized by the natives as an efficatious remidy in the cure of the bite of the rattle snake, or Mad dog"; a tin box containing an assortment of insects and mice; and three cages, one holding "four liveing Magpies," an-other "a liveing burrowing Squirel of the praries," and the last "containing one liveing hen of the Prarie."

The winter months had been well spent. By replacing the boat that had carried them to Fort Mandan with six dugout canoes Lewis counted on being able to travel at the smart rate of

"20 or 25 miles pr. day as far as the falls of the Missouri. beyond this point, or the first range of rocky Mountains situated about 100 miles further, any calculation with rispect to our daily progress, can be little more than bare conjecture. the circumstances of the Snake [Shoshone] Indians possessing large quantities of horses, is much in our favour."

They carefully stowed away the iron frame that Lewis had designed especially for shallow water, which had been so perfected as to "enable us to prepare it in the course of a few hours" with a covering of hides. Game had been plentiful and hunting profitable, and they were "thus enabled to reserve the parched meal, portable Soup," and other prepared foods "for the more difficult parts of our voyage." Item by item Lewis was robbing the unknown of its dangers and perils; in a quiet, prosaic manner he could write: "We do not calculate on completeing our voyage within the present year"; therefore Jefferson must not expect him at Monticello before September 1806.

Lewis's letter exudes an assurance, a confidence born of the information he had secured about the upper Missouri not only from the Indians "who have visited that country" but from fur traders—French *voyageurs*, Montrealers, and Americans from the Illinois country—who had been as far as the Roche Jaune (Yellowstone River) and knew of the significant landmarks farther west. There is a ring of optimism, not bravado, in his assertion that he can

"foresee no material or probable obstruction to our progress, and entertain therefore the most sanguine hopes of complete success . . . At this moment, every individual of the party are in good health, and excellent sperits; zealously attached to the enterprise, and anxious to proceed . . . with such men I have every thing to hope, and but little to fear."

A sizable party accompanied Lewis and Clark: twenty-six soldiers and *voyageurs;* Clark's Negro servant, York; Georges Drouillard, a Frenchman from St. Louis whose knowledge of

Indian sign language and "uncommon skill as a hunter and woodsman" served the party well; Toussaint Charbonneau, an interpreter whom they found living in the Hidasta village near Fort Mandan, and "one Indian woman, wife to one of the interpreters." Thus Jefferson was given details and highlights, a suggestion of how they had spent their time, and a promise that their enterprise would succeed. On April 7, 1805, the two groups parted; the keelboat sailed back for St. Louis, and a small flotilla started westward.

Lewis described their start in his diary:

"Our vessels consisted of six small canoes, and two large perogues. This little fleet altho' not quite so rispectable as those of Columbus or Capt. Cook, were still viewed by us with as much pleasure as those deservedly famed adventurers ever beheld theirs; and I dare say with quite as much anxiety for their safety and preservation. we were now about to penetrate a country at least two thousand miles in width, on which the foot of civilized man had never trodden . . . these little vessells contained every article by which we were to expect to subsist or defend ourselves."

In this entry there is a tension not found in his letter to Jefferson and the world. There is also another difference. Here the list of the party ends with "an Indian Woman wife to Charbono [Charbonneau] with a young child." This last, this youngest, the thirty-third member of the party—not quite two months old—was not mentioned in the letter; it would have made the picture too preposterous—a babe carried on his mother's back on a journey for which only the strongest, the bravest, the most daring had been deemed eligible.

But no equipment and preparations, inquiries and plans, none of what had been so carefully considered and constructed, not all the wisdom that had been concentrated on the expedition, was to be more valuable than that child's mother. Her name was not even listed at first, and yet so crucial was the role she played as guide and interpreter (and as a visible proof of the peaceable purposes of this large, strange, and intrusive party) that were credit and honor fully accorded, beside the names of Lewis and

Clark would stand that of the "Indian squar" Sacajawea, "Canoe Pusher."

Squat and strong, self-effacing, obedient, unassertive, Sacajawea was externally the typical drudging Shoshone squaw. But by nature as well as experience she was exceptional; she was not an ordinary daughter of the wilderness, not just another young Indian woman who had been stolen from her tribe as a girl and sold, far from home, to a Frenchman—a man of another race who, when she reached puberty, added her to his collection of Indian wives. From the anonymity that had hidden her until recently, from the diaries that contain most of what is definitely known of her, she emerges with title to an overdue rightful recognition. She was hired because she was a Shoshone, familiar with the formidable rocky face of the country whose features they would have to recognize; she stayed on because she too had the compelling curiosity of the explorer, because of her high loyalty to the aims of the expedition. For twenty months with a cradleboard strapped to her back she was a valued member of the group that made its way from the Mandan village across the Rockies to the Pacific and back; asking no special consideration, she shared the fortunes of the trail; she had stamina and sweetness, and unflaggingly she guarded and served and saved and guided the party. She was a woman accepted fully as an equal—no sentimentality, no belittling chivalry, no fuss; in her was epitomized the stuff demanded of generations of women who went westward into the wilderness.

Sacajawea's unusual qualities of heart and mind shimmer through the course of events. There is much about her that is tantalizing and provocative of speculation, but her motives escape the strong light of scrutiny; never once does she speak out. Only her actions are recorded, and from them her intelligence and personality must be judged. Conversely, it is in relation to her that the two leaders are most clearly defined. Lewis, the unhappy neurotic, who at the peak of his fame and honors committed suicide, who from boyhood on had been happiest when alone in the woods—Lewis, who, because he could not evaluate people, disposed of them by fitting them into obvious categories—always regarded her as a squaw, a dull insensitive slavey, a creature of another sex and species from the ladies he knew at home. To Clark she became "Janey," as if she had been a sister or dear and close cousin; to him her son was "Pomp," the Shoshone word for eldest son, which is what his mother must have called him, and "my little dancing boy Baptiest" (the baby's name was Jean-Baptiste); to Clark, who was warm and easy and delightfully human, she was a woman who commanded his respect, his affection, his undying gratitude. Through Clark's eyes, Sacajawea can be seen and prized.

Like a legend with its pristine happy setting, its combination of innocence and violence, its known facts and implied drama, the story of Sacajawea starts. Born into the Lemhi band of the Shoshone tribe, she grew up along the height of land that separated the headwaters of the Missouri from those of the Salmon, which, emptying into the Snake, twists and turns until at last it joins the mighty Columbia. From their tribal cousins the Comanche, the Shoshone acquired horses stolen from Spanish rancherías in Texas and Mexico and, with horses, mobility, importance, advantages, and a widespread celebrity. Across the Plains, in the Mandan village, Lewis had heard of the Shoshone's "large quantities of horses," by which, as he figures, "the transportation of our baggage will be rendered easy and expeditious over land, from the Missouri to the Columbia river." Before they had horses, the Lemhi had lived half-starved along the western slopes of the Bitter Root Mountains, precariously depending on salmon, a little game, edible roots, and berries; with horses they could swoop down on the plains that lay to the east of their mountain retreat, secure quantities of buffalo meat, and return before their fierce neighbors could stop them. North and south along that high plateau, horses passed in trade; the Shoshone were the envy and target of the neighboring Plains Indians, who still hunted the buffalo on foot and used dogs for transportation. The Lemhi loomed large in the plans and worries of Lewis and Clark: they held the high passes that led to the West; they had the horses that would make that critical crossing possible. By blood, by upbringing, by language, Sacajawea belonged to that tribe and that band. She was the key that would unlock the western door, a precious, essential key that the expedition had casually picked up fifteen hundred miles away in a Mandan village.

Aboriginal America, with its villages and camps, its plains and mountains and waters, was the silent witness of bloodshed and heartbreak, of a pattern of war that was constant and sudden and ruthless, in which small war parties seeking booty and honor pocked the land like a plague. Fire and the earth have received the dead, and the wind has swallowed up the sighs, the rivers washed away the tears of the pitiful living victims of this deadly game; their history was never written, and today it no longer matters; but at that time the scalp dance had a dreadful rhythm, and war paint was the pure pigment of terror. Almost Sacajawea had been broken in such a bubble of primitive blitz. What actually happened that clear happy midsummer morning—the action, the sequence, the sounds and emotions, the slaughter and struggle—when a band of Minnetarees or Hidatsa captured her, is proper food for the imagination; the facts are few. When it happened, in 1800, she was about twelve, enjoying the brief Indian spring between girlhood and motherhood. She was already promised in marriage; as soon as she had become a woman she would be given—for such was Shoshone custom—to the man from whom her father had chosen to accept horses. With her people she had come down from the mountains onto the plains, and there, by the Three Forks where the Jefferson, the Madison, and the Gallatin unite to form the Missouri, the young girl was captured by an enemy war party. From that day on she was a captive, more pitiful even than an orphan, driven fifteen hundred miles away to live among a strange group who spoke an alien tongue.

This nightmare did not crush Sacajawea. Some spirit must still have vigorously bespoken her inner quality, for Charbonneau singled her out to buy. Maybe he thought her pretty; vaguely he must have reflected that some day she might be useful; eventually she would become his wife, but while she was still too young for that she could fetch and carry and haul for his other wives. The years passed quickly. She learned the Siouan language spoken in the Hidatsa village where she lived; from an upheaval that provided illuminating comparisons and contrasts free of schooled social reactions, she learned as people can who have the capacity; her perceptions deepened and her understanding broadened. Formative years were spent in this bitter, lonely school of exile; it made her unafraid of change; it fostered a curiosity to see more; it left her a wanderer for the rest of her long life. At fourteen she was a woman, and Charbonneau married her. Soon after, when she was big with child, Lewis and Clark came up the river to the Mandan village; they asked about the upper Missouri and the Shoshone country. Charbonneau told them he had a woman who belonged to the tribe that held the pass they must cross. Because of her and the bridge of languages she and Charbonneau offered—English to French to Siouan to Shoshonean—Lewis and Clark included them in the expedition.

On February 11, 1805, Sacajawea's baby was born. From a *voyageur* who had lived many years among the Indians, Lewis borrowed a suggested treatment to hasten the delivery. "Having the rattle of a snake by me I gave it to him and he administered two rings of it to the woman broken in small pieces with the fingers and added to a small quantity of water. Whether this medicine was truly the cause or not I shall not undertake to determine," but ten minutes later Sacajawea had brought her Pomp into the world.

"I continue to Draw a connected plott from the information of Traders, Indians & my own observations & ideas. from the best information, the Great falls is about (800) miles nearly West," Clark noted as they started westward. The Great Falls of the Missouri was their first objective.

Their first season had made them experienced rivermen. Head winds and shallow water, rapids, sandbars and caving banks, snags, sawyers, and quicksands were all in the day's work; the light canoes and pirogues were much easier to handle than the heavy boat at which they had strained before. In a few days they reached the mouth of the Little Missouri, passing the outer fringe of the fantastic Bad Lands, through the heart of which the tributary cuts its way. There the level, naked plain covers vast smoldering beds of lignite coal that "throws out considerable quantities of smoke which has a strong sulphurious smell." The sides of the hills and even the flats in the river are white with alkali, and the water is so strongly impregnated with sulphate of soda that it "is extremely unpleasant to the taste and has a purgative effect." At the mouth of the Little Missouri (*April 14*) they found the hoops of small whiskey kegs, positive testimony that Assiniboines and Crees had hunted buffalo there for the North West Company; out of the "Buffaloe meat and grease they procure" they had made pemmican "by means of which [the North

West Company] are enabled to supply provision to their engages on their return from . . . the Athabaskey country where they winter; without such resource those voyagers would frequently be straitened for provisions." The system Peter Pond had initiated was still serving the Montrealers.

That day Lewis and Clark reached the farthest point on the Missouri visited up till then by white men. Before them all was new.

Spring came. The prairie was green, cottonwood began to leave, plum bushes bloomed, and they noted "some Boxalder, ash and red Elm. the under brush, willow, rose bushes, Honeysuccles, goosbury, currant and servicebury." White cranes, gray brant, geese, turkey, in great numbers nibbled the tender new grass; overhead, bald eagles and sparrow hawks circled, choosing their prey. The horizon penned in great quantities of gentle game—elk, antelopes, and herds of buffalo; the creeks and rivers were full of beaver "larger, fatter, more abundant and better clad with fur" than any they had yet seen. In mud and sand were found the huge track of the grizzly bear—*Ursus horribilis*, unknown until found by Lewis and Clark—whose ferocity was equaled by his thick invulnerability; he could not be killed "unless shot thro' head or heart." The first victory over this "turrible looking animal" by Clark and Drouillard was fully reported in Lewis's diary: "it was a most tremendious looking anamal, and extreemly hard to kill, notwithstanding he had five balls through his lungs and five in other parts he swam more than half the distance across the river to a sandbar, & it was at least twenty minutes before he died." His weight they estimated at between five and six hundred pounds; he measured "8 Feet 7½ Inches from the nose to the extremety of the hind feet. . . his tallons which were five in number on each foot were 4⅜ Inches in length." They skinned him and boiled down his oil—"as hard as hogs lard when cool"; the yield was about eight gallons, which they put in a cask for future use. "His heart was as large as that of a large Ox."

In that land of plenty, exploration was versatile and on many levels; it even included food. Everything that was not too lean found its way into their pots; "the flesh of the beaver is esteemed a delecacy among us; I think the tale a most delicious morsal, when boiled it resembles in flavour the fresh tongues and sounds [air-bladders] of the codfish." Of the buffalo the hump and the tongue were the preferred parts, but when Lewis was served "the small guts of the buffaloe cooked over a blazing fire in the Indian stile without any preparation of washing or other clensing," he found them very good. Through Sacajawea they were introduced to some wild plants with which the Indians supplemented their diet.

"When we halted for dinner the squaw busied herself in serching for the wild artichokes which the mice [pocket-gophers] collect and deposit in large hoards. this operation she performed by penetrating the earth with a sharp stick about some small collections of drift wood. her labour soon proved successful, and she procured a good quantity of these roots. the flavor of this root resembles that of the Jerusalem Artichoke."

Later she collected wild licorice and the tuber called whiteapple, which the Missouri Indians used. Collected in the summer and fall, the latter was eaten fresh or carefully dried and stored for future need; beloved of the bears, who dug it up with their talons, Lewis found it "a tasteless insippid food of itself, tho' I have no doubt it is a very healthy and moderately nutrious food. I have no doubt but our epicures would admire this root very much, it would serve them in their ragouts and gravies instead of the truffles morella." But the favorite dish, made whenever they had the requisite ingredients, was Charbonneau's "white pudding." His masterpiece was produced to the running culinary comment and the frivolous but sure gestures of a master chef. Taking the large lower gut of the buffalo "that is covered with a good coat of fat," knotting one end and skillfully turning it inside out, he made a casing and stuffed it—"with a brisk motion of the finger and thumb"—with finely chopped tidbits of meat mixed with kidney suet, pepper and salt, and flour. When it "is compleatly filled with something good to eat, it is tyed at the other end, but not any cut off, for that would make the pattern too scant; it is then baptised in the missouri with two dips and a flirt, and bobbed into the kettle; from whence, after it be well boiled it is taken and fryed with bears oil untill it becomes brown, when it is ready to esswage the pangs of a keen appetite." Buffalo sausage *à la Charbonneau!*

"A delightfull land," notes Lewis; and "a delightfull morning" is the oft-repeated start to the record of days happily spent in side trips—deep inland circuits—days when he saw a new world with fresh eyes, days employed in profitable hunting. For the two leaders shared both responsibility and adventure. While one went by canoe to supervise and direct the progress of their little fleet, the other, relieved of the monotonous vexations of that duty, was free to wander off and hunt. It is a duet of work and play; the former was their main concern, but the latter gave a flavor of glorious excitement to each new day. On these jaunts Lewis commonly went alone, while Drouillard or Charbonneau usually accompanied Clark, often with Sacajawea carrying her baby. At night, when all were together again, there would be stories and news to exchange. If the river or weather had been particularly wayward, grog would be issued to each man, and "this soon produced the fiddle, and they spent the evening with much hilarity, singing & dancing, and seemed perfectly to forget their past toils."

Often the idyllic note is lost. Day after day the wind blew with a violent, unopposed strength; it was "verry" cold on those high plains, even though May had come: "the water friezed on the oars this morning as the men rowed"; snow fell and "formed a singular contrast with the vegetation which was considerably advanced." Or suddenly they saw, like a column of thick smoke, a dust storm that whirled down on them and blotted out the opposite bank of the river, and then the air would be saturated with fine, irritating particles that made their eyes sore; "so penitrating is this sand that we cannot keep any article free from it; in short we are compelled to eat, drink, and breath it very freely."

These were but petty annoyances, and they were reduced to their proper size when real danger struck, when on an instant confusion, excitement, fear threatened many lives and jeopardized the expedition. The fourteenth of May was such a day, when on both land and water sudden death stalked the expedition. It began ominously with "Some fog on the river this morning which is a very rare occurence." A bear, old, fierce, and fighting for his life, was the villain of the first incident; Charbonneau, inept and cowardly, precipitated the second. Late that afternoon two men in one of the rear canoes spotted a large bear and with four others, all good hunters, landed to shoot him. It was prudently decided that two should hold their fire in case the others missed. Taking advantage of a small hill that concealed them, they were able to crawl within forty paces, and four guns fired simultaneously; all the bullets hit the bear, two of them passing through the lungs.

"In an instant this monster ran at them with open mouth, the two who had reserved their fire discharged their pieces at him as he came towards them, boath of them struck him, one only slightly and the other fortunately broke his shoulder, this however re-tarded his motion for a moment only, the men unable to reload their guns took to flight, the bear pursued and had very nearly overtaken them before they reached the river; two of the party betook themselves to a canoe and the others seperated and con-cealed themselves among the willows, reloaded their pieces, each discharged his piece at him as they had an opportunity they struck him several times again but the guns only served to direct the bear to them, in this manner he pursued two of them sepe-rately so close that they were obliged to throw aside their guns and pouches and throw themselves into the river altho' the bank was nearly twenty feet perpendicular; so enraged was this ana-mal that he plunged into the river only a few feet behind the second man he compelled to take refuge in the water, when one of those who still remained on shore shot him through the head and finally killed him; they then took him on shore and butchered him when they found eight balls had passed through him in different directions."

It is Clark who tersely and truly supplies the bear's epitaph: "& indeed he had like to have defeated the whole party." The scene of this fight received the unwieldy and soon forgotten name of Brown-bear-defeated Creek.

Of a different order was the other incident, so paralyzing in its implications that Lewis could not recall it without "the utmost trepidation and horror," for it clearly demonstrated that the issue would be not simply between success and failure, but be-tween life and death. Several unusual factors set the stage: both Lewis and Clark were on shore, back from the river; Lewis had "felt an inclination to eat some veal," and had gone on shore and killed a buffalo calf. And Charbonneau, who "cannot swim

and is perhaps the most timid waterman in the world," instead
of Drouillard was steering the pirogue on which were loaded
"our papers, Instruments, books, medicine, a great part of our
merchandize and in short almost every article indispensibly necessary to further the views, or insure the success of the enter-
prize in which we were now launched to the distance of 2200
miles." Returning from their separate hunting excursions, the
two captains stood helplessly on the shore, "too far distant to be
heard or do more than remain spectators." The sun was just setting when a violent gust of wind struck the pirogue and almost
turned her over. Charbonneau, inexperienced, frightened, lost
his head; the force of the wind whipped the sail out of the hand
of the man holding it, upset the pirogue, and "would have turned
her completely topsaturva" if the sail, now flat on the water, had
not opposed the will of the wind.

"Such was their confusion and consternation at this moment,
that they suffered the perogue to lye on her side for half a minute
before they took the sail in, the perogue then wrighted but had
filled within an inch of the gunwals; Charbono still crying to his
god for mercy, had not yet recollected the rudder, nor could the
repeated orders of the Bowsman, Cruzat, bring him to his recol-
lection until he threatend to shoot him instantly if he did not
take hold of the rudder and do his duty."

The experienced Cruzatte took command over the hysterical
Charbonneau and ordered two men to bail as hard as they could
while with two others he rowed the pirogue to the shore, which
she reached barely afloat.

The danger to the pirogue had been so imminent—besides Charbonneau there were two other men who could not swim and
"who must have perished had she gone to the bottom"—that for
a moment Lewis, unmindful of the futility of such a gesture,
overwhelmed by despair, prepared to swim three hundred yards
to the sinking boat against high waves and a rapid current. "had I
undertaken this project, there was a hundred to one but what I
should have paid the forfit of my life for the madness of my
project, but this had the perogue been lost, I should have valued
but little." Though Charbonneau had lost his head, Sacajawea,
seated in the rear, holding her baby, calmly salvaged packages

bobbing about on the waves; so marked was the contrast that Lewis, recalling it the next day, when they had estimated their losses and dried the swamped cargo, wrote: "the Indian woman to whom I ascribe equal fortitude and resolution, with any person on board at the time of the accedent, caught and preserved most of the light articles which were washed overboard." As they camped there they must have constantly been reminded of their narrow escape—all day long dead buffalo were seen floating down the river, "those buffalow either drown in swiming the river or brake thro' the ice."

As they reached the Missouri's important tributaries one after another, they were pleased to check them against the information they had gathered from the Indians and traders. On the twenty-sixth of April they had traveled one hundred and fifty miles to arrive at the junction of the Missouri and the river known to French trappers as the Roche Jaune; Lewis translated this literally to Yellowstone, descriptive of the vividly colored rocks through which the canyon had been cut. Another hundred and fifty miles brought them (*May 8*) to the mouth of a river "called by the Minitares *the river which scoalds at all others*," which they more prosaically marked down as the Milk because its water was of a "peculiar whiteness, being about the colour of a cup of tea with the admixture of a tablespoonfull of milk." The very next day they passed "the bed of the most extraordinary river that I ever beheld. it is as wide as the Missouri is at this place or ½ mile wide and not containing a single drop of runing water." It was the Big Dry. By then they had gone almost two thousand miles from St. Louis, and they were beginning to wonder if the Missouri would ever end.

". . . the river for several days has been as wide as it is generally near it's mouth, tho' it is much shallower or I should begin to dispair of ever reaching it's source . . . the water also appears to become much clearer, it has changed it's complexin very considerably. I begin to feel extreemly anxious to get in view of the rocky mountains."

Possibly it was their impatience for at least a glimpse of the mountains that left them untouched by the strange splendor of the country through which they were passing, a country in

which wind and water and weather had freakishly modeled the
gypsy-colored sandstone rocks into bizarre forms—cathedrals,
pillars, castles, and other traditional forms created by man—a
country to which they applied the simple adjective "broken."
Or it may have been that to these men scenery as such was not
an entity to be remarked on, a purely esthetic reaction distinct
from an appraisal of a countryside as good for farming or hunting. Casual mention is made of the colorful configurations
through which the Missouri flows between the Milk and the
Musselshell; equal space is given to describing one of the many
little creeks—Blowing Fly Creek—named for the clouds of pests
that stung them there; they dryly noted the irregular horizontal
strata of varicolored stones—freestone, ironstone, clay, and sand
—and seemed more preoccupied with the "immence quantities of
the Prickley pear" that covered the land and tore their moccasins
to ribbons.

On the twenty-sixth of May, Lewis climbed a high bluff and
beheld as a reward "the Rocky Mountains for the first time."
Covered with snow, glittering under a downpour of sun, they
were as brilliant as his hopes; but with joy came anxiety as he
read in those peaks a resolute obstacle to his westward passage.
Putting this fear aside, he held to the promise of the mountains
that soon the endless Missouri must end.

A week later those men who were making geography faced
their first major test: they reached a fork formed by the junction
of two large rivers, and nothing in the information they had
received had prepared them for this. Which was the Missouri?
The one northern tributary mentioned by the Indians had been
the Milk, the "River which scolds at all other Rivers." Even
Sacajawea knew nothing of this fork, knew not how to advise
them. The only positive identification they could rely on was
that the true Missouri had great falls. They camped at the fork
and sent parties out along both rivers in an effort to decipher
the geographical riddle: Clark went forty-five miles up the
southern branch and found nothing conclusive; Lewis explored
even farther along the northern branch with the same negative
result. In the face of this and even though all their men believed
that the northern river was the Missouri, both Lewis and Clark
deduced from valid topographical factors that their route lay
along the southern river. Rather than rush into action and make

a costly—maybe fatal—error in time and effort and enthusiasm, they decided to be cautious. While Clark stayed with the main party, made necessary repairs, and cached surplus ammunition and supplies, to follow when all was completed, Lewis went ahead on foot with a few men to explore the southern branch.

Early on the eleventh of June, Lewis started out. Despite a sudden violent attack of dysentery, which weakened and delayed him, he pushed forward, and "having brought no medecine with me I resolved to try an experiment with some simples"; he drank "an astringent bitter" concoction brewed out of chokecherry leaves and twigs, which quickly relieved "me of every symptom of the disorder." Two days later, about ten in the morning, not far beyond Clark's farthest reconnaissance, "my ears were saluted with the agreeable sound of a fall of water and advancing a little further I saw the spray arrise above the plain like a collumn of smoke"; against a stiff wind the sound carried fifteen miles—a "roaring too tremendious to be mistaken for any cause short of the great falls of the Missouri"; a two-hour walk brought him to some rocks opposite the center of the falls, where he could "gaze on this sublimely grand specticle . . . which has from the commencement of time been concealed from the view of civilized man."

Doubts, problems, indecisions, hesitations, all were swept away by the imperious rush and thunderous sound of the falls: this was the Missouri! A delighted and reassured leader watched the mighty river he had traced for twenty-two hundred and forty wicked miles fall down the giant steps it had carved out of rock; in prose that is at once precise and triumphant, full of measurements and emotion, Lewis describes the ten miles in which the wide river falls over four hundred feet, half this amount in four major falls, the rest in "one continued sene of rapids and cascades." As he watched the Big Muddy, smooth as a stucco wall, hurl itself over a rocky ledge to be transformed into the "whitest beaten froath," he longed for the pen of a writer, the brush of a painter, the cunning of a "crimee obscura" (camera obscura) to catch truly and completely the magnitude of the scene as he saw and felt it. Four hours he sat on the rocky bank and watched the gigantic drama of water and stone locked in unrelenting, unending combat.

"My fare is really sumptuous this evening; buffaloe's humps, tongues and marrowbones, fine trout (*caught in the falls*) parched meal pepper and salt, and a good appetite." This was one of the vastly rewarding moments, heightened and made sweeter by the recent dilemma; relaxed, relieved, his ears received the roar of the water like a surging, exultant victory march.

4.

(*13 June–25 July*)

From out the welter of crises, adventures, labors, alarms, dangers, annoyances, when it seemed as though earth and sky added their malevolence to the great hurdle of the Missouri, a simple shining fact emerges: nothing could stop their forward advance. Lewis and Clark had welded a living machine of strength and spirit. Of another order was the darkest threat that overhung them, the severe sickness that struck Sacajawea just as they were approaching the threshold of the Shoshone country. Certainly their troubles never came singly.

Lewis, having dispatched a man back to Clark to tell of his discovery of the Great Falls (the collective name given to the series of four falls), proceeded to explore the river to learn the nature and extent of the obstruction. Led on by a series of rapids, cascades, cataracts, and the sound of still more distant falls, he walked mile after mile past the frenzied falling water until he saw Medicine River, the Indian name for the stream that "fell into the Missouri just above the falls." Enchanted with his discoveries, exhilarated by the certainty that this *was* the Missouri, he was still sensible of the gentle view beyond where "the missouri . . . lies a smoth, even and unruffled sheet of water nearly a mile in width bearing on it's watry bosome vast flocks of geese." He loathed having to turn back from a reconnaissance that beckoned him on; and to be prepared, in case he decided to spend the night out on the prairie, he "scelected a fat buffaloe and shot him very well." Watching the mortally wounded buffalo, waiting for the animal "to fall every instant, and having entirely forgotten to reload my gun," he suddenly turned and saw that a large grizzly bear had crept within twenty paces of him. His first impulse was to shoot, but his gun was empty; he wanted to reload, but the bear was too close and advancing too rapidly. His only hope was to hide and charge his rifle, but he was on "an open level plain, not a bush within miles nor a tree within less than three hundred yards of me; the river bank was sloping and not more than three feet above the level of the water"; there was no hiding place for him. He thought he might walk briskly toward that nearest tree, but as he turned, the bear "pitched at me, open mouthed and full speed. I ran about 80 yards and found he gained on me fast, I then run into the water." He waded out to a depth where he could still stand but where the bear would have to swim, for he figured that these odds would give him a chance to defend himself with his heavy club. As he took his stand, waist-deep in water, his club ready, the bear, which was at the edge of the river, "sudonly wheeled about as if frightened, declined the combat on such unequal grounds, and retreated with quite as great precipitation as he had just before pursued me . . . the cause of his allarm still remains with me misterious and unaccountable."

Slowly Lewis came ashore and reloaded his gun. A little later he shot at an animal "of the tiger kind" that crouched, tensed to spring at him, but strangely disappeared into a burrow. Then, almost immediately he was amazed to see that three bull buffaloes "seperated from the herd and ran full speed towards me"; when they were within a hundred yards, they took a good look at him and turned around and fled.

"I did not think it prudent to remain all night at this place which really from the succession of curious adventures wore the impression on my mind of inchantment; at sometimes for a moment I thought it might be a dream, but the prickley pears which pierced my feet very severely once in a while, particularly after it grew dark, convinced me that I was really awake, and that it was necessary to make the best of my way to camp."

But his queer encounters persisted, for when he awoke, he "found a large rattlesnake coiled on the leaning trunk of a tree under the shade of which I had been lying at the distance of about ten feet from him." No wonder that he felt "that all the beasts of the neighborhood had made a league to destroy me."

Meanwhile Clark had his own assorted troubles to contend with. The river was swift and deep and troubled, and the canoes could advance only slowly; he had "two men with the Tooth Ake 2 with Tumers, & one man with a Tumor & a slight fever"; but worst of all Sacajawea had been "complaining all night & excessively bad this morning. her case is somewhat dangerous." On the tenth of June, the night before they broke up their camp at the fork—the northern branch had finally been named Maria's River, in honor of a cousin of Lewis's—Sacajawea had suddenly become very ill. "I blead her which appeared to be of great service to her," says Clark hopefully; but the next day she was so "*sick* that I move her into the back part . . . of the Perogue which is cool, her own situation being a verry hot one in the bottom . . . exposed to the sun." For the next few days there runs through his entries, like the bitter refrain to a ballad, the line, "the Indian woman verry sick." The entries are brief, the notations terse, for his mind, his heart, and his time were filled with her illness, with his unceasing efforts to cure her. "Our Indian woman sick & low spirited. I gave her the bark & apply it exteranely to her region which revived her much . . . the Indian woman much wors this evening, she will not take any medison."

On the sixteenth they joined Lewis at a creek—they called it Portage Creek—just below the lowest falls. Lewis immediately prescribed "two dozes of barks and opium" and made her drink copiously of water from a near-by spring "strongly impregnated with sulpher, and I suspect Iron also . . . precisely similar to that of Bowyer's Sulpher spring in Virginia." He continued the "cataplasms of barks and laudnumn which had previously been used by my friend Capt. Clark" and was delighted when her "pulse had become regular and much fuller and a gentle perspiration had taken place." So worried was Lewis—"as well for the poor object herself, then with a young child in her arms, as from the consideration of her being our only dependence for a friendly negociation with the Snake Indians on whom we depend for horses to assist us in our portage from the Missouri to the columbia river"—that her cure became his first concern. His treatment of medicines and mineral water succeeded, and he was soon permitting her to eat "broiled buffaloe well seasoned with pepper and salt and rich soope of the same meat;

I think therefore that there is every rational hope of her recovery." There is in this last sentence, under its muted medical phrasing, the same feeling of success and certainty that had filled him with thanksgiving when he heard the thundering falls and knew that he was on the Missouri. In these assorted conquests over indecision and illness Lewis and Clark showed an intrinsic heroism that could take the full measure of the most varied situations.

All this was but the prelude to the tremendous task they faced in portaging their boats and baggage past the Great Falls. Their cargo was still considerable, and so was the distance; here was no Grand Portage where one set of canoes were unloaded and their cargoes transferred over a known trail to another waiting fleet. From Portage Creek the trail as surveyed and staked out by Clark measured eighteen and a quarter miles over a cruel broken terrain. The upper camp was established at Whitebear Island, named for the many grizzlies there that lunged at these two-legged invaders. The portage was too long "to think of transporting the canoes and baggage on the men's shoulders"; so the men were detailed to look for timbers large enough to fashion into wheels on which they could roll their canoes across the plain. "We were fortunate enough to find one cottonwood tree . . . that was large enough to make our carrage wheels about 22 Inchis in diameter; fortunate I say because I do not beleive that we could find another of the same size perfectly sound within 20 miles of us." Even so the cottonwood proved "illy calculated for [the work] being soft and brittle"; the masts of their pirogues were utilized for the axles.

Other preparations went forward simultaneously: the canoes and pirogues were unloaded, baggage was sorted and suitably packed for transportation, the canoes were dried out in the sun to lighten them; another cache was prepared in which were stored, along with extra food and ammunition, Lewis's desk, some of his books, and the specimens of plants and minerals collected since Fort Mandan. Lewis planned on hiding one pirogue near the cache, replacing it with his iron boat, whose frame needed only to be covered with elk skins to furnish them with a capacious light vessel. Hunters went out to secure the necessary number of elk, a difficult task in a country that seemed to abound in all game but that: "the hunters returned; they had

killed 10 deer but no Elk." Other men went out to kill and
prepare quantities of buffalo meat so that those who hauled the
baggage would not have to stop to secure food:

"we eat an emensity of meat; it requires 4 deer, an Elk and a
deer, or one buffaloe, to supply us plentifully 24 hours. meat
now forms our food prinsipally as we reserve our flour, parched
meal and corn as much as possible for the rocky mountains which
we are shortly to enter, and where from the indian account game
is not very abundant."

One item—distinct from their rich impressions and adventures
and extraneous to their preparations—stands out from the activity
of those days. When at last all was in readiness and the expedition, snaillike, was ready to move forward carrying everything
on its back, Clark writes:

"Not haveing seen the Snake Indians or knowing in fact whither
to calculate on their friendship or hostillity, we have conceived
our party sufficiently small, and therefore have concluded not
to dispatch a canoe with part of our men to St. Louis as we
entended early in the Spring. we fear also that such a measure
might also discourage those who would in such a case remain,
and might possibly hazard the fate of the expedition. We have
never hinted to any one of the party that we had such a scheem
in contemplation, and all appear perfectly to have made up their
minds to Succeed in the expedition or perish in the attempt. We
all believe we are about to enter on the most perilous and dificuelt
part of our Voyage, yet I see no one repineing."

Their reasons for not sending some of the men back were
excellent, but it caused worry and concern to Jefferson and
others who had counted on news from them before they crossed
the Rockies. Safety for the expedition, not reassurance for
those at home, was the motto Jefferson had enjoined on the
leaders.

Nearly two weeks were spent in that portage. A small number
of men—usually those who were ill or spent or occupied with
specific tasks—stayed around the terminal camps, guarding the
possessions, hunting for game, and cooking, while the rest made

the long trek, carrying, hauling, pushing, pulling for eighteen miles, and then returning for more. The wheels split; the tongues and axles broke—they were renewed with sweet willow, and when that splintered uselessly, the men bound loads on their backs and kept on. The ground over which they walked was murderous: prickly pears pierced their moccasins with long, sharp thorns; buffalo herds had trampled the ground during recent rains, and then the earth had been dried and baked by the sun so that it preserved the imprint of hooves with iron ridges:

"this is particularly severe on the feet of the men who not only have their own weight to bear in treading on those hacklelike points but have also the addition of the burthen which they draw . . . they are obliged to halt and rest frequently for a few minutes, at every halt these poor fellows tumble down and are so much fortiegued that many of them are asleep in an instant; in short their fatiegues are incredible; some are limping from the soreness of their feet, others faint and unable to stand for a few minutes, with heat and fatiegue, yet no one complains, all go with cheerfullness."

Despite the hardships and length of the portage and the confused account of comings and goings, the activity was well organized; everybody worked, each at what he was best fitted and able to do. Clark supervised the start from Portage Creek, making certain that everything had been either cached or carried, while Lewis remained at Whitebear Island to receive the goods and assemble his iron boat. Between these two camps the men shuttled, and at both ends they always found food for their ravenous appetites and rest for their weary bodies. Sometimes the fiddle played for their pleasure and relaxation. For those who could not make the entire distance in one lap there was a wayside shelter at "willow run which always had a plentiful supply of good water." Away from the river, water was the determining factor of a camp site; food was everywhere for the shooting.

Rattlesnakes, bears, thorns, were not the only afflictions. The weather was so extreme and capricious that often it ceased to be a subject for scientific notation and assumed the vicious aspect of a hostile force. Either the sun was so hot that the men worked "mostly naked," or their unprotected bodies were chilled and bruised by hail—"7 Inches in circumference and waied 3 ounces"—which lashed at them as sudden storms, accompanied by lightning and thunder, roared across the plains. "the hail was as large as musket balls and covered the ground perfectly," reads one entry; "we had some of it collected which kept very well through the day and served to cool our water!" A violent wind swept over the country and beat the burdened men to the ground; undismayed, savoring its power, they "hoisted a sail in the canoe and [the wind] had driven her along on the truck wheels. this is really sailing on dry land." But their ingenuity could make nothing of the mosquitoes, which were "extreemly troublesome," and the fiendish large black gnat, "which dose not sting, but attacks the eye in swarms and compells us to brush them off or have our eyes filled with them."

While Nature hammered at them with a variety of weapons, she also showed them her "prodegies . . . which she seems to have dealt with a liberal hand." Always there were the vast herds of buffalo ("at least ten thousand at one view"). The men watched the herds press down the steep banks to water at the river's edge; the vanguard, pushed "out of their debth," were instantly swept over the cataracts

"where they are instantly crushed to death without the possibility of escaping. . . . their mangled carcases ly along the shores below the falls in considerable quantities and afford fine amusement for the bears wolves and birds of prey; this may be one reason . . . that the bears are so tenatious of the right of soil in this neighbourhood."

Strange subterranean noises sometimes burst like shots or again rumbled on and on.

"I am at a great loss to account for this Phenomenon. I well recollect hereing the Minitarees say that these Rocky mountains make a great noise, but they could not tell me the cause . . . this phenomenon the philosphy of the engages [French *voyageurs*] readily accounts for; they state it to be the bursting of the rich mines of silver which these mountains contain."

Then there was the Giant Spring that Clark discovered close to one of the four falls:

"this fountain the largest I ever beheld . . . is about 25 yds. from the river . . . the water of this fountain is extreemly transparent and cold; nor is it impregnated with lime or any other extranious matter, but is very pure and pleasent . . . [it] boil up with such force near it's center that it's surface in that part seems even higher than the surrounding earth which is a firm handsom terf of fine green grass."

This spring, one of the largest outside Yellowstone Park, covers about a quarter of an acre in the shape of a fan and throws out the enormous and constant volume of six hundred and eighty cubic feet per second.

Much of Clark's time during this period was spent in making an accurate survey of the intricate, complex staircase by which the Missouri steps from the feet of the shining mountains down to the great central plain. Accompanied by York, Charbonneau, and Sacajawea, he was thus engaged one day (*June 29*) when he saw a threatening black cloud—a cyclone—advancing swiftly over the plain. "I looked for a shelter but could see no place without being blown into the river if the wind should prove as turbulant as it is at some times." The only likely spot near by was

"a Deep riveen in which was shelveing rocks under which we took shelter near the river and placed our guns the compass &c. &c. . . . in a place which was verry secure from the rain, the first rain was moderate accompanied with a violent wind, the effects of which we did not feel, soon after a torrent of rain and hail fell more violent than ever I saw before . . . like one voley of water falling from the heavens and gave us time only to get out of the way of a torrent of water which was Poreing down the hill with emence force . . . tareing every thing before it takeing with it large rocks & mud, I took my gun & shot pouch in my left hand, and with the right scrambled up the hill pushing the interpreters wife (who had her child in her arms) before me, the Interpreter [Charbonneau] himself makeing attempts to pull up his wife by the hand much scared and nearly without motion, we at length reached the top of the hill safe where I found my servant in serch of us greatly agitated for our well-far . . . I scercely got out before [the water] raised 10 feet deep with a torrent which was turrouble to behold, and by the time I reached the top of the hill, at least 15 feet water. I derected the party to return to the camp . . . where Clothes could be got to cover the child whose clothes were all lost, and the woman who was but just recovering from a severe indisposition, and was wet and cold, I was fearfull of a relaps."

At the camp they met the men

"who had returned in great confusion leaveing their loads in the Plain, the hail & wind being so large and violent . . . and them naked, they were much brused, and some nearly killed one knocked down three times, and others without hats or any thing on their heads bloody & complained verry much, I refreshed them with a little grog . . . I lost at the river in the torrent the large *compas*, an elegant fusee, Tomahawk *Humbrallo* [umbrella]. . . . The Compass, is a serious loss, as we have no other large one."

The next day two men sent "in serch" of the compass found it "in the mud & stones near the mouth of the raveen, no other articles found, the place I sheltered under filled up with hugh Rocks." Thus Clark tells the slim margin by which the party escaped destruction from the cloudburst; had the outcome been other than lucky it is certain that, without his friend to share the responsibility and command, Lewis would not have had the heart to continue, while without Sacajawea the expedition could hardly have had dealings with her tribesmen, the Shoshone Indians.

Meanwhile, at Whitebear Island, Lewis was getting his iron boat ready. To cover the frame, thirty-six feet long, four and a half feet wide, and two feet two inches deep, required the skins of twenty-eight elk and four buffalo. The skins had to be properly prepared, fitted to the outline, and sewed together into one piece; a top dressing to seal the seams and make it waterproof was compounded, after much trial and tribulation, out of a mixture of buffalo tallow, beeswax, and charcoal. Dear to his heart was this creation of Lewis's; the men called her "the Experiment and expect she will answer our purpose." But intimations of failure sound long before the complete collapse of his hopes.

For six days (*July 3–9*) Lewis wrestled with his problem:

"our tar-kiln has yealded no tar as yet and I am much affraid my boat will be useless. I fear I have committed another blunder also in sewing the skins with a nedle which has sharp edges these have cut the skin and as it drys I discover that the throng dose not fill the holes as expected . . . I had the boat removed to an open situation, scaffolded her off the ground, turned her keel to the sun and kindled fires under her to dry her more expediciously. . . . The day being warm and fair the boat was sufficiently dry to receive a coat of the composition. this adds much to her appearance whether it will be effectual or not. it gives her hull the appearance of being formed of one solid piece. after the first coat had cooled I gave her a second which I think has made it sufficiently thick . . . we launched the boat; she lay like a perfect cork on the water . . . I now directed seats to be fixed in her and oars to be fitted."

But just as they were ready to leave a storm came up and tied them down, and in a few hours they found that, for one reason or another, the boat would not hold together: "to make further experiments in our present situation seemed to me madness . . . I therefore relinquished all further hope of my favorite boat and ordered her to be sunk in water . . . and I bid adieu to my boat and her expected services."

Replacing the *Experiment* with two dugout canoes hastily fashioned from the only wood they were able to find, they finally (*July 15*) started for the Shoshone country. "We now found our vessels eight in number all heavily laden, notwithstanding our several deposits; tho' it is true we have now a considerable stock of dryed meat and grease." Their first definite awareness that they were already in Shoshone country came the next morning when they passed about forty willow wickiups only recently abandoned:

"we supposed that they were snake Indians. they appeared to have a number of horses with them . . . as we were now anxious to meet with [them] to obtain information relative to the geography of the country and also if necessary, some horses we thought it better for one of us either Capt. C. or myself to take a small party & proceed up the river some distance before the canoes, in order to discover them . . . before the daily discharge of our guns, which was necessary in procuring subsistence for the party, should allarm and cause them to retreat to the mountains and conceal themselves, supposing us to be their enemies who visit them usually by way of this river."

On the meeting with the Shoshone and on the outcome rested the entire fortunes of the expedition.

The tension with which they sought the encounter has the almost unbearable quality of a shrill, prolonged note; expectancy marks every moment of the days, guides every action. From the time they left the Great Falls, each day pitched their nervous hope higher.

Each day brought changes in the scenery, so different from the persistent pattern of the prairies over which they had traveled for long months; now the current was faster, and the river made sharper, shorter twists, through which the canoes stumbled and groped; steep cliffs crowded down to the water and on their perpendicular faces ibex, "Big-horned anamals . . . walked about and bounded from rock to rock with apparent unconcern where it appeared to me that no quadruped could have stood . . . they are perfectly secure from the pursuit of the wolf, bear, or even man himself." The land of the buffalo was behind them, though from bleached bones it appeared that "the buffaloe sometimes struggle into this valley . . . our harvest of white puddings is at an end!" Pine grew sparsely on the mountains, aspen added its loveliness to sumac and red willow, cottonwood and chokecherry; berry bushes laced the trees together—"two species of goosbirris," currants "red yellow perple & black," the last a "really charming fruit" preferable to "any current now cultivated in the U. States"; wild onions and wild flax, along the bottom lands, were mixed with "a luxuriant growth of grass and weeds; among the last the sun-flower holds a distinguished place . . . the Indians of the Missouri particularly those who do not cultivate maze make great uce of the seed of this plant for bread, or use it in thickening their soope. they most commonly first parch the seed and then pound them between two smooth stones untill they reduce it to a fine meal."

Everywhere, constantly, there were signs of the Indians. As Clark was walking on ahead of the canoes to hunt and keep an eye out for the Shoshone (*July 18*), he "passed over a mountain on an Indian rode by which rout I cut off Several Miles of the Meanderings of the river, the roade which passes this mountain is wide and appears to have been dug in maney places." The next day they saw more willow wickiups that had been used during the spring. "Saw where the natives had peeled the bark off the pine trees about the same season. this the indian woman with us informs that they do to obtain the sap and soft part of the wood and bark for food." Nothing, it would seem, that the region offered was dismissed or neglected by the Indians as material for food, clothing, or shelter; a people still living the precarious hand-to-mouth existence of the New World's Stone Age, they had only the horse to lighten their drudgery and to help them extend their meager resources.

Expectancy mounted as day after day, both afloat and afoot, the men pushed forward, looking always for the Shoshone. On the nineteenth the river silently led the canoes through a magnificent somber gorge, a deep romantic chasm that Lewis dramatically named the Gates of the Rocky Mountains. Almost without warning they were enclosed by black granite cliffs that stood up from the river to

"the hight of 1200 feet. every object here wears a dark and gloomy aspect. the towering and projecting rocks in many places seem ready to tumble on us. the river appears to have forced it's way through this immence body of solid rock for the distance of 5 ¾ Miles and where it makes it's exit below has thrown on either side vast collumns of rocks mountains high . . . [the water] is deep from side to side. nor is ther . . . a spot on which a man could rest the soal of his foot."

At the other end "the hills retreated from the river" and the valley widened out. The next morning, some miles up the valley, Lewis saw smoke rising "as if the country had been set on fire." Was it a signal? Was it a signal of Indians, or of Clark and his men? "The first however proved to be the fact, [the Indians] had unperceived by us discovered Capt. Clark's party or mine, and had set the plain on fire to allarm the more distant natives and fled themselves further into the interior of the mountains." To the Shoshone, watching from a safe distance, men who broke into their territory could belong to only one group, Blackfeet —could fit into only one category, enemies; and, seeing the size of the party and judging by past experience, they retreated as fast as Lewis and Clark advanced. This unwelcome game of hide-and-seek must have been maddening to the explorers, and yet the leaders could do nothing to stop the terrified flight. Clark was careful to leave a train of signs and signals—clothes, paper, pieces of linen—"to inform the indians should they pursue his trale that we were not their enemies, but *white men* and their friends." Day after day Clark, his feet torn and blistered, followed the Indian road, driving himself in search of Indians he could never catch up with.

On the twenty-second, Sacajawea recognized the country

"and assures us that this is the river on which her relations live, and that the three forks are at no great distance. this peice of information has cheered the sperits of the party who now begin to console themselves with the anticipation of shortly seeing the head of the missouri yet unknown to the civilized world."

Two days later she pointed out a bold crimson bluff which supplied her people with pigment for paint; and that day Clark spied a horse in the distance and left the trail in the hope of meeting its owner, of standing at last face to face with an elusive Shoshone. "On approaching he found the horse in fine order but so wild he could not get within less than several hundred paces of him. he still saw much indian sign but none of recent date." As shy as the horse were the Shoshone. But complaints were generally confined to

"our trio of pests [that] still invade and obstruct us on all occasions, these are the Musquetoes, eye knats and prickley pear, equal to any three curses that ever poor Egypt laiboured under, except the *Mahometant yoke*. the men complain of being much fateigued. their labour is excessively great."

Despite the many signs, despite Sacajawea's reassurances, they reached the Three Forks without having met any Indians. Clark arrived there first, early on the twenty-fifth.

"those three forks are nearly of a Size, the North fork [Jefferson] appears to have the most water and must be Considered as the one best calculated for us to assend Middle fork [Madison] is quite as large about 90 yds. wide. The South fork [Gallatin] is about 70 yds wide & falls in about 400 yards below the middle fork . . . on the North Side the Indians have latterly Set the Praries on fire, the Cause I can't account for. I saw one horse track going up the river, about four or 5 days past."

Only his terrible eagerness to meet the Shoshone can account for the way Clark drove himself, spending every ounce of strength in pushing forward to make that necessary friendly contact. In a note, left where Lewis would see it, he told of his intention to explore the northern river before the canoes reached the Three Forks. "He ascended this stream about 25 miles and encamped, much fateigued." The next day he went on another twelve miles and then made a wide swing to the middle fork, which he explored on his way back to where Lewis awaited him. He arrived at the rendezvous so exhausted and ill—"a high fever and frequent chills & constant aking pain in all his mustles" —that Lewis ordered him "a doze of Rushes pills, which I have always found sovereign in such cases and to bath his feet in warm water and rest himself."

The illness of his friend, brought on by a desperate effort to find the Indians, and his own clear awareness of how much hinged on this meeting added to Lewis's impatience and worry.

"If we do not find them [the Shoshone] or some other nation who have horses I fear the successfull issue of our voyage will be very doubtfull or at all events much more difficult in it's ac-complishment. we are now several hundred miles within the bosom of this wild and mountanous country . . . without any information with rispect to the country not knowing how far these mountains continue, or wher to direct our course to pass them to advantage or intersept a navigable branch of the Columbia."

This was the critical point in their transcontinental crossing. So far, though the Missouri had been a long and hard path, it had been clear to follow. But where were they to go now? How were they to find the pass that would let them through the mountains? Where should they look for the upper reaches of the Columbia?

Watching his sick, spent friend, Lewis wrote: "I still hope for the best, and intend taking a tramp myself in a few days to find these yellow gentlemen if possible."

5.

August 1805 was the most critical of the twenty-eight months that elapsed between the expedition's leaving St. Louis and its triumphant return.

The events have a dramatic unity; their elements were subordinated to the pervading taut atmosphere. The setting was the high plateau along the continental divide where the waters of the Missouri finally peter out in shallow, rushing, stone-strewn streams, in soggy highlands crisscrossed by beaver dams, in a country so poor in game that sheer physical hunger became an important protagonist. The actors, each motivated by his own needs and fears and hopes, are not only the party of white men united and commanded by Lewis and Clark, but a band of one hundred Shoshone warriors, an atomistic agglomeration in which "every man is a chief." In Cameahwait, the native chief—a formal term applied to an informal recognition of the man "who happens to enjoy the greatest share of confidence of the other members of the community"—Lewis and Clark dealt with a man of dignity, courage, and understanding; he happened also to be Sacajawea's brother.

The camp at Three Forks where the white men rested, waiting for Clark to recover, was, Sacajawea told them,

"precisely on the spot that the Snake Indians were encamped
at the time the Minnetares of the Knife R[iver] first came in
sight of them five years since. from hence they retreated . . .
and concealed themselves in the woods, the Minnetares pursued,
attacked them, killed 4 men 4 women a number of boys, and
made prisoners of all the females and four boys."

It was then that she had been captured, Sacajawea said, recalling how the outnumbered men, to save their precious horses,
galloped away as soon as the attack began. The women and
children had scattered wildly, widely, and she herself, even as
she was running across a ford in the river, was caught and held
by her pursuers. Lewis, unaccustomed to Indian behavior, seems
to have expected the place to unseal her sorrow, but he could not
see "that she shews any immotion of sorrow in recollecting this
event."

On the first of August the two leaders decided to separate.
Lewis, with three men, was to go "in quest of the Snake Indians"
while Clark worked the canoes up the river as far as possible.
Their first week's story, unvarying from day to day, is soon told:

"Capt. Clark continued his rout early this morning . . . shoals
or riffles succeed each other every 3 or four hundred yards;
at those places they are obliged to drag the canoes over the stone
there not being water enough to float them, and betwen the
riffles the current is so strong that they are compelled to have
recourse to the cord; and being unable to walk on the shore
for the brush wade in the river . . . this has increased the pain
and labour extreemly; their feet soon get tender and soar by
wading and walking over the stones. these are so slipry that they
frequently get severe falls. being constantly wet soon makes
them feble also."

All their efforts netted them less than ten miles a day. But
still they followed the Jefferson as it curved and raced; it led
them into lush valleys that were cut off from one another by
rocky outcroppings pierced by dark, narrow gorges. Meanwhile Lewis roamed and ranged on ahead. Near a region that
was one day to be one of the greatest mining camps in the world

—Butte and Anaconda—Lewis discovered a new species of pheasant; walking over this terrain, he did not suspect that one day men would strip off its covering of berry bushes and honeysuckle and roses to get at the gold and silver and copper underground. His burning ambition was not to amass a fortune in precious metals, but to effect a speedy and successful meeting with the Shoshone. In that maze of valleys filled with swampy beaver meadows he crossed and recrossed the river searching the high land on both sides in vain for Indian trails.

On the fourth he came to another fork, where two streams joined the Jefferson, and left a note for Clark urging him to take the middle river, along which he would look for him. The next afternoon when Clark's boat party in turn reached the fork they were at a loss to know how to proceed, for the note "had unfortunately been placed on a green pole which the beaver had cut and carried off together with the note; the possibility of such an occurance never once occurred to me when I placed it on a green pole. this accedent deprived Capt. Clark of any information." Two days later, despite the beaver, the parties were reunited. Together the leaders named the Jefferson's tributaries: "the bold rapid and clear stream *Wisdom,* and the more mild and placid one which flows in from the S. E. *Philanthropy,* in commemoration of those two cardinal virtues, which have so eminently marked that deservedly selibrated character through life"; the former is now known and charted as the Big Hole, the latter as Stinkingwater. Cloudy weather prevented observations being taken on the eighth, but Sacajawea recognized a landmark near where her tribe summered; "this hill her nation calls the beaver's head . . . [and] she assures us that we shall either find her people on this river or on the river immediately west of it's source."

This last information decided Lewis. Clark was suffering from an ugly and painful boil on his ankle that was not "yet matured," and the men were so exhausted "that they wished much that navigation was at an end that they might go by land." He knew that they had gone almost as far as they could by water; the Jefferson was clearly shrinking to its source. It had become imperative that they find the Indians and from them get information and assistance. "In short it is my resolusion to find them or some others, who have horses if it should cause me a trip of one month."

Lewis, with Drouillard and two other men, started out on the ninth to find the Shoshone. On Sacajawea's advice they traced the Jefferson to where it divided into two equal streams; beyond this point navigation was impossible. Here he hopefully left a note—on a dry willow pole—telling Clark "to halt at this place untill my return," and then, swinging to the right, he followed some horse tracks into a rolling watered valley encircled by hills —Shoshone Cove. Soon the horse tracks disappeared.

The eleventh was a fateful day. Heading straight for the pass that led to the "river immediately west," he spread out his small forces so that there was less chance for them to miss any Indian trail. Drouillard paced him on his right, another man on his left; the third man he kept by his side.

"After having marched in this order for about five miles I discovered an Indian on horse back about two miles distant coming down the plain toward us . . . I was overjoyed at the sight of this stranger and had no doubt of obtaining a friendly introduction to his nation provided I could get near enough to him to convince him of our being whitemen."

When they were within a mile of each other the Indian stopped. Lewis stopped. Using the widespread sign-language symbol for friendship, he raised his blanket, threw it over his head, and spread it on the ground. This he did three times, as if "spreading a robe or skin for ther gests to set on when they are visited." But the Indian's suspicious eyes saw not the invitation in Lewis's gesture but the menace of the two scouts, who continued to advance. If only they would halt! Lewis dared not call out to them lest his shouts feed the Indian's fears; he could only try to counteract their frightening behavior by leaving his gun and pouch behind and advancing unarmed, proffering beads and other trinkets as proof of his peaceful intentions. When he was near enough for his voice to carry, he called out the words Sacajawea had taught him, "*tab-ba-bone*, which in their language signifyes *white-man*." But the Indian had eyes only for the scouts, "neither of them haveing segacity enough to recollect the impropriety of advancing when they saw me

thus in parley with the Indian." He risked making the signal
to halt; Drouillard obeyed, but the other man, failing to see
the command, kept on. Again, and in an effort to nullify that
threat, Lewis "repepeated the word tab-ba-bone and held up
the trinkits and striped up my shirt sleve to give him an opportunity of seeing the colour of my skin and advanced leasurely
towards him."

Not words nor baubles nor the sight of pale flesh could still
the terror and fears of the horseman.

"He suddonly turned his horse about, gave him the whip leaped
the creek and disapeared in the willow brush in an instant and
with him vanished all my hopes of obtaining horses for the
preasant. I now felt quite as much mortification and disappointment as I had pleasure and expectation at the first sight of this
indian."

Especially toward the scout who had endangered his parley,
Lewis "felt soarly chargrined . . . and could not forbare abraid-
ing" him; but his greatest fear was that the Indian would warn
the whole tribe and that they would quickly scatter. The horse's
tracks led toward some high hills from which the Shoshone
could keep a lookout for intruders. More than ever it was imperative now that they do nothing to alarm the tribe. "After
meeting with the Indian today I fixed a small flag of the U'.S. to
a pole," which he had one of the men carry.

Early the next morning they continued looking for Indians.

"The road took us to the most distant fountain of the waters
of the Mighty Missouri in surch of which we had spent so many
toilsome days and wristless nights. thus far I had accomplished
one of those great objects on which my mind has been unal-
terably fixed for many years, judge then of the pleasure I felt
in allaying my thirst with this pure and ice-cold water which
issues from the base of a low mountain. . . . two miles below
McNeal [the standard-bearer] had exultingly stood with a foot
on each side of this little rivulet and thanked his god that he had
lived to bestride the mighty & heretofore deemed endless Missouri. after refreshing ourselves we proceeded on to the top
of the dividing ridge from which I discovered immence ranges

of high mountains still to the West of us with their tops partially covered with snow. I now decended the mountain . . . to a handsome bold runing Creek of cold Clear water. here I first tasted the water of the great Columbia river."

The Indian road had led them to the Lemhi Pass, and that night they camped beyond the Missouri drainage basin, beyond the farthest limit of the vast Louisiana Territory. The twelfth of August had been a most momentous day—but their need to make contact with the Shoshone was greater, not less, than it had been.

Very early the next morning they walked along the Indian road, and had gone only four miles when about a mile away they "saw two women, a man and some dogs." This time Lewis took no chances, but alone, unarmed, carrying the flag and holding an assortment of trinkets, he walked unhurriedly towards the little party.

"I now haistened to the top of the hill where they had stood but could see nothing of them. the dogs were less shye than their masters [and] I thought of tying a handkerchief about one of their necks with some beads and other trinkets and then let them loose to surch their fugitive owners thinking by this means to convince them of our pacific disposition towards them but the dogs would not suffer me to take hold of them; they also soon disappeared."

A second attempt, a second desperate wooing of a strange tribe, a second effort to bridge the ever-diminishing distance that separated the two races—a second failure.

And then, that same afternoon, they unexpectedly surprised "three female savages. the short and steep ravines which we passed concealed us from each other untill we arrived within 30 paces. a young woman immediately took to flight, an Elderly woman and a girl of about 12 years old remained." At last, at last, Lewis was able to throw down his gun and actually touch—make physical contact with—a person belonging to the tribe they had sought so long, so ardently. The scene is reminiscent of Mackenzie's resolute and awkward self-introduction to the

panic-stricken women in the house along his westward trail.
Like them, these women too felt caught and doomed and

"seated themselves on the ground, holding down their heads as
if reconciled to die . . . I took the elderly woman by the hand
and raised her up repeated the word *tab-ba-bone* and striped up
my shirt sleve to shew her my skin [his face and hands the sun
and wind had made quite as dark as an Indian's]; . . . they appeared instantly reconciled, and the men coming up I gave these
women some beads a few mockerson awls some pewter looking-
glasses and a little paint."

Through Drouillard he told the old woman to recall the
younger one who had fled, lest she alarm the camp; when,
breathless, she returned he gave her presents.

"I now painted their tawny cheeks with some vermillion which
with this nation is emblematic of peace. after they had become
composed I enformed them by signs that I wished them to
conduct us to their camp that we wer anxious to become acquainted with the chiefs and warriors of their nation. they
readily obeyed and we set out, still pursuing the road down
the river."

A satisfaction as profound as that of tasting in quick succession
the waters of the Missouri and the Columbia filled Lewis as he
followed his guides to their camp.

How could he parley with people whose language he did not
speak? Sacajawea was far away with the rest of the party. On
his negotiations depended the fate of their mission. Happily the
language barrier was not insurmountable; the Plains Indians had
perfected a system of signs by which tribes with different languages and even fundamentally different concepts of language
were able to converse. This was the means Lewis used, for
Drouillard, "who understood perfectly the common language
of jesticulation or signs which seems to be universally understood
by all the Nations," stood at his side. "It is true that this language
is imperfect and liable to error but is much less so than would
be expected. the strong parts of the ideas are seldom mistaken."

The precision and explicitness of such communication explains the remarkable conversations that followed.

"We had marched about 2 miles when we met a party of about 60 warriors mounted on excellent horses who came in nearly full speed . . . I advanced towards them with the flag leaving my gun with the party about 50 paces behind me. the chief and two others who were a little in advance of the main body spoke to the women, and they informed them who we were and exultingly shewed the presents which had been given them these men then advanced and embraced me very affectionately in their way which is by puting their left arm over your wright sholder clasping your back, while they apply their left cheek to yours and frequently vociforate . . . I am much pleased, I am much rejoiced. bothe parties now advanced and we wer all carresed and besmeared with their grease and paint till I was heartily tired of the national hug. I now had the pipe lit and gave them smoke . . . after smoking a few pipes with them I distributed some trifles. . . . I now informed the chief that the object of our visit was a friendly one . . . I gave him the flag which I informed him was an emblem of peace among whitemen."

With excitement and pleasure on both sides and with the flag flying, Lewis and his party were led by Cameahwait to the Indians' encampment, where a willow wickiup had been specially prepared for them by men sent on ahead.

Shoshone honors were showered on the white men. Seated on green boughs and antelope skins, they were welcomed by the tribe in an impressive ceremonial smoke.

"After the cerimony of the pipe was over I distributed the remainder of the small articles I had brought with me among the women and children. by this time it was late in the evening and we had not taisted any food since the evening before. the Chief informed us that they had nothing but berries to eat and gave us some cakes of serviceberries and Choke cherries which had been dryed in the sun; of these I made a hearty meal."

The hospitality and the generosity of these people who had "nothing but berries to eat" and whom hunger was forcing out onto the open plains to hunt buffalo—always at the peril of death from deadly war parties—was most touchingly expressed when later that evening

"an indian called me into his bower and gave me a small morsel of the flesh of an antelope boiled, and a peice of fresh salmon roasted; both which I eat with a very good relish. this was the first salmon I had seen and perfectly convinced me that we were on the waters of the Pacific Ocean."

The Shoshone, whom the leaders found so open-handed with what little food they had, who were gay and pleasant and poor and dirty, whose chief Cameahwait was "a man of Influence, Sence & easey & reserved manners, [and] appears to possess a great deel of Cincerity," were not stout and proud like the Sioux, nor lean and fierce like the Blackfeet. "These people are deminutive in stature, thick ankles, crooked legs, thick flat feet and in short but illy formed, at least much more so than any of the nation of Indians I ever saw." Unprepossessing they were, but they are notable in the long list of native tribes for their qualities of heart and understanding.

It had been a long, an eventful, a most successful day. Lewis fell asleep to the sound of singing and dancing. "I was several times awoke in the course of the night by their yells but was too much fatiegued to be deprived of a tolerable sound night's repose."

The account of the next three days (*August 14–17*) reads like a fever chart with its mounting hope and chilling worries; it flouts the precise division of hours, now dragging, now rushing. He had found the Shoshone; now to hold them. His problem was simple: to get them to accompany him the forty miles over the divide to the fork of the Jefferson where he had left a note bidding Clark await him; and to secure horses from them with which to transport the baggage. He had to do this in the face of their need for food, their capriciousness, their latent distrust of all strangers. His immediate plans were to allow enough time for Clark to reach the fork and in the meantime to secure food, "as we had nothing but a little flour and parched meal to eat except the berries which the Indians furnished us." His hunters went out and came back with nothing; the young warriors went hunt-

ing and also returned empty-handed. "Notwithstanding the ex-
treem poverty of these poor people they are very merry they
danced again this evening untill midnight." The amazing bounty
of the plains was behind, and henceforward hunger, the unin-
vited guest, was with them.

"This morning [the fifteenth] I arrose very early and as hungary
as a wolf. I had eat nothing yesterday but one scant meal of the
flour and berries except the dryed cakes of berries which did not
appear to satisfy my appetite as they appeared to do those of my
Indian friends . . . we had only about two pounds of flour remaining. this I directed [McNeal] to divide into two equal parts
and to cook the one half this morning in a kind of pudding with
the burries as he had done yesterday and reserve the ballance
for the evening. on this new fashioned pudding four of us
breakfasted, giving a pretty good allowance also, to the
Chief who declared it the best thing he had taisted for a
long time."

Soon it was time for the Indians to start with him for Shoshone Cove. "The Chief addressed them several times before
they would move they seemed very reluctant to accompany
me." Lewis finally learned that their unwillingness sprang from
a rumor that the white men were in league with their enemies
and had been sent as decoys to lead them into ambush. Answering their fears and quivering doubts, he pleaded and argued, he
baited their hopes with the promise of trade goods, and shamed
them, questioning their pride and courage. It was the slurs he
cast on their bravery that finally turned the argument. Cameahwait showed that he did not fear death;

"he now mounted his horse and haranged his village a third time
. . . and was joined by six or eight only and with these I smoked
a pipe . . . being determined to set out with them while I had
them in the humour. several of the old women were crying and
imploring the great sperit to protect their warriors as if they
were going to inevitable distruction. we had not proceeded far
before our party was augmented by ten or twelve more, and before we reached the Creek . . . it appeared to me that we had
all the men of the village and a number of the women with us.

this may serve in some measure to ilustrate the capricious disposition of those people, who never act but from the impulse of
the moment. they were now very cheerfull and gay, and two
hours ago they looked as sirly as so many imps of satturn."

Late that afternoon they reached the upper level of Shoshone
Cove, where they camped. Drouillard, the expert and successful
hunter, who had been sent out to get some meat, joined them
after dark; he had nothing for them. "I now cooked and divided
among six of us the remaining pound of flour stired in a little
boiling water."

So far Lewis's task had been comparatively easy; the next day
was more difficult. Clark's heartbreakingly slow advance, the
best he could do, threatened to wreck Lewis's attempts to hold
the Shoshone to his purpose. Luckily, in Cameahwait he had
found a man of authority who responded to his imperative mood,
who was convinced of the validity and urgency of the story
told by the stranger. Tenaciously, desperately, Lewis held them
to his will, using every device to gain his end and still their suspicions and fears. Drouillard at last had luck in securing game, and
the Indians raced to the spot and "like a parcel of famished dogs"
devoured the "intestens" which Drouillard had thrown away.
Of the three deer killed, Lewis kept only a little and gave the rest
to the natives, "who eat the whole of them even to the soft parts
of the hoof." He and his men changed clothes with the Indians
so that by no outward mark could their friends differentiate
between them. He gladly let an Indian carry their flag. As they
set out for the Jefferson, Lewis again repeated

"the possibility of the party not having arrived at the place . . .
lest by not finding them at the forks their suspicions might arrise
to such hight as to induce them to return precipitately . . .
when we arrived in sight I discovered to my mortification that
the party had not arrived, and the Indians slackened their pace.
I now scarcely new what to do and feared every moment when
they would halt altogether, I now determined to restore their
confidence cost what it might and therefore gave the Chief my
gun and told him that if his enimies were in those bushes before
him . . . if I deceived him he might make what uce of the gun
he thought proper or in other words that he might shoot me.

the men also gave their guns to other indians which seemed to inspire them with more confidence."

Finally Lewis "had recource to a stratagem." Knowing that his note was still where he had left it, he sent Drouillard with an Indian—who was to witness his taking the note—to fetch it. Using his own note, he told Cameahwait that it had been left by his "brother Chief" to inform him "that he was just below the mountains and was coming on slowly up, and added that I should wait for him." To give credibility to this ruse, Lewis suggested that he would send one of his men, accompanied by a warrior, who was induced to go by the promise of a knife and some beads, to meet the canoes while he stayed behind with the main party. He wrote a note stating his predicament and told Drouillard to be ready to set out early, "being confident that there was not a moment to spare." Racking his brains for other ways to detain the Indians, Lewis told Cameahwait that in the canoe party was "a woman of his nation who had been taken prisoner by the Minnetares, and that by means of her I hoped to explain myself more fully that I could do by signs," Drouillard told them that they would see a "man who was black and had short curling hair, this had excited their curiossity very much. and they seemed quite as anxious to see this monster as they were the merchandize which we had to barter for their horses." As Lewis lay down by his fire to sleep, he saw that only Cameahwait and five or six others were brave enough to do the same; all the others hid themselves, still fearful of an ambush.

"I slept but little as might well be expected . . . my mind was in reallity quite gloomy." He knew that if the Indians left him they would hide and never reappear, they would warn the other bands; and the alarm thus spread would prevent his obtaining horses, "which would vastly retard and increase the labour of our voyage and I feared might so discourage the men as to defeat the expedition altogether." Before the next day's light appeared he dispatched Drouillard and the Indian down the river.

As Lewis and Cameahwait were having a light breakfast on Saturday, the seventeenth of August, "an Indian who had straggled some little distance down the river returned and reported that the whitemen were coming." Thus sweetly and happily the long tension was spent. Everyone was "transported with joy, &

the chief repeated his fraternal hug." In this rapturous release can be seen a little of what Cameahwait on his side must have suffered: he had forgotten almost his traditions and his race in responding to and believing in this white stranger; the conflicts within him must have been strong, his isolation as an intermediary between two races acute.

That same morning Clark, with Charbonneau and Sacajawea, was walking on ahead of the canoes. They had not gone far when Clark saw several Indians on horseback. At their appearance Sacajawea suddenly began to dance "for the joyful sight," and by sucking her fingers made him understand that these men were of her band. One of the men was Drouillard, who delivered the note. Clark and the Indians hurried forward, light of heart and foot, and "those Indians sung all the way to their Camp where . . . the Three Chiefs with Capt. Lewis met me with great cordiallity." As Sacajawea joined the main group a woman ran toward her, recognized her, and hugged her. They had been friends from childhood and had been taken prisoner together; where Sacajawea had gone forward to slavery and exile, the other had escaped, found her way back to her people, and thought of her friend as one dead. And now Sacajawea stood before her, alive, honored, with a man-child strapped to her back. For both it was a wonderful and precious moment. By noon the canoes arrived, and Lewis's worries vanished as he beheld the two groups mingling joyously. Never had the prospects of the expedition looked more hopeful.

The canoes were unloaded, the baggage arranged, and gradually the excitement abated. Sacajawea had been restored to her friends, the Indians had gazed on the undreamt-of sight of a man perfectly black; no longer did fear of ambush becloud the blue sky. Under a canopy made by one of the large sails, Lewis and Clark addressed the assembled warriors. When they sent for Sacajawea, she came, glad to be able to speak more fully, sat down, and was beginning to interpret when she recognized Cameahwait as her brother. She jumped up and ran and embraced him, throwing her blanket over him, and wept profusely. The chief himself was moved, though trained not to show such womanish feelings. After some conversation between them she resumed her seat and attempted to interpret; but her new situation seemed to overpower her, and she was frequently interrupted by her tears. In this atmosphere charged with emotion, Lewis stated the object of their mission, the power and goodwill of the new father in Washington, the Shoshone's favorably critical position in transcontinental trade (which he took pains to point out could only start flowing after the expedition had safely returned), and the white men's urgent need to buy horses. Cameahwait replied that "they had not horses enough with them at present to remove our baggage to their village over the mountain, but that he would return tomorrow and encourage his people to come over with their horses and that he would bring his own and assist us." Presents were given, more speeches made, food distributed, and the council broke up.

The two leaders decided that when the Indians returned to their camp, Charbonneau and Sacajawea should accompany them to "haisten the return of the Indians with their horses to this place." Clark, now fully recovered from his assorted ills, would go with them and would take eleven men furnished with axes and other tools for making canoes, "in order to examine the river and if he found it navigable and could obtain timber to set about making canoes immediately." Lewis was to remain behind and get everything ready for their overland ride: air, sort, and repack their baggage into "proper parsels," cache all heavy equipment, sink the canoes in the river, where they would be safe from theft, flood, and fire against their return; out of oar blades and rawhide thongs he would improvise sturdy pack-saddles. The seventeenth of August had been a wonderful and fruitful day, as Lewis soberly reflected: "The sperits of the men were now much elated at the prospect of geting horses." Clark, delighted with Sacajawea's band, noted that "those people are not begerley but generous, only one has asked me for anything and he for powder." From such people anyone could be proud to accept assistance.

In some respects the expedition reached the Shoshone at a most inopportune time. The calendar of their yearly movements was closely governed by their constant search for food.

"From the middle of May to the first of September these people reside on the waters of the Columbia [the Lemhi and the Salmon that eventually find their way to the Columbia] where they consider themselves in perfect security from their enimies . . . during this season the salmon furnish the principal part of their subsistence and as this fish either perishes or returns about the 1st of September they are compelled at this season in surch of subsistence to resort to the Missouri . . . here they move slowly down the river in order to collect and join other bands either of their own nation or the Flatheads, and having become sufficiently strong venture on the Eastern side of the Rockey mountains into the plains, where the buffaloe abound. but they never leave the interior of the mountains while they can obtain a scanty subsistence, and always return as soon as they have acquired a good stock of dryed meat in the plains; when this stock is consumed they venture again into the plains; thus alternately obtaining their food at the risk of their lives and retiring to the mountains, while they consume it."

This seasonal ebb and flow, this hunger, this perilous need for food, was moving them eastward just when Lewis and Clark wanted to be guided to the west.

Though the days were still very warm, the last of August hinted at approaching cold weather: "This morning was very cold. the ice ¼ of an inch thick on the water which stood in the vessels exposed to the air. some wet deerskins . . . are stiffly frozen. the ink friezes in my pen." On the twenty-second, Cameahwait, Charbonneau, and Sacajawea, leading about fifty warriors and many women and children, reached Lewis's camp by the Jefferson. Lewis's men had worked hard to have everything in readiness for the overland journey. To keep the Indians' enthusiasm high, Lewis made more speeches and gave more presents. "I gave him [Cameahwait] a few dryed squashes which we had brought from the Mandans he had them boiled and declared them to be the best thing he had ever tasted except sugar, a small lump of which it seems his sister [Sacajawea] had given him." Lewis concentrated on buying horses. A few days before he had purchased three for which he had paid "an uniform coat, a pair of legings, a few handkerchiefs, three knives and some other small articles which did not cost more than about 20 $ in the U' States"; but now they did not want to sell any until "we had reach their camp beyond the mountains." The next day another party arrived on their way to the river. Lewis noticed that "there was a good deal of anxiety on the part of those who had promised to assist me over the mountains to accompany this party. I felt some uneasiness on this subject but as they still said they would return with me as they had promised, I said nothing to them." Three more horses and a mule raised his total of pack animals to ten, and by hiring two more he felt ready to leave the river for the mountains.

On the twenty-fourth, the horses were loaded, "the Indian women took the ballance of the baggage," and the trip to the Shoshone camp started. He now had the "inexpressible satisfaction to find myself once more under way with all my baggage and party," and he was soon aware that it would require many more horses to transport them "along such roads as I expect we shall be obliged to pass in the mountains."

A week had passed since the two groups had met and saluted each other, a whole week in which game had been scarce, seven empty-bellied days that were forcing the Indians eastward to the plenty of the plains, seven preparatory days in which the expedition readied itself for its westward trek. The conflict in needs and directions had been overlaid by the first great joy, but time and the pressing pangs of hunger brought it into the open. Sacajawea first learned of the danger to the expedition. Again her motives are not known, only the action that seals her allegiance not to the people of her blood, but to the strangers by whom she had been treated with dignity and kindness. Had not Lewis only yesterday given Charbonneau articles with which to purchase a horse for her, so that she rode as might an honored chief? Had not Clark, when all were tired and ill-humored from the long struggle up the Jefferson, threatened Charbonneau if ever he beat her again? The reasons for her loyalty to the Americans are not known, but because it possessed and animated her, she warned Charbonneau of the Indians' plans, which, born of necessity, appeared to the expedition as deceit.

Charbonneau had not the wit to understand the seriousness of the threat and later mentioned to Lewis

"with apparent unconcern that he expected to meet all the Indians from the camp . . . on their way to the Missouri. allarmed at this information I asked him why he expected to meet them. he then informed me that the 1st Cheif [Cameahwait] had dispatched some of his young men this morning to this camp requesting the Indians to meet them tomorrow and that himself and those with him would go on with them down the Missouri."

Lewis instantly understood that he and his baggage would be stranded on the mountain. "I was out of patience with the folly of Charbono . . . I saw that there was no time to be lost in having those orders countermanded." He called a council and after a ceremonial smoke reminded the warriors of their promises to help, of his liberality with food and presents, and of the great advantages that would come to them as friends of the white man. At length his arguments and pleading prevailed; the orders were canceled, and a young man was sent to the camp "to whom we gave a handkerchief in order to insure dispatch and fidelity." On the twenty-sixth, Lewis, reassured, resumed the march to the mountain camp. Always alert, he noticed that one of the Indian women who had been helping with the baggage dropped behind the party and sent on the two pack horses she had been leading with one of her

"female friends. I enquired of Cameahwait the cause of her detention, and was informed by him in an unconcerned manner that she had halted to bring fourth a child and would soon overtake us; in about an hour the woman arrived with her new-born babe and passed us on her way to the camp apparently as well as she ever was."

That afternoon they reached the camp, where Lewis found a note from Clark.

For several days Clark and his men had been sampling the country into which they had come and out of which the men and horses and baggage would have to make their way to reach the Columbia and the Pacific. On his arrival with the Indians at their camp on the twentieth of August, Cameahwait introduced him to an old man "well acquainted with the country to the North of this river," who told him that the river did join the Columbia, but that as a route it was useless. Clark spent a few days in checking the Indian's information. The Salmon flowed through the Sawtooth Mountains, an incredible region.

"Rocks were So sharp large and unsettled and the hill sides [so] Steep that the horses could with the greatest risque and dificulty get on. . . . the passage of [the river] with Canoes is entirely impossible, as the water is Confined between huge Rocks & the Current beeting from one [side] against another for Some distance. . . . below my guide and maney other Indians tell me that the Mountains Close [in, and there] is a perpendicular Clift on each Side, and Continues for a great distance and that the water runs with great violence from one rock to the other on each Side foaming and roreing thro rocks in every direction, So as to render the passage of any thing impossible. those rapids which I had Seen he said were Small & trifleing in comparrison to the rocks and rapids below, & The Hills or mountains were not like those I had Seen but like the Side of a tree Streight up."

Clark's note told that he was "perfictly satisfyed as to the impracticability of this rout either by land or water, and informed the old man, that he was convinced of the varacity of his assertions."

Clark was disappointed but not discouraged. There must be some way that would lead them to the Columbia, and that way he was determined to discover. A close questioning of Cameahwait revealed nothing. An old man told him of an overland road that connected with the Colorado and led to the "gulph of Callifornia," a road described as of such horrors that it was obviously no possible future path for commerce, even if they had wanted to go south instead of north to the Columbia. Unsatisfied but still determined, Clark again questioned Cameahwait, "his ferce eyes and lank jaws grown meager for the want of food," as to how their friends the Nez Percé, who lived below the mountains, joined the Shoshone on the Missouri. By his shrewd questions he forced the reluctant chief at last to mention a road

"to the north, but [he] added that the road was a very bad one as he had been informed by them and that they had suffered excessively with hunger being obliged to subsist for many days on berries alone as there was no game in that part of the mountains which were broken, rockey and so thickly covered with timber that they could scarcely pass. . . . My rout was instantly settled in my own mind. I felt perfectly satisfyed, that if the Indians could pass these mountains with their women and Children, that we could also pass them; and that if the nations on this river below the mountains were as numerous as they were stated to be that they must have some means of subsistence which it would be equally in our power to procure in the same country. . . . In this manner I spent the day smoking with them and acquiring what information I could with respect to their country."

Patiently, perseveringly, Clark had found the road; he had also hired an old Shoshone "who was better informed than any of them" as their guide. August was drawing to an end, and with it, as the Indians had warned, any hope of finding food in the mountains. Berries and a few salmon, which they kindly shared with their white friends, made "pleasant eateing" even though, as Clark found, it "weakened me verry fast and I find my flesh declineing." On the eve of their departure Lewis "directed the fiddle to be played and the party danced very merily, much to the amusement and gratification of the natives."

Parting speeches were made, the last bright gifts given. The expedition turned westward toward the mountains where hunger held sovereignty; the Indians started for the Missouri and the plenty of the plains. Farewell Cameahwait! Farewell Shoshone! Only later when Lewis and Clark had completed their crossing of the continent and met and dealt with dozens of tribes would they appreciate how rare and how essential to their success had been the unselfish, happy assistance given by these poor people who opened the door to the western coast. Sacajawea had good reason to hold her head high with pride for her tribesmen. The two human streams started moving, one west, the other east. They did not meet again.

6.

The Lolo Trail

If August 1805 was the most critical month, surely September was the hardest. The anxiety that had preceded their meeting with the Shoshone had been dispelled; they did not now need to woo friends delicately to obtain horses and information, but had to meet the simple immediate problem of staying alive. As Saca-

jawea had been their mainstay before, now it was her old kins-
man—the men called him Toby—who guided them, reassured
them, and finally delivered them alive, though half-starved, to
the region inhabited by the Nez Percé.

Their party had been augmented not only by Toby, but also
by one of his sons. As they started from the Shoshone camp, they
saw that the valleys had been set on fire "for the purpose of Collecting the different bands."

Lewis and Clark had few provisions left, and they knew that
they would find very little in the mountains they had to cross;
they imagined that they would follow a trail—the very same that
the Indians used—but the trail was a direction rather than a road,
and it pointed across the mountains to the Bitter Root valley,
down the valley, over the Lolo Pass, and across more mountains
to the valley of the Clearwater. Their route, with its backtrack-
ings and needless detours, its lost wanderings and its eventual
happy ending, was traced a hundred years later by Olin D.
Wheeler; it is enough to know that they did get through to a
river leading to the Columbia, enough to share a little in their experiences over those trying, bitter miles. When the expedition
left the canoes and rode from the Jefferson to the Shoshone
camp, they crossed the divide at the Lemhi Pass. Unlike Balboa
and Mackenzie, who climbed to the continental divide, crossed
it, and raced down the western slope to the Pacific, Lewis and
Clark in their journey to and from the Pacific crossed the western
mountains seven times at six different places, twice using the
same pass.

The entries in the journals for this period are variations on the
themes of hunger and hardship. Immediately a terrible terrain
closed about them.

"In the after part of the day the high mountains closed the Creek
on each Side and obliged us to take on the Steep Sides of those
Mountains, So steep that the horses Could Scurcelly keep from
Slipping down, Several sliped & Injured themselves verry much
. . . but little to eate I killed five Pheasents & the hunters 4 with
a little Corn afforded us a kind of Supper, at dusk it began to
Snow, at three oClock Some rain."

Surely they must have dreamed of the great game that was
always at hand when they were on the plains, a whole buffalo

consumed every twenty-four hours. A few days of climbing and
cold, and they came down a "verry Steep decent" to a wide
valley (*September 4*) where they found the "Tushepau nation,
of 33 Lodges about 80 men 400 Total and at least 500 horses
. . . we Encamped with them & found them friendly but nothing but berries to eate a part of which they gave us." They had
crossed from the waters of the Salmon to those of the Bitter
Root; they had had a taste of what they might expect on the
still longer, still hungrier trail that led from the Bitter Root
valley to that of the distant Clearwater.

The next day they held a council with the Indians and

"Spoke to them with much difcuelty as what we Said had to
pass through Several languages before it got into theirs, which is
a gugling kind of language Spoken much thro the throught. . . .
in the Course of the day I purchased 11 horses & exchanged 7
. . . those people possess ellegant horses."

On the sixth they bought two more horses, "took a Vocabelary
of the language, litened our loads & packed up." In Pvt. Joseph
Whitehouse's diary is the explanation that "Capt. Lewis took
down the names of everry thing in their Language, in order that
it may be found out whether they are or whether they Sprang
or origenated first from the Welch or not." They had about
forty horses and three colts, enough for their needs; they were
ready to start down the long, narrow valley, "which is pore
Stoney land," following a winding creek. This extensive valley
had been at one time a lake and under its surface of gravel and
boulders had such fertile soil that it became one of the most
productive and highly cultivated parts of Montana, covered
with rich orchards. Still following the "handsome stream," they
were amazed to learn from their guides that its headwaters
were

"in the mountains near the Missouri to the East of us and passed
through . . . a generally open prarie which forms an excellent
pass to the Missouri. the point of the Missouri where this Indian
pass intersects it, is about 30 miles above the *gates of the rocky
Mountain,* or the place where the valley of the Missouri first
widens into an extensive plain after entering the rockey moun-

tains. the guide informed us that a man might pass to the missouri from hence by that rout in four days."

This information was something the leaders would remember for the homeward trail. They called the stream Traveller's Rest Creek.

Before them lay rugged, ragged hills, steep, unfriendly mountains separated by narrow canyons littered with rocks and brush: beyond lay the Columbia.

The ten days from the twelfth to the twenty-second of September were desperate. The entries are sparse and factual.

"*12 September:* a white frost . . . The road through this hilley Countrey is verry bad passing over hills & thio' Steep hollows, over falling [fallen] timber &c. &c. . . . the Indians have pealed a number of Pine for the under bark which they eate at certain Seasons of the year . . . our hunters Killed only one Pheasent. *13 September:* Capt. Lewis and one of our guides lost their horses, Capt. Lewis & 4 men detained to hunt the horses . . . passed Several Springs . . . I tasted this water and found it hot & not bad tasted. in further examonation [of another spring] I found the water nearly boiling hot at the places it Sprouted from the rocks . . . the mountains Closed on either Side crossing the Creek Several times & Encamped. One Deer & Some Pheasants killed this morning. The road over the last mountain was thick Steep & Stoney as usial. *14 September:* a cloudy day in the Valies it rained and hailed, on the top of the mountains Some Snow fell . . . we Crossed at a place where the *Tushepaws* or Flat head Indians have made *2 Wears* [weirs] across to Catch Sammon and have but latterly left the place I could see no fish, and the grass entirely eaten out by the horses. . . . Encamped opposit a Small Island . . . here We were compelled to kill a colt for our men & Selves to eat for the want of meat. . . . The Mountains which we passed to day much worst than yesterday . . . 9 miles over a high mountain steep & almost inaxcessible much falling timber which fatigues our men & horses exceedingly . . . all wet and cold."

At Colt-Killed Creek, as they called it, the party somehow left the trail and wandered without even that slight aid to help them.

The fourteenth and fifteenth were spent marching up the hill and then marching down again. On the sixteenth they finally corrected their blunder.

"*15 September:* We set out early, the Morning Cloudy . . . the road leaves the river and assends a *mountain* winding in every direction . . . 4 miles up the mountain I found a Spring and halted for the rear to come up and to let our horses rest & feed. . . . Several horses Sliped and roled down Steep hills which hurt them verry much the one which Carried my desk & Small trunk Turned over & roled down a mountain for 40 yards & lodged against a tree, broke the Desk the horse escaped and appeared but little hurt. Some others verry much hurt. . . . Two of our horses gave out, pore and too much hurt to proceed on and left in the rear. nothing killed to day except 2 Phests . . . we camped on a high Pinical of the mountain near a Bank of old Snow . . . we melted the Snow to drink, and cook our horse flesh to eat."

"*16 September:* began to Snow about 3 hours before Day and continued all day the Snow in the morning 4 inches deep on the old Snow, and by night we found it from 6 to 8 inches deep. I walked in front to keep the road and found great difcuelty in keeping it as in maney places the Snow had entirely filled up the track. . . . The Knobs Steep hill Sides & falling timber Continue to day, and a thickly timbered Countrey of 8 different kinds of pine, which are so covered with Snow, that in passing thro' them we are continually covered with Snow, I have been wet and as cold in every part as I ever was in my life, indeed I was at one time fearfull my feet would freeze in the thin Mockirsons which I wore . . . we Encamped at this Branch . . . which was scurcely large enough for us to lie leavil, men all wet cold and hungary. Killed a Second Colt which we all Suped hartily on and thought it fine meat . . . this day would be a repitition of yesterday except the Snow which made it much worse."

The seventeenth indeed, was a repetition, even to the snow and the colt killed for food.

"*18 September:* a fair morning cold. I [Clark] proceeded on in advance with Six hunters (*and let it be understood that my object was*) to try and find deer or Something to kill (*& send back to the party*). (*The want of provisions together with the dificulty of passing those emence mountains dampened the sperits of the party which induced us* [the leaders] *to resort to Some plan of reviving ther sperits. I deturmined to take a party of hunters and proceed on in advance to Some leavel Country, where there was game Kill Some meat & send it back.*) we passed over a countrey Similar to the one of yesterday . . . made 32 miles and Encamped on a bold running Creek which I call *Hungery* Creek as at that place we had nothing to eate."

"*19 September* [Clark]: Set out early proceeded on up the Creek passing through a Small glade at which place we found a horse. I derected him killed and hung up for the party after takeing a brackfast off for our Selves which we thought fine . . . nearly 22 miles on a Direct Course & at double the distance winding around falling timber . . . (*as we decend the mountain the heat becomes more proseptable* every mile)."

"*20 September* [Clark]: I set out early and proceeded on through a Countrey as ruged as usial . . . passed the head of several dreans of a divideing ridge, and decended the mountain to a leavel pine Countrey . . . a Small Plain in which I found maney Indian lodges, at the distance of 1 mile from the lodges, I met 3 (*Indian*) boys, when they saw me [they] ran and hid themselves (*in the grass. I desmounted gave my gun and horse to one of the men,*) serched (*in the grass,*) found (*2 of the boys,*) gave them Small pieces of ribin & sent them forward to the village. (*Soon after*) a man Came out to meet me, (*with great caution*) & Conducted me to a Large Spacious Lodge . . . those people gave us a Small piece of Baffalow meat, Some dried Salmon beries & roots. . . . They call themselves *Cho pun-nish* or *Pierced noses.* Their diolect appears verry different from the flat heads [Tushapaws], altho origineally the Same people. . . . I find myself verry unwell all the evening from eateing the fish & roots too freely. Sent hunters out they killed nothing."

Clark and the hunters had found their way through the mountains, and as they straggled down from the snow and bitter cold they closed the last link in their great crossing. The roots Clark had eaten were called kamas, quamash, or camas—the bulbous root of a liliaceous plant. They "grow much like an onion in marshey places; those people have an emence quantities of Roots which is their Principal food. those roots are like onions, sweet when Dried, and tolerably good [when made up into] bread."

The Chopunnish were an outpost of the Nez Percé, a tribe that was spread westward from the Bitter Root Mountains to the lower Columbia and its tributaries. Clark's immediate tasks were to establish friendly contacts with these people and to get some food back to the main party. He was told that the chief and all the men had set out three days before "to war . . . & would return in 15 or 18 days. the fiew men that were left in the Village and great numbers of women geathered around me with much apparent signs of fear . . . I gave them a fiew Small articles as preasents, and proceeded on with a Chief to his Village 2 miles in the Same Plain." The same integrated village-clusters that Mackenzie had encountered along the Fraser, so different from the amorphous political structure of the Shoshone, among whom the explorers "made chiefs" on whom to pin medals, appeared first among these people of the Kamas plain. Early the next morning Clark sent out his hunters while he himself stayed with "the Chief to prevent Suspission and to Collect by Signs as much information as possible about the river and Countrey in advance." Then with the few articles he had in his pockets he bought as much salmon, bread roots, and berries as they would sell, and sent one of his hunters with an Indian to meet Lewis and his party. The warm weather, so sudden and so marked after their months on the cool high plateau, as well as their sudden change in diet made them all uncomfortable and sick: for months they had eaten nothing but meat, then they had hungered, and now they were trying to satisfy their ravenous appetites with kamas roots and berries. But despite his acute discomfort—"I am verry sick to day and puke which relive me"—Clark set out that same afternoon (*September 21*) to meet a "greater Chief . . . [who] was fishing at a river half a days march" from the village. With an Indian to guide him he reached the river, where Chief Twisted-Hair had his camp on the opposite bank. Though it was almost midnight, the guide called to the chief, who crossed the river and

"Soon join'd me. I found him a Chearfull man with apparant siencerity, I gave him a Medal and Smoked untill 1 oClock a.m. and went to Sleep. . . . This river is the one we killed the first Coalt on near a fishing *were* [weir]."

Meanwhile (*September 18*) Lewis and the main party continued their journey as quickly as they could. Their miseries were many and marked their days. That morning they had eaten the last scraps of their last colt, and so

"we dined & suped [elegant words that bore no relation to what they ate] on a skant proportion of portable soupe, a few canesters of which and about 20 lbs. of bears oil form our stock of provision, the only recources being our guns & packhorses. the first is but a poor dependence in our present situation where there is nothing upon earth except ourselves and a few small pheasants, small grey Squirrels, and a blue bird of the vulter kind."

They were in one of those rare deserts, pockets empty of all game. Wheeler, who followed their trail a hundred years later, says: "There never was any [game], so far as I can learn, in the country immediately adjoining this trail. There was none in 1805, there is none now." The next day they were still struggling over the steep mountains and had reached a most dangerous part of the trail, where a narrow stony ledge led around the face of a precipice.

"Fraziers horse fell from this road in the evening, and roled with his load near a hundred yards into the Creek. we all expected that the horse was killed but to our astonishment when the load was taken off him he arose & . . . in 20 minutes he proceeded with his load. this was the most wonderfull escape I ever witnessed."

That day there is mention of something less dramatic but far more serious. This was scurvy, the first really ominous consequence of the privations and starvation they had suffered since leaving the immense buffalo herds of the plains. The signs of the dread and debilitating scourge were evident: "several of the men

are unwell of the disentary. brakings out, or irruptions of the
Skin, have also been common with us for some time."

The next morning (*September 20*) they rejoiced to find "the
greater part of a horse which Capt. Clark had met with and
killed for us." There they halted and

"made a hearty meal on our horse beef much to the comfort of
our hungry stomachs. here I [Lewis] larnt that one of the Packhorses with his load was missing. . . . The load of the horse was
of considerable value consisting of merchandize and all my stock
of winter cloathing. I therefore dispatched two of my best
woodsmen in surch of him, and proceeded with the party."

Despite hunger, accidents, sickness, fatigue, the miseries of the
march, Lewis was able to remember the scientific inquiries he
had been requested to pursue; he noted the quality of the soil,
the nature of the rock formations, the flora—"a kind of honeysuckle . . . not common but to the western side of the rockey
mountains"—and collected his specimens as he stumbled along.
It was the minor heroism of a responsible man.

Valuable time was lost (*September 21*) rounding up the horses;
so when they camped, Lewis "directed the horses to be hubbled
to prevent delay . . . being determined to make a forced march
tomorrow to reach, if possible the open country." A stew spiced
only by starved appetites was concocted out of a few pheasants,
"a prarie woolf together with the balance of our horse beef and
some crawfish obtained in the creek," and provided them with
"one more hearty meal." The great timber characteristic of the
western slopes began to appear: "I saw several sticks today large
enough to form eligant perogues of at least 45 feet in length."
The men went to sleep that night satisfied that they had put the
worst behind them, that on the morrow they would be quit of
the mountains and traveling along an easy path to a land that
offered food. For days this hope had sustained them, and when
next day the hunter sent by Clark brought them dried fish and
roots, it was with a sweet certainty that they bridged the last
miles. "the pleasure I now felt in having tryumphed over the
rockey Mountains and descending once more to a level and fertile
country where there was every rational hope of finding a comfortable subsistence for myself and party," wrote Lewis on the

twenty-second of September, "can be more readily conceived than expressed, nor was the flattering prospect of the final success of the expedition less pleasing." Of the main party's reaching the kamas prairie, Clark says:

"The planes appeared covered with Spectators viewing the white men and the articles which we had, our party weakened and much reduced in flesh as well as Strength . . . much rejoiced to find something to eate of which they appeared to partake plentifully I cautioned them of the Consequences of eateing too much."

There is no exulting chorus at their victory over the terrible mountain march. They had come through; it was enough that they had survived, that they had unraveled the dark secrets of that labyrinth; they still had to navigate the Columbia to reach the Pacific. This was just another battle won; the campaign still had more battles ahead before their real victory would be secured. For a few days these tired warriors paused.

7.

The Columbia River establishes the limit of eccentricity in river courses. Rising in British Columbia, it makes an almost complete loop around the Selkirk Range, and heading southward, receives the waters of the Okanagan, the Kootenay, and the Pend d'Oreille; crossing the international border, it curves like a sickle around an extensive lava field, is joined by the mighty Snake, and at last turns due west toward the Pacific Ocean. Fourteen hundred miles long, it reaches northward toward the Fraser and southward through the thousand-mile-long Snake toward Yellowstone Park, near to the headwaters of the Colorado, which flows into the Gulf of California; with its two long, greedy arms it drains much of the country west of the Rockies. From its sources in the high timbered mountains it cuts through a triste, arid region—bare hills that sport a few straggling pines—and finally a savage, naked country stripped even of grass, devoid of game, with only the river to give it life. For the Columbia is one of the principal highways for the migratory salmon that bless the poor country through which it flows. Here were no buffalo herds to sustain tribes, no deer or antelope that families might hunt, but a desert that the swarming salmon had peopled with many villages, large communities. By its falls and rapids, where fish were easily caught, lived hundreds of Indians fiercely guarding sites, rights, and privileges; there they laid up vast stores of dried fish, and from there they migrated annually into the mountains, where roots and berries were gathered and some game was found. The river was their life: it gave them their staple food, it was their thoroughfare between mountains and sea.

Two of the three widespread linguistic groups found along the Columbia the expedition had already met: the Nez Percé and the Flatheads, whose many different bands were native to the tributaries and the main river as far west as the Dalles; from the Dalles to the mouth of the Columbia were the Chinook. It was these last who named the Flatheads in contempt, for the Chinook successfully imposed their own standard of beauty on nature by pressing the malleable skull of their infants into a high, backward slanting point. The Chinook were similar to the coastal tribes Mackenzie had met: they had well-built, seaworthy canoes and permanent wooden houses, they had well-defined social classes from chief to slave, and they were shrewd, aggressive traders. A Chinook jargon—combining Chinook, Nootka, some few other Indian languages, English, and Canadian French—became a lingua franca used by white and Indian fur traders along the northwest coast as far as Alaska; but the stunning totemic art of the more northerly tribes was not part of Chinook culture.

To reach the Pacific the expedition had to go down the Clearwater—Kooskooskee, the Indians called it—to its junction with the Snake, thus into the Columbia, and so to their journey's end, the sea. Their path led through a country of sharp contrasts: from the open timber-fringed plains, whose moist soil grew an abundance of kamas roots, across a dry belt, and without warning into the continuous, drenching Pacific rains; from a country where wood was so scarce that the Indians used dried fish for fuel, to the dense vegetation of the coast, where junglelike undergrowth knitted great trees into a wall that the hunters could not penetrate; from the Nez Percé, who were honest people and trusted friends, to the thieving, flea-ridden Chinook. But all this lay before them. Now they were on wide plains where hot breezes welcomed them after the numbing, icy mountain air; now they must rest a bit and eat a lot and get canoes ready for the last step of their journey.

So urgent was their hunger that despite Clark's caution to eat sparingly of fish and roots and berries, they gorged themselves. The next day

"all Complain of a *Lax* & heaviness. . . . We All set out for the River and proceeded on by the Same rout I had previously traveled and at Sunset [*September 24*] we arrived at the Island on which I found the [Chief] *Twisted hare*, and formed a Camp on a large Island a little below, Capt. Lewis scercely able to ride on a jentle horse which was furnished by the Chief, Several men So unwell that they were Compelled to lie on the Side of the road for Some time others obliged to be put on horses. I gave rushes Pills to the Sick this evening."

All the men reacted to the enervating heat of the plains, and their diet caused violent gastric disorders; Clark doctored them heroically and searched doggedly for trees with which to make canoes: "we deturmined to go where the best timber was and there form a Camp." Still weak, still sick, still taking assorted medication—"*Salts* Pils Tarter emetic"—the men started building the canoes. "Men complaining of their diat of fish & roots. all that is able working." To save them hard "labour we have adopted the Indian method of burning out the canoes." Days passed. October came; "Northing to eate except dried fish & roots . . . Capt. Lewis and myself eate a Supper of roots boiled, which Swelled us in Such a manner that we were Scerely able to breath for Several hours."

At last on the sixth of October they were ready and strong enough to start down the river.

"Had all our horses 38 in number Collected and branded . . . delivered them to the 2 brothers and one son of one of the Chiefs who intends to accompany us . . . they promised to be attentive to our horses untill we Should return . . . had all our Saddles Collected, a whole dug and in the night buried them, also a Canister of powder and a bag of Balls."

Their ammunition had been very cleverly packaged: the powder was put into lead "canesters which were filled with the necessary proportion of powder to discharge the lead when used, and those canesters well secured with corks and wax . . . all the Canoes finished this evening ready to be put into the water," and next day they started for the Pacific.

Besides their old Shoshone guide Toby and his son they had two Nez Percé chiefs, Twisted-Hair and Tetoh, "who had promised to accompany us, we took them on board after the Serimony of Smokeing." Immediately, hurriedly, secretly, Toby was

"Seen running up the river Several miles above us, we could not account for the cause of his leaveing us at this time, without receiving his pay for the services he had rendered us, or letting us know anything of his intention. we requested the Chief to Send a horseman after our old guide to come back and receive his pay, which he advised us not do as his nation [the Nez Percé] would take his things from him before he passed their camps."

Later they were glad to learn that Toby and his son had taken their pay—each had appropriated one of the expedition's horses when he rode off.

On the tenth they reached the junction of the Clearwater and the Snake.

"The Indians Came down all the Courses of this river on each side on horses to view us as we were decending . . . our diet extremely bad haveing nothing but roots and dried fish to eate. all the Party have greatly the advantage of me, in as much as they all relish the flesh of the dogs, Several of which we purchased of the nativs."

They had learned from some of their Frenchmen that it was possible to prefer "dogflesh to fish."

Their progress down the Snake (*October 10–16*) led them uneventfully through "an open plain leavel & fertile . . . not a tree of any kind to be Seen on the river." Wherever the river had rapids, there on the banks were Indian houses; at each of these settlements they stopped and purchased fish, roots, and dogs. "[Sacajawea] we find reconsiles all the Indians, as to our friendly intentions. a woman with a party of men is a token of peace." It is an illuminating commentary from Clark, for it is clear that while the size of their party gave them a feeling of security in facing unknown tribes, it was the mere presence of Sacajawea that assured them a good reception and was a guarantee of their peaceable motives being understood by the Indians; she was their flag of truce.

Despite delays and accidents they made good speed and reached

"the junction of this river and the Columbia. . . . We halted above the point . . . to smoke with the Indians who had collected there in great numbers to view us, here we met our 2 chiefs who left us two days ago and proceeded to this place to inform those bands of our approach and friendly intentions towards all nations. . . . We formed a camp near the place where I saw a fiew pieces of Drift wood . . . a Chief came . . . at the head of about 200 men singing and beeting on their drums Stick and keeping time to the musik, they formed a half circle around us and Sung for Some time, we gave them all Smoke," [speeches, medals, and small presents].

In return they were offered fish, "Some fuil Such as the Stalks of weeds or plants and willow bushes [and] one man made me a present of about 20 lb. of verry fat Dried horse meat."

Thus they celebrated, after so long a time and so much effort, their arrival at the Columbia. Here the water was so full of salmon that it almost seemed a different element:

"This river is remarkably clear and crouded with salmon. I observe great numbers of salmon *dead* on the shores, floating on the water and in the Bottom which can be seen at the debth of 20 feet . . . emence quantities of dried fish. large scaffols of fish drying at every lodge, and piles of salmon lying, the squars engaged prepareing them for the scaffol."

They stayed for two days while "Capt. Lewis took a Vocabelary of the Language of those people," and Clark explored a little up the river. Wood being imported from afar, the   .

"Houses or Lodges of the tribes of the main Columbia is of large Mats made of rushes, those houses are from 15 to 60 feet in length

generally of an Oblong squar form, Suported by poles on forks
. . . the roughfs [roofs] are nearly flat, which proves to me that
rains are not common in this open Countrey."

They decided that the people along the river

"appear to live in a State of comparitive happiness: they take a
greater share in the labor of the woman, than is common among
Savage tribes, and as I am informed are content with one wife.
. . . We purchased forty dogs for which we gave articles of
little value, such as beeds bells & thimbles, of which they are
verry fond. at 4 oClock we set out down the great Columbia
accompanied by our two old Chiefs."

The current carried them swiftly, and their progress was interrupted only to buy food, make friends, and do honor to a
tribe by making speeches and presenting medals to the chiefs.
Soon (*October 19*) they encountered some panic-stricken Indians who had not been forewarned of their arrival, those who had
been busy drying fish "hid themselves in their Lodges and not
one was to be seen untill we had passed." A few miles beyond
they reached a "verry bad rapid," which could only be passed
with lightened canoes. "I deturmined to walk [ahead] with the
2 chiefs the interpreter & his woman." It was a wise precaution,
for at the next lodges the people appeared

"in the greatest agutation, Some crying and ringing there hands,
others hanging their heads . . . as Soon as they Saw the Squar
they pointed to her . . . and immediately all appeared to assume
new life. The sight of This Indian woman confirmed those people of our friendly intentions, as no woman ever accompanies a
war party."

News of the expedition spread swiftly down the river and
when they camped that night

"about 100 Indians came from different Lodges, and a number
of them brought wood which they gave us, we Smoked with all
of them and two of our party played on the *violin* which delighted them greatly. . . . This day we made 36 miles."

From a "high clift" Clark

"descovered a high mountain of emence hight covered with
Snow, this must be one of the mountains laid down by Vancouver, as seen from the mouth of the Columbia . . . I take it
to be Mt. St. Hellens [it was Mount Adams], destant about 120
miles . . . a conical mountain S.W. toped with snow."

This was the Cascade Range, through which the Columbia
would lead them to the ocean. Now the river was alive with
"a great numbers of Pelicons on the wing, and black Comerants";
near by were the three Memaloose Islands (Place of the Departed).

"We discovered an Indian Vault. our curiosity induced us to
examine the method those nativs practiced in depositeing the
dead, the vault was made by broad boards and pieces of Canoes
leaning on a ridge pole which was Suported by 2 forks Set in the
ground six feet in hight . . . about 60 feet long and 12 feet wide,
in it I observed great numbers of humane bones of every description perticularly in a pile near the center of the vault, on the
East End 21 Scul bomes forming a circle on Mats; in the wester-
ley part of the *Vault* appeared to be appropriated for those of
more resent death, as many of the bodies of the deceased *raped*
up in leather robes, lay [in rows] on boards covered with mats,
&c (*when bones & robes rot, they are gathered in a heap & sculls
placed in a circle*) we observed, independant of the Canoes which
served as a covering, fishing nets of various kinds, Baskets of
different Sizes, wooden boles, robes Skins, trenchers, and various
kind of trinkets, in and suspended on the ends of the pieces
forming the vault; we also Saw the Skeletons of Several
Horses."

Gradually the open plains were crossed. Making from thirty
to forty miles a day, they put behind them the smooth rounded
hillocks into which the sand had been piled and shaped, where
wood was so scarce that often they lacked fuel for cooking.
From the twenty-second, when they reached the western end
of the pass the Columbia had carved for itself through the Cascade Mountains, until the beginning of November, when they

had negotiated the last hazard and found themselves surrounded by sea otters in the Columbia's deep tidal basin, they were in a country where rock and river carry on the ancient titanic struggle of fire and water. The literary spirit that had saluted the Great Falls of the Missouri found no similarly glowing words to hail the stupendous scenery through which they carefully advanced; their eyes were glued to the river in its twisting and turning—now wide, now suddenly and dangerously narrowed, falling, shooting between rocks, over rocks. Now their hearts were not filled with eager anticipation of meeting the friendly Shoshone but rather were on guard against the warlike Chinook, from whom the two chiefs, who had come so far to act as good-will ambassadors, wanted to flee. For a long time now the explorers had been "verry fateigued," for a long time they had lived on dried fish and roots and dog flesh—not fat elk and buffalo and Charbonneau's marvelous white pudding. Except for the immense bounty of fish this was not a country in which they could take delight; the sense of high adventure was replaced by a mood of dogged determination.

From Celilo Falls, through both the Short and the Long Narrows between the Dalles and down to the Cascades, the Columbia traverses a volcanic region, which at one time was flooded with white-hot liquid lava. With the power and urgency of its sprawling length behind it, the river fights for a way to the ocean—cutting through lava beds, creating sooty brown palisades that tower majestically two to three thousand feet high; terraces, towers, chimneys, obelisks are carved in the lava banks. Before the molten rock congealed, it tried to trap the river in a series of colossal dams; across the river, through the river, the remains of these obstructions, battered and eroded, still torture the water into a succession of angry rapids and falls, tricky swirls and cross-currents, into narrow, deep channels. Mighty rocks still stud the river bed, dwarfed by the towering height of the Cascade Range. The falls were a dividing line not only between the plain and the mountains, the dry interior and the rainy coast, but between major Indian groups: there the Flathead and the Nez Percé stopped; and below were the Chinook, unknown and very numerous.

The falls did not constitute a major problem, and were easily coped with.

"We landed and walked down accompanied by an old man to view the falls, and the best rout for us to make a portage which we Soon discovered . . . we returned and droped down to the head of the rapids and took every article except the Canoes across the portage where I had formed a camp on an ellegable Situation for the protection of our Stores from thieft . . . Indians assisted us over the portage with our heavy articles on their horses";

It gave them a perfect chance to pilfer at will, so that constant precautions had to be taken against thieving. The Indians came from five large lodges, where they dried and prepared fish for sale

"to the white people who visit the mouth of this river as well as to the nativs. I observe great numbers of Stacks of pounded Salmon neetly preserved in the following manner, after being sufficiently Dried it is pounded between two Stones fine, and put into a speces of basket neetly made of grass and rushes which is lined with the Skin of Salmon Stretched and dried for the purpose. in this is it pressed down as hard as possible, when full they Secure the opening with the fish Skins which they fasten thro'. . . . their common custom is to Set 7 as close as they can Stand and 5 on top of them, and secure them with mats which is raped around and made fast with cords. these 12 baskets of from 90 to 100 lbs. each form a Stack. thus preserved those fish may be kept Sound and sweet Several years . . . I counted 107 stacks of dried pounded fish . . . which must have contained 10.000 lb. of neet fish."

The next day (*October 23*) the men carried the canoes "across the portage of 457 yards" and were

"nearly covered with flees which were so thick amongst the Straw and fish Skins . . . that every man was obliged to Strip naked dureing the time of takeing over the canoes that they might have an oppertunity of brushing the flees off . . . one of the old Chiefs who had accompanied us from the head of the river, informed us that he herd the Indians Say that the nation below intended to kill us, we examined all the arms, complete the ammunition to 100 rounds. The natives leave us earlyer this evening than usial, which gives a Shadow of confermation to the information . . . as we are at all times & places on our guard, are under no greater apprehention than is common."

Having passed the falls, the chiefs Twisted-Hair and Tetoh

"expressed a desire to return to their band, Saying 'that they could be of no further Service to us, as their nation extended no further down the river' (*they could no longer understand the language of those below the falls, till then not much difference in the vocabs.*) . . . we insisted on their staying two nights longer with us, untill we should pass the next falls, which we were told were very bad . . . at this place the water of this great river is compressed into a chanel between two rocks not exceeding *forty five* yards wide and continues for ¼ of a mile when it again widens to 200 yards and continues this width for about 2 miles when it is again intersepted by rocks . . . as the portage of our canoes over . . . would be impossible with our Strength, and the only danger in passing thro those narrows was the whorls and swells arrising from the Compression of the water, and which I thought (as also our principal water-man Peter Cruzat) by good Stearing we could pass down Safe, accordingly I deturmined to pass through this place notwith-standing the horrid appearance of this agitated gut swelling, boiling & whorling in every direction, (which from the top of the rock did not appear as bad as when I was in it;) however we passed Safe to the astonishment of all the Indians who viewed us from the top of the rock . . . this place being verry bad I sent by land all the men who could not Swim and such articles as was most valuable to us."

Before them were the Long Narrows.

"Capt. Lewis and my Self walked down to See the place the Indians pointed out as the worst place in passing through the gut, which we found difficuelt of passing without great danger, but as the portage was impracticable with our large canoes, we concluded to Make a portage of our most valuable articles and run the canoes thro . . . this chanel is through a hard rough

black rock, from 50 to 100 yards wide, swelling and boiling in
a most tremendious maner."

Having taken every precaution, the canoes ran the narrows
and reached the end where "the river widens and becoms a
butifull jentle Stream of about half a mile wide, Great numbers
of the Sea orter about those narrows and both below and above."
There they had a "parting Smoke with our two faithful friends
the chiefs who accompanied us from the head of the river, (who
had purchased a horse each with 2 robes and intended to return
on horseback)." To "make Some Selestial observations" they
made a camp there.

"The face of the Countrey on both Side of the river is Steep,
ruged and rockey," say the journals of the extraordinary scenery
that surrounded their camp. They were at the Dalles, a descriptive word preserved from the French Canadians whose canoes
were to be familiar with every turn and twist of the Columbia.
Dalles, in French, means slabs or flagstones, and accurately con-
veys the unique structure of the enormous basaltic blocks that
line the river and stud the stream. Instead of descriptions, the
journal entries stress the everlasting problem of food and the
armies of fleas, which "they can't get rid of, perticularly as they
have no clothes to change those which they wore"; there was
an endless succession of meetings with chiefs who were received and addressed and decorated before great crowds of
natives for whose delight and goodwill Cruzatte played his violin
and York danced. The explorers took a vocabulary of Chinook
with its predominating "clucking tone," and observed the manner by which these Indians made their infants' foreheads slope
sharply backward. Now there were signs in increasing number
and variety of European contact; clothes and muskets, "a Cut-
lash and Several brass Tea kittles." Whether they had received
them from British or American traders it was impossible to learn;
the Indians could say only that the traders spoke English, the
same as the explorers, and proved the truth of their claims "by
repeating . . . musquet, powder, shot, knife, file, damned
rascal, son of a bitch &c." Below the Dalles they were stopped
by strong head winds, "which do not retard the motions of the
Indians at all, as their canoes are calculated to ride the highest

waves." Timber began to appear, and lacy waterfalls festooned the high banks. "The Countrey rises with steep assent."

They had reached (*October 30*) the Coastal Range and the Cascades. This, the last, was a serious and tricky obstacle, for here the river falls sixty feet in three miles without any perpendicular break. Not only does the river twist and turn and then turn and twist back again on itself, but it is constricted, and its bed is studded with high, dangerous rocks. At first the water rushes over a sloping reef where, as in a giant sluice, it gathers momentum, and, tearing at the high obstructing rocks, it begins to boil and foam with fury. Still it rushes downhill, forming whirlpools and eddies as if some puissant pressure from below were trying to roll back the flood. To Clark the Cascades were "the Great Shute." A careful survey convinced him that a portage must be made, and two days later "We got all our baggage over the Portage of 940 yards, after which we got the 4 large canoes over by slipping them over the rocks on poles placed from one rock to another, and at some places along partial Streams of the river." The thirty miles below "the Great Shute [was] high and rugid," but then "the mountains leave the river on each Side. . . . The bottoms below appear extensive and thickly covered with wood. river here about 2½ miles wide. . . . The ebb tide rose here about 9 Inches."

The tide signaled the close presence of the Pacific Ocean; this bald mention of it marks the beginning of the end of their long, long journey. The difficulties posed by the Columbia had been successfully resolved; with consummate skill they had negotiated a mighty river whose temper was strange and new. And then, almost powerless, they were to be bewildered by fogs, buffeted by winds, and bullied by drenching rains, as they advanced down the ever-widening tidal estuary.

A "Fog so thick this morning [*November 3*] that we could not see a man 50 Steps off" introduced them to the northwest coast in November. When the fog lifted, they were delighted to see that the country was heavily timbered and "emence numbers of fowl flying in every direction, Such as Swan, geese, Brants, Cranes, Storks, white guls, comerants & plevers . . . on which we made a Sumpteous supper." At a large and prosperous village they were introduced to "a roundish root about the Size of a Small Irish potato which [the Chinook] roasted in the embers until they became Soft. This root they call *Wap-pa-to* . . . it has an agreeable taste and answers verry well in place of bread. we purchased about 4 bushels."

In contrast to the Indians they had met along the river, they found the Chinookan tribes

"assumeing and disagreeable, however we Smoked with them and treated them with every attention & friendship . . . dureing the time we were at dinner those fellow Stold my pipe Tomahawk which they were Smoking with, I imediately serched every man and the canoes, but could find nothing of my Tomahawk, while Serching for the Tomahawk one of these Scoundals Stole a cappoe [*capotte*, or great coat] . . . which was found Stufed under the root of a tree, near the place they Sat."

Such unmitigated, unabashed thieving of their diminishing supplies was not only annoying, it was dangerous; "we were more fearfull of [it] than their arrows."

They continued westward toward the sea:

"Rained all the after part of last night, rain continues this morning [*5th*], I slept but verry little last night for the noise Kept up dureing the whole of night by Swans, Geese, white & Grey Brant Ducks; they were emensely noumerous, and their noise horid . . . we met two canoes from below . . . the Shore bold and rockey. I saw 17 Snakes today, but little appearance of Frost in this place. . . . This is the first night which we have been entirely clear of Indians since our arrival on the waters of the Columbia River."

And on the sixth: "Cloudy with rain all day. we are all wet and disagreeable. No place for Several Miles sufficiently large for our camp, we at length Landed at a place which by moveing the stones we made a place sufficiently large for the party to lie leavel on the Smaller Stones clear of the *Tide* . . . had large fires made on the Stone and dried our bedding and kill the flces

which collected in our blankets at every old village we encamped near . . . made about 29 miles."

Would the river never end? Would they ever be rid of the
fleas? Would they ever again enjoy some food other than
wappato roots, salmon, and dog meat? Would the rain and fog
ultimately admit the sun so that they could dry out their clothes?
There is almost a sodden battle fatigue about the men, who had
spent their strength and spirit and were now only automatically
going on with a task. They wanted rest and filling food and
warmth. Even the entry for the seventh of November has a
kind of warmed-over enthusiasm:

"Great joy in camp we are in *view* of the *Ocian*, (*in the morning
when fog cleared off just below the last village*) this great Pacific
Octean which we been so long anxious to See. and the roreing or
noise made by the waves brakeing on the rockey Shores (as
I suppose) may be heard distinctly."

But it was not the ocean that they saw—it was the wide bay
into which the river opened, which to eyes long accustomed
to the confinement of rivers seemed oceanic. An end, an end,
their tired bodies must have cried in seeking to place the sea
there. Before they were to gaze on the Pacific they still had
miseries to endure:

"We found the Swells or Waves so high that we thought it
imprudent to proceed . . . our present Situation a verry disagreeable one in as much as we have not leavel land Sufficient
for an encampment and for our baggage to lie clear of the tide,
the High hills jutting in so close and steep that we cannot retreat back, and the water of the river too Salt to be used. added
to this the waves are increasing to Such a hight that we cannot
move from this place, in this Situation we are compelled to
form our camp between the hite of the Ebb and flood tides,
and rase our baggage on logs. . . . The Seas roled and tossed
the Canoes in such a manner this evening that Several of our
party were Sea Sick . . . wind Hard from the South and rained
hard all fore part of the day [*9th*] . . . the flood tide came in
with emence waves and heavy winds, floated the trees and Drift

which was on the point of which we Camped and tosed them
about in such a manner as to endanger the canoes verry much.
every exertion . . . was scercely sufficient to Save our Canoes
from being crushed by those monsterous trees maney of them
nearly 200 feet long . . . our camp entirely under water dureing
the hight of the *tide,* every man as wet as water could make them
all the last night and today all day as the rain continued. . . . At
this dismal point we must Spend another night as the wind &
waves are too high to proceed."

And yet courage was burning with a steady flame; the men
were tired, but far from beaten: "notwithstanding the disagreeable Situation . . . they are all chearfull and anxious to See
further into the Ocian." Clark noted this camping spot on his
charts as Point Distress; the men thought Blustery Point a fitter
name.

Six days they were there on drift logs endowed with destructive motion by the hard wind and high tides, between the
high bank and the formidable waves, with the rain soaking them
day and night.

"Nothing to eate but pounded fish which we Keep as a reserve
and use in Situations of this kind . . . The rain &c. which has
continued without a longer intermition than 2 hours at a time for
ten days past has destroyed the robes and rotted nearly one half
of the fiew clothes the party has, particularley the leather clothes.
fortunately for us we have no very cold weather as yet. and
if we have cold weather before we can kill & Dress Skins for
clothing the bulk of the party will Suffer verry much. . . . The
wind lay about 3 oClock, we loaded in great haste and set out
passed the blustering Point."

They reached an abandoned Chinook village, "36 houses deserted by the Indians & in full possession of the flees, a small
creek falls in at this village." Immediately in front of them was
the "ocean at this time more raging than pacific."

Nineteen months after they had left St. Louis they had completed the crossing by the route Jefferson had suggested—up
the Missouri, thence across to the Columbia, and so to the western ocean. They still had the winter months to get through

before they could start on the long trail home. Fort Clatsop, where they spent their second winter, was named, like Fort Mandan, for the tribe in whose territory it was situated, and Christmas Eve found "all employed in finishing their huts and moving into them."

The start for home was made March 25, 1806. They said farewell to the chiefs who had visited and traded with them during their stay there, and with them they left notices to be given to traders—hoping thus, should misfortune overtake them on their return, to leave some proof of their living presence on the Pacific coast.

8.

The homeward journey was delayed until winter should have left the mountain passes. By the beginning of May they had reached their old friend Chief Twisted-Hair, to whose family's keeping their horses had been entrusted. After the persistent and expert thieving of the rascally Chinook, it was a relief to be back among friends, among people who instead of taking property restored it. "A man of this lodge produced us two canisters of powder which he informed us he had found by means of his dog where they had [been] buried . . . as he kept them safe and had honesty enough to return them we gave him a fire steel by way of recompense." Their fear lest the snowy mountains detain them until too late to return to St. Louis the same season caused them to start out too early. A few weeks later, when June was almost ended, they were en route again, guided by an Indian who now thought they might get through; and with no greater suffering than on the outward journey they reached the lovely valley of Traveller's Rest. A fat deer made them a pleasant supper; their gaunt horses had grass, and, having camped beside the hot springs, "both men and indians amused themselves with the use of a bath this evening."

Now was the place and the time (*July 1*) for them to "accomplish the objects we have in view," as they had planned at Fort Clatsop.

"Capt. Clark & myself consurted the following plan viz: from this place [Camp Traveller's Rest] I determined to go with a

small party by the most direct rout to the falls of the Missouri, there to leave [three men] . . . to prepare carriages and geer for the purpose of transporting the canoes and baggage over the portage, and myself and six volunteers to ascend Maria's river with a view to explore the country and ascertain whether any branch of that river lies as far as Latid. 50, and again return and join the party who are to decend the Missouri, at the entrance of Maria's river. . . . The other part of the men are to proceed with Capt. Clark to the head of Jefferson's river where we deposited sundry articles and left our canoes. from hence Sergt. Ordway with a party of 9 men are to decend the river with the canoes; Capt. Clark with the remaining ten including Charbono and York will proceed to the Yellowstone river at it's nearest approach to the three forks of the missouri, here he will build a canoe and decend the Yellowstone river . . . to the missouri, where should he arrive first he will await my arrival. Sergt. Pryor with two other men are to proceed with the horses by land to the Mandans and thence to the British posts on the Assinniboin with a letter to Mr. Heney whom we wish to engage to prevail on the Sioux Chiefs to join us on the Missouri, and accompany them with us to the seat of the general government. these arrangements being made, the party were informed of our design and prepared themselves accordingly. our hunters killed 13 deer in the course of this day of which 7 were fine bucks . . . we had our venison fleeced and exposed in the sun on poles to dry."

Two days later (*July 3*) all the arrangements were "compleated for carrying into effect the several scheemes we had planed for execution on our return, we saddled our horses and set out. I took leave of my worthy friend and companion Capt. Clark and the party that accompanyed him." Like Balboa, they were not content to return by their outward trail. They had learned much about the land, its contours, the flow and direction of its rivers; they were eager at once to test this knowledge and to extend it. The plan they had worked out utilized their personnel, their experience, their equipment; it dovetailed separate efforts and individual schedules so that all should meet and together travel from Fort Mandan to St. Louis. In six weeks they would all be together again, but much was to happen in that period.

With twenty men, Charbonneau, Sacajawea and her son, and fifty horses, Clark headed straight for Shoshone Cove. As soon as they neared the headwaters of the Wisdom, Sacajawea was in familiar country and led them to the

"place we Sunk our Canoes & buried some articles. . . . The most of the Party with me being Chewers of Tobacco become so impatient to be chewing it that they scercely gave themselves time to take their saddles off their horses before they were off to the deposit. I found every article safe, except a little damp."

It must have delighted Clark to descend the river up which he had toiled so desperately: in three days—it had taken eighteen days to ascend—he was at the Three Forks. Ordway with nine men took the canoes down to the Great Falls to meet Lewis, while Clark, with the remaining men and all the horses, swung eastward toward the Yellowstone into unknown country. "The indian woman . . . recommends a gap in the mountain more south which I shall cross"—she had pointed out Bozeman Pass, the one now used by the Northern Pacific Railway. As they quickly advanced down the river on their horses, they saw smoke signals—for good or ill, they knew not—"raised by the Crow Indians." That same day they had to alter their plans: "Gibson . . . fell on a Snag and sent it nearly two inches into the Muskeler part of his thy . . . a verry bad wound and pains him exceedingly . . . complains of great pain in his Kne and hip as well as his *thy*." Gibson's wound could not stand even the gentlest riding, and Clark was forced to hurry toward the nearest timber to make canoes.

The next morning half their horses were gone: "I am apprehensive that the indians had Stolen our horses, and probably those who had made the Smoke." They were on the Plains, where horses were scarce, terribly desirable, and a recognized target for raids—yet they never took precautions. When the canoes were ready, Clark gave Sergeant Pryor the letter he was to carry and their remaining twenty-six horses and started his small party overland on their mission. In his "little flotilla" Clark and the rest swept down the Yellowstone. Able thus to lie still, Gibson found his wound healing nicely, and he was soon walking and hunting. The only delays were caused by the vast numbers of buffalo that crowded the valley. "I was obliged to land to let the Baffalow cross . . . the river was crouded with those animals for ½ an hour . . . two gangues of Buffalow crossed a little below us, as noumerous as the first." On the third of August they reached the mouth of the Yellowstone, where game was scarce and the "Musquetors was so troublesom that no one of the party Slept half the night"; leaving a note for Lewis, Clark went a short distance down the Missouri to "an elligable Situation," where he hunted "to precure as many skins as possible for the purpose of purchaseing Corn and Beans of the Mandans, as we have now no article of Merchandize nor horses to purchase with."

On the eighth he was surprised to see Pryor's party coming "down the river in two canoes made of Buffalow Skins." Two nights after they had parted, the sergeant told Clark, all twenty-six of their horses disappeared. The Crow, the most expert horse thieves of the Plains, had made a rich haul; they now had all fifty of the expedition's horses.

"*August 12,* noon: Capt. Lewis hove in Sight with the party which went by way of the Missouri as well as that which accompanied him . . . I was alarmed on the landing of the Canoes to be informed that Capt. Lewis was wounded by an accident. I found him lying in the Perogue, he informed me that his wound was slight and would be well in 20 or 30 days. this information relieved me very much. . . . Capt. Lewis informed me the accident happened the day before by one of the men Peter Crusat [Cruzatte] misstaking him in the thick bushes to be an Elk . . . from the colour of his clothes which were of leather . . . Capt. Lewis thinking it was indians who had Shot him hobbled to the canoes as fast as possible and was followed by Crusat, The Mistake was then discovered. This Crusat is near Sighted and has the use of but one eye."

Yet it was this one-eyed, near-sighted Cruzatte who had steered their canoes down the worst rapids, through the most perilous waters. The wound was disconcerting, but the story

Lewis had to tell, the story that explained why he thought it was Indians who had shot him, was more serious. As they drifted down the Missouri, Lewis told his friend of the sudden, terrible adventure that had befallen him.

Upon parting from Clark, Lewis, guided by Indians, took the "most derect rout" to the Missouri along a trail "through a tolerable leavel plain"—the total distance from his starting point being "only 150 miles." By the twelfth of July he had arrived at Whitebear Island, "and in the morning he discovered that the Indians had taken off seven of his best horses." When he opened the cache he found that the "river had risen so high that the water had penitrated. my bearskins entirly destroyed, all my specimens of plant also lost. the Chart of the Missouri fortunately escaped. opened my trunks and boxes and exposed the articles to dry. found my papers damp. . . . Had the carriage wheels dug up"—those precious, irreplaceable, useful wheels —"found them in good order." On the sixteenth he was ready to start exploring up the Marias. He took with him only Drouillard and the two Fieldses, the brothers Reuben and Joseph, and six horses. He left Sergeant Gass with six men and four horses at the portage and told him that if all went well "he would meet up at the mouth of the Maria's river on the 5th of August."

At the portage Gass's party was augmented by Ordway's group, who had floated the canoes down from the Three Forks, and by the twenty-seventh of July the portage had been effected. The next day canoes and horses reached the mouth of the Marias. So far the intricate timetable was working out as the leaders had planned.

Up to a certain point Lewis's side trip up the Marias was a routine horseback excursion, made to determine whether the northern source of that river afforded a direct connection with the Columbia. But his route lay through the country of the Blackfeet, a tribe not previously encountered by the party. The Blackfeet and Minnetaree! Even their names struck terror into Sacajawea's heart, for those were the nations whom her people feared most when they went out on the plains to hunt.

"The Minnetares of Fort de prarie and the blackfoot indians rove through this quarter of the country and as they are a vicious lawless and reather an abandoned set of wretches I wish to avoid an interview with them if possible. I have no doubt but they would steel our horses if they have it in their power and finding us weak should they happen to be numerous wil most probably attempt to rob us of our arms and baggage."

This opinion and this fear were the prelude to a fatal struggle.

Meanwhile on the twenty-second, Lewis had reached his farthest point and

"thought it unnecessary to proceed further (I now have lost all hope of this river ever extending to N. Latitude 50°) and therefore encamped resolving to rest ourselves and horses a couple of days at this place and take the necessary observations . . . game of every discription is extreemly wild which induces me to beleive that the indians are now, or lately have been in this neighborhood."

A steady rain prevented his taking observations, and after hoping and waiting in vain, he started for the mouth of the river. Riding over "broken" country, suddenly, from the top of a hill, he saw

"an assembleage of about 30 horses, I halted and used my spye glass and . . . discovered several indians . . . about half the horses were saddled. this was a very unpleasant sight, however I resolved to make the best of our situation and to approach them in a friendly manner . . . when we had arrived within a quarter of a mile of them, one of them mounted his horse and rode full speed towards us, which when I discovered I halted and alighted . . . and becconed to him to approach but he paid no attention to my overtures. on his return to his party they all . . . mounted their horses and advanced towards us, we also advanced to meet them. I counted eight of them but still supposed that there were others concealed as there were several other horses saddled . . . when we arrived within a hundred yards of each other, the indians except one halted. . . . I advanced singly to meet the indian with whom I shook hands . . . I asked if there was any cheif among them and they pointed out 3. I did not believe them however I thought it best to please them and gave to one a medal to a second a flag and to the third

a handkerchief, with which they appeared well satisfyed . . .
as it was growing late I proposed that we should . . . encamp
together."

That, he thought, would be the best way to keep a close watch
on the group.

The Indians put up a large tipi, which Lewis and Drouillard
shared, while the Fields brothers "lay outside near the fire in
front of the shelter." Using the sign language, Lewis and the
Indians held a council that night; conversing thus, the red men
seemed gentle and friendly.

"I found them extreemly fond of smoking and plyed them with
the pipe untill late at night. . . . I took the first watch and set
up untill half after eleven; the indians by this time were all
asleep, I roused up R. Fields and laid down myself; I directed
Fields to watch the movements of the indians and if any of them
left the camp to awake us all. . . . This being done I fell into a
profound sleep and did not awake untill the noise of the men
and the indians awoke me a little after light in the morning.
. . . At daylight the indians got up and crouded around the
fire."

One chief—to whom Lewis had given the medal the previous
night—unperceived, took the Fieldses' guns that had been care-
lessly laid down; another at the same instant took Drouillard's,
and a third snatched Lewis's, and immediately they all started
running. Joe Fields saw this and shouted to his brother, who "instantly jumped up and pursued the indian with him, whom they
overtook . . . seized their guns and rested them from him. R. Fields
as he seized his gun stabed the indian to the heart with his knife,
the fellow ran about 15 steps and fell dead . . . having recovered their guns they ran back instantly to the camp; Drewyer
[Drouillard] who was awake saw the indian take hold of his
gun," and wrenched it from him, but failed to secure his powder
pouch. Lewis, awakened by the shouts and the struggle, saw
the Indian making off with his gun. He ran after him and,
threatening to shoot him with his pistol, "bid him lay down my
gun." One by one the four guns had been recovered; Lewis's
men wanted to shoot the Indian who had returned his gun, but

he forbade it. As the excitement was subsiding, this Indian, still bent on securing something valuable, started driving off Lewis's horses. In a running fight to save his horses Lewis shot the thief and barely escaped being wounded by him; "he overshot me, being bearheaded I felt the wind of his bullet very distinctly."

Two Indians were dead, their rascally plans frustrated; they had fled, leaving their camp to Lewis. An Indian version of this battle that was given much later to the anthropologist Grinnell confirmed Lewis's account.

"We left one of our horses [Lewis continues] and took four of the best of those of the indian's; while the men were preparing the horses I put four sheilds and two bows and quivers of arrows which had been left on the fire, with sundry other articles; they left all their baggage at our mercy. they had but two guns and one of them they left . . . the gun we took with us. I also retook the flagg . . . we took some of their buffaloe meat and set out."

However conclusive their victory had been, they were much too close to the main Indian band. The four men rode for their lives. Pushing the horses as hard as they could, by midafternoon they had covered about sixty-three fast miles, when "we halted an hour and a half took some refreshment and suffered our horses to graize; . . . by dark we had traveled about 17 miles further." A two-hour stop for food and rest, and

"we set out again by moonlight . . . we continued to pass immence herds of buffaloe all night . . . we traveled untill 2 oClock . . . we now turned out our horses and laid ourselves down to rest. . . . I awoke as day appeared, I was so soar from my ride of yesterday that I could scarcely stand and the men complained of being in a similar situation however I encouraged them by telling them that our lives as well as those of our friends depended on our exertions."

They had covered about one hundred and twenty miles in twenty-four hours.

And (*July 28*) as they were speeding toward the Missouri,

"we heared the report of several rifles. . . . we quickly replied to this joyfull sound and on arriving at the bank of the river had the unspeakable satisfaction to see our canoes coming down. we hurried down from the bluff on which we were and joined them striped our horses and gave them a final discharge imbarking without loss of time with our baggage."

Such was the story Lewis told Clark; it was the first, the only meeting with Indians to end on a note of violence and death. Despite all their adventures and accidents everyone was alive, the wounded were doing well, their papers were intact; reunited, they drifted down the Missouri toward home.

They approached the "Minetares Grand Village" on the fourteenth of August. They were back at Fort Mandan. Here they discharged Colter, who immediately turned back for the Yellowstone country with two traders; there he was to gain fame by his daring exploits. Here, too, they "Settled with Charbono for his services . . . in all amounting to 500$ 33⅓ cents." Clark offered the trader

"to take his little son a butifull promising child who is 19 months old to which both himself & wife wer willing provided the child had been weaned. they observed that in one year the boy would be sufficiently old to leave his mother & he would then take him to me if I would be so freindly as to raise the child for him in such a manner as I thought proper, to which I agreeed."

They said farewell to Charbonneau and his wife Sacajawea and their son Pomp, and left the Mandan village: they had left, it seemed to the men, something of themselves, for Sacajawea and her baby had tied themselves to all their hearts.

Bit by bit, civilization came back to them. Early in September they met a trader; "our first enquirey was after the President of our country and then our friends and the State of the politicks of our country." Three days later from another trader "we purchased a gallon of whiskey . . . and gave to each man a dram which is the first sprituous licquor which had been tasted by any since the 4 of July 1805." Soon the mere sight of grazing cows made the men shout for joy. The poor hamlets of La Charette were the first to welcome them:

"every person, both French and americans seem to express great pleasure at our return, and acknowledged themselves much astonished in seeing us return. they informed us that we were supposed to have been lost long since, and were entirely given out by every person."

Bit by bit, they came back to civilization. First La Charette, then St. Charles, then St. Louis,

"at which place we arived about 12 oClock [*September 23*]. we Suffered the party to fire off their pieces as a Salute to the Town. we were met by all the village and received a harty welcom from its inhabitants . . . I sleped but little last night however we rose early and commenced wrighting our letters."

To Jefferson—who had fathered this bold and now, after so long a time, successful journey—to the nation and to the world the news was sent out.

The realization that their expedition had made history, that the full account of their trip was a vital part of their mission, is implied in Clark's last entry of his long journal: "a fine morning we commenced wrighting."

Jefferson's Western Dream

UNTIL Mackenzie and Lewis and Clark made their transcontinental crossings, the profile of North America north of the Gulf of Mexico had not been drawn. The outline had indeed been mapped, save for the far northern coasts, and the four highways that invited ocean-going ships deep into the interior had been explored: Hudson Bay, which opened up the far north; the St. Lawrence and the fiordlike Hudson River, which offered two easy approaches to the Great Lakes at the center of the continent; and the Mississippi, leading into the enormous south central plain. Tocqueville, though a political scientist, not a geographer, thought that he could perceive, some time after those two great westward expeditions, "a sort of methodical order [that] seems to have regulated the separation of land and water, mountains and valleys. A simple but grand arrangement is discoverable amid the confusion of objects and the prodigious variety of scenes." From the accumulation of detailed descriptions and of authentic information on conditions of soil and climate, flora and fauna, that had been noted by explorers from the Atlantic to the Pacific, he envisioned the massive continental scheme with its great interior valleys, each of them with its mighty river-system. Separated by an almost imperceptible height of land, one poured its waters into northern seas, the other drained into the Gulf of Mexico. The southern valley, the valley of the Mississippi, spanned the distance from the "rounded summits" of the Appalachians that paralleled the Atlantic from Newfoundland to Alabama all the way west to the sharp, high, jagged cordillera that paced the Pacific coast and appeared "like the bones of a skeleton whose flesh has been consumed by time."

In the quarter of a century that elapsed between the Lewis and Clark expedition and Tocqueville's famous visit to America in 1831, two other westward pioneering expeditions were commissioned by the United States government. Lieutenant Pike, on horseback, ranged from the Kansas River to Spanish settlements along the Río Grande, and Major Long made a wide sweep into the mountains of Colorado by going up the Platte and returning down the Canadian River. From these probings of the trans-Mississippi West, from fur traders who hurried into that vast and varied territory to hunt and explore, to add fine, precise details, and to enlarge the total picture of the country, the great western trails took shape—the Santa Fe Trail, the Oregon Trail, the Mormon Trail—the heroic highways that carried commerce and immigrants westward across the continent, planted settlements in the wilderness, and brought democracy to the frontier.

Distinct from the traders, the men and women who, setting their faces toward the west, took their homes with them in prairie schooners, as still earlier comers had confided their lives and earthly goods to tiny barques ferrying across the Atlantic, carried with them in their hearts and thoughts the fight for the chance of a better life: their hope and heritage were the struggle against restrictive authority. Men and women who had fought by Wolfe Tone's side for an Irish republic, Chartists from Great Britain, Utopian socialists from France and England, Scottish radicals, religious dissidents, moved westward along those trails to find land where they could build their better world. The wilderness offered them the chance for which they searched, and they stamped the frontier with their robust belief in liberty and a resounding equalitarianism. Lemuel Gulliver never kept better company or made a more extraordinary journey than when Swift's work traveled with the earliest band of hunters bound for the Kentucky country. Rousseau "crossed the Rockies," the Beards say in explaining the spirit of the social compact drafted by the Oregon settlers in 1843.

The seed of irresistible growth planted in the New World was fertilized by Old World revolutionary theories—new political and social principles aimed at breaking the centuries-old iron grip of the system of power and privilege—that inspired and sustained settlers to seek a freer world; they were shared and understood by Thomas Jefferson. Western Virginia, in which he grew up, was then frontier country, and his home was thoroughly seasoned with democratic frontier ideas; his father, like other small farmers, had built his cabin in the wilderness, a section not as yet dominated by lords and landowners such as possessed princely tidewater plantations.

A substantial element always reckoned with in the southern planter economy was the frontier. Men who wanted to obtain furs, to accumulate capital for themselves or their backers, went ever deeper into wild lands; wealthy, large-scale tobacco planters, with a crop as valuable as the silver mined annually in Mexico and Peru, were always hungry for fresh lands to replace the quickly exhausted tidewater soil. These two groups in 1749 formed themselves into the Ohio Company, which, by royal charter, secured half a million acres across the mountains in the triangle formed by the Ohio and the Mississippi. In the next decade, Virginia, whose charter delimited her western boundary only in case of its touching on a foreign frontier, made grants of six times as much trans-Appalachian acreage. To stake out these claims, before the fur trader, before the frontiersman, went the land speculator and surveyor, in an orderly, propertied expansion. Fur trading, small farms, land speculation—all summed up in the one word, the West—were in the air that the growing Jefferson breathed in the Virginia piedmont. He was twenty when the Royal Proclamation of October 1763 at one stroke barred Virginia and the other British colonies from the coveted West. Now, forbidden, still desirable, and yearly more urgently needed, the West loomed in on Jefferson's consciousness and colored his judgment of Great Britain.

In a rough mental picture of North America today, Canada, the United States, and Mexico stretch from ocean to ocean in broad horizontal lines of national demarcation. By the peace settlement of 1763 after the French and Indian War—which had been started by colonists who were determined to keep the French out of "their" land, the Ohio country—North America south of the Great Lakes was divided between Spain and Great Britain, with the Mississippi as the boundary. France was wiped out in North America: she had lost Canada to the British; for safekeeping, Louis XV of France had ceded the Louisiana Territory to his Bourbon cousin in Spain the previous year. Thereafter vertical lines slashed the length of the continent: a narrow fringe of Atlantic colonies was divorced from the deep hinterland extending from the crest of the mountains to the Mississippi

—a region rich in furs and good land that was now reserved for the Indians and a few licensed traders; beyond, all belonged to Spain.

The Royal Proclamation of 1763—coming a short eight months after the peace settlement—that excluded the Atlantic colonies from expanding westward was not merely, despite the colonials' claims, an act of royal stupidity or deliberate injustice. It was a quick reflection of the pressure brought by British fur interests who wanted to protect their steady and ready profits. Furs accounted for two thirds of Canada's exports to England. In the peace settlement, some Englishmen had wanted to take not Canada but France's rich sugar-producing island of Guadeloupe —a lucrative, desirable market for slaves and manufactured goods; but British fur traders strengthened the colonists' insistence that the French threat be forever eliminated, and the combination forced Great Britain to claim Canada as the price of victory.

And so to the colonists western exclusion had only one clear meaning: they had lost men and spent monies to drive the French out of the northwest country, the French whom they despised so thoroughly that the word "frenchmen" was used along Chesapeake Bay to describe spindling, good-for-nothing tobacco plants; but the prize they had helped win was denied them. The proclamation substituted Great Britain for France as the hated enemy; it rallied the southern planter to the side of commercial New England against a common, restrictive, frustrating authority; it established a bond; it started a process. The proclamation of 1763—in spite of changes and amendments made later—was a link in the intricate chain of conflicting interests that led inevitably, once the French peril was resolved, to the firing of the shot heard round the world.

Up to that time, hostility had followed a national tack, the British against the French. With peace, the colonists, united under a common flag, expected an untroubled expansion. In the proclamation they heard the faint but clear announcement of another long and bitter struggle, a life-and-death battle between two economies: that of the fur trade, which needed to preserve the wilderness and the Indians, and that of the settler, who wanted to invade and plant communities in the inviting virgin West and who, to possess the land and obtain security, had to clear the great oak and maple forests and exterminate the Indians. The conflict thus annunciated flared openly into an embattled stand of farmers who, by their victorious revolution, procured considerable territory and a little time to gather strength before renewing the same struggle farther to the west in the War of 1812; still the issue escaped solution—the seat of the fur-traders' empire shifted, after Mackenzie, to the far West, and there the Compromise of 1818 postponed the problem of the Oregon Territory until the final settlement in 1846. In the eighty-odd years from 1763 to 1846 the Northwest receded two thousand miles; as the settlers pushed westward, the scene of unresolved tension went with them. For over eighty years British fur interests piled up political levees to guard the wilderness against the flood of farmers.

These antagonistic economies were not an inheritance from differing European backgrounds—the French in Canada, the English along the Atlantic—but were dictated by the basic structure of North America. Almost the stage had been set in geological times, when four or five glacial waves passed over northern North America and, like gigantic bulldozers, scraped clean the rock foundation that forms three fourths of the continent, pushing the soils and the elements of future soils before them. When the last ice wave receded, it left exposed the enormous area of the Canadian Shield—two thirds of northern and eastern Canada—and the ancient, leveled plateau covered its brutal scars with coniferous forests, tough tundra, marshes, and swamps, and tied them decently together with lakes and rivers. This was a country created for the fur trader. Very different was the interior of the United States, blessed with the dumpings of rich, fertile, top soils, a region marvelously rewarding to the farmer. From the Atlantic coast, from Europe, this specially created fecundity drew the dispossessed but spirited; it made Tocqueville pronounce the valley of the Mississippi "the most magnificent dwelling place prepared by God for man's abode."

The men of Hudson Bay and the Pedlars of the St. Lawrence had fought each other to determine who, not what, was to dominate; both groups represented the fur trade. In the war between the fur interests of Canada and the agrarian appetite of the colonies, on the contrary, the struggle settled which of two economies was to triumph. Mackenzie could propose a merger to the rivalrous fur companies as the sensible and fitting solution; to the antithetical economies, the only answer was one-sided survival and victory.

Hope and hatred, the winged seeds of dreams, had been planted in Jefferson; thus was his western dream born; it grew in scope and complexity, in purpose and meaning, as he matured and as world events moved ever faster. The creative expressions of his preoccupation were many; the forms that disclosed it— the Northwest Ordinance, the Louisiana Purchase, the Lewis and Clark expedition—clearly bespoke the bold innovator.

In 1784, one year after the United States had been formally recognized by Great Britain as a nation with her western boundary at the Mississippi, Jefferson was ready with a proposal for dealing with the immense empty territory beyond the Appalachians. Herein was the germ of the famous Northwest Ordinance of 1787. During the war years, George Rogers Clark, the explorer's much older brother and an ex-surveyor for the Ohio Company, won military control of the then Northwest by a brilliant and strenuous campaign against the British; political authority over this territory was finally yielded to the Federal government by the several States that, like Virginia, claimed rights of domain as far as the Spanish border. The greatness of Jefferson's concept lay in a plan—a plan made before the region was settled, not a compromise or a solution effected after the event—whereby the trans-Appalachian country, thrown open to eager farmers, would, by a prescribed, time-limited process, be organized as States having perfect equality with the original thirteen. The West must never be subservient to the East, where powerful interests were entrenched; the West must create its own democratic life in the light of its own genius. Congress, accepting its responsibility, modified Jefferson's plan without changing his aim—incorporating certain features that had proved successful in the New England township system— and passed the Northwest Ordinance.

It instituted, as John Bartlet Brebner has said,

"a political apparatus which showed that the offspring of an imperial people could produce imperial statesmanship which was superior to the original brand. For the first time since ancient Greece, a growing nation laid down in detail the formal steps by which its colonies could progress with self-respect and certainty from a generous measure of autonomy to free federal association with it." [4]

Grandeur, historical imagination, political creativity, clothed Jefferson's western dream as he translated it into reality.

Jefferson submitted his proposed ordinance and then, as newly appointed minister to the court of Paris, sailed to assume his duties abroad. To Paris, a little later, Ledyard came. The excitement of that meeting! Those two, so different in their training and temperament, revealed to each other the dream that was the common passion of both—the exquisite luxury of this discovery like the relaxation of a mutually avowed love; and though each had fashioned his own dream, his own hope, the images flowed together effortlessly; each brought a special original emphasis that combined to make the result richer, more expansive. Ledyard had found in the numerous exotic tribes of the Pacific coast a provocative resemblance to the Indians of the eastern seaboard; both were native to America, different from other Pacific peoples living on the islands Cook's ships had touched at, and the shared characteristics that united the Indians of North America across so vast a distance held a thrilling promise for the future pattern of the United States. Ledyard's plans for commerce along the northwest coast changed, from his conversations with Jefferson, to an obsession with exploring the trans-Mississippi West. For Jefferson, the West that had ended with the Mississippi was stretched to embrace the unknown country beyond, even to the Pacific; to his hope of settlements of strong, self-reliant, independent yeomen the element of commerce was added; the leisurely pace of the frontier's extension suddenly broke into an accelerated tempo to meet the impatient rush of Europe to the North Pacific. In Jefferson's own mind the western dream was not only enormously enlarged: it also became more complex and extremely urgent. The changing scene and the rate of this change Tocqueville found peculiarly American: "Twelve years are more in America than half a century in Europe."

Ledyard had done well to impart this sense of urgency to

---

[4] John Bartlet Brebner: *North Atlantic Triangle* (New Haven, 1945), p. 75.

Jefferson. A scant twenty years after the young explorer vainly pleaded for a ship to trade in the Pacific, almost twoscore American vessels were going annually to the mouth of the Columbia and Nootka Sound. Their captains traded with the Russians; they traded with China, with India. And knowing the importance of this commerce to the young nation's economy, Jefferson must often have remembered his ardent friend who had foreseen the concerted movement of men and ships engaged in lucrative enterprise. Surely Jefferson pondered the reasons for Ledyard's expulsion from Siberia. Ledyard himself never knew them. An eyewitness to his arrest affirmed that the imperial warrant charged him with being a French spy. Obviously this was a pretext—a French spy begging his way across the wilderness of Siberia!—and a ludicrous one at that. Twenty-five years later Jefferson, writing his autobiography, "remembered" that Catherine the Great had immediately refused her permission because she considered Ledyard's venture "entirely chimerical," had arrested and expelled him to save the foolhardy American from certain death. It would have been more in character for her to shrug her shoulders and leave him to the fate he deserved—or, consistent with her policy of furthering scientific work, to help him reach Kamchatka and the northwest coast of America. For Catherine to allow herself to be branded by Lafayette as "illiberal and narrow-minded, and . . . ungenerous" in her treatment of Ledyard implies her response to some strong pressure, some cogent argument. Had Ledyard known the real reason for his removal, it might have minimized his bewilderment and heartbreak; his fate would not have appeared, darkly, as an impersonal, pitiless force that struck at him even as he was about to succeed after having surmounted so many obstacles; he would have seen it in its true perspective, as a coup to be expected from a grasping and jealous competitor.

Ledyard appeared in Siberia, in 1787, at just the wrong moment. Nobody could have forewarned him. Unknowingly he walked into a situation that was still formless—the secret, ambitious beginnings of a driving plan that grew into the powerful Russian American Company. It achieved for Russia's far eastern trade and possessions what the Montreal Pedlars' North West Company had for Canada's western empire: independent traders were united, competition was eliminated, trading posts were established, Russian influence and territory were expanded; the company assumed important commercial and political force. Ledyard probably never met Gregory Shelekhov, a moving power in this Russian enterprise, and yet it was Shelekhov who intrigued to have him ousted from Siberia. The Russian fur trader was nicknamed "the Russian Columbus" in recognition of his boldness in exploring the Kurile and Aleutian Islands and in acknowledgment of his ascendency in Russia's Pacific possessions. Three years before, he had formed a partnership with the brothers Golikov, built some ships at Okhotsk, and sailed across the Pacific to start a factory or agency on Kodiak Island. Shelekhov had great plans: while his company extended its holdings in America, he would consolidate his position by an imperial monopoly. It was at this critical time that Ledyard arrived in Irkutsk, the district capital from which Shelekhov directed the policies of his incipient empire and to which his men brought reports of foreign traders collecting fine seal and sea-otter skins from the Indians to the south of his factory. He knew that foreign competition had already started; he hoped to keep it at a safe distance, and he wanted no prying foreign eyes to assay his activity and strength in Siberia and America. Suspicious of this young man who had suddenly appeared, Shelekhov invoked high political aid to have the unwary traveler hauled back to Russia and expelled from the empire.

Shelekhov's company prospered. A few years after Ledyard had been summarily disposed of, the Russians, under the dynamic direction of Alexander Baranov, began to play an important role in America and international commerce. Baranov, a man of small stature, of great force and considerable genius, began to make his influence felt when in 1790 he was appointed resident director of the Kodiak Island post, the headquarters for Russian trade in Northwest America. Eight years later, Shelekhov's original company was reorganized into the Russian American Company. Its charter gave it the authority to administer justice in Russia's Pacific colonies along with a monopoly in trade. While a member of the Shelekhov family was technically the head of the new monopoly, Baranov, its manager, was the real power, virtually an independent ruler. The story of the man, from that time until his death thirty years later, in 1819, is the story of his plans and attempts to make Russia supreme in the North Pacific. He shrewdly gauged his competitors: the Spaniards he could disregard—they had shown their weakness in the Nootka Sound Convention; he could dismiss the British, who, though they had already made their way across Canada, were hamstrung for concerted aggressive action by their separate conflicting monopolies; with the Yankee shipmasters he could do business.

John Jacob Astor, operating out of New York through the American Fur Company, which he had organized in 1808, and Baranov, directing the Russian American Company from New Archangel, as Sitka was then called, entered into a mutually satisfactory and highly promising trade alliance. Here were two audacious schemers, vastly different, who for a while joined hands to achieve the daring, gigantic desires that each independently nursed: Astor to capture the fur market of the world and dominate a large part of the world's commerce; Baranov to extend Russian influence so that the North Pacific Ocean would become a Russian sea. There must have been a contagion in the air of that day, the Napoleonic era, that infected many men with the belief that a world awaited their mastery. Both Astor and Baranov failed in their objectives. The fate of the Pacific trading post, the keystone in Astor's global edifice, is familiar from Washington Irving's account of it in *Astoria.* Baranov's efforts are worth recalling.

Baranov's plan to control the North Pacific meant securing the two remaining sides of a triangle whose first side, running from Kamchatka south to a Japan tightly sealed against all intruders, was already his. The second side, along the American coast, needed only to be extended as far as the Spanish settlements in California; the third side, crossing the Pacific through the Sandwich Islands, must be controlled to close off the northern seas and give him a base for provisioning his ships and settlements. In 1812, he built a post later known as Fort Ross, at Bodega Bay just north of San Francisco; in 1815, he tried in vain to gain a foothold on the Sandwich Islands. It was an ambitious scheme, as ambitious as Astor's had been. When Baranov died, he had no successor; his plan was cut off by his death. Fort Ross was left a lonely outpost, a relic of a grandiose design. In 1844 it was bought by the Swiss-born Sutter, who called his vast estate New Helvetia. Sutter is remembered for his mill near which in 1848 fabulous gold deposits were found. The ebb-tide of Baranov's hopes was reached in 1867, when, to satisfy the territorial interests of the United States, Russia sold Alaska for a nominal sum.

Long was the process that shaped Jefferson's western dream. In the sixty years from his birth in the frontier home his father built in western Virginia to the time when he dispatched Lewis and Clark on their magnificent mission, he saw the frontier reach the Mississippi, saw States carved out of what had been a north-west territory. Jefferson was impatient to extend his country's sovereignty to the Pacific. Beyond the Mississippi, the West was still too vast, too distant, to be thought of in terms of immediate settlement. Trade and commerce would open it up and secure it; farms and towns and States would follow. The United States was hesitating a brief moment before the full, slashing vigor of its great expansion took it in one leap across the treeless plains to the wooded, watered Pacific coast. Had Jefferson been alive sixty years after the Lewis and Clark expedition, he would have beheld the deluge of men and women who poured without pause across the Mississippi and, with a ruthless, righteous belief in their destiny, by cash or clash or compromise, claimed for the United States the continental territory—including Alaska—that it occupies today.

Jefferson would have seen how, despite his warm humanitarianism, his abiding conviction that all men have inalienable rights, he had been unable to encompass the problem of developing and populating the West without destroying its original inhabitants, the Indians. On one hand he sent out Lewis and Clark, his ambassadors provided with full powers to negotiate treaties of friendly alliance with the tribes along their route; on the other hand he had to accept as agents of western penetration the fur traders, whose liquor debauched the Indians. An Arikara chief near the Mandan village that had long been accustomed to traders' visits rebuked Clark for offering the Indians whiskey: it "makes them fools." The result of this policy was already obvious twenty-five years later, when Tocqueville acidly noted its brighter side:

"The conduct of the Americans of the United States towards the aborigines is characterized . . . by a singular attachment to the formalities of law. . . . They treat [the Indians] as independent nations and do not possess themselves of their hunting-grounds without a treaty of purchase; and if an Indian nation happens to be so encroached upon as to be unable to subsist upon their territory, they kindly take them by the hand and transport them to a grave far from the land of their fathers.

"The Spaniards were unable to exterminate the Indian race by those unparalleled atrocities which brand them with indelible shame, nor did they succeed wholly in depriving it of its rights; but the Americans of the United States have accomplished this twofold purpose with singular felicity, tranquilly, legally, philanthropically, without shedding blood, and without violating a single great principle of morality in the eyes of the world. It is impossible to destroy men with more respect for the laws of humanity." [5]

When Jefferson sailed for France in 1784, he was going to his second home: as the frontier had shaped him as a growing man, so the writings of the French liberals had molded his growing intellect. Hope and hatred had started his western dream; it was made great by great ideas. The ideational sources of his obsession endowed it with splendor. One of the most widely read men of his day, he was steeped in the intellectual independence expressed by the seventeenth-century English liberals and the wider implications of the eighteenth-century French liberals—and between the two he had already chosen.

Parrington traces in the quality of Jefferson's social outlook the marked influence of the French school's

"back-to-nature philosophy, with its corollary of an agrarian economics and its emphasis on social well-being, a philosophy more consonant with Virginian experience and his own temperament than Locke's philosophy of property."

When Jefferson drafted the Declaration of Independence, his profound allegiance to

---

[5] Alexis de Tocqueville: *Democracy in America* (New York, 1945), Vol. I, p. 355.

"French humanitarianism [was] revealed in the passage on slavery that was stricken out on the floor of Congress, and more significantly in the change in the familiar phrasing of the several natural rights. Samuel Adams and other followers of Locke had been content with the classical enumeration of life, liberty, and property; but in Jefferson's hands the English doctrine was given a revolutionary shift. The substitution of 'pursuit of happiness' for 'property' marks a complete break with the Wiggish doctrine of property rights that Locke had bequeathed to the English middle class, and the substitution of a broader sociological conception; and it was this substitution that gave to the document the note of idealism which was to make it so perennially human and vital." [6]

The humanitarianism that marked much of French political thinking cast back to Montaigne. The seventeenth-century essayist was one of the rare men whose thought has, down the centuries, shaped and kept vigilant the conscience of mankind. The New World—its strange, innocent life, its savage, dreadful fate—was known to Montaigne through the writings of Columbus, Peter Martyr, Las Casas, and others. The indignant, passionate, religious outcry raised by Las Casas became a simple moral problem to be quietly, thoughtfully voiced by Montaigne. What right had Europe, where the Four Horsemen of the Apocalypse pastured their mounts, to call any people barbarous? He questioned the civilization that could perpetrate insensate cruelties on defenseless savages. As if to answer those who justified the enslavement and dismissed the extermination of the Indians because they were subhuman or barbarous, Montaigne did not invoke God's inscrutable purpose in creating differences; rather, with originality and insight, he examined the moral superiority of the Europeans.

In his famous essay "On Cannibals," Montaigne's method is bold, explicit, direct:

"I am not sorie we note the barbarous horror of [cannibalism], but grieved, that prying so narrowly into their faults we are

---

[6] Vernon Louis Parrington: *Main Currents in American Thought* (New York, 1930), Vol. I, p. 344.

so blinded in ours. I thinke there is more barbarisme in eating men alive, than to feed upon them being dead; to mangle by tortures and torments a body full of lively sense, to roast him in peeces, to make dogges and swine to gnaw and teare him . . . (as wee have not only read, but seene very lately, yea & in our own memorie, not amongst ancient enemies, but our neighbours and fellow-citizens; and which is worse, under pretence of pietie and religion) than to roast and eat him after he is dead."

Again, through one of the Brazilian cannibals who were exhibited to Charles IX's court at Rouen, Montaigne itemized some of the monstrous inequalities present in civilized Europe and suggested a remedy for what he saw. The cannibals

"had perceived, there were men amongst us full gorged with all sortes of commodities, and others which hunger-starved, and bare with need and povertie, begged at their gates: and found it strange, these moyties so needy could endure such an injustice, and that they tooke not the others by the throte, or set fire to their houses."

Moytie (*moitié*), which means a half of, or a part of, was, as Montaigne explained, the savages' expression "whereby they call men but a moytie one of another."

Montaigne lifted the protest of Las Casas and his sort out of its narrow theological setting. He secularized the cruelties of acculturation and placed the responsibility solidly on the shoulders of thinking, feeling men everywhere. In his resentment of the tragic impact of Europe on America, Las Casas was guided by the teachings of Jesus; Montaigne searched out the answer in his own heart and soul. Where Las Casas illuminated the skies with his flaming fanaticism, Montaigne used exquisite logic and polished tact to speak privately to all who would hear him; where Las Casas evoked powerful, militant enemies, Montaigne's wit disarmed and charmed those at whom he pointed a well-bred but accusing finger. Montaigne transformed Las Casas's argument and transmitted it to a wider world; his persuasive voice was heard everywhere, for everywhere he was read from the time his book was first published in 1580. Such men stand out like mountain-tops.

As he created a new literary form in the essay, Montaigne also devised other patterns that recurred significantly in later writers. The inhabitants of the New World, hauntingly pictured for their Catholic Majesties, he fixed in the imagination of Europe as citizens who enjoyed the sweet felicities of a golden age "that hath no kinde of traffike. . . . no name of magistrate, nor of politike superioritie; no use of services, of riches or of povertie." Here was the natural man, whom Rousseau found good before institutions perverted and corrupted him; here was a free, happy, independent yeomanry, with government reduced to a minimum, operating by common consent and for the common good, as the physiocrats interpreted it. From these latter came the vision that Jefferson added to his western dream.

The same books that gave substance and purpose to Jefferson's western dream went into the wilderness in the earliest wave of expansion. Dream and dreamer, plan and fulfillment, hope for a better world and a waiting continent, rushed irresistibly to an epic climax as the nineteenth century started. The United States was young, and the West was its first love.

Three hundred years before, Columbus had sailed west to find the East. North America blocked him, and the problem he left behind was the conquest of the continental obstacle. Balboa to find gold for his king, Mackenzie to amass furs for his company, Lewis and Clark to secure a highway for their nation's commerce, provided bridges from the Atlantic to the Pacific by the paths they traced across North America.

SOURCES AND BACKGROUND BOOKS

Scholars can quite easily make up bibliographies listing comprehensively and minutely the items large and small that they consulted in a particular investigation. This book, making use of scholars' researches, is written for the wider public that often supposes scholarly research to be tedious, technical, and esoteric. But scholarship should not be confused with pedantry and should not have to pay for the sins of the latter. Those who have enjoyed reading of the magnificent adventures of Balboa, Mackenzie, and Lewis and Clark and whose appetites have been whetted for authentic recitals of achievement will realize that an account by a person who was party to an adventure has a flavor that no later historian can impart. Like an artist's sketch, it gives in bold, sure strokes the impact of the event as it happened; it is simpler and more direct than the finished, worked-over canvas. But there is more to such accounts than their naïve charm. They are part of a long and stirring epic: they are the sequel to what has gone before and the introduction to what is to follow in man's struggle to explore the planet he inhabits, and each episode becomes more interesting, more significant, if placed in relation to this whole.

So I have listed first, for each section of my book what the scholars call primary source material: journals, letters, what not, occasionally even works of later historians valuable for the documentary evidence they present. There is, for example, an especially good translation of Balboa's famous letter in Anderson's book about him. Afterward, to provide background, I have listed some few additional books including biographies—what the scholars call secondary material. My bibliography, then, is not so much an accounting of what I have used in fashioning this book as it is a guide for those who would like to read further in this field.

The list does not include the best single account of the course of exploration in North America. This is John Bartlet Brebner's *The Explorers of North America 1492–1806* (London: A. & C.

Black, Ltd., 1933). I must urge my readers to begin with this, for it is unsurpassed both as an introduction and as a guide to the vast subject it surveys.

Then, too, there are great collections of early travels, which the interested reader might very profitably investigate: the superbly edited publications of the Hakluyt Society, the Champlain Society, the J. F. Jameson collection of *Original Narratives of Early American History*, and the multivolumed histories compiled by H. H. Bancroft. Though these collections are very large, they are well indexed and can be used to the individual's taste and capacity. My list can and indeed should be augmented in another way: by reference to the research of certain eminent scholars. These can be located through any good card catalogue under the names of Herbert E. Bolton, Elliott Coues, Herbert I. Priestley, James A. Robertson, Reuben G. Thwaites, and Ralph E. Twitchell. Only a couple of samplings of this mass of material are incorporated in my list.

GOLD FOR THE CROWN

For Source Material:

D'ANGHERA, PETER MARTYR, *De Orbe Novo*. Translated from the Latin with notes and introduction by C. F. MacNutt. 2 vols. New York: G. P. Putnam's Sons, 1912.

ANDAGOYA, PASCUAL DE, *Narrative of the Proceedings of Pedrárias Dávila in . . . Tierra Firme or Castilla del Oro*. Translated by C. F. Markham. London: Hakluyt Society, 1865.

ANDERSON, C. L. G., *Life and Letters of Vasco Núñez de Balboa*. New York: Fleming H. Revell Co., 1941.

——— *Old Panama and Castilla del Oro*. Boston: Page Co., 1914.

IRVING WASHINGTON, *Voyages and Discoveries of the Companions of Columbus*. 3 vols. New York and London: Cooperative Publications Society, n.d.

DÍAZ DEL CASTILLO, BERNAL, *The True History of the Conquest of New Spain*. 4 vols. Edited by A. P. Maudslay. London: Hakluyt Society, second series, 1908–16.

For Background:

BOURNE, EDWARD GAYLORD, *Spain in America 1450–1580*. New York: Harper & Bros., 1906.

PRIESTLEY, HERBERT INGRAM, *The Coming of the White Man 1492–1848*. New York: The Macmillan Co., 1930.

GHENT, W. J., *The Early Far West. A Narrative Outline, 1540–1850*. New York and Toronto: Longmans, Green & Co., 1931.

WEBB, WALTER P., *The Great Plains*. Boston: Ginn & Co., 1931.

SIMPSON, LESLEY BYRD, *The Encomienda in New Spain; Forced Labor in the Spanish Colonies, 1492–1550*. Berkeley: University of California Publications in History, Vol. 19, 1929.

MACNUTT, C. F., *Bartholomew de Las Casas: His Life, his Apostolate, and his Writings*. New York: G. P. Putnam's Sons, 1909.

MORISON, SAMUEL ELIOT, *Admiral of the Ocean Sea. A Life of Christopher Columbus*. 2 vols. Boston: Little, Brown & Co., 1942.

HUMBOLDT, ALEXANDER DE, *Political Essay on the Kingdom of New Spain*. Translated from the original French by John Black. 3 vols. Third edition. London: 1822.

PRESCOTT, WILLIAM HICKLING, *History of the Conquest of Mexico*. 3 vols. New York: Harper & Bros., 1843.

———— *History of the Reign of Ferdinand and Isabella, the Catholic*. 3 vols. Tenth edition. New York: Harper & Bros., 1845–6.

MERRIMAN, R. B., *The Rise of the Spanish Empire in the Old World and in the New*. 4 vols. New York: The Macmillan Co., 1918–34.

TREND, J. B., *The Civilization of Spain*. New York & London: Oxford University Press, 1944.

CLARK, G. N., *The Seventeenth Century*. Oxford: Clarendon Press, 1931.

FURS FOR THE COMPANY

For Source Material:

MACKENZIE, ALEXANDER, *Voyages from Montreal through the Continent of North America to the Frozen and Pacific*

Oceans in 1789 and 1793, with an Account of the Rise and the State of the Fur Trade. 2 vols. New York: Allerton Book Co., 1922.

INNIS, HAROLD A., *Peter Pond, Fur Trader and Adventurer.* Toronto: Irwin & Gordon, Ltd., 1930.

THWAITES, R. G., *Peter Pond's Journal.* Madison: Wisconsin Historical Collection, xvii, 1908.

DAVIDSON, G. C., *The North-West Company.* Berkeley: University of California Press, 1918.

HENRY, ALEXANDER, *Travels and Adventures in Canada and the Indian Territories, between the Years 1760 and 1776.* Edited by J. Bain. Toronto: G. N. Morang & Co., Ltd., 1901.

For Background:

INNIS, HAROLD A., *The Fur Trade in Canada: An Introduction to Canadian Economic History.* New Haven: Yale University Press, 1930.

CREIGHTON, D. G., *The Commercial Empire of the St. Lawrence.* Toronto: Ryerson Press, 1937.

MORTON, ARTHUR S., *A History of the Canadian West to 1870–1.* London: Thomas Nelson & Sons, Ltd., 1939.

GOLDER, F. A., *Russian Expansion on the Pacific, 1641–1850.* Cleveland: A. H. Clark Co., 1914.

——— *Bering's Voyages: An Account of the Efforts of the Russians to Determine the Relation of Asia and America.* 2 vols. New York: American Geographical Society, 1922–5.

MIRSKY, JEANNETTE, *To the North! The Story of Arctic Exploration from Earliest Times to the Present.* New York: Viking Press, 1934.

COMMERCE FOR THE NATION

For Source Material:

LEDYARD, JOHN, *A Journal of Capt. Cook's Last Voyage to the Pacific Ocean.* Hartford: N. Patten, 1783.

SPARKS, JARED, *The Life of John Ledyard, The American Traveller; Comprising Selections from his Journals and Correspondence.* Second edition. Cambridge: Hilliard & Brown, 1829.

History of the Lewis and Clark Expedition . . . Faithfully Reprinted from the only Authorized Edition of 1814, etc. Edited by Elliott Coues. 3 vols. and atlas. New York: Francis P. Harper, 1893.

The Original Journals of Lewis and Clark. Edited by R. G. Thwaites. 7 vols. and atlas. New York: Dodd, Mead & Co., 1904–5.

The Journals of Captain Meriwether Lewis and Sergeant John Ordway. Edited by Milo M. Quaife. Madison: Wisconsin State Historical Society, 1916.

GASS, PATRICK, *Journal of the Voyages and Discoveries of a Corps of Discovery, under the Command of Captain Lewis and Captain Clarke . . .* Fourth edition. Philadelphia: Mathew Carey, 1812.

HEBARD, R. G., *Sacajawea.* Glendale, California: The Arthur H. Clark Co., 1933.

For Background:

WHEELER, OLIN D., *The Trail of Lewis and Clark, 1804–1904.* 2 vols. New York: G. P. Putnam's Sons, 1904.

IRVING, WASHINGTON, *Astoria.* New York: G. P. Putnam's Sons, 1881.

TOCQUEVILLE, ALEXIS DE, *Democracy in America.* Edited by Phillips Bradley. 2 vols. New York: Alfred A. Knopf, Inc., 1945.

TURNER, F. J., *The Frontier in American History.* New York: Henry Holt & Co., 1920.

BREBNER, JOHN BARTLET, *North Atlantic Triangle. The Interplay of Canada, the United States, and Great Britain.* New Haven: Yale University Press, 1945.

MORISON, SAMUEL ELIOT, *The Maritime History of Massachusetts, 1783–1860.* Boston: Houghton Mifflin Co., 1921.

CHINARD, GILBERT, *L'Exotisime Américain dans la Littérature Française au XVI.* Siècle d'après Rabelais, Ronsard, Montaigne, etc. Paris: Hachette et Cie., 1911.

INDEX

i

A NOTE ON THE TYPE IN WHICH
THIS BOOK IS SET

This book was set on the Linotype in *Janson*, a recutting made direct from the type cast from matrices made by Anton Janson some time between 1660 and 1687.

Of Janson's origin nothing is known. He may have been a relative of Justus Janson, a printer of Danish birth who practised in Leipzig from 1614 to 1635. Some time between 1657 and 1668 Anton Janson, a punch-cutter and type-founder, bought from the Leipzig printer Johann Erich Hahn the type-foundry which had formerly been a part of the printing house of M. Friedrich Lankisch. Janson's types were first shown in a specimen sheet issued at Leipzig about 1675. Janson's successor, and perhaps his son-in-law, Johann Karl Edling, issued a specimen sheet of Janson types in 1689. His heirs sold the Janson matrices in Holland to Wolffgang Dietrich Erhardt, of Leipzig.

The book was composed, printed, and bound by H. Wolff, New York. The typography is by James Hendrickson and the binding scheme is based on original designs by W. A. Dwiggins.

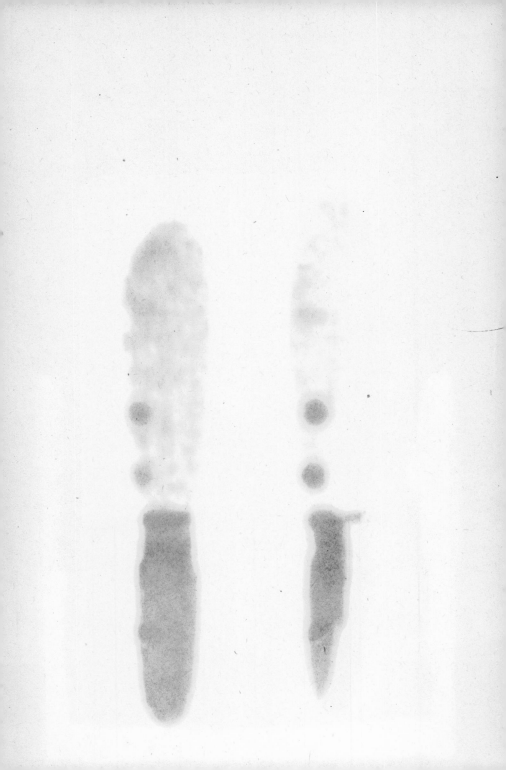

28403

E
27
M5

MIRSKY, JEANNETTE
   THE WESTWARD CROSSINGS.